STRATEGIC RESPONSES TO CRIME

Thinking Locally, Acting Globally

International Police Executive Symposium Co-Publications

Dilip K. Das, *Founding President-IPES*

PUBLISHED

Global Trafficking in Women and Children
By Obi N.I. Ebbe and Dilip K. Das, ISBN: 978-1-4200-5943-4

Contemporary Issues in Law Enforcement and Policing
By Andrew Millie and Dilip K. Das, ISBN: 978-1-4200-7215-0

Trends in Policing: Interviews with Police Leaders Across the Globe, Volume Two
By Dilip K. Das and Otwin Marenin, ISBN: 978-1-4200-7520-5

Criminal Abuse of Women and Children: An International Perspective
By Obi N.I. Ebbe and Dilip K. Das, ISBN: 978-1-4200-8803-8

Urbanization, Policing, and Security: Global Perspectives
By Gary Cordner, AnnMarie Cordner, and Dilip K. Das, ISBN: 978-1-4200-8557-0

Global Environment of Policing
By Dilip K. Das, Darren Palmer, and Michael M. Berlin, ISBN: 978-1-4200-6590-9

Trends in Policing: Interviews with Police Leaders Across the Globe, Volume Three
By Otwin Marenin and Dilip K. Das, ISBN: 978-1-4398-1924-1

Police Without Borders: The Fading Distinction between Local and Global
By Cliff Roberson, Dilip K. Das, and Jennie K. Singer, ISBN: 978-1-4398-0501-5

Effective Crime Reduction Strategies: International Perspectives
By James F. Albrecht and Dilip K. Das, ISBN: 978-1-4200-7838-1

Strategic Responses to Crime: Thinking Locally, Acting Globally
By Melchor de Guzman, Aiedeo Mintie Das, and Dilip K. Das, ISBN: 978-1-4200-7669-1

FORTHCOMING

Policing Neoliberal Societies
By Allison Wakefield, Bankole Cole, and Dilip K. Das, ISBN: 978-1-4398-4135-8

Terrorism, Counterterrorism, and Internal Wars: Examining International Political Violence
By Austin Turk, Dilip K. Das, and James Ross, ISBN: 978-1-4398-2104-6

Justices of the World: Their Views, Opinions and Perspectives
By Chandrika M. Kelso and Dilip K. Das, ISBN: 978-1-4200-9978-2

Cross Cultural Profiles of Policing
By Dilip K. Das, Osman Dolu, and Bonnie Mihalka, ISBN: 978-1-4200-7014-9

Trends in Corrections: Interviews with Corrections Leaders Around the World
By Jennie K. Singer and Dilip K. Das, ISBN: 978-1-4398-3578-4

Trends in Policing: Interviews with Police Leaders Across the Globe, Volume Three
By Bruce F. Baker and Dilip K. Das, ISBN: 978-1-4398-8073-9

International Police Executive Symposium Co-Publications

Dilip K. Das, *Founding President-IPES*

Interviews with Global Leaders in Policing, Prisons, and Courts Series

PUBLISHED

Trends in Policing: Interviews with Police Leaders Across the Globe, Volume Three
By Otwin Marenin and Dilip K. Das, ISBN: 978-1-4398-1924-1

Justices of the World: Their Views, Opinions, and Perspectives
By Chandrika M. Kelso and Dilip K. Das, ISBN: 978-1-4200-9978-2

FORTHCOMING

Trends in Corrections: Interviews with Corrections Leaders Around the World
By Jennie K. Singer and Dilip K. Das, ISBN: 978-1-4398-3578-4

Trends in Policing: Interviews with Police Leaders Across the Globe, Volume Three
By Bruce F. Baker and Dilip K. Das, ISBN: 978-1-4398-8073-9

STRATEGIC RESPONSES TO CRIME

Thinking Locally, Acting Globally

Edited by

Melchor de Guzman
Aiedeo Mintie Das
Dilip K. Das

International Police Executive Symposium
Co-Publication

CRC Press
Taylor & Francis Group
Boca Raton London New York

CRC Press is an imprint of the
Taylor & Francis Group, an **informa** business

CRC Press
Taylor & Francis Group
6000 Broken Sound Parkway NW, Suite 300
Boca Raton, FL 33487-2742

First issued in paperback 2017

Version Date: 20110719

ISBN-13: 978-1-4200-7669-1 (hbk)
ISBN-13: 978-1-138-11247-6 (pbk)

Library of Congress Cataloging-in-Publication Data

International Police Executive Symposium (13th : 2006 : Ayvalik, Balikesir Ili, Turkey)
Strategic responses to crime : thinking locally, acting globally / editors, Melchor de Guzman, Aiedeo Mintie Das, Dilip K. Das.
p. cm.
Papers presented at the 13th Annual Meeting of the International Police Executive Symposium held in Ayvalik, Turkey, in 2006.
Includes bibliographical references and index.
ISBN 978-1-4200-7669-1 (alk. paper)
1. Community policing--Congresses. 2. Police--Congresses. 3. Crime--Congresses. I. De Guzman, Melchor. II. Das, Aiedeo Mintie. III. Das, Dilip K., 1941- IV. Title.

HV7936.C83I57 2006
363.2'3--dc23 2011028350

Visit the Taylor & Francis Web site at
http://www.taylorandfrancis.com

and the CRC Press Web site at
http://www.crcpress.com

Table of Contents

Section 4

INTERNATIONAL POLICE PRACTICES AND CULTURES

INTERNATIONAL POLICE EXECUTIVE SYMPOSIUM
Co-publication Preface

The *International Police Executive Symposium* (IPES) was founded in 1994 to address one major challenge, i.e., the two worlds of research and practice remain disconnected even though cooperation between the two is growing. A major reason is that the two groups speak in different languages. The research is published in hard to access journals and presented in a manner that is difficult for some to comprehend. On the other hand, police practitioners tend not to mix with researchers and remain secretive about their work. Consequently there is little dialogue between the two and almost no attempt to learn from one another. The global dialogue among police researchers and practitioners is limited. True, the literature on the police is growing exponentially. But its impact upon day-to-day policing, however, is negligible.

The aims and objectives of the IPES are to provide a forum to foster closer relationships among police researchers and practitioners on a global scale, to facilitate cross-cultural, international and interdisciplinary exchanges for the enrichment of this law enforcement, to encourage discussion, and to publish research on challenging and contemporary problems facing the policing profession. One of the most important activities of the IPES is the organization of an annual meeting under the auspices of a police agency or an educational institution. Now in its 17th year, the annual meeting, a five-day initiative on specific issues relevant to the policing profession, brings together ministers of interior and justice, police commissioners and chiefs, members of academia representing world-renown institutions, and many more criminal justice elite from over 60 countries. It facilitates interaction and the exchange of ideas and opinions on all aspects of policing. The agenda is structured to encourage dialogue in both formal and informal settings.

Another important aspect of the meeting is the publication of the best papers presented by well known criminal justice scholars and police administrators who attend the meetings. The best papers are selected, thoroughly revised, fully updated, meticulously edited, and published as books based upon the theme of each meeting. This repository of knowledge under the co-publication imprint of IPES and CRC Press-Taylor & Francis Group chronicles the important contributions of the International Police Executive Symposium over the last two decades. As a result, in 2011 the United Nations awarded IPES a Special Consultative Status for the Economic and Social Council (ECSOC) honoring its importance in the global security community.

In addition to this book series, the IPES also has a research journal, *Police Practices and Research: An International Journal* (PPR). The PPR contains research articles on police issues. It is an international journal and is distributed worldwide. For more information on the PPR visit **http://www.tandf.co.uk/journals/GPPR**

This unique volume, titled, *Strategic Responses to Crime: Thinking Locally, Acting Globally*, includes selected articles that were originally presented by police executives and scholars from several countries who attended the 13th Annual Meeting of the International Police Executive Symposium held in Ayvalik, Turkey, in 2006. However, the articles have been updated and several papers outside of the conference have been added to capture the theme of the book. The volume is divided into four sections, each of which includes perspectives of police administrators and members of the academia from different countries. These chapters encompass topics in law enforcement from operations to organizations including pervading issues that the police confront both locally and globally. The chapters provide a comprehensive survey of police practices across police jurisdictions. This book is a useful reference for practitioners and researchers.

IPES advocates, promotes, and propagates that POLICING is one of the most basic and essential avenues for improving the quality of life in all nations; rich and poor; modern and traditional; large and small; as well as peaceful and strife-ridden. IPES actively works to drive home to all its office bearers, supporters, and admirers that, in order to reach its full potential as an instrument of service to humanity, POLICING must be fully and enthusiastically open to collaboration between research and practice, global exchange of information between police and academics in every country, universal disseminations and sharing of best practices, generating thinking police leaders and followers, and reflecting and writing on the issues challenging to the profession.

Through its annual meetings, hosts, institutional supporters, and publications, IPES reaffirms that POLICING is a moral profession with unflinching adherence to the rule of law and human rights as the embodiment of humane values.

—**Dilip K. Das**
Founding President, *International Police Executive Symposium*, www.ipes.info

Book Series Editor for:

Advances in Police Theory and Practice, CRC Press-Taylor & Francis Group

Interviews with Global Leaders in Policing, Courts, and Prisons, CRC Press-Taylor & Francis Group

PPR Special Issues as Books, Routledge-Taylor & Francis Group

Founding Editor-in-Chief, *Police Practice and Research: An International Journal*, PPR, http://www.tandf.co.uk/journals/GPPR

Introduction

MELCHOR C. DE GUZMAN

AIEDEO MINTIE DAS

DILIP K. DAS

This unique volume includes selected studies originally presented by police executives and scholars from several countries who attended the thirteenth annual meeting of the International Police Executive Symposium held in Ayvalik, Turkey, in 2006. The theme for this volume describes how local police agencies are addressing issues of crime that have global implications. In addition, the chapters show variations of policing practices that seem to have transcended global boundaries such as community policing. Although some of the original articles were solicited from the participants to the Turkey conference in 2006, they have been updated by their respective authors for this current volume. In addition, several chapters outside of the conference have been added to capture the theme of the book.

The volume is divided into four sections, each of which includes views of police administrators and members of academia from different countries. The book intends to capture perspectives from different lenses. The first lens aims to provide a combination of academic scholars and practitioners in the field of policing, specifically policing problems and practices. Oftentimes, scholars and practitioners are in opposite poles; however, much could be learned from the merger of both views. On one hand, the scholarly ideas could provide the empirical evidence required for practitioners to hone their craft of policing. On the other hand, the practitioners' ideas could provide clues for scholars on the dimensions and appropriate indicators for the way their research is conceptualized, designed, and conducted.

The second lens aims to provide varying world perspectives about policing. This approach would enable practitioners, academicians, policy makers, and general readers to capture glimpses of policing issues and practices in various cultural settings. In this way, readers can be informed about police innovations. Furthermore, this approach intends to awaken the social consciousness of citizens about policing practices and compare their own to those of the rest of the world. However, the main concentration of the chapters is on police services in democratic countries, both emerging and long-established. This is a limitation that readers must keep in mind.

Section 1: Global Innovations in Policing

These chapters provide insight into the contemporary policing innovations especially with regard to variations in the adoption of community policing. Community policing is a policing paradigm that has blossomed in the United States, but other countries have already adopted bits and pieces of the community policing strategies. These policing practices have been organized around the overarching philosophy of community-oriented policing.

This section opens with a discussion by James Albrecht, a former New York Police Department captain, on the evolution of community policing in the United States. Albrecht argues that the events of 9/11 have heightened the need to counter the threat of terrorism, a development that has negatively affected community policing in the United States. On the other hand, Albrecht maintains that community policing is becoming an international phenomenon and goes on to describe the development of community policing in the Scandinavian countries and in Israel.

The other chapters discuss police innovations in various countries. Goraz Mesko and Darko Maver, from the faculty of criminal justice at the University of Kotnikova in Slovenia, discuss the creation of 125 safety and security councils established on the local level in Slovenia to deal with everyday criminality, disorder, drugs, and traffic offenses. These practices might be synonymous with the COMPSTAT model that originated in New York City.

Terry Coleman, chief of police in Moose Jaw, Saskatchewan, Canada, and director of the Canadian Association of Chiefs of Police, discusses a study that attempted to measure and compare organizational performance in the private and public sectors to determine the organizational structures applicable to contemporary policing. As part of the study, Canadian police executives were surveyed to determine the extent to which organizations are managed strategically and performance management systems congruent with quality, value, and public sector reforms that might have been implemented in Canadian police organizations. The findings are that many police organizations in Canada are not managed strategically and still employ output measures of performance as opposed to measures of outcomes or results.

Section 2: Responding to Transnational and Emerging Law Enforcement Issues

The second section in this volume focuses on drugs cultivation and trafficking, a novel approach to counter international terrorism, the appropriate approaches to policing and handling of the mentally ill, and the promotion of cyber safety for special populations. Drugs and terrorism are transnational crimes. Practitioners will appreciate the chapters that touch on this subject. The movements of drugs and the knowledge about recruitment of terrorists are vital information to enable local police officers to handle these problems. The other chapters in this section deal with a common local law enforcement challenge—the mentally ill. Regardless of jurisdiction, policing the mentally ill presents a dilemma for police officers. This special group of people dictates police officers to wear two masks—the law enforcement mask and the social worker mask. The balanced performance of these two roles is required in the handling of the mentally ill. The last chapter deals with twin special issues of children and cyber crime. These two issues are becoming common problems of law enforcement everywhere especially in a digital age. In addition, this problem of cyber crime has the potential of becoming transnational; therefore, other law enforcements in the world could learn from the information provided in this chapter.

The section opens with the discussion of drugs and terrorism. The cultivation and trafficking of cocaine, heroin, and marijuana from Colombia and Mexico to Chicago are discussed by Gad Bensinger and Arthur Lurigio, two Loyola University Chicago criminologists, and Thomas Lemmer, a Chicago police department captain. They maintain that despite the many efforts undertaken by the U.S. government to counter the cultivation, production, trafficking, and distribution of illegal drugs, the ultimate responsibility for successfully fighting the so-called war on drugs lies with local law enforcement. The authors conclude that the Chicago police department's antidrug and antigang efforts have disrupted the local drug trade to a greater extent than the federal efforts.

A new and innovative approach to deal more effectively with the problem of international terrorism is presented by Mutlu Koseli. Drawing conclusions from the literature on the motivations for joining terrorist organizations and the recruitment activities of a terrorist organization, Koseli outlines these different factors. He also confirms the relative importance of these factors by presenting data that were gathered through interviews of several terrorist organization members. Koseli's interviews and lived-experiences approach provide valuable insights into individuals' motivations to participate in terrorist organizations.

The problems dealing with mentally ill subjects are discussed in two chapters, both of which present the complexities of policing this special population. Avdi Avdija's chapter deals with the issues surrounding this population from U.S. perspectives. He proposes an organizational model that may be used to address this issue. The other chapter presents an international view by Duncan Chappell, discussing the standards that need to be in place for handling the mentally ill. Chappell argues that the manner of handling people with mental illness reflects on the nation's commitment to human rights and respect for individual freedom. Particular attention is devoted to the way police exercise their powers of apprehension and detention within the framework of the United Nations (UN) Code of Conduct for Law Enforcement Officials, the UN Basic Principles on the Use of Force Firearms by Law Enforcement Officials, and the UN Principles for the Protection of Persons with a Mental Illness and the Improvement of Mental Health Care.

The section closes with the chapter by Julia Davidson and Elena Martellozo of the University of Westminster, England, on dealing with a two-pronged police problem—special populations and cyber crime. Another element of vulnerability in society affecting police practices is sexual abuse of young children, especially with the use of the digital media. Davidson and Martellozo suggest that not enough is currently being done in England to educate children about sexual abuse or to safeguard them from the danger of the Internet. The authors suggest that there is a need for greater cooperation among government, the police, and schools protecting children from sexual abuse. Several programs in New Zealand and in England do just that. In England, for example, the Metropolitan Police Safer Surfing Internet Programme, designed in 2002 and evaluated by the authors, has proven effective in raising the awareness of children exposed to the program's safety strategies messages. Based on their research, the authors suggest that the police should work systematically with schools to educate children about sexual abuse in their neighborhoods and in cyberspace.

Section 3: Knowledge Management: Capturing, Sharing, and Sustaining

Stefan Holgersson of the Swedish Police Authority in Stockholm and Peter Gottschalk of the Norwegian School of Management in Oslo classify and describe different types of knowledge that are part of patrolling police officers' practice. In their discussion, they address five primary activities: initial crime scene assessment, assessment of incoming information, selecting appropriate lines of enquiry, case development, and postcharge case management.

Katrina Berger and Dee Wood Harper discuss jurisprudence, law, and empirical research dealing with racial profiling in the United States. They discuss the relevant legal jurisprudence on the limits of police action relative to minority populations. Their study also identifies the complexities of researching or establishing profiling incidents in policing. Finally, the authors provide guidelines for investigating terrorism and immigration issues.

Brion Sever and colleagues investigate a municipal police departments' attention to crime analysis. Their study examines the use of such strategies in New Jersey police departments in jurisdictions with a population of more than 15,000. They surveyed 90 police departments in New Jersey in an effort to determine the type of computer technology they possess as well as the extent and manner to which they use crime analysis. They found that although most departments use crime analysis, few use modern strategies in such endeavors. Thus, the outcome of their study could potentially inform police practitioners of the utility and acceptability of crime analyses tools and models.

John Middleton-Hope, Chief of the Lethbridge Regional Police Service in Alberta, Canada, shares with the reader his concepts of emerging police administration strategies for the twenty-first century. Middleton-Hope notes that police leaders must deploy new strategies to confront emerging challenges in policing. His discussions included the ethical challenges that have eroded the image of the police as well as political challenges emanating from the community. He argues that in this new environment police chiefs should be more like corporate chief executive officers rather than just top cops. Thus, he suggests that the police executives must adopt the practices of corporations to develop human resources, ensure fiscal accountability, and create strategies for organizational effectiveness and efficiency.

Section 4: International Police Practices and Cultures

In the final section, scholars and police executives from Norway, Canada, the United States, and India present ideas and research on emerging police practices. The chapters stress the importance of social and organizational cultures and how they shape police behaviors and values.

Rune Glomseth of the Norwegian Police University College and Petter Gottschalk of the Norwegian School of Management present data based on questionnaires, interviews, and observations conducted to measure the dominating values among police officers assigned to the Norwegian Counter Terrorist Unit, which is a special unit within the Norwegian Police Service.

Helen Rosenberg of the University of Wisconsin at Parkside and her associates report on their examinations of police officers' attitudes toward various aspects of a community policing program in Racine, Wisconsin. Their study, based on a 40-item survey, documents officer perceptions to gradual changes implemented over a 6-year period in the Racine Police Department. They report that, despite the fact that an attempt was made to integrate community policing into a unified policy, departmental subcultures across rank signified divisions in the organization.

K. S. Subramanian provides an in-depth view of policing services in India and the adherence to democratic principles. The chapter provides a thorough synopsis of the Human Rights Watch Report, a comprehensive study of the Indian Police. Subramanian provides valuable insights on police behavior and reform efforts. He claims that although the Human Rights Watch efforts were commendable, police abuses were being perpetuated. He touches on the role of culture and politics in policing as an explanation for the occurrence of these abuses.

Altogether, this volume promises a wide array of topics and perspectives. The chapters present and examine current and emerging police practices involving diverse issues in crime and disorder. The collection also touches on issues of accountability, legality, and control on the use of force and performance of police functions. One little caveat: The reader might see an emerging trend of the internationalization and uniformity of police practices in this volume. Furthermore, the body of literature, both theoretical and pragmatic, found in these chapters seems to converge. These latter phenomena are not intentional. Thus, the reader should remember that policing viewed from the local perspective tends to project the bias of the cultures and social organizations where the police operate. Therefore, readers are advised to reflect and critique these chapters based on these various cultures from which they originated.

The Contributors

James F. Albrecht
New York City Police Department (Retired)
New York City, New York

Avdi S. Avdija
Indiana State University
Terre Haute, Indiana

Gad J. Bensinger
Loyola University
Chicago, Illinois

Katrina W. Berger
Department of Homeland Security
Washington, D.C.

Duncan Chappell
University of Sydney
New South Wales, Australia

Simon Fraser University
British Columbia, Canada

Terry G. Coleman
Chief of Moose Jaw Police (Retired)
Saskatchewan, Canada

Julia C. Davidson
University of Westminster
London, United Kingdom

Venessa Garcia
Kean University
Union, New Jersey

Rune Glomseth
Norwegian Police University College
Oslo, Norway

Petter Gottschalk
Norwegian School of Management
Oslo, Norway

Dee Wood Harper, Jr.
Loyola University
New Orleans, Louisiana

Stefan Holgersson
Linköping University
Linköping, Sweden

Arthur J. Jurigio
Loyola University
Chicago, Illinois

Mutlu Koseli
Turkish National Police
Ankara, Turkey

Thomas J. Lemmer
Chicago Police Department
Chicago, Illinois

Scott Lewis
City Attorney's Office (Retired)
Racine, Wisconsin

Elena Martellozzo
University of Westminster
London, United Kingdom

Darko Maver
University of Maribor, Slovenia
Faculty of Criminal Justice and Security
Ljubljana, Slovenia

Gorazd Meško
University of Maribor, Slovenia
Faculty of Criminal Justice and Security
Ljubljana, Slovenia

John Middleton-Hope
Chief of Police (Retired)
Alberta, Canada

Helen Rosenberg
University of Wisconsin–Parkside
Kenosha, Wisconsin

Brion Sever
Monmouth University
West Long Branch, New Jersey

Robert T. Sigler
University of Alabama–Tuscaloosa
Tuscaloosa, Alabama

K. S. Subramanian
Council for Social Development
New Delhi, India

Antonia Tsiandi
Monmouth University
West Long Branch, New Jersey

1 Global Innovations in Policing

Analyzing the Implementation and Evolution of Community Policing in the United States and Scandinavia

1

JAMES F. ALBRECHT
New York City Police Department (Retired)

Contents

Introduction

In the 1980s, police administrators in the United States implemented community policing initiatives based on research conducted by Herman Goldstein (1990) and Robert Trojanowicz (1988). Quickly becoming the buzzword of law enforcement executives and aided by federal funding under the COPS (Community-Oriented Policing Services) program community policing became a recognized program in almost every local American police agency. Police commanders routinely boasted of their strong ties and cooperation with their communities.

However, in the late 1990s, the success of the more proactive zero-tolerance philosophy and computerized crime analysis in some large municipalities drew attention away from community-oriented policing, as crime rates declined nationally. Law enforcement agency funding shifted to enhanced technology and crime mapping. At the same time, the more proactive approach resulted in a small number of sensationalized tragedies involving shootings that were criticized by minority group leaders. Ultimately, the tragic events of September 11, 2001, brought an end to community policing as the predominant emphasis of law enforcement agency deployment in the United States. The contemporary need for counterterrorism measures and the ready availability of federal grants to undertake these new responsibilities have brought community policing to the brink of extinction within the United States. While no police commander would openly note any decline in their police–community partnership, the reality is that these endeavors have dramatically declined at a time when many constituents, particularly those from minority communities, allege police abuse and racial bias.

Meanwhile, community policing and the problem-solving concept have brought increased vigor to law enforcement practices in other nations. Community policing programs implemented in Europe, particularly in Scandinavian countries, have been comprehensively examined, but ultimately these evaluations appear to reflect the trend witnessed in the United States, albeit at a slower pace. Technology has superseded the personal touch of community policing and actually has again moved local law enforcement officials away from direct contact with the population that they serve.

This has caused unwanted criticism of the police, more so in the United States, due to the loss of the once existent and relatively strong community–police partnership. Effective strategies involving crime analysis, geographic information system (GIS) mapping, and "Hot Spot" deployment are the contemporary trends in the arena of modern law enforcement. Unfortunately, the recent emphasis on counterterrorism and emergency incident response and the dramatic reduction in federal community policing funding for U.S. police agencies have brought community policing closer to extinction, and this pattern is being copied in other democratic countries across the globe.

Community Policing in New York City and the United States

In January 1994, Republican candidate Rudolph W. Giuliani was sworn in as New York City's (NYC's) mayor. His platform promoted a hard stance against crime and the improvement of quality of life throughout the city. To spearhead these efforts, Mayor Giuliani appointed former Boston Police Chief William Bratton as the New York City Police Commissioner. His first month in office saw the total restructuring of the upper executive corps with highly motivated youngblood administrators taking over the top executive positions.

Under the supervision and guidance of former New York City Police Department (NYPD) chief Louis Anemone, a number of initiatives have been undertaken since 1994. Since their implementation and continuing through 2010, a dramatic 85% reduction in violent crime and a notable improvement in quality of life have resulted. The following initiatives represent some of the more significant and successful programs instituted by the NYPD:

1. Zero-tolerance proactive policing
2. The COMPSTAT Process
3. Twelve new police strategies
4. Crime reduction principles
5. Vehicle safety checkpoints
6. Truancy sweeps
7. Surveillance cameras
8. Enhanced intelligence gathering
9. Suspect background identification

Zero-Tolerance Proactive Policing

The NYPD crime reduction strategists theorized that individuals who committed lower level offenses may later be responsible for participating in more violent criminal activity. By targeting and detaining offenders for less serious infractions, the police may be preventing a more tragic incident from occurring. While this concept may sound like a recent innovation, it was first introduced by Patrick Colquhoun (1795) in the 1700s, when he advocated targeting nonviolent unlawful activity, such as gambling and public intoxication, to deter more serious illegal activity. The NYPD quickly initiated a zero-tolerance policy and began proactively enforcing lower-level offenses including panhandling, public intoxication, excessive noise, and disorderly conduct. All NYPD patrol personnel were supplied with pocket-sized cards outlining legal references and procedural guidelines involving the lower-level infractions. An additional goal of this strategy was to improve the quality of life in public areas. In line with Wilson and Kelling's (1982) "Broken Windows," both sociologists and practitioners believed that addressing the quality of life concerns of the community should improve public confidence in the police and reduce the level of fear in the traditionally higher crime neighborhoods in the city.

Since its inception in January 1994, this initiative has been highly effective and has greatly contributed to the impressive 80% decrease in Federal Bureau of Investigation (FBI) Index crime levels in New York City through the start of the new millennium. As a result, New York City is now regarded as the safest city in the United States with a population exceeding 1 million residents, and this remarkable improvement in quality of life resulted in the easy and overwhelming reelection of Mayor Giuliani for a second term.[1]

The COMPSTAT Process

Since his appointment in 1994, former NYPD chief Anemone advocated holding police executives completely accountable for the operation of their commands. Police commanders have now been granted the discretion to assign their personnel as they deem necessary and no longer as per predesignated staffing percentage guidelines. To be best informed and to appropriately deploy manpower, it is clear that police commanders must have information regarding current crime trends and productivity indicators readily available. Due to the archaic handwritten fashion in which criminal incidents were recorded in the past, statistical information regarding index crimes, arrests, and summary activity was routinely available 90 days to 6 months after the fact. To remedy this situation, the NYPD undertook the task of inputting all crime incident reports and arrest information into a computerized database. Precinct commanders and police executives now receive a weekly report that outlines summary statistics involving command demographics, precinct and unit staffing levels, civilian complaints, overtime, summons activity, sick rate, radio runs, and response time with comparisons with prior year and citywide data. Of even more importance is the weekly comparison report that documents criminal incident, arrest, and summons activity on a week-, month- and year-to-date basis. Each commander must prepare a weekly response delineating efforts being made by his or her respective units to further improve the statistics and reduce serious crime.

To ensure that police commanders are continually analyzing this information and addressing necessary concerns, they are summoned to unannounced COMPSTAT meetings at police headquarters, at least once each month. These commanders are subjected to direct questioning by the police commissioner, the chief of the department, and other higher-ranking executives regarding the efforts being conducted to address recent violent crimes in their respective jurisdictions and to ensure that crime reduction strategies, as instituted, are effective.

Twelve New Police Strategies

To give precinct commanders and police executives direction in their crime reduction endeavors, the NYPD has outlined 12 department-wide strategies that address important issues such as gun control, youth violence, drug dealing, domestic violence, quality of life concerns, auto theft, police corruption, traffic problems, professional and courteous public interaction, and the apprehension of fugitives.

Crime Reduction Principles

The NYPD has outlined four crime reduction principles that apply the problem-solving philosophy to the crime reduction strategies: (1) accurate and timely intelligence; (2) effective tactics; (3) rapid deployment of personnel and resources; and (4) relentless follow-up and assessment.

In line with this initiative, each precinct now has a special operations lieutenant whose responsibility is to assist the precinct commander in analyzing crime patterns and quality of life conditions and to design a customized strategic response. The special operations lieutenant additionally establishes and maintains liaison with other NYPD units (e.g., narcotics, vice enforcement, emergency services) and government and public agencies that can assist in the suppression of crime and the improvement of the quality of life in the neighborhood concerned.

Vehicle Safety Checkpoints

Each precinct and uniformed enforcement unit has been directed to conduct regularly scheduled vehicle safety checkpoints (using the constitutionally permitted nonarbitrary method that allows police personnel to stop vehicles in a systematic fashion, e.g., every vehicle, every fifth vehicle, every green vehicle, every vehicle with Pennsylvania registration plates, every taxi). Police officers are directed to conduct driver license and criminal warrant checks on all individuals stopped and to arrest or summons violators. While this may appear at face value to be purely an income-generating operation, it has led to a dramatic reduction in auto thefts and a decrease in both vehicle accidents and pedestrian fatalities throughout the city. To obtain a greater benefit, the checkpoints are regularly conducted at accident-prone intersections, in higher-crime areas, or on streets where a crime pattern has been identified. The checkpoints are normally conducted for 1- to 3-hour periods, and the increased uniform presence will act as a deterrent to violent crime in the surrounding public areas. The checkpoints may also be used to facilitate the exchange of information whereby wanted person bulletins and crime prevention information are distributed to vehicle occupants who may reside in, drive through, or frequent the area.

Truancy Sweeps

It is widely recognized that juveniles and adolescents are responsible for a significant portion of violent crime and community complaints. The New York City Education Law allows police officers to detain individuals during school hours who appear to be 17 years of age or younger. The pedigree information is recorded, criminal warrant checks are conducted, parents and guardians are notified, and the truants are returned to their respective schools if within the precinct boundary or to truant drop-off locations designated by the New York City Board of Education. School personnel also conduct truant debriefings and make additional parental notifications. NYPD guidelines also allow police officers to frisk or handcuff the truants as the situation dictates for safety reasons per *Terry v. Ohio* guidelines (*Terry v. Ohio,* 392 U.S. 1(1968)). Countless weapons have been discovered and removed as a result of this initiative, and those responsible have been further charged as juvenile delinquents or youthful offenders in both family and criminal courts. Locations that have been found to routinely harbor truants, such as billiard halls, bars, and small convenience stores that sell alcohol and cigarettes, have also been targeted for increased enforcement activity to deter catering to underage or truant teenagers.

Surveillance Cameras

By monitoring television screens that are connected to video cameras placed in public areas, a single police officer can maintain observation of a widespread area that, in all likelihood, would require the assignment of a team of patrol officers. The NYPD has conducted a number of pilot programs to measure the crime reduction potential of video cameras strategically placed in problem-plagued public areas, such as city parks, school yards, and the public areas surrounding socialized housing developments. Initial results have indicated a dramatic decline in reported criminal and community complaints and have resulted in an expansion of the program. It appears that the mere presence of the video camera itself acts as a deterrent to illegal activity. The operation is very cost-effective in that a restricted duty (injured) police officer is assigned to monitor the television screens in lieu of the deployment of a squad of police officers to cover the same area, thus saving valuable man-hours and allowing the redeployment of these personnel to other initiatives and enforcement functions.

Enhanced Intelligence Gathering

To solve crimes and apprehend offenders, extensive effort has been applied to obtain as much intelligence information as possible. After the police respond and gather information and evidence at a serious criminal event, or if it is determined that a pattern (serial) crime has occurred, the precinct commander or precinct detective squad supervisor will direct a community policing beat officer or detective to respond to the incident location and conduct an investigative debriefing of area residents and business persons. This canvass may occur immediately after an incident, the next day at approximately the same time of occurrence, during evening hours when residents are more likely to be home, or, if warranted, repeatedly at different times.

Another extremely effective initiative to obtain criminal intelligence is to have precinct detectives approach persons in police custody and thoroughly debrief them using a list of prepared general questions such as, "Do you know anyone that sells drugs?" or "Do you know anyone that possesses illegal weapons?" and a list of relevant questions dealing with current ongoing investigations such as, "Last Thursday a homicide occurred at First Avenue and 55th Street not far from your residence. Do you know anything about this? Did you hear any rumors?" While there are apparent restrictions regarding the questioning of suspects (per the Miranda guidelines), suspects often have no reservations about discussing criminal conduct that has been committed by others.

In addition, arrested individuals who have waived Miranda protections and have chosen to be questioned by investigators are thoroughly debriefed regarding other criminal participants (e.g., "Who sold you the narcotics? Who offered to buy the stolen property from you? Who else participated in the planning of this crime?"). Detailed information should be obtained in an effort to procure arrest and search warrants with the assistance of the prosecutor's office. The ultimate goal is to remove as many violators from the streets as possible.

Suspect Background Identification

Many violators, when arrested, refuse to identify themselves, use a fictitious identity, or are released on their own recognizance without a thorough background investigation (e.g., parole or probation status, arrest warrant, recidivist status, suspended or revoked driver's license, bench warrant history). NYPD arresting officers can no longer release an individual by issuing a desk appearance ticket or universal summons without first positively identifying the suspect. Only certain select forms of identification (i.e., photo driver's license, valid passport, citizenship or naturalization papers, and resident alien card) are acceptable. Without proper identification, the individual will not be released and will be processed as an arrest and delivered directly to the court system. If the suspect does provide legitimate identification, a thorough background investigation will be conducted before the person may be issued a court appearance ticket. If a person fails any stage of the background check, he or she will be removed directly to court for a prompt arraignment before a judge.

Millennium Statistics

At the start of 2010, New York City progressed through the new millennium as the safest city in America with a population over 1 million people. While New York City had consistently ranked in the top 10 crime-ridden cities in the United States through the early 1990s, NYC now ranks near the bottom of the more than 220 American cities with a population over 100,000 (U.S. Department of Justice, 2009). The strategic deployment of NYPD personnel, coupled with the zero-tolerance philosophy, has resulted in continuing reductions in serious crime through 2010, which continues the crime reduction trend that started in 1994. Since the COMPSTAT and zero-tolerance initiatives have commenced, serious crime in New York City has decreased more than 80%, and this trend continues, with the largest and most impressive reduction in the former bellwether crime of murder, which has declined almost 85% since 1994. The number of individuals injured by gunfire in NYC in the last 6 years also declined approximately 75%. It is estimated that this dramatic reduction in murder since the inception of the new policing philosophy in NYC has spared over 20,000 lives from the murder rolls.[2] While the costs of policing the streets of New York City can be concretely defined, there is no way to estimate the value on the lives of the thousands of people that are alive today because of the NYPD's successful endeavors. Of interesting note, due to the lack of gunshot victims medical professionals have raised the issue that new medical interns no longer obtain sufficient trauma training at hospitals located throughout NYC.

Tourism and Revenue

The heightened sense of safety and security on the streets of New York City has had a drastic impact on business and tourism. Recent statistics indicate that in excess of 200,000 tourists visit NYC on average daily. The tourist trade, coupled with the success of flourishing new businesses, had resulted in annual tax surpluses surpassing $4 billion through the start of the new millennium. Unfortunately, the September 11, 2001, terrorist attack reversed that trend for a number of years, but the economic condition of NYC has steadily improved since that time to approach a $5 billion tax surplus in both 2006 and 2007. More importantly, New York City continues its designation as the safest big city in America.

A Look Back to the 1990s: Community Policing in NYC

As previously outlined, not only was crime rampant in New York City in 1990, but police–community relations were also at an all-time low. Due to NYC's high crime rate (with a murder rate that surpassed 2,200 in 1990) and a highly publicized corruption and perjury scandal, the public had little confidence or support for the police. In 1990, NYPD police commissioner Lee Brown was appointed by Mayor David Dinkins to rectify the sad state of affairs. Brown immediately instituted community policing as the department-wide philosophy. The entire police department was evaluated and reorganized, and thousands of police officers were reassigned from administrative tasks to patrol and enforcement responsibilities, with new civilian employees hired as their replacements. In addition, 5,000 new police officers were appointed over 5 years with supplementary funding supplied by New York State and the implementation of a new police tax. The community policing implementation plan, titled "Safe Streets/Safe City" (City of New York, 1990), called for precinct patrol personnel to be assigned to foot patrol in every neighborhood in the city. In fact, the contractual agreement between NYC and New York State mandated the deployment of between 30 to 70 police officers to foot patrol on community policing beats in each of the NYPD's 75 police stations or precincts, some of which are only 2 to 3 square miles (4 to 6 square kilometers) in area. The goal of this tactic was to increase the visible uniform presence in an effort to deter crime and increase the sense of public security.

Brown also instituted a dramatic change in management style by directing all precinct commanding officers to chair monthly Community Council Meetings that are held directly in each police station and that are open to all precinct residents and business persons. The purpose of these gatherings is to allow all members of the public to relay their concerns and complaints directly to the precinct commander, who was given the new responsibility as problem-solving coordinator for the jurisdiction. In addition, Brown, in an effort to strengthen the police–community partnership, mandated that an elected panel of five representatives from each precinct would designate the five priority problems to be addressed by precinct personnel and would evaluate the progress of the efforts and conditions each month. This clearly established the community as an equal participant in the police–community partnership.

The implementation of the community policing philosophy resulted in the stabilization of serious crime and a dramatic increase in citizen satisfaction in the police and an enhanced feeling of public security. Supporters of community policing note that there are two important components: enhancing community involvement while at the same time using a problem-solving approach against crime and other community concerns. Brown's implementation plan did much to enhance community participation but in reality left the responsibility of developing and implementing problem-solving strategies in the hands of front-line patrol officers. The community policing scale in the early 1990s, therefore, favored the community partnership half of the equation.

On the other hand, the new zero-tolerance crime analysis-oriented policing philosophy swings the scale to the other side by holding the precinct commander strictly accountable for the crime reduction problem-solving efforts within the jurisdiction. While community policing continues to be an important aspect of policing in New York City, the proactive and assertive enforcement efforts have placed a burden on police–community relations since the mid-1990s, most notably in communities with large African American and Hispanic populations.

Police–Community Relations

Mayor Giuliani's "get tough on crime" stance has had a clear impact on illegal and violent conduct and improved the quality of life on New York City's streets. Thorough analysis of crime has resulted in the strategic deployment of NYPD resources in the neighborhoods with the highest crime rates. In New York City, these areas tend to be predominantly minority communities at the lower end of the socioeconomic scale. The dramatic increase in uniformed police presence initially drew cries of a police state in these neighborhoods, but once violent crime subsided most community leaders quickly supported the new initiatives. It is now relatively safe to walk on the streets again, even in precincts that traditionally had high crime rates. However, some minority leaders and political activists have publicly extolled that the increased police presence in minority neighborhoods is racially motivated and is a coordinated effort to target only African Americans and Hispanics for summary action and arrest. Some of these minority community leaders often refuse to publicly acknowledge the positive impact of the statistical analysis of violence and crime trends and the strategic deployment of police personnel to high-crime neighborhoods and refuse to accept the reality that the majority of serious crime in New York City is committed by minority males (85%), most of whom are African American (55%; Ridgeway, 2007). The same leaders maintain that relying on statistics will result in stereotyping, which in essence promotes racism.

Racism and the Police

Is there racism within the police? Does racial profiling exist? Is there a clear definition of racial profiling? These are difficult questions to answer. Each person in society and each police officer have personal opinions and prejudices that may change after extended experience and exposure to the harsh realities of the street. The NYPD mandates that all personnel remain professional and neutral at all times. Is it possible that police officers can totally put aside personal beliefs or perceptions and take unbiased police action? Do police officers suspect that young African Americans driving fancy new cars are actually drug dealers or car thieves? Are police officers themselves being stereotyped as being antiminority and racially motivated? These questions cannot be concretely answered in general terms, and the responses will differ on an individual basis.

In 2000, the U.S. Department of Justice concluded that the NYPD did participate in widespread racial profiling and recommended an independent monitor of the police. The Justice Department came to this conclusion by stating that, since approximately 54% of the NYC population is non-White yet 90% of the persons stopped by NYPD officers with "reasonable suspicion" of criminal conduct as per *Terry v. Ohio* guidelines (U.S. Supreme Court, 1968) are minorities, NYPD officers are therefore using racial profiling as their justification to stop these suspicious individuals (U.S. Commission for Civil Rights, 2000).

These minority leaders and the U.S. Department of Justice failed to comprehend a major reality. While arrest and crime reporting data reveals that the criminal population in New York City is composed mainly of members from minority groups, most police officers (approximately 61% in the NYPD) are White males. This therefore creates the likelihood that male White police officers will routinely interact with minority suspects. This results in numerous occasions for minority leaders and the media to label sensitive incidents, such as police shootings and allegations of police brutality or misconduct, as being racially motivated. There have been an isolated number of highly sensationalized NYPD incidents that have drawn the attention of the media and the scrutiny of the public.

The 70th Precinct Police Brutality Case

In August 1997 in the early morning hours, as a crowd was leaving a dance club that was closing for the night, a large group of Haitian immigrants began fighting with each other. When 70th Precinct police personnel responded to the call for assistance, they themselves were turned upon by the intoxicated crowd. After further police officers arrived and the crowd was finally separated, one of the original combatants, Abner Louima, punched a uniformed police officer in the face without provocation. That officer, Justin Volpe, placed the individual under arrest. What happened next was clearly bizarre and difficult to comprehend. Later the same day, the suspect made the sensational allegation that his arresting officer had brutally and sexually attacked him in the police station bathroom. The Haitian and African American communities immediately staged large-scale demonstrations. The media grasped the allegation as the major headline for months, relying mainly on the fabricated claim by certain African American leaders that this single, isolated incident was an indication that police brutality against minorities in New York City was widespread. Almost 2 years later, in summer 1999, Police Officer Volpe pleaded guilty to this unbelievable crime. This brutal attack on an unarmed and handcuffed suspect was the first of a small number of incidents that have drained police–community relations in minority neighborhoods and have initiated a sense of mistrust in the New York City Police Department.

The Bronx Street Crime Unit Shooting

In February 1999, the elite plainclothes Street Crime Unit, with its reputation for arresting large numbers of violent and armed suspects throughout New York City, was deployed in the Soundview section in the Bronx in search of a violent serial rapist. One evening while patrolling the streets in their unmarked vehicles, two officers observed a male in a dimly lit doorway that they believed resembled the sketch of the wanted suspect. As they exited their auto, the first two officers were joined by two colleagues who had also observed the suspect. The four officers identified themselves as police officers and directed the suspect to stop and raise his hands. The suspect, in apparent defiance, started turning away and reached into his pocket while standing in the dark apartment building doorway. The officer standing closest to the suspect observed the male remove a black object from his pocket, yelled the word "Gun!" to his colleagues, and in self-defense drew his firearm and fired. The three other officers also fired, believing that the ricocheting bullets were actually bullets being fired at them. At the conclusion of the event, which lasted only 5 seconds, the four officers had fired 41 bullets, and the suspect lay dead in the building doorway. The object in the suspect's hand turned out to be a black wallet. It is unclear why the suspect made the evasive and furtive movements, but the suspect was an illegal alien from Africa who may have incorrectly believed that he would be deported if apprehended by authorities. All four officers involved in the incident were White, and the same African American leaders once again proclaimed that the incident was a clear example of racism and racial profiling and called for large-scale demonstrations and civil disorder. The media also fueled the antipolice environment by reporting that the police had shot and killed an unarmed street peddler, when the victim's occupation had nothing to do with the incident. The Bronx prosecutor, Robert Johnson, himself an African American, in an apparent effort to gain political favor, charged the four officers with intentional premeditated murder.

The media attention and public outcry compelled the New York City Police Department to evaluate recent trends in the stopping of criminal suspects. The African American community alleged that NYPD personnel engage in racial profiling and thus target mainly African American and Hispanic individuals when conducting criminal investigations.

The NYPD analyzed documents to ascertain if these claims were true. The results of this investigation were interesting and notable. Although 90% of suspects described by crime victims were minorities, only 85% of the suspects stopped and investigated by police were African American or Hispanic, and 13% were White. These statistics therefore counter the claim that NYPD officers engage in racial profiling by intentionally detaining a larger proportion of minority suspects. It appears that police officers in New York City are merely stopping suspects in response to descriptions provided by crime victims, who in 81% of violent crime incidents are minorities themselves (NYPD, 2000). Mayor Giuliani and NYPD executives were quick to emphasize that their own findings counter the claim made by the U.S. Department of Justice that NYPD personnel engage in widespread racial profiling.

The four officers were tried in Criminal Court and in February 2000 were found not guilty of all charges, having been found to have acted in self-defense. The African American leaders disregarded the jury's findings and continued to cause more controversy. In two subsequent cases in which African American suspects were killed by police in New York City, these same leaders claimed that racism played a role, even though the police officers involved were themselves minorities and in both cases were involved in life-and-death situations in which the suspect was trying to take the officer's firearm. It often appeared as if the media enjoyed causing increased sensationalism and community unrest by emphasizing inaccurate information in their headline reports.

Courtesy, Professionalism, and Respect

In August 1997, in response to the 70th Precinct police brutality case, the NYPD released a new strategy aimed at improving the professional image of the police by emphasizing increased courtesy and respect to the public, criminal suspects, and NYPD supervisors and peers. A copy of the report, titled "Courtesy, Professionalism, Respect" (CPR; NYPD, 1997), was distributed to each of the 41,000 police officers and 9,000 civilian employees of the NYPD. The ultimate goal of this strategy was to breathe the new life into police–community relations.

The report emphasized positive interaction with the public and noted that if "crime levels decline, but members of the community are reluctant to approach police for fear of a negative encounter, then the police have not met their obligations to the public." The document continued that "negative perceptions of police behavior toward the public" may emanate "not only from incidents of actual misconduct, but also from situations where proper police actions were mistakenly viewed by the public as inappropriate" (NYPD, 1997). This is a clear reference to the media's continuous sensationalizing of controversial or questionable police actions and reporting of contradicting information, which in itself has repeatedly caused community unrest and, on occasion, rioting.

The NYPD has undertaken considerable effort to improve the image of the police. New initiatives have been instituted to enhance the quality of newly hired police officers. The applicant screening process has been revised to emphasize the "screening in" of candidates with desirable characteristics, rather than the "screening out" of unqualified candidates. In addition, efforts have been made to recruit most candidates from the pool of New York City residents, not from the surrounding suburbs. Many sociologists believe that persons who reside outside of major American cities may not appreciate the diversity and comprehend the cultural differences in the various communities in the neighboring metropolis. New York City residents now receive extra points toward the final score on hiring and promotional exams, and efforts have increased to conduct recruitment drives at colleges and schools in minority neighborhoods. Minimum educational requirements for newly hired police officers have also been increased from a high school diploma to 2 years of college education or 2 years of military service.

In 1994, the NYPD introduced the "Verbal Judo" concept when interacting with suspects and other members of the public. Every member of the NYPD has attended the "Verbal Judo" course, which emphasizes verbal deescalation techniques to help police officers avoid and defuse conflicts while obtaining voluntary compliance, improve communication skills, and reinforce concepts of professionalism and respect to ensure use of minimum necessary force (Thompson, 1983).

In addition to attending mandatory community meetings with representatives from the respective neighborhoods that they serve, all police officers have obtained and will continue to receive both ethical and cultural awareness training and now have the opportunity to obtain language instruction to overcome barriers and better communicate with neighborhood residents.

The NYPD has six separate performance monitoring programs designed to proactively identify and track police officers who present discipline problems, appear to use excessive force, or have personal difficulties that may impact their job performance. This computerized early warning system supplies numerical points to incidents that occur within a police officer's career. When a police officer obtains a target number of points, the individual is called into police headquarters and is interviewed by a peer counselor who apprises the officer of the situation and the negative impact it may have on his or her career aspirations. If the negative conduct fails to improve, then the officer concerned is assigned to a nonpatrol function. In addition, precinct and unit commanders are apprised of the special monitoring status of personnel within their command and must then reevaluate the progress of the individual officers.

The most important aspect of the CPR initiative is the regularly scheduled community meeting attended by police commanders in each of NYC's neighborhoods that allows an open dialogue between the public and the police. In addition, many highly successful programs have been instituted that involve community youth in sporting and other positive activities, where police officers can interact directly with the juvenile population in an informal and friendly environment.

Civilian Complaints Against Police

While some minority leaders and the media contend that the new zero-tolerance philosophy would create a police state in minority communities and that there would be an overwhelming increase in negative interactions with the police, civilian complaint statistics clearly indicate that the opposite is true. From 1995, when the new policing style was fully institutionalized, through the turn of the millennium, the number of civilian complaints filed against the NYPD has decreased by 20%, and the number of excessive force complaints has declined 32% (New York City Civilian Complaint Review Board, 2001). This impressive reduction occurred at the same time that the complement of police officers in the NYPD increased by approximately 12,000, which reflects a 40% increase in police personnel through 2001. However, once the New York City Civilian Complaint Review Board permitted online reporting of abuse allegations against members of the NYPD, the number of complaints increased dramatically (New York City Civilian Complaint Review Board, 2006). However, it should be noted that well less than 2% of all civilian complaints filed against NYPD members, including the more than 10,000 civilian staff (e.g., parking enforcement agents, school safety officers, 911 operators) are found to be substantiated.

Police Corruption and Misconduct

Of the approximately 35,000 police officers presently in the NYPD, there are over 500 investigators assigned to the Internal Affairs Bureau, which is responsible for thoroughly investigating allegations of corruption and police misconduct. With the dramatic increase in police resources in recent years, there has been a notable decrease in the number of corruption complaints filed against NYPD employees. In the period between 1997 and 2001, these complaints have declined approximately 33% and continue a trend that commenced in 1994 (NYPD, 2002).

In proactive fashion, Internal Affairs Bureau investigators routinely conduct integrity tests either randomly or involving targeted police personnel. These tests evaluate a police officer's reaction to found currency or narcotics and ensure that legal and police department procedural guidelines are complied with. From 1997 through 2001, only one police officer has failed a random integrity test, and approximately 40 police employees have failed targeted tests (NYPD, 2002). Individuals failing an integrity test are subsequently arrested and suspended, and all efforts are made to terminate them from their employment with the NYPD.

All police officers are administered tests for illegal drug usage. These urine and hair sample tests are given to all newly hired police candidates, to all promoted and newly transferred personnel, to officers suspected of using drugs illegally based on allegations and observation, and to all police personnel on a random basis. In 1998, 16 and in 1999, 25 police officers failed the illegal drug examinations and were subsequently and automatically fired from the NYPD. The numbers of drug test failures continues to decline (NYPD, 2002).

Fatal Shootings Involving the Police

In 1990, at the peak of the rising crime rate, there were 41 fatal shootings by NYPD personnel, which declined to 30 in 1994, when the zero-tolerance philosophy was initially instituted. In 1999, there were 11 fatal shootings, a 75% reduction since 1990 and a 65% drop since 1994. In addition, the number of shooting incidents involving NYPD officers has decreased over 50% since 1994, and the number of bullets shot by NYPD personnel has decreased more than 45% over the same time frame (NYPD, 2001). These dramatic reductions occurred as the firearms carried by NYPD officers were improved from the six-shot revolver to the 16-shot 9 mm handgun. To better appreciate these statistics, one must consider that the number of sworn officers in the NYPD increased almost 40% over the same period. When compared with other metropolitan police departments in the United States, the NYPD is actually one of the most restrained law enforcement agencies. These figures have remained relatively stable through the new millennium.

As the streets of New York City have become safer for the public, they have also become safer for NYPD officers. From 1999 through early 2003, no members of the NYPD were killed by gunfire. However, that figure has unfortunately changed through 2004 and 2005 with three line-of-duty deaths annually involving NYPD enforcement personnel (NYPD, 2006). Clearly, though, this is much lower than line-of-duty death trends witnessed in New York City and across the United States from the 1970s to the early 1990s.

The Effective and Professional NYPD

Not only has the 1994 reorganization of the NYPD and the institutionalization of the zero-tolerance philosophy resulted in the dramatic 85% reduction in serious crime in New York City since that time, but also all indications are that the New York City Police Department has continued to evolve into a highly professional police agency. From 1994 through 2002, the sworn officer complement of the NYPD had increased by approximately 12,000 police officers (or about 40%), yet the number of civilian complaints filed against the police, fatal police shootings, police shooting incidents, police brutality complaints, and corruption and misconduct allegations made against the NYPD have all drastically declined.

It appears that the negative perspective that the media and certain minority leaders are portraying of the police is inaccurate and that the opposite is actually true. The stereotyping of NYPD personnel as being brutal, abusive, and racist is based not on fact or reality but on isolated incidents or fabricated allegations, and it often appears that the media is merely relying on the sensationalism created by opportunistic minority leaders to sell more newspapers and obtain more television advertisement revenue.

It should be noted, though, that a certain amount of racism and prejudice exists in many individuals regardless of profession. But the strong probability that a male White police officer will become involved in a "negative" incident (e.g., arrest, shooting, physical confrontation) with a minority suspect is not based on racism but is merely the most likely police–suspect interaction encountered in New York City. The public and the media both have to acknowledge that reality.

It also should be emphasized that all efforts should be made to gain the respect and cooperation of community members, and the NYPD and police agencies throughout the world should ensure that their personnel are educated in cultural diversity and in courtesy, professionalism, and respect. Recruitment of new officers should target all facets of the community at large. Diversity in police agencies will improve public confidence and satisfaction in the police. No effort should be spared to improve and strengthen the police–community partnership. The support and trust of the population that is served is an important and necessary aspect of effective policing and is just as relevant an indicator of police department success as crime reduction.

The Post-September 11, 2001 World

Stating that the September 11, 2001, terrorist attacks on American soil have changed life in the United States and the role of law enforcement is an understatement. On September 11, 2001, over 3,000 innocent lives were lost in a surprise dramatic attack by extremist Middle Eastern terrorists. The loss of 420 rescue personnel in New York City, including 72 law enforcement officers, coupled by extensive and exhausting counterterrorism measures, has dramatically caused a drop in morale and the retirement and resignation of over 15,000 NYPD officers since 2001. The complement of officers has steadily declined from a high of almost 42,000 in 2001 to the current level of approximately 31,000 enforcement personnel, a steep decline of almost 30%.

This terrible tragic attack did have one positive result. Public support for police and rescue personnel dramatically improved. This immense tragedy did not cause dissension but actually drew Americans and the international community together. Unfortunately, another intention of the perpetrators was to cause an economic decline in NYC and the United States, which did occur but has slowly improved.

Mayor Giuliani, who had lost much of his public support, particularly from minority communities within New York City, quickly emerged as a strong leader in the darkest hours in U.S. history. The NYPD, faced with extensive and new counterterrorism responsibilities, continues the successful crime reduction trend to this day. But the NYPD continues to receive criticism from the African American community after each incident in which a White officer interacts with a minority (non-White) suspect under media sensationalized circumstances.

The Future of Community Policing in the United States

So where does all this leave community policing? Do the two basic subcomponents community participation and problem solving still warrant a role in contemporary law enforcement? The answer is a definitive yes. With the additional responsibility of counterterrorism, the community has been called upon to provide law enforcement with as much assistance as possible. Given the gravity of the situation, it is imperative that everyone acts as the additional eyes and ears of the police. In addition, community input and feedback are critical aspects (and measures) of agency success. If the population served is not content with the police service, then community unrest could result. And as public servants, the police hold an important stake in ensuring that the public has both trust and confidence in law enforcement.

The second aspect of community policing (i.e., problem solving) has clearly become an important factor in the national crime reduction trend. While the emphasis has shifted from the front-line beat cop back to the local commander, instituting a strategy that addresses the root cause of the problem or crime trend can save considerable effort in the long run. With the assistance of computerized crime analysis and crime mapping, major police departments can strategically deploy personnel to disorder-ridden areas. The use of the broken windows theory and the zero-tolerance enforcement initiative has had a dramatic effect on improvement of the quality of life as well as on unforeseen decreases in violent and serious crime.

What then has affected the concept of community policing in America the most? Clearly the emphasis on homeland security, not only in local law enforcement deployment but more importantly in the drastic shift in federal funding, has played a major role in the contemporary trend away from local community policing efforts. COPS and other traditional grants for local law enforcement agencies have become practically extinct, as the emphasis has shifted to counterterrorism and emergency preparedness. While community policing clearly has merit and is the basis for recent dramatic crime reductions both locally and nationally, the concept as originally depicted unfortunately may go the way of the dinosaur.

Community Policing in Scandinavia

The crime reduction successes in the United States have drawn the attention of international police executives over the last decade. During the dawn of the American crime decline of the mid-1990s, many law enforcement leaders placed responsibility for this dramatic accomplishment on the community policing strategies that they had been publicly endorsing. The promotion of this accomplishment caught the attention of the federal government, and the

COPS funding initiative was created. No police executive could turn down federal funding for additional personnel and equipment. The crime reduction trend continues in the United States to this day, and police executives in other nations have been paying attention. As crime rates increased in Europe and globally, the public there called for action. If this strategy worked in one Western democracy, then why not in another? The national police administrations in Scandinavian countries and other nations such as Israel, South Africa, Haiti, and Brazil have opted to implement community policing as the crime fighting initiative for the new millennium (Davis, Henderson, & Merrick, 2003).

Policing in Sweden

The Scandinavian country of Sweden is protected by the National Police Administration composed of a national headquarter, 21 subordinate county police authorities, and 23,000 employees. Annually 1.2 million criminal offenses are reported to the Swedish police. The most frequent grounds for police interaction involves public disorder complaints (35% of all incidents), followed by 16% for violent crime and 15% for theft (Swedish Police, 2005a).

Following the U.S. trend, the Swedish National Police Administration instituted the community and problem-oriented policing models as the new law enforcement ideology in the early 1990s. In addition, an effort was made to incorporate community involvement in crime fighting. A complement of 1,500 auxiliary (volunteer) police officers now assist Swedish police in uniformed patrol and rescue operations. The Goldstein model involving fixed localized assignment, and front-line problem solving was selected as the methodology to be instituted. Regional commanders were also granted the discretion to deploy personnel as needed (over 6-week periods), which permitted the assignment of resources to reflect crime trends. The result has been the stabilization of crime in Sweden over the last decade (Swedish Police, 2005b).

Another initiative has been the development of a comprehensive survey to measure the quality of police service. The Swedish Police Balanced Scorecard, which examined crime victimization, fear of crime, and fear of disorder (quality-of-life offenses), has been in use since 1998. Over 200,000 surveys have been administered nationally resulting in the following significant findings:

- The main public fear of disorder involved interaction with intoxicated persons and drug users in public places.
- The fear of crime was highest in transportation facilities such as train stations and bus depots.

- The fear of crime was dramatically higher in cities than in suburban and countryside regions.
- The public preferred visible foot police patrols over longer vehicular patrol shifts.
- The public is increasingly dissatisfied with the processing and investigation of criminal complaints.

The Swedish police have thus created a mechanism to obtain public feedback and have used the citizen survey as a measure of police effectiveness (Swedish Police, 2005b). In summary, the National Police Administration in the 1990s accepted the Goldstein model of community policing as its crime reduction ideology. However, over time the regional commander, and not the front-line foot patrol officer, has been designated the chief problem solver and strategist, which reflects more the crime analysis (COMPSTAT) prototype than the delineated problem-oriented practices of Goldstein. The results have, however, been impressive with crime rates remaining steady since the initiative's inception. The use of the citizen survey as a major measure of police efficiency does reflect the country's desire to use public input to impact police performance.

Policing in Norway

The Norwegian Police is a national agency under the supervision of the National Police Directorate. Specialized national investigative units and the National Police Academy join 27 regional police districts with a total complement of 12,000 employees. Theft-related crimes account for the vast majority of criminal complaints followed by a small number of drug-, violence-, and vandalism-related crimes (Norwegian Police, 2005).

In 2002, the Norwegian police instituted crime prevention policing, which emphasized the Goldstein problem-oriented policing methodology. However, keeping in line with the American trend, the district commander was designated the problem-solving strategist (not the front-line patrol officer), which reflects the COMPSTAT model. As a result, national crime rates, which had been stable since the end of the 1990s, commenced an impressive decline overall and in each category but drug-related offences (Norwegian Police, 2006).

The crime analysis and problem-oriented model is now the mandated crime reduction strategy with a directive that all districts receive specific training in the concept by the end of 2006. The emphasis is now on proactive enforcement over reactive response. In line with the community policing model, the police receive training in contact with both public and private agencies to foster the involvement of social agencies to deter delinquency and drug usage and the use of security personnel and architects to promote safety through environmental design. In addition, fixed patrol assignment has been directed, but very few officers are routinely assigned to foot patrol, which is the most recognized form of community policing within the Goldstein (1990) and Trojanowicz (1988) perspectives. Efforts have been made to emphasize community involvement, and the Night Raven civilian patrol program has become highly regarded and extremely successful (Norwegian Police, 2006).

In summary, the police of Norway have incorporated accepted community policing and problem-oriented practices into their crime fighting initiatives. In line with recent American successes, the task of coordinating problem-solving strategies has been delegated to the local commander. The initiative has been successful as crime continues to decline. Efforts to engage the public in crime prevention endeavors also has proven to be beneficial. The one drawback has been the difficulty of police executives to deploy additional personnel during days and time frames needed as reflected by crime trends. Cultural norms and lack of union cooperation have made it challenging for commanders to assign supplementary personnel to weekend and evening patrols, when street-level crime and disorder conditions are most visible. Regardless of this drawback, the Norwegian police appear to be moving in a positive direction.

The Future of Community Policing

It is clear that the paradigm of community policing as described by both Goldstein (1990) and Trojanowicz (1988) never reached its advertised fruition. While appealing and successful in small-scale pilot projects, when expanded to large agencies the expected goals were rarely, if ever, achieved. However, the problem-solving concept did evolve into the crime analysis and proactive strategic response model most clearly exhibited by the COMPSTAT practices of New York City and copied elsewhere. Most law enforcement executives and many criminologists give this aspect of the community policing ideal credit, at least partially, for crime reduction trends in large cities and nationally in America and for crime declines in other nations such as Norway and Sweden.

It would therefore appear that community policing in its purest form is facing extinction both in the United States and internationally, but the concept is still being promoted by law enforcement executives as a means to advocate enhanced police–community cooperation and partnership. Computer analysis and proactive strategic deployment (based on crime mapping and "hot spot" deployment) appear to be the more desirable (and clearly more effective) forms of problem-oriented policing and crime fighting. In the United States, budgetary shifts emphasizing counterterrorism have taken funding away from most community policing-related endeavors. While no police executive will publicly admit this reality, community policing in its classical form has never been fully realized and faces extermination in both the United States and abroad. It can be concluded that in the contemporary world technology has taken away the personal touch within local law enforcement. This trend is clearly being duplicated internationally.

References

Colquhoun, P. (1975). *A Treatise on the Police of the Metropolis.* Patterson Smith Reprint Series in Criminology, Law Enforcement and Social Problems, Publication No. 42. 7th ed. (reprinted 1969).

City of New York. (1990). *Safe Streets/ Safe City.* Published by the Office of the New York City Mayor.

Davis, R., Henderson, N., & Merrick, C. (2003). Community Policing: Variations on the Western Model in the Developing World. *Police Practice and Research,* Vol. 4, No. 3, pp. 285–300.

Goldstein, H. (1990). *Problem-Oriented Policing.* New York: McGraw Hill Publishers.

Israeli Police (2004). *Israel Police.*

New York City Civilian Complaint Review Board. (2001). *New York City Civilian Complaint Review Board Annual Report 2000.*

New York City Civilian Complaint Review Board. (2006) *New York City Civilian Complaint Review Board Annual Report 2005.*

New York City Police Department. (NYPD). (1990). *NYPD Staffing Needs Plan.*

New York City Police Department. (NYPD). (1994). *The COMPSTAT Process.*

New York City Police Department. (NYPD). (1997). *Courtesy, Professionalism, Respect.*

New York City Police Department. (NYPD). (1994–2009). Police Department—City of New York Public Information Division Media Advisory (Daily press bulletins).

New York City Police Department. (NYPD). (2000). *NYPD Response to the draft "Police Practices and Civil Rights in New York City."*

New York City Police Department. (NYPD). (2001). *NYPD Firearms and Tactics Section Annual Firearms Discharge and Assault Report 2000.*

New York City Police Department. (NYPD). (2002). *NYPD Internal Affairs Bureau Annual Report 2001.*

New York City Police Department. (NYPD). (2006). *NYPD Firearms and Tactics Section Annual Firearms Discharge and Assault Report 2005.*

Norwegian Police. (2005). *Politiet: The Police in Norway.*

Norwegian Police. (2006). *Strategy Plan—Crime Prevention Policing 2002–2005.*

Ridgeway, G. (2007). *New York: Analysis of Racial Disparities in the New York City Police Department's Stop, Question and Frisk Practices.* Rand Corporation.

South Africa. (1995). *South African Police Service Act 68 of 1995.*

South African Department of Safety and Security. (1997). *Policy Framework and Draft Guidelines.*

South African Department of Safety and Security. (1997). *White Paper on Safety and Security.*

Swedish Police. (2005a). *Presentation of the Swedish Police Service.*

Swedish Police. (2005b). *Activity Control within the Swedish Police Force.*
Terry v. Ohio, 392 U.S. 1 (1968).
Thompson, G. J. (1983). *Verbal Judo: Words as a Force Option.* Springfield, IL: Charles C. Thomas Publishers.
Trojanowicz, R. C. (1988). *The Meaning of Community in Community Policing.* National Neighborhood Foot Patrol Center, School of Criminal Justice, Michigan State University.
U.S. Commission for Civil Rights. (2000). *Police Practices and Civil Rights in New York City.*
U.S. Department of Justice. (2009). *Statistics: FBI–2009 Crime Statistics: Preliminary Semiannual Uniform Crime Report.* U.S. Department of Justice, Criminal Justice Information Services Division.
Weisburd, D., Shalev, O., & Amir, M. (2001). *Community Policing in Israel: An Evaluation Study.* University of Jerusalem.
Wilson, J. Q., & Kelling, G. L. (1982). Broken Windows: The Police and Neighborhood Safety. *Atlantic Quarterly, 256*, 29-38.

Notes

1. The author was a member of the New York City Police Department from 1984 to 2003, and his firsthand exposure to the various elements of community policing from its inception in the early 1980s through his promotion to police station commander at the turn of the millennium make it difficult to reference many aspects since programmatic elements and statistics were obtained while in service and were common knowledge to NYPD practitioners, particularly those in executive ranks.
2. This statistic is calculated by comparing the base level of 2,000 murders each year in New York City in the early 1990s and comparing it with the contemporary figure, which hovers around 500 murders annually.

Think Globally, Solve Locally

Security Threats—From Public Opinion to a Proper Response

2

GORAZD MEŠKO
Faculty of Criminal Justice and Security

DARKO MAVER
Faculty of Criminal Justice and Security

Contents

Introduction: Safety and Security Issues in Slovenia

This chapter is organized in the following fashion. First, ideas on safety and security from a general point of view will be presented; second, security threats in Slovenia will be presented and ranked; and third, security and new ideas about shared responsibility on a local level in Slovenia will be presented and discussed. This chapter seeks to stimulate thinking about perceptions of security threats and ways of decision making when threats are identified.

Slovenia's period from the old millennium to the new one has been termed the transition period, as it is characterized by different processes related to economic and political transition and to the country becoming a member of both the North Atlantic Treaty Organization (NATO) and the European Union (EU). While discussions of these processes try to present a comprehensive explanation and convincing arguments within the framework of European and world history, they fail to recognize that Europe, as well as the entire world, is facing a more long-term and far-reaching transition of the society from the modern era to the so-called postmodern era. The absence of a thorough understanding of this transitional period evident in today's world is also characteristic of the discussion surrounding Slovenia and its security environment both present and future.

Postmodern society is characterized by unpredictable and explicitly contradictory economic, political, and social developments. Capitalist society today is characterized by the following:

1. Economic and political globalization,[1] which is becoming increasingly similar to economic and cultural imperialism. Among other things, it aggravates the polarization between the so-called developed and underdeveloped world.[2] Furthermore, it widens the gap between different cultures and civilizations, encourages religious fundamentalism and, consequently, terrorism; increases poverty (in the developed and underdeveloped world),[3] neglect, and exclusion of vulnerable social groups (e.g., minorities, youth, the elderly); and diminishes the possibility of individual countries working out a strategy of their own economic and general development.
2. Neoliberal capitalist economy. It is forcing its functional, market, and profit logic upon different areas of social relations (including those where it has nothing to offer).[4]
3. Political and economic integration efforts, in particular in European regions, which appeal to, for example, common goals and values, multiethnic cooperation, coexistence, and tolerance. Yet at the same time, these efforts bring about a worrying increase in isolationism, xenophobia, populism, and ideological and political (neo) conservatism.
4. Digitalization and informatization of social processes that are changing the foundations of the modern world. This era is alternately referred to as the *information, digital, postindustrial, postmodern, hypermodern, hypertechnological,* and *cyber* age.
5. A critical and skeptical approach in the field of social studies. This has undermined the authority of the disciplines and puts the emphasis on the relativity and limits of its cognitive potentials in search of the truth about man (see Wicks, 2003, pp. 1–6, 293–299).

6. The appearance of critical postmodern approaches in philosophy. These approaches stress the position that ratio should be defined not only as the central progressive force of historical development but also as means and a tool that has been used throughout history in different, but more or less subtle ways, by protagonists of different ideological and political backgrounds to dominate and to preserve the achieved social position. Such trends have undermined the foundations of modern enlightenment's "big story" about the exclusive role of science and rationalism in the emancipation of mankind (compare Wicks, 2003, pp. 217–242, and Litowitz, 1997, pp. 65–86).
7. Transformation of social values and lifestyles that has led to experimenting with life practices and their increasingly flexible, plural, and atomistic nature. It has also strengthened ideological, religious, and moral traditionalism.
8. A number of dramatic discoveries in astronomy, physics, genetics, and medicine. These have sharpened the contrast between largely liberal ideas about the world and man on one hand and more or less dogmatic ideas on the other.
9. The appearance of new, complex forms of extremely intensive and far-reaching threats to individual and collective security.

These new threats to individual and collective security comprise the subject of this chapter. In such circumstances, the general and political discourse, as well as the discourse in the security profession (which has to be underlined in this article), is becoming increasingly contradictory, ideological, and inefficient. Inefficient, contradictory, and legally and morally controversial also describe the approach to certain factors, which represent the central, most far-reaching, and intensive threat to security in the present world, such as international terrorism and organized crime, both of which are becoming phenomena of global proportions. The official security discourse has focused largely on the abstract security of the international community and international organizations and institutions or individual states and state institutions. This ultimately implies security of the elite or members of those groups that play a central role in society. Additionally, it implies security against "internal" and "external" threats, criminal victimization, and others that are all widely held to be rooted in culturally, economically, and socially deprived environments.

Security is nowadays one of the most frequent words used and is often ideologically misused (Kanduč, 2003). The official "understanding" of security problems and the ways of solving them have been obviously biased toward the interests of the so-called civilized world, its well-to-do individuals, and central (integrated) social groups. It is this security culture that forms the basis of the current security policy that is building walls.

A part of such security culture are new developments of safety and security councils in local municipalities in Slovenia (Meško & Lobnikar, 2005a), which represent so-called new old strategies in local responses to crime and disorder problems in addition to everyday policing (Meško & Klemenčič, 2007).

Security Culture and Threat Sources in Present Society

Security culture refers to the possibility of perceiving real dangers and threats, an understanding of the need for state and civil society security mechanisms and instruments, as well as a willingness for cooperation and sacrifice (Sotlar, 2000). Security culture can be "imposed" by the state in the sense of promotion of certain values (e.g., glorification of military service in the defense of the state), or it can be effected, in part, through threat sources. The central issue related to security culture is what and to what extent, if at all, citizens are willing to risk and to make sacrifices to safeguard certain social (and personal) values.

In October and November 2005, the Defence Research Centre (FDV–IDV) carried out the National and International Security opinion poll, in which 1,002 people were surveyed. The results show that, on average, Slovenians are willing to take risks and sacrifices themselves pertaining to several values.

As seen from Table 2.1, the values for which more than half of the polled are willing to take risks and make sacrifices emphasize particularly well-being—political and social rights, freedom, peace, and environmental protection. These are followed by state defense, gender equality, and fight against

Table 2.1 What Is Worth Risk and Sacrifice?

Values	Percent
Fight against poverty	59.9
World peace	57.2
Human rights	57.1
Environmental protection	53.4
Individuals rights	36.6
Defense of Slovenia	33.7
Fight against racism	27.6
Gender equality	25.8
Unification of Europe	17.3
Religious belief	10.2
Nothing from the above, undecided	5.0

Source: ORC, FDV-IDV (http://nato.gov.si/slo/javno-mnenje/nacionalna-varnost.pdf), April 5, 2009.

racism. In light of this, it can be surmised that these results are to a great extent influenced by perceived threat sources in Slovenia.

On a daily basis, states, societies, and individuals face different influences that potentially pose many threats. These threats represent a latent risk for their physical, psychological, spiritual, material, or other type of well-being. Threat sources can be classified into several dichotomies such as military and nonmilitary, internal and external, natural and anthrophogenous. Protection against threat sources at the state level can be effected either by decreasing vulnerability or by eliminating and preventing threat sources (Buzan, 1991; in Sotlar, 2000). Military, political, societal, economic, ecological, and other threat sources (Sotlar, 2000) are among the most important. Since the end of the cold war, military sources of threats have no longer been regarded as more important than any other threat sources in the political and social sense as well as media-wise. However, this equanimity of threat classification does not mean that there have been fewer of them. The danger of global military conflict has largely ceased to exist, but there have been outbreaks of many other local and regional military conflicts, even in Europe, Asia, the Middle East, and elsewhere (Prezelj, 2001).

It has been noted already that postmodern society is characterized by the fact that threats and dangers are individualized and personalized. Kanduč (2004, pp. 7–13), for example, says that nowadays an individual is in fact not threatened by crime so much as by different forms of "structural violence," particularly in the fields of heteronymous work, consumer practices, and family relations. This perception is shaped partly due to the fact that security policy is still, to a large extent, related to collective entities (e.g., national and public security) rather than to the provision of international legal and constitutional human rights. In addition, crime policy is too often limited only to the penal policy (criminal justice system). It is precisely due to these varied ways of perceiving threats and dangers that security appears in different forms as a need, value, goods, or commodity, with the notion of *security* surpassing its past physical and repressive context.

Sources of threats often appear to be abstract and distant. They do not reveal the extent of the reality of their threats. Thus, the extent of the threat is the result of perceptions as defined only by the experts in the field and by the general public. In short, the intensity and time frame of a certain security threat play a very important role in creating certain perceptions. In other words, if certain conditions are not fulfilled, the potential sources of threats by the state, society, and individual are not correctly assessed. In turn, these incorrect assessments decrease the possibility of a timely deployment of the necessary security mechanisms and instruments to counter the threat. Following the end of the cold war and the reduction of imminent military threats, developed industrial societies formulated the concept of security challenges and security threats. The main (positive) characteristic of this new conceptualization was to abandon the traditional thinking regarding the threat as immediate and imminent (Kotnik-Dvojmoč, 2000, p. 144). There is actually a scale of the intensity of threat sources, with *security challenges* graded the lowest, followed by *security risks*, which can also act as an intervening factor for security challenges. *Security threats* represent the highest level, reached after security risks are transformed or aggravated (Kotnik-Dvojmoč, 2000). The results of the aforementioned research, summarized in Table 2.2, indicate that in 2006 the great majority of polled participants (82%) felt secure and only 9% threatened, while 9% of those responding were undecided.

Table 2.2 Do You Feel Safe or Threatened?

Feeling	Responses
Safe	82%
Threatened	9%
I do not know, cannot assess, without an answer	9%

Source: ORC, FDV-IDV (http://nato.gov.si/slo/javno-mnenje/nacionalna-varnost.pdf), April 5, 2009.

Table 2.3 Security Threat Factors in Slovenia

Source of Threats	Average Value
Unemployment	3.24
Drugs, narcotics	3.21
Crime	3.20
Low birth rate	3.14
Traffic accidents	3.12
Environment destruction	3.06
Sale of public assets	2.96
Economic problems	2.85
Suicides	2.77
Natural and technological accidents	2.73
Lagging behind in the field of science and technology	2.55
Refugees and illegal immigrants	2.49
Domestic political instability	2.45
Contagious diseases	2.28
Conflicts in the area of former Yugoslavia	2.22
Extreme nationalism	2.15
Terrorism	1.90
Military threats by other countries	1.68

Source: ORC, FDV-IDV (http://nato.gov.si/slo/javno-mnenje/nacionalna-varnost.pdf), April 5, 2009.

Note: Measured using a five-point scale with 1 = no threat and 5 = high level of threat.

Of even more interest were the data on the perceptions of threats to Slovenia as shown in Table 2.3. At first glance, it appears that two traditional threats—terrorism and military threats by other countries—rank as the least important factors of security threats to Slovenia. Those that were ranked highest were unemployment, drugs, narcotics, crime, low birth rate, and environment destruction (between 3.24 and 3.06). The lowest assessment values were accorded to domestic political instability, contagious diseases, conflict in the area of former Yugoslavia, terrorism, and military threats by other countries (between 2.49 and 1.68).

Threat sources have a twofold relation to the design of a national security policy. First, they are a part of such a policy, which has to answer the question of how the state will deal with individual sources threatening it. Second, in the process of designing and implementing security policy, security threats play not only the role of an output but also a decisive factor as a pressure tool. Therefore, it can be argued that the process of deciding on a security policy is determined also by the reality and intensity of the threat sources (Sotlar, 2000).

It would be ideal if the national security system were established on the basis of realistically perceived and assessed threat sources. The problem with the ideal always lies in the fact that it is difficult to find an ideal state in nature, let alone in society. The perception and adequate assessment of different sources and types of threats is therefore a complex, demanding, and ungrateful task. In particular, it takes place at different levels—individual level, group level, expert level, institutional level, as well as the level of political elites. These entities have to provide a basic normative and legal framework for facing or tackling security risks and threats (Sotlar, 2002).

Outcomes and actions can become dangerous if the general public can allow itself misperceptions and inaccurate assessments of threat sources. However, it becomes much more dangerous if the authors and practitioners of the national security system (e.g., police, the military, intelligence security services), experts in the field (e.g., research institutes and universities), and those in charge of making decisions (i.e., the government and the parliament) make the same mistakes. It is therefore necessary for the political elites that exert power over the executive and legislative branch of power to shoulder additional responsibilities in this field. Only through the accurate perception and understanding of the sources of threats can adequate and consistent policies and decisions be designed and implemented by the actors of the security system. Above all, the elites should not use the security field to further their own interests, as theoretician Mills (Heywood, 1997) argued was the case with the elite in power in the United States. Mills argues that the United States is in fact run by only a small number of groups—the power elite. Among such groups he counts large enterprises (e.g., the military industry), the military, and the political clique surrounding the president. Such a combination of economic power, bureaucratic control, and access to the highest levels of the executive power (government) allows the power elite to adopt key historically important decisions, particularly in the field of defense and foreign policy, as well as strategic economic policy (Heywood, 1997, pp. 77–78).

Security solutions should be found at the system level, in the form of some sort of standby mechanisms to ensure that the security system would operate regardless of the security situation. Therefore, it is necessary to anticipate different possible events and situations that could take place in the parliament or its surroundings and would have a direct or indirect influence on the parliament. These sources of threats can be grouped under the following classifications:

- Military threats (particularly during wartime, when the country as a whole represents a military target, which comes before all else for its institutions of power)
- Domestic security threats (crime, such as burglary, theft, robbery, physical attack on a person under protection, members of parliament or visitors; terrorism, such as attack on a person or persons under protection, military police, the staff of the parliament and visitors; hostage taking, planting of explosives; other disturbing events, such as violent demonstrations, massive violations of public order, disturbing the work of the parliament, serious violations of the house rules)
- Threats caused by natural and other disasters (ecological accidents, floods, earthquake, fire)

A survey on values, fears, and perception of real threats in Slovenia was conducted on a sample of 1,100 respondents by the first author of this chapter at the end of 2003 (Meško, 2003, 2006). All studied items are presented from the highest to the lowest rank as follows:

1. Values: family, health, personal happiness, love, friendship, money, education, employment/work
2. Fear of illness, death, war, natural disasters, violence, unemployment, failure, bad social conditions
3. Perception of threats: pollution, congestion, violent crimes, psychological pressures or stress, illnesses, drugs, questionable politics, inefficient economy

The example of local securitization on one hand and democratization of local community on the other are recently established local safety and security councils, which take place in about one-half of Slovenia municipalities (Meško & Lobnikar, 2005a). The role and other characteristics of such councils are described in the following section.

Local Crime Prevention and Safety Efforts in Slovenia

Recent trends in crime prevention and community safety in Slovenia have been characterized by the influence of ideas of crime prevention in Western societies, especially with the idea of community responsibility and involvement of local administration in setting priorities in safety and security efforts and preventing everyday criminality and communal disorder.

The safety councils have been situated within the local town, city, or municipality administration as a consultative body in crime and safety matters. The legal bases for such councils are the Police Act (paragraph 21) and the Local Self-Administration Act (paragraph 29). Both paragraphs in the two acts are, however, more or less recommendatory. Therefore, a consultative body (a safety council) can be established by a municipality council. No piece of national legislation determines the obligations of such councils (Strategy of Community Policing in Slovenia, 2002).

This chapter presents research findings on some aspects of the councils' performances of their duties. The analysis includes the definition of local crime prevention, community policing, disparities between proclaimed goals and reality, everyday practice of crime prevention, the role of safety councils in everyday life, conducting a criminological analysis of local crime and safety problems, and the influence of the police presentation of crime problems and public opinion about the root causes of criminality in their environments. Research findings would also show whether the respondents were more inclined to the ideas of authoritarian communitarianism and avoidance solving crime and safety problems or of moral minimalism (Hope, 1995, pp. 67–68). More specifically, groups of people involved were studied in the sense of crime prevention activities and safety councils in Slovenian towns.

The Studies of Local Safety Councils in Slovenia

Before 1991, when Slovenia was a republic of the Socialist Federative Republic of Yugoslavia, safety councils were situated in every local community. With the independence of Slovenia in 1991, all such councils were abolished. Between 1991 and 1997, no such councils existed in Slovenia. Since 1997 more than 100 local safety councils have been established mostly initiated by the police. In this sense, discussions could be focused on reinvented strategies of crime prevention and public safety, which once were directed by the communist party (Social Self-protection, orig. *družbena samozaščita*) and now by responsible individuals and groups of local communities and sometimes populists.[5] These efforts can also be described as a story about help and support versus power, and such activities are sometimes characterized by the ideas of informal for the purpose of formal, thinking globally and reacting locally without substantial financial support (Meško & Lobnikar,

2005a). This study was an attempt to gain information on the extent to which the *European Urban Charter* (1992) and "Prevention of Violence—A Guide for Local Authorities" (2002) might be applicable to local communities in Slovenian cities. In addition, the study aimed to explore the ways the local safety councils were started and established and how they performed.

Meško and Lobnikar (2005b) dealt with the Western ideas of community policing and other modes of policing imported into Slovenian police and security practices. These practices consist of community policing and problem-oriented policing; both forms of policing consist of the analysis of security threats before taking action. The main characteristic of community policing in regard to democratization of police function is the inclusion of other partners into setting priorities in crime prevention and crime control activities.

General Perception of Solving Local Safety Problems

Part one of this study shows that the respondents perceived safety and security problems in their communities as by far the biggest problem, which was typical for an average Slovenian community. Local safety and security problems in their communities are solved on the basis of a temporary partnership and use *ad hoc* approaches without a profound analysis of the problems. In effect, a common sense approach prevails. More than one-half of the respondents were of the opinion that the police were the most active in this field, while other institutions were seen as more or less apathetic. A feeling of security and reassurance was good where police officers appeared to be in the streets and interacting with local citizens. Social policy was not balanced with the needs of crime prevention.

In the respondents' opinion, the police force was seen as having the greatest responsibility for the control of local crime and safety problems. However, this responsibility was not seen as the sole monopoly of the police. Other agencies were also seen as responsible in this field. The first to be mentioned was the local city administration, followed by individuals, schools, social services, and family. Most respondents thought that the police and local administration should cooperate more closely in solving local safety and crime problems. Priorities in the prevention and control of local problems should be set in cooperation, and this was seen as a shared responsibility.

Analysis of local safety problems and crime was not an everyday practice in the towns studied. Only about 40% of the respondents stated that they did an analysis of problems before taking action. Notably, police officers in particular said that they conducted analyses of the local problems of crime, disorder, and safety. These analyses were then presented to local citizen safety councils. The dominant position of the police was also reflected in the fact that these analyses were mainly based on police statistics. As a rule, the police undertook these analyses of crime and local safety problems either monthly or quarterly and in towns where local safety councils have been established. The police delivered an annual safety and crime report to these councils. If necessary, this report was produced to cover a shorter period.

Most Appropriate Preventive Activities

Social crime prevention measures were recognized as necessary priorities in local crime prevention. In addition to the professional (accountable) policing, respondents understood crime and disorder problems as activities of the young and neglected citizens; those alienated from their communities; and problem pupils at schools. The least appropriate preventive measures seemed to be citizens' patrols (holding a notion of vigilantism), private security at schools (despite the fact that school areas were being progressively controlled by private security), police repression and strict law enforcement, designing out crime (almost impossible due to suburban neighborhoods characterized by high blocks of flats with a high density of population), private security (affordable only to the well-off), situational crime prevention (seems to be too impersonal and costly), and personal and property insurance.

Proximity of Dangers and Everyday Routines—Perception of Local Dangers

Violence (including domestic violence, violence in public, at school or committed by youth, in combination with bullying and vandalism) was the most urgent and serious safety problem. Drugs (alcohol included), traffic safety, property crimes, and public disorder followed as the perceived urgent and serious safety concerns. These findings implied a very narrow understanding of threats or security issues by the respondents.

Responsibility for Problem Solving

Responsibility for solving these safety and security problems was attributed to the police. Respondents also stressed that police should cooperate with other institutions, civil society, and local administrations. Analysis of local safety problems was performed mainly by the police, and it was also the police who were supposed to reassure citizens and reduce fear of crime with their presence in local communities. In this sense, a paradoxical situation emerged—the majority of the most appropriate crime prevention activities were so-called social. The attribution of responsibility to perform these activities was reposed with the police. They were considered to be universal solvers of societal and social problems. The ranking of responsibility for solving local safety/security and crime problems was as follows: the police, social care institutions, prosecutors' office, courts, other law enforcement agencies, nongovernmental organizations (NGOs), and educational institutions. In solving problems of the young, at least one representative of the young should take part in reaching a decision about any actions. The results of the study showed that a low level of responsibility, seriousness, coordination, slow response, training, and knowledge were the main obstacles in common efforts in local community safety and crime prevention efforts.

Suggestions for better policing of their communities were related to more police officers on the beat in local communities, greater visibility and approachability of police officers, better cooperation and communication between the police and local citizens, adequate police training in communication skills, social diversity, and multicultural society. In the view of the respondents, to promote "community policing" it was suggested that it would be necessary to pay more attention to professional policing, learning skills for solving problems, the development of a sense of belonging to the community, and solving social problems.

The respondents familiar with the idea of community policing emphasized citizen–police cooperation, support of local citizens in organizing "crime control networks," and education about what people can do for their safety. The results implied that the most significant obstacles in local safety endeavors were as follows: the unclear roles of institutions and representatives of civil society in such activities, diverse understanding and conceptualization of safety problems, diverse understanding of partnership, vertical relations among partners, just a discussion on diverse problems and the lack of executive powers, lack of political will and departmentalism, one's questionable willingness to listen to those who do not share the same view of the problem, feeling that such councils are an extended police arm (in all cases the police initiated the establishment of such councils), ignorance and apathy of local citizens (crime prevention is not an attractive and "profitable" activity), centralized arrangements and local problem solving (no firm legal background), "informal for the purpose of formal"—cooperation based only on good will of representatives on state and local institutions, and local administration and civil society without any responsibility or legal framework.

Advantages of such councils could be as follows: democratization of formal social control and control over the police, cooperation of (responsible) citizens and knowing each other, development of more active cooperation among all local key persons, facilitating of safety consciousness and discussions on local problems and "communities that care" mentality.

Implementation of Local Safety Efforts

Since 1997, more than 130 such councils have been established. Some of the councils have overcome child diseases and have set goals and used modern knowledge and information-based approaches in solving local safety problems (i.e., the city of Ljubljana). Recently established councils are still in the stage of defining their mission.

The comparison between police officers and other respondents showed that about one-half of the police officers did not believe such councils were effective, whereas the majority of the other respondents thought that these councils served the community and contributed to a greater social cohesion and safety in the area. This is a remarkable finding because the local safety councils were initiated and facilitated by the police. The police appeared to have high expectations on the safety councils. Police views of the councils as an expanded police arm were probably too ambitious. The meetings of the councils should rather be a place for democratic debate and the exchange of different views on local problems. Sometimes the views on solving local safety problems of other partners involved differed significantly from those of the police. A recent solution for such a disparity is the Local Police Act, adopted in the Slovenian Parliament in 2006, which requires a local annual safety and security plan to be prepared by local administration in cooperation with the police.

Conclusion

Planned, systematic, and coordinated communal and common crime prevention and efforts for local safety and security are still at an early stage mainly due to the problems of centralized local institutions and consequently of the financing of activities on the local level. The results imply that a role of local municipalities in the field of crime prevention and local safety has not yet been clearly defined. Despite all of these obstacles, numerous activities are taking place at the local level, especially those of the local governmental (state) institutions, NGOs, and civil society initiatives. A national crime prevention program, which should stress the organization of crime prevention and local safety and security efforts, has not yet been adopted. Due to its complexity, a consensus on its contents has not been totally agreed upon. Likewise, it is also necessary to learn from others' experiences who have witnessed that crime prevention and local safety and security activities can become a subtle "people-friendly control." It is only about net-widening and has nothing to do with the real crime prevention and reassurance. Authoritarian and non-democratic organization of such activities can only lead to *policeization* of the local communities where the primary goal is serving the police with information for criminal investigation and order maintenance. Other functions of common safety endeavors are neglected in this scenario. Such scenarios can be prevented if institutions, agencies, and representatives from all parts of society are included into local decision-making bodies (i.e., safety councils).

An effective safety policy depends on close cooperation between the police and the local community. This is also the main principle underlying the concept of community policing. With regard to the role of local safety councils and community policing, the police have contributed substantially, perhaps even too eagerly. A crucial question is the extent to which the police can achieve consent with local citizens in solving crime and safety problems. There are still substantial obstacles, resulting from the current formal rules, which do not allow police discretion in the field of achieving police–community consensus, and from the restrictive policing mentality, which relies upon the idea of law enforcement and control. Cooperation of the police with local communities and local administrations is still limited to informal communication without any obligation and real consequences for everyday practices of the institutions. It seems that these activities have more influence on the reduction of fear of crime or feelings of insecurity than on the reduction and elimination of crime in the community. It will take quite some time for the police and the community to learn how to cooperate and solve problems together more effectively.

It is also necessary to emphasize that local experts in security issues and crime prevention perceive problems from their local perspective and often neglect the global perspective of their local safety and security problems. It is necessary to learn about global and local trends in security threats for more effective provision of safety and security and crime prevention on the local level.

References

Beck, U. (2003). *Kaj je globalizacija?* Ljubljana: Krtina.

European Urban Charter (1992). Council of Europe: Strasbourg.

Hanžek, M., & Gregorčič, K. (2001). *Poročilo o človekovem razvoju: Slovenija 2000–2001.* Ljubljana: Urad za makroekonomske analize in razvoj.

Heywood, A. (1997). *Politics.* Houndmills: Macmillan Foundations.

Hope, T. (1995). Community crime prevention. In M. Tonry & D. P. Farrington (Eds.), *Building a safer society, Strategic approaches to crime prevention.* Chicago: University of Chicago Press.

Kanduč, Z. (2000). *(Ne)varnost in (ne)varnostna politika v poznomodernih družbah.* Dnevi varstvoslovja. Bled, Ljubljana: Visoka policijsko-varnostna šola.

Kanduč, Z. (2003). O sodobnih tveganjih, grožnjah in nevarnostih—postmoderna družba vslogu staromodne »hiše strahov«. *Revija za kriminalistiko in kriminologijo, 54*(4), 356–371.

Kanduč, Z. (2004). Poznomoderno stanje in družbeno nadzorstvo. *Revija za kriminalistiko in kriminologijo, 55*(1), 1, 3–21.

Kotnik-Dvojmoč, I. (2000). *Preoblikovanje oboroženih sil sodobnih evropskih držav (študija primera Slovenije).* PhD thesis. Ljubljana: Fakulteta za družbene vede.

Litowitz, D. E. (1997). *Postmodern philosophy and law.* University Press of Kansas.

Meško, G. (2003). Rezultati pilotske javnomnenjske študije o vrednotah, strahu in oblikah ogrožanja. Ljubljana: Fakulteta za policijsko-varnostne vede, 3 pp.
Meško, G. (2006). Perceptions of security: Local safety councils in Slovenia. In U. Gori & I. Paparela (Eds.), *Invisible threats* (pp. 69–88). Amsterdam: Ios Press.
Meško, G., & Lobnikar, B. (2005a). The contribution of local safety councils to local responsibility in crime prevention and provision of safety. *Policing: An International Journal of Police Strategies and Management, 28*(2), 353–373.
Meško, G., & Lobnikar, B. (2005b). Policijsko delo v skupnosti: razumevanje uvoženih idej, njihova kontekstualizacija in implementacija. In G. Meško, M. Pagon, & B. Dobovšek (Eds.), *Izzivi sodobnega varstvoslovja* (pp. 89–109). Ljubljana: Fakulteta za policijsko-varnostne vede.
Meško, G., & Klemenčič, G. (2007). Rebuilding legitimacy and police professionalism in an emerging democracy: The Slovenian experience. In T. Tyler (Ed.), *Legitimacy and criminal justice*. New York: Russell Sage Foundation.
Prezelj, I. (2001). Vojaško ogrožanje nacionalne in mednarodne varnosti po koncu hladne vojne. *Teorija in praksa, 38*(5), 848–860.
Sotlar, A. (2000). *Analiza sprejemanja odločitev v procesu oblikovanja obrambnih politik v sodobnih državah*. Master's thesis. Ljubljana: Fakulteta za družbene vede.
Sotlar, A. (2002). *Vloga političnih elit pri zagotavljanju varnosti.* Dnevi varstvoslovja. Bled junij 2002, Ljubljana: Visoka policijsko-varnostna šola.
Strategija v skupnost usmerjenega policijskega dela (Strategy of Community Policing in Slovenia). (2002). Ministrstvo za notranje zadeve Republike Slovenije. Ljubljana: MNZ.
The Local Self-Government Act. (1993). *Official Gazette of the Republic of Slovenia,* No. 72/93.
The Police Act, *Official Gazette of the Republic of Slovenia* (1998). *Official Gazette of the Republic of Slovenia,* No. 49/98.
Urban Crime Prevention—A Guide for Local Authorities (2002). Strasbourg: Council of Europe.
Uredba o varovanju določenih oseb, objektov in okolišev objektov, v katerih so sedeži državnih organov (2000). *Official Gazette of the Republic of Slovenia,* No. 103/00.
Wallerstein, I. M. (1999). *Utopistike ali izbira zgodovinskih možnosti 21. stoletja. Dediščina sociologije: obljuba družbenih ved.* Ljubljana: Založba.
Wicks, R. (2003). *Modern French philosophy: From existentialism to postmodernism.* Oxford: One World Publications.
Zakon o občinskem redarstvu. (2006). (Local Police Act, Official Gazette of the Republic of Slovenia, No. 139/2006.

Notes

1. For a detailed explanation of the notion, nature, and characteristics of the globalization processes see Beck (2003).
2. The worth of the 225 richest people in 1998 amounted to the annual income of 47% of the world's population (i.e., 2.5 billion people). Since 1994 their fortunes have increased an average of US$500 per day. The wealth of the three richest people in the world is said to be larger than the total annual gross domestic

product (GDP) of the 48 poorest countries, whereas the wealth of the 64 richest people in the world is said to be greater than the GDP of China, with a population of 1.2 billion (Hanžek & Gregorčič, 2001).

3. In the context of increasing social, political, and economic inequalities, the reference literature in the field of social studies discusses the tragic nature of the Western social system (which tends to be considered superior compared with other systems and civilizations). It is argued that large social inequalities are rooted in its most praised quality, the imperative for a constant increase of product value. Because product (added) value has always been historically bigger in Western economies than in other parts of the world, the difference in wealth and social power among various social groups and strata was also larger than in other social systems (Wallerstein, 1999, p. 58).
4. "In [the] post-modern era, markets and anonymous market rules took over the key control function in almost all segments of the society… Market control is not exerted only over individuals, but also over groups, institutions, and even states…. Neo-liberal 'hyperbolic' capitalism is abolishing certain typically modern forms of human subjectivity…" (Kanduč, 2004, pp. 7–8).
5. " 'Community policing' and local safety councils existed in Slovenia prior to its independence in 1991. The underlying principle of such social control practices was however as much or more about social and political control in all spheres of community as about safety, security and problem solving. It was an endeavour of 'big brothers and sisters' controlling 'little brothers and sisters'. Because of this experience, contemporary community policing is not perhaps as popular as it could and should be; coupled with the historical experience it can even produce negative results" (Meško & Klemenčič, 2007, p. 35).

2010! But Is Anyone Counting?

3

TERRY G. COLEMAN
Chief of Moose Jaw Police (Retired)

Contents

Introduction

Since the mid-1970s, most police leaders in Canada have touted community policing as being the operating philosophy of their police organizations.[1] Nonetheless, evidence indicates that the culture change in Canada from traditional policing[2] to community policing[3] is generally incomplete. The literature suggests this might be because police organizations have often failed to make the shift to organizational structures and practices consistent with what is required for community policing to succeed. Two of these structures are those of strategic management and a results-based performance measurement system.

This chapter discusses the extent to which Canadian police organizations have actually implemented strategic management and performance measurement, thereby making them outcome-focused organizations that, thus, operate congruently with the successful contemporary public and private organizations. This chapter examines this implementation aspect by comparing traditional policing with contemporary policing and considers the environmental influences, specifically of the public sector reform movement, that have affected the requirements for change. A questionnaire was subsequently constructed to determine whether Canadian police organizations are managed strategically and outcome focused.

Traditional Versus Contemporary Policing

Since the establishment of modern policing in the mid-nineteenth century, police organizations have adopted the paramilitary and bureaucratic structures within which police have often been socially isolated from the community. As pointed out by such leading authorities on the evolution of policing (see Kelling & Moore, 1998; Trojanowicz & Bucqueroux, 1990), the traditional models of policing have been problematic. These police scholars argued that these models were bureaucratic responses characterized by rigid and centralized organizational controls; a tendency toward a functional structure with high degrees of specialization, isolationism, and conservatism; a failure to be innovative; limited discretion afforded to employees; organizational inflexibility; and clearly defined lines of authority, responsibility, and communication. Such police departments[4] were closed systems, described by Trojanowicz and Bucqueroux as *paternalistic hierarchies* (p.24) that were unresponsive to the external environment.

In their book *Underwriting the Risky Investment in Community Policing: What Social Science Should Be Doing to Evaluate Community Policing*, David Kennedy and Mark Moore (1997) observed that traditional police culture manifested itself as inertial pressures that made it difficult for organizations to adapt their strategies and structures in response to environmental change. In addition, they posited that a rational framework, such as the framework inherent in traditional policing (i.e. quasi-military, bureaucratic, and hierarchical) inhibited as well as discouraged employee participation.

Criminologist George Kelling (1999), a pioneer in recognizing the difficulties of traditional policing, found that because the culture of traditional policing was rooted in scientific management and a military command structure, which valued and emphasized efficiency over effectiveness, the outcome of policing was not addressed. In their work, *How Organizations Measure Success: The Use of Performance Indicators in Government* (1992), Neil Carter, Rudolph Klelin, Patricia Day, were concerned that traditional indicators of performance had not helped in understanding the impact of policing. For example, they explained that police budgets were often justified based on the notion that there was a direct relationship between the numbers of police and the crime rate. However, as numerous researchers and contemporary observers of the public sector and policing, including George Kelling, David Kennedy, Mark Corriera, Jihong Zhao, Neil Carter, Rudolph Klein, and Patricia Day as well as David Osborne, Ted Gaebler, Larry Hoover, and David Bayley have pointed out, although this traditional, and still prevalent, model of policing casts the community as passive participants, the success of policing relies on mutually beneficial relationships and shared values. This is developed through internal and external consultation, accountability, decentralization of authority, the sharing of power both internally and externally, and a primary focus on results. Because of the realization by progressive police leaders that there must be a better way to reduce crime and social disorder, starting in the 1960s the more open system of community policing began to evolve. This transition received added impetus in the 1980s with the advent of substantial reforms across the public sector.

Influences of Public Sector Reform

In their seminal work *Reinventing Government: How the Entrepreneurial Spirit is Transforming the Public Sector,* David Osborne and Ted Gaebler (1992) commented that public sector reform[5] emerged when the concerns of taxpayers about what is achieved with public funds not only increased demand for public service but also significantly increased expectations of equity, fairness, responsiveness, accountability, and value for money[6] with respect to public services. To satisfy customers and clients[7] and their expectations of quality service, the public sector began to implement private-sector performance-based management practices, such as value-added management, corporate reengineering, total quality (TQ),[8] and strategic management. These approaches focused attention on measurement[9] to improve the performance of public sector services.

Traditionally, as noted in the *Report of the Auditor General of Canada: Moving Toward Managing for Results* (1997) from the Canadian Auditor General, public sector managers were "held accountable for the prudent use of the resources they were given, the authorities they used and the activities they carried out" (para. 11.9). This led to a narrow cost-centered focus of staying within budget and strictly following policies and procedures. Christopher Lovelock and his colleagues (Lovelock, Lewin, Day, & Bateson, 1987) identified this as a problem with respect to organizational performance. They argued that although public sector services must satisfy the needs of the public at an acceptable cost, personnel have tended to focus inward on the operation rather than outward to clients and customers when they operated in a cost-centered environment. They concluded that a compliance culture emerged instead of a culture focused on results. Hatry (1999) shared this perspective and recommended that public organizations instead of focusing just on inputs, processes, and outputs must think and act strategically by focusing on "measurement on a regular basis of the results (i.e., outcomes) and efficiency of services or programs" (p. 3). It is the consensus among contemporary business management and public sector experts that the achievement of agreed upon outcomes should be the overall goal of management. Therefore, because outcomes are derived from inputs through the application of processes and the generation of outputs, it is necessary to establish what each of these terms mean.

In the context of policing, organizational inputs are twofold. First, inputs are the funds received from taxpayers to finance policing activities. These inputs are quickly converted by managers into human resources and various technologies. Second, and arguably more importantly, inputs include the authorities of the state, which are used, as necessary, by police to create safe communities and thus address the quality of community life (Moore, Thacher, Dodge, & Moore, 2002, p. 26).

Processes are the means by which inputs are converted to services, and thus outputs, delivered to the customers and clients. Outputs, in turn, are the means to the end—the outcome. They are generated through the processes and are usually the immediately visible and tangible results of police activities such as arrests made or charges laid. Outcomes are the aggregate of the outputs and are the results experienced by a member of a community or by the community as a whole. In the case of policing, these outcomes are safe streets and communities free from a fear of crime and social disorder. However, because it is apparent from the literature that the meanings of outputs, outcomes, and objectives might vary slightly depending on the source, Table 3.1 provides a consolidation of these terms as they are applied to this study.

Appropriate measurements of police performance have perplexed police practitioners for many years. Increasingly, there has been an agreement that the traditional measurement of outputs alone is not sufficient. Many authorities on policing in Britain, the United States, and Canada, including Larry Hoover and David Bayley in the United States, have concluded that traditional police organizations have focused almost entirely on the *processes* and *outputs* achieved through rigid adherence to bureaucratic processes and the finite measurement of easily determined performance indicators.[10] These include the crime rate, the number of arrests made, crimes solved or cleared, the clearance rate per police officer, response times, workloads of police officers, traffic enforcement, and charges laid (Bayley, 1996; Hoover, 1996). However, they argued, because police officers apply discretion to many of these activities, measurement is necessary beyond recording and relying on this type of data. Further, they observed that activity measures have traditionally been popular because they are usually easily tabulated and collected. Hoover (1996) pointed out that, despite widespread media coverage and public interest in activity measures, enlightened police practitioners and academics have criticized these traditional simplistic tallies as being inadequate indicators of police effectiveness because they do not relate to the impact (i.e., the outcome) of police activities. The relevance and importance of a focus on outcomes is reinforced by Carter et al. (1992, p. 5) when they characterize successful reform in the public sector as being evidenced by the presence of three critical and mutually dependent components:

- The specification of objectives
- The allocation of costs to activities and programs
- The development of performance indicators and output measures sufficient to assess the degree of success in achieving agreed upon outcomes

Further support for the use of outcome-based measurement, in the context of quality service and value for money, can be found in the public sectors of several countries. For example, in 1995, the Canadian federal government recognized the public's demand for quality of service with a Declaration of Quality Service Principles (Report of the Auditor General of Canada. Moving Toward Managing for Results, 1997). As the president of the Urban Institute in the United States stated, "Regularly measuring the outcomes of

Table 3.1 Performance Measurements Derived from the Literature

Category	Descriptors
Inputs	The resources required to operate the organization. In police organizations, these are the funding raised through taxes and the authorities of the state. The latter includes society's ultimate sanctions: the use of force and the authority to restrict a person's freedom
Processes	The ways outputs are generated and service is delivered
Outputs	Produced through the processes and activities of the organization (e.g., in a police organization, they include the number of arrests and charges and the number of calls for service answered)
Outcomes	Events, occurrences, or conditions that are of direct importance to the clients or customers—the community. The net sum of the outputs generated by programs and tactics to achieve the end result for the consumer—safe communities without a fear of crime and disorder. Service quality, such as the timeliness with which the service was provided, is often an important aspect of outcome measurement.
Intermediate Outcomes	Outcomes that are expected to lead to a desired end but are not an end in themselves. Examples include service response time, which is of concern to a member of the community requesting service but does not inform directly about the success of the service. An intermediate outcome could be a reduction in crime or a reduction in social disorder.

Sources: Carter, N., Klein, R., & Day, P., *How organisations measure success: The use of performance indicators in government,* London: Routledge, 1992. Osborne, D., & Gaebler, T., *Reinventing government: How the entrepreneurial spirit is transforming the public sector,* Don Mills, ON: Addison-Wesley, 1992. Moore, M. H., & Poethig, M., in R. H. Langworthy (Ed.), *Measuring what matters: Proceedings from the Policing Research Institute Meetings* (pp. 151–167), Washington, DC: U.S. Department of Justice, National Institute of Justice, 1999. Morley, E. Bryant, S. P. & Hatry, H. P. *Comparative performance measurement,* Washington, DC: Urban Institute Press, 2001. *What works: Management applications of performance measurement in local government,* Washington, DC: ICMA (International City/County Management Association) Centre for Performance Measurement, 2001.

services provided by government to its citizens, and using those measures to improve outcomes, is as worthy a goal for the next millennium as it has been for this one" (Hatry, 1999, p. xx). As cited by Nyhan and Marlowe (1995), the American Society of Public Administration (ASPA) expressed similar support in 1992 when they endorsed the development and adoption of permanent measures by all levels of government. William Bratton, the chief of police in Los Angeles, and former commissioner of the New York Police Department, William Andrews, pointed the out in *Leading for Innovation & Results in Police Departments* that an outcome focus facilitates accountability. They maintained that this is important for policing because, historically, a lack of accountability has been viewed as "a hallmark of police [organizations]" (Bratton & Andrews, 2002, p. 260). In Britain, Richard Common, Norman Flynn, and Elizabeth Mellon (1992) observed that when an organization manages for results then the process of agreeing on the desired results, measuring the results to improve performance and effectively reporting on overall performance fosters the necessary organizational culture of accountability. They argued that such accountability is further achieved by an important characteristic of public sector reform—the decentralization of decision making. This revitalizes managerial motivation and improves service to clients by being responsive to local needs. Those to whom authority has been delegated are, therefore, held accountable to follow the strategy of the organization and achieve organizational goals through the effective measurement of the various activities, programs, and work units. They can then assess and report their contribution to the goals of the organization such as the satisfaction of clients and consumers of services.

Even though most organizations, including those in the public sector, have traditionally focused on inputs, processes, and outputs rather than on outcomes achieved, the reinvention of government has created "a new way of doing business" (Rohm, 1996, p. 6). It requires the public sector to get "closer to the customer" and to put the "customer in the driver's seat." (Osborne & Gaebler, 1992, p. 167). Despite the necessity for probity and prudence, this emphasis encourages and facilitates the introduction of systems so that desired results can be better identified and achieved. However, Flynn (1997) observed that even though focusing on results leads to better results and enhances the external credibility of the organization, staying within budget has often been considered the most important criterion for public sector success. Such a continuing focus on inputs, rather than on outcomes, is problematic in that not only does it ignore the quality of the outputs and thus the outcomes but it also provides little incentive to strive for improved performance. On the other hand, as Osborne and Gaebler (1992) stated, when performance is funded based on desired outcomes organizations quickly focus on results (p. 139). Nonetheless, this can be complicated because outputs are sometimes easier to identify and measure. Moreover, because the identification and measurement of results in government is not as straightforward as in the private sector, it is sometimes necessary to use measurements of processes and outputs as proxy measures of the ultimate outcome.

Regardless, it is still a problem when organizations measure only processes and outputs without an ultimate focus on the outcomes. This is particularly true in policing, which has had difficulty in understanding and establishing relationships among inputs, processes, and outcomes. As Flynn (1997) observed, although it is "difficult to quantify quality" (p. 43) with respect to the public sector, this can change when public administrators, partners, elected officials and the public think in terms of outcomes rather than inputs. Osborne and Gaebler (1992) said that when outcome-focused performance measures are used in the public sector, the right questions are asked to redefine the problem such that it can be diagnosed from a different perspective to generate suitable solutions for the benefit of the respective community (p. 147).

While the public sector differs from the private sector on customer and client expectations, leadership, performance management strategies, and organizational cultures, the public expects good quality service regardless of the provider. They do not generally make a distinction between public and private sector services. This expectation is also true in assessing policing services. Due to the often enthusiastic marketing of community policing by police authorities and police leaders, the transition to community policing has not only changed public attitudes about policing but has also increased the expectations of police performance (Friedman & Clark, 1999). The public expects and demands quality and value through client-focused services instead of the previous rigid bureaucratic-based systems and services. Consequently, performance measurement in the environment of contemporary policing must include measurement of quality and value.

As a result, the principles of TQ, which has been widely applied in the private sector and is considered by Common et al. (1992) as an "acronym for good management" (p. 112), is now used in the public sector as a means of addressing the demand for quality public services. TQ, which derives its success primarily from a strategic approach and continuous improvement based on performance monitoring and data analysis, emphasizes quality and valued service. Posner and Rothstein (1994) concluded that TQ is "appropriate in the public sector to help it decentralize control and identify with its customers ... [by getting] people from different areas of expertise working on the same problem" (p. 137). While the business practices and contemporary management philosophies of the private sector have had a significant effect on the evolution of policing, the impact of TQ has been such that community policing can be considered to be "the application of quality management to police organizations" (Carter, 1996, p.79) to maximize service and to achieve value for money. Similarly, Peak and Glensor (1999) viewed TQ as a means for police organizations to meet the expectations of effectiveness, efficiency, and accountability now expected of public sector agencies including police services. Herman Goldstein (1993), who has been credited as being the architect of problem-oriented policing, determined that the use of "total quality management (TQM) in policing has demonstrated very positive results, holds much promise [and can teach us important lessons]" (p. 12). However, the literature is clear that shifting a police organization to a culture of contemporary policing and thus to a TQ culture requires the integration of the fundamentals of contemporary policing into all aspects of a police organization including the evaluation of organizational performance (see Table 3.2).

Trojanowicz and Bucqueroux (1990) observed that police organizations "must [therefore] not only change the way they think, but the way they act" (p. 7) if they are truly committed to a culture change. For instance, if police organizations are to move to the contemporary model, not only must they change human resource management practices, work structures, reward systems, information systems, and decision-making processes, but they also must have the ability to successfully apply problem-solving skills and be able to continuously learn by collecting as well as interpreting relevant data. Community policing achieves this by focusing organizational attention on

Table 3.2 The Fundamentals of Contemporary Policing

The Fundamentals of Contemporary Policing
Due process, equity and fairness
A customer and client focus
Consultation and collaboration with the community
Quality and valued customer service
Continuous evaluation, continuous improvement and change
Teamwork
Decentralization of authority and decision making
Total involvement
Participative leadership
Increased communication
Internal and external alignment
Outcome focused

Sources: Carter, N., Klein, R., & Day, P., *How organisations measure success: The use of performance indicators in government*, London: Routledge, 1992. Hoover, L. T., in L. T. Hoover (Ed.), *Quantifying quality in policing* (pp. 1–22), Washington, DC: PERF, 1996. Swanson, C. R., Territo L., & Taylor, R. W., *Police administration—Structures, processes, and behavior*, Toronto, ON: Prentice Hall, 1998. Dantzker, M. L., *Police organization & management: Yesterday, today & tomorrow*, Boston: Butterworth Heinemann, 1999.

the measurement of performance and the implementation of performance management systems to produce actionable data that are easily accessible to those who make decisions. The desired outputs and outcomes must, therefore, be clearly identified and developed and their relative importance established so that the quality of the outputs and outcomes is monitored and measured for the purpose of continuous improvement.

Because community policing is driven by demands of the customer or client[11] and is concerned about providing valued and quality service, the client is naturally of primary concern. Organizational success from their perspective can be determined, therefore, through surveys similar to the market research conducted in the private sector. This direct communication with the customer and the consequent feedback enables organizations to recognize opportunities and reduce their vulnerability to trends that are otherwise unforeseen. Poister and Henry (1994) considered customer surveys to be useful tools in the public sector because surveys view the public as consumers whose attitudes about service delivery in the absence of market competition can be considered as an expression of the bottom line of government. Kennedy and Moore (1997) considered conducting surveys of communities[12] to be a practical way for police organizations to obtain the necessary feedback even though tools such as focus groups of police and the public, after-action audits of problem-solving initiatives, as well as systems to measure corruption and abuse of authority are usually also necessary. However, caution is required when interpreting responses to surveys not only because customer assessments of service quality are subjective but also because assessments tend to change in proportion to the number of employees encountered by customers/clients. Nonetheless, Stephens (1996) commented that when appropriately designed and interpreted, surveys are a useful gauge of clients and customers satisfaction on the quality and value of the services they received. In a policing context, surveys could also identify the extent to which the community has a fear of crime, the number of repeat calls for service and the degree of social disorder in public spaces,[13] all potentially affecting the outcome of policing. Additionally, rather than relying on just the crime and disorder that is reported to police, community surveys can provide superior information such as the extent of the nonreporting of crime. For instance, the degree to which crime and disorder is not reported is important when assessing the performance of police.

Wholey and Hatry (1992) stated that although "regular monitoring of service quality and program results is a key component of informed public management," it is not necessary to be a TQ organization to realize substantial benefit from implementing performance measures. However, if leaders of the organization have not embraced the concept of TQ, then strategic performance management will have difficulty flourishing. When a leader uses a combination of TQ and strategic performance management, Kaydos (1999, p. 150) maintained that the organization will move toward delivering the necessary quality and value by:

- Focusing management's attention on satisfying external and internal customers
- Raising questions about strategy
- Identifying previously unrecognized quality and waste problems
- Providing objective information to establish priorities
- Providing feedback about the success of performance initiatives
- Getting support from managers and employees for further change when they see tangible improvements in performance
- Increasing employee involvement by enabling managers to delegate responsibility

Nevertheless, one challenge is the difficulty in articulating the bottom line of public sector agencies (p. 430). This gives rise to challenges in identifying and then collecting the necessary performance data. Another challenge is that there is often a failure to understand that when TQ is implemented it must be implemented strategically as a total organizational culture, as opposed to being implemented as just a program added to the existing organizational structure. This is relevant to this study because, as Trojanowicz and Bucqueroux (1990) stressed, it is important that it is understood as being the dominant philosophy of a police service operationalized through an organizational strategy rather than as a specific program tactic technique or "an add-on deploying a handful of [community policing officers]" (p.6). Unfortunately, in police organizations this has often not been the case. This is supported, at least in part, by the results of a study by Coleman (2002), which indicated that the failure to manage human resources strategically was likely a factor in the incomplete evolution of community policing in Canada.

Despite challenges to the implementation of TQ in the public sector, Gore (1993), with respect to public sector reform in the United States, recommended that public sector organizations could improve performance through the implementation of TQ and by taking a strategic approach to management. Michael Porter (1996), the Bishop William Lawrence University Professor at Harvard Business School and an authority on strategic planning and strategic management, emphasized in his work *What Is Strategy?* that even though the development of a clear organizational strategy is often not straightforward and requires strong leadership, a strategic approach is critical if an organization is to achieve superior performance. Moore and Trojanowicz (1988) explained that the necessary strategic approach is achieved when "the executive [of the police service] discovers the best way to use [the] organization to meet the challenges or exploit the opportunities of the environment" (p. 2).

Strategic management, according to Janet Vinzant and Douglas Vinzant (1999), is a "comprehensive management approach that helps organizations align organizational direction with organizational goals to accomplish strategic change" (p. 516) through the establishment and implementation of a corporate strategy.

A corporate strategy is important to a police organization because it not only enables internal understanding of the mission and organizational objectives but also communicates to those outside the organization what the organization proposes to do and how it will be achieved. Consequently, as Osborne and Gaebler (1992) identified, police leaders in collaboration with the community and employees must establish a clear strategic direction through a decentralized and results-oriented organizational mission to be used to develop budgets that fund outcomes rather than outputs. The content of the mission statement is thus significant because, as Moore et al. (2002) pointed out, when constructed appropriately it "embodies a shared collective conception of what police [services] should try to achieve, and how they ought to behave in trying to achieve their goals" (p. 31). This is important because if the management control system is incompatible with the corporate strategy and thus the appropriate information is not available to decision makers, the strategy is likely to fail.

Strategic performance management, in contrast to traditional performance management that was output focused, has a future perspective, is concerned about the achievement of strategic goals, is customer and client driven, and is outcome focused. This difference is important to police leaders because, as Bayley (1996) pointed out, they are frequently pushed internally and externally to demonstrate that their organizations are led and managed effectively and delivering value for money (p. 39). Strategic performance management enables them to embrace political accountability for achieving goals and objectives through the development of measurable goals based on their mission, as well as establishing internal measurement systems to ensure all employees are accountable and working toward the achievement of organizational goals. When widely and clearly communicated so that employees are motivated as well as able to understand organizational expectations and how well they and the organization are performing strategic performance management is an effective means of achieving and demonstrating the necessary accountability. Such accountability is dependent on measurement systems that not only record the activities and outcomes of the organization but also enable analyses and decision making.

However, a performance management system is of little value unless it is also reliable, valid, and credible. It must not only indicate what is observed and experienced but also be able to adjust to the internal and external environments by accommodating changes such as those affecting policies, priorities, resource availability, program delivery mechanisms, and restructuring of the organization. Furthermore, the design of a measurement system should change as the vision of the organization changes and must therefore be tied to the organization's strategic vision in what Carolyn Brancato (1995) describes as "an iterative loop" (p. 10). Because organizations are complex systems, caution is necessary, however, when designing measurement systems so that measuring performance in one part of the organization does not create a problem in another part.

Although public sector organizations have usually had only a *cost-line*, which made it difficult to assess compromises between service improvement and cost reduction, according to Carter et al. (1992) the evolution of strategic performance measurement in the public sector has been driven by the desire of the public not only to control public expenditure but also to ensure managerial competence and increased accountability. Strategic performance management facilitates this by maintaining meaningful links among the organization's vision, mission, and strategic goals. Furthermore, while it enables the necessary accountability and facilitates decision making, overall it provides for effective planning, budgeting, program evaluation, the appropriate allocation of resources, the direction of operations, internal and external communication about the effort expended by the agency for the financial investment, and the provision of information to the public about what is achieved with their taxes. Taken as a whole, it improves the service delivery of the organization.

Strategic performance measurement is also necessary for organizational learning as well as for building consensus for change. Organizations that attend to the required skills and expertise of employees and embrace organizational learning as part of a strategic approach will be able to "stay relevant and responsive to the changing needs of clients" (Report of the Auditor General of Canada. Moving Toward Managing for Results, 1997, para. 11.55). Organizational innovation, for example, is "stillborn" (Osborne & Gaebler, 1992, p. 151) unless the organization is outcome focused and has feedback on results. Consequently, because organizational learning is imperative to quality and valued customer focused service, it is important to assess the ability of the organization "to learn to cope with change and to improve through its people, its systems, and its infrastructure" (Wisniewski & Dickson, 2001, p. 6). In addition, to maximize the benefit of results-oriented management, employees require expertise in strategic planning, the concepts and practices of performance measurement, and the use of performance information in decision making.

Kaydos (1999) maintained that strategic performance management is not only an integral part of delegated management but also "a catalyst for creating a culture of excellence, teamwork and continuous improvement" (p. xv). Moreover, a Conference Board study, cited by Gates (1999), found teamwork and risk taking by employees with respect to creativity and innovation was greater in "measurement-managed companies" (p. 11). While some of those organizations used performance measurement as a management and accountability tool and for continuous improvement, and some linked it to incentive compensation, progressive organizations, as Osborne and Gaebler (1992) pointed out, use performance measurement for all three purposes.

Methodology

Contemporary policing literature makes it abundantly clear that for policing to be relevant and to meet the expectations of the community it must be managed strategically and have an outcome focus rather than a continuing reliance on output measures of performance. The goal of this study was to determine the extent to which Canadian police organizations had done this—that is, whether they had moved to the contemporary model of policing not only by operating strategically but also by changing their traditional narrow focus on outputs to a focus on outcomes. To determine what shift, if any, had occurred, a self-report survey of police leaders was constructed.[14] More specifically, this two-part survey was designed to obtain information from police leaders about strategic management and the performance measurement systems of their organizations. It is important to note that care was taken when constructing the survey to use language that is common in the police management universe and when there could have been a possibility that terminology might be misinterpreted, an explanation or definition was provided in the survey instrument. The survey was distributed by mail to leaders of 75 Canadian police organizations that were selected from Police Resources in Canada (2004) based on the criteria that they were staffed with 50 or more police officers.[15] This criteria, although it might appear to be arbitrary, was established because, based on observations of the author,[16] smaller police organizations such as those with less than 50 police officers, usually have insufficient capacity, even if they have the desire, to measure and analyze performance outside of measuring and reporting the traditional outputs necessary to comply with the mandated Uniform Crime Report (UCR) data collection.[17] The information obtained in the responses was used to determine where the respective organizations are located on the continuum from traditional policing to fully evolved strategic community policing—contemporary policing.

Survey Findings

Of the 75 surveys mailed to Canadian police leaders, 39 responses were received from all provinces.[18] This was a return rate of 52% and represented approximately 56% (33,500) of the 59,906 federal, provincial, and municipal police officers across Canada (Police Resources in Canada, 2004). Because there are more police organizations in Ontario than in any other province, 32 of the 75 surveys (42.7%) were distributed to police leaders in that province. The 16 responses received (n = 39) from Ontario represented 41% of all those returned. The province with the second largest number of police services is Quebec. Surveys were mailed to 19 chiefs of police in Quebec, which represented 25% of the total distribution across Canada. Although the survey was not translated into French,[19] 5 of the 19 surveys were completed and returned, which represented 6% of those originally distributed nationwide. Of the 75 police organizations initially surveyed, 65.3% were staffed with between 51 and 300 police officers; 59% of the returned surveys were from this group. Police organizations with more than 300 police officers represented 34.6% of the surveys distributed and accounted for 41% of those returned. As a result, the responses can be considered as a reasonably representative cross-section of Canadian police organizations based on province and size of the organization.

To understand the of strategic community policing in Canada and, thus, the shift, if any, from traditional policing, the responses to the surveys were separated into seven groups of findings for the purpose of analysis and discussion. These groups were identified because they can be considered individually, as well as in aggregate, to be indicators of a police organization's commitment to strategic management and a results-based organizational focus. Because community policing must be implemented and managed strategically, the first of the groups to be considered was whether the respondents understood what was meant by "community-policing must be an organizational strategy." Of the 37 respondents (n = 39) who considered their organization to be a community-policing organization, 17 of them did not appear to understand the concept of an "organizational strategy." An additional eight appeared to have only a partial understanding. While 13 respondents (n = 39) identified community policing to be an "organizational strategy," only seven of these seemed to understand, either fully or partially, what is meant by an organizational strategy.

Even though the literature tells us community policing should be implemented as the organizational strategy of a police organization, these findings suggest that some Canadian police leaders might not understand this. It is particularly interesting given that community policing had been present in canada for 30+ years that even though 37 respondents (n =39) considered their organizations to be community policing organizations, only 13 considered community policing to be an organization strategy. These respondents clearly did not understand that if the organization is to be a community-policing organization then "community-policing must be the organizational strategy." Overall, of the 37 respondents (n = 39) who considered their organization to be a "community-policing" organization, only 14 seem to understand, at least partially, what is meant by an "organizational strategy" and only 7 of the 14 considered community policing to be an "organizational strategy." This suggests that the majority of the respondents do not understand that "community policing must be an organizational strategy" and thus their respective organizations might not be led and managed strategically.

Seventeen of the 34 police leaders who reported their organization had a corporate plan or a business plan when asked to articulate the *organizational strategy* of their organization, did not seem to understand the concept of an organizational strategy. This suggested that, while 34 of the organizations represented in the study reported that they had a business plan or corporate plan, many of these might not be led and managed strategically.

Because community policing is results focused, it is important to determine what police leaders understand as being the outcome of policing.[20] Therefore, the third group of findings to be considered was whether police leaders understood the bottom line—the outcome—of policing. Even though the identification of the bottom line is challenging and the literature offers more than one perspective, the extent to which a police leader understands what constitutes the outcome of policing can provide insight into whether they are strategic and outcome focused. In turn, this can provide assistance in determining whether their organization is strategic and results based. Although there were some differences in how respondents articulated their understanding of the bottom-line, overall 29 ($n = 39$) identified the bottom line—the outcome—as being "a safe community" or as being "community trust and satisfaction." It is of interest that, while 25 of these 29 respondents who seemed to understand the bottom line of policing directly surveyed their communities, only 5 of the 33 who reported they used community surveys also used performance data for the primary purpose of determining "how safe the community is" or to gauge the "degree of community satisfaction."

This raises the question: if most of the participant organizations survey the community directly but do not use the resulting data for the primary purpose of identifying the outcomes of "community safety" or "community trust and satisfaction" what data are they seeking through the survey and to what use are they putting that data? While there might be reasons for this that are outside of the control of the police organization, one inference that could be made is, that notwithstanding, 29 leaders ($n = 39$) indicated they understood what is meant by the bottom line of policing; only five of the organizations that participated might actually be results based. That is, while not conclusive and more research is necessary, this might indicate that most of the organizations represented in these findings were not actually outcome focused. Of further interest is that five respondents ($n = 39$) advised that their primary use of performance data was to learn "information such as the number of arrests made, the number of cases cleared and the amount of traffic enforcement." This is output data that suggests these organizations might still be predominantly output focused. A further seven respondents ($n = 39$) advised that their primary use of data was for "providing information to the governance authority of my police organization." While to some degree this might satisfy the need to be accountable, if the information communicated to the governance body is not outcome focused then that body might be getting incomplete and misleading information.

The literature is clear that a mission statement in a strategically managed organization should be measurable. Consequently, the fourth group of findings to be considered to identify whether the participating police organizations operate strategically was an assessment of the measurability of their mission statements. While all respondents ($n = 39$) advised that their organizations had a mission statement, and even though all respondents ($n = 39$) considered the measurement of the goals in their mission statement to be important (4/39 slightly important, 25/39 important, and 10/39 very important) when assessing the performance of their organization, a qualitative review of the submitted mission statements indicated that at least 15 ($n = 39$) are not written in language that can clearly enable performance measurement. Although a further 22 mission statements ($n = 39$) were classified by the author as measurable and thus potentially able to form a base for strategic performance measurement, the categorization errs on being generous. Overall, the mission statements of the respondent organizations tended to be a blend of a vision statement and vague objectives. In general, they failed to provide a clear picture of the purpose of their organization such that an assessment could be made about whether the mission is being achieved. While the findings from this analysis might not be conclusive when considered alone, it does provide an indication that the respective organizations might not be managed strategically.

In a strategic environment, performance data should be used to make decisions. Conversely, unless performance data are routinely used to aid decision making, the organization might not be led and managed strategically. Therefore, the fifth group of findings to be considered when determining if the organization was operating strategically was how the organization used performance data, whether it employed a strategic analyst, and whether the leaders and managers were trained in strategic planning and strategic management as well as how to use performance data to make decisions. For example, if an organization reports that it uses performance data to make decisions but the leaders and managers have not been trained how to do this, it is possible that the data are either not actually used to make decisions or are not used as effectively as they could be.

Similarly, data that have been processed by a strategic analyst are likely to be of more value to decision makers than if they have not been expertly analyzed. It could also be argued that the presence of strategic management is evidenced by the employment of a strategic analyst and by the training of leaders and managers in strategic management.

Of the 30 organizations (n = 39) that reportedly used performance data to make strategic decisions, only 17 (57%) of these organizations employed a strategic analyst. Furthermore, 19 (59%) of these 30 organizations reportedly did not train their leaders and managers in how to use performance data to make decisions, and 11 did not train their leaders and managers in strategic planning and strategic management. Although most of the participant organizations reported that they used performance data to make strategic decisions, the absence of a strategic analyst and relevant training for managers or leaders in many of the organizations questions the extent to which these organizations were operating strategically. As with the findings of the other groups, while not conclusive when taken alone, these findings are an indication that many of the organizations that participated in the study might not be totally strategic and thus may not yet have evolved to be a community-policing organization.

An indicator of a commitment to a strategic approach and an outcome focus is whether the organization has a system and personnel to determine how well it is performing and meeting the needs of the customer—the community. Therefore, the sixth group of findings used to cast light on where the respondent organizations were situated on the community-policing continuum is a consideration of the type of performance systems and the performance measurement expertise that they have in place. Even though an organization might report that they have a performance measurement system in place, unless expertise is applied to the management of the system and to the interpretation of results it is likely to focus on easily measured outputs rather than on outcome measurement required of contemporary organizations. Achieving the outcome of a safe community and maintaining community trust and satisfaction also include dealing with the perception of crime and disorder in the community. Because the perception of the prevalence of crime and disorder, and thus the extent of the fear of crime and disorder, in a community is a potential criminogenic factor and, therefore, affects the outcome of policing, whether a police organization tries to determine the extent of the fear of crime in the community is one indication of an outcome focus.

Of the 23 organizations represented in the responses (n = 39) that reportedly had a performance measurement system to determine how well their organization was performing, 21 of these used community surveys. Of those that use surveys, 17 (81%) reportedly also measured the fear of crime. On the other hand, 16 of the participating organizations (41%) reported that they did not have a performance measurement system, yet 12 of these conducted community surveys.[21] These findings suggest that while 17 of the police organizations (n = 39) might have moved toward a contemporary performance measurement culture, many might not have yet realized the need to change. Viewed from another perspective, of the 23 organizations that reportedly had a contemporary performance measurement system, only 9 employed a performance measurement specialist and only 12 reported that they employed a specialist to evaluate programs. While not conclusive evidence, these findings suggest that because many of the surveyed organizations were not systematically measuring performance and using the relevant expertise, they might not be managing performance well. Further research is necessary to determine if this is the situation or if it is a capacity issue for the respective organizations.

Because the focus of contemporary police organizations should be on the aggregate of all activities—the outcome—the seventh, and final, group of findings looked at the indicators of performance that the organizations used, or did not use, to measure organizational success. Respondents were provided with a list of performance indicators, both traditional and nontraditional, and were asked to identify "which of the following indicators of performance (performance indicators) does your police organization use to measure how well your organization is performing overall?" It was intended that this would provide an indication of whether the organization tended to collect traditional output data or nontraditional performance indicators when determining how well they are meeting needs of the community. Not surprisingly, most organizations collected output data such as the number of reported criminal offenses, the clearance rate of reported crime, and the crime rates, all of which are necessary to satisfy UCR requirements, to determine how well they are performing. In addition, most of the organizations also collected non-UCR output data such as the amount of traffic enforcement, the number of arrests made, the caseload per officer, and the number of calls for service to determine how well they are performing. What is of interest, though, is that the majority of the surveyed organizations did not factor in the extent of unreported criminal offences (82.1%) or the extent of the incidents of disorder not reported to police (89.7%) when making a determination of how were are performing. Given the apparent continued reliance by the surveyed organizations on performance indicators such as the *clearance rate* of crime, the *crime rate* and the *caseload per officer*, the unreported incidents of crime and disorder should be of relevance.

Public trust and confidence are essential for successful contemporary policing. It can be argued that if the community is not reporting incidents of crime or disorder, it might be because they have insufficient trust and confidence that police will take the complaint seriously and take action even if it is reported. The extent of unreported incidents, whether of crime or disorder, could therefore be taken as an indicator of public trust and confidence and should consequently be of relevance to the organizational measurement of contemporary policing. By not considering this as important, the question arises: Is the organization operating strategically and working to achieve the outcome of policing—a safe community free from a fear of crime in which the community has trust and confidence in the police? Overall, although these findings as presented might not be definitive indicators of whether an organization is output or outcome focused, they do provide some assistance in that it is clear many organizations still use data such as the crime rate and the caseload per officer, yet relatively few organizations take into consideration the amount of unreported crime and disorder.

Of further interest is that 64% of the respondent organizations ($n = 39$) reportedly still used the time taken to respond to a nonemergency call for service as an indicator of their performance. While additional research is required to determine how and why they use this output data, it appears that it is used despite research cited by Bayley (1994), which pointed out that those who call for service in other than an actual emergency are not concerned about receiving a quick response but are concerned about the police responding within a promised time frame. Overall, based on the responses of the surveyed organizations, police in Canada continued to use a wide range of outputs, most of which were traditional outputs, to determine how well they were performing. However, it was outside the scope of this study to determine if, or how, they aggregate this output data to measure outcomes.

Conclusion

Historically, police organizations have been paramilitary and bureaucratic organizations that have been socially isolated from the community. This traditional police culture made it difficult for organizations to adapt their strategies and structures in response to the dynamic environment and thus be able to effect necessary organizational change. Police departments were closed systems, which used defensive strategies and tended to ignore developments in their external environment. Moreover, the outcome of policing was not usually addressed. Starting in the 1960s, and gaining momentum during the 1980s and 1990s, some observers and practitioners of policing, as well as some community leaders, realized that the real success of policing is built on internal and external relationships and shared values through cooperation and collaboration. They noted that this requires consultation, accountability, decentralization of authority, the sharing of power, both internally and externa.

The environment with respect to the public sector, of which policing is but one part, has changed substantially during the past 20–30 years in that the public now has not only increased expectations of receiving quality and value from their public sector agencies but also increased demand for accountability in general. As a result, the public now expects to know what is achieved by their police organization as well as knowing whether the resources they provide for it are used wisely. This has led to increased attention to the outcome of what is achieved by all policing activities. To achieve this, police organizations are entrusted with two important resources—the authority of the state and financial resources—with which to maintain or improve community safety and thus the quality of life of those living and working in our communities. It is incumbent upon police leaders to use these resources wisely such that the police organizations are effective, efficient, and abide by the rules of a democracy while striving to achieve the desired outcome of policing. This can be achieved only by taking a strategic approach to the application of resources so that the goals of the organization are clearly identified through collaboration with their respective communities and the accomplishment of these important goals is achieved through a structured and systematic process. Moreover, the progress made in achieving the desired goals must be constantly monitored and measured so that not only is it demonstrated that resources are used prudently but that also corrective decisions can be made, when necessary, to improve performance. The literature is clear that contemporary policing will not succeed and achieve what is intended if it is not implemented as an organizational strategy. The literature tells us also that when contemporary policing has been implemented as an "add-on" program to a traditional structure, it is likely to fail or at least not be as effective and efficient as it should be.

While most of the Canadian police leaders who responded to this study described their organizations as community-policing organizations, which suggests they have rejected the business practices of traditional policing and have embraced those of contemporary policing, the situation does not appear to be so straightforward. When considered in aggregate as well as individually, the findings of the seven groups show that some police services are clearly more progressive than others by being strategic and outcome focused to at least some degree. What is of interest, however, although it varies a little between each group of findings, is that despite community policing having been present in Canada for 30 years and that each respondent organization considers itself to be a community-policing organization, indications are that many did not appear to have fully embraced strategic management and might still be primarily output, instead of outcome, focused. That is, the findings suggest that many of the surveyed police organizations, despite their claims to the contrary, have yet to make the culture shift to contemporary policing. For instance, while most respondents (74%) seemed to understand the concept of the bottom-line of policing, there are indications from the study that more than a few police leaders instead of using a strategic approach to leading and managing their organizations have not sufficiently—and in some cases possibly not at all—implemented contemporary policing as an organizational strategy. Without an organizational strategy with which to guide the organization, it is unlikely that the organization has a strategic performance management system that is really focused on the bottom-line. Even if they do have a performance measurement system, without taking a strategic approach that system will exist in an organizational vacuum and thus probably will not have a true outcome focus.

Overall, the results of the study indicated that many police organizations were not managed strategically and still primarily employed output measures of performance as opposed to measures of outcomes—results. That is, these police organizations were still using measures of their activities rather than focusing on the results achieved through these activities. This apparent absence of a strategic approach to policing and an apparent failure to implement performance accountability mechanisms such as are found in successful public and private sector organizations suggests these police organizations had yet to fully move into the era of community policing (i.e., contemporary policing) despite their claims to the contrary.

Having identified signs that many Canadian police organizations had yet to be sufficiently strategic and establish the appropriate systems to measure and report on outcomes, further research is necessary to determine the actual performance indicators that will afford an assessment of the achievement of outcomes and, thus, whether a police organization is delivering value for money through its methodology and findings, the study has raised the awareness and understanding of police leaders about the value of strategic management, and the necessity to focus on the outcome of police activities, then it has contributed to the essential discussion that is necessary to further the evolution of contemporary policing.

References

Bayley, D. H. (1994). *Police for the future.* New York: Oxford University Press.

Bayley, D. H. (1996). Measuring overall effectiveness: Or police force show & tell. In L. T. Hoover (Ed.), *Quantifying quality in policing* (pp. 37–54). Washington, DC: PERF.

Brancato, C. K. (1995). *New corporate performance measures.* New York: The Conference Board.

Bratton, W. J., & Andrews, W. (2002). Leading for innovation & results in police departments. In F. Hesselbein, M. Goldsmith, & I. Somerville (Eds.), *Leading for innovation and organizing for results* (pp. 251–262). New York: Jossey-Bass.

Carter, D. L. (1996). Measuring quality: The scope of community policing. In L. T. Hoover (Ed.), *Quantifying quality in policing* (pp. 73–94). Washington, DC: PERF.

Carter, N., Klein, R., & Day, P. (1992). *How organisations measure success: The use of performance indicators in government.* London: Routledge.

Coleman, T. (2002). *A study of the relationship between strategic human resource management in Canadian police services and the evolution of contemporary policing.* Unpublished paper. Regina, SK: University of Regina.

Common, R., Flynn, N., & Mellon, E. (1992). *Managing public services: Competition and decentralization.* Oxford, UK: Butterworth-Heinemann.

Dantzker, M. L. (1999). *Police organization & management: Yesterday, today & tomorrow.* Boston: Butterworth Heinemann.

Flynn, N. (1997). *Public sector management,* 3d ed. Toronto, ON: Prentice Hall/Harvester Wheatsheaf.

Friedman, W., & Clark, M. (1999). Community policing: What is the community and what can it do? In R. H. Langworthy (Ed.), *Measuring what matters: Proceedings from the Policing Research Meetings* (pp. 121–131). Washington, DC: U.S. Department of Justice, National Institute of Justice.

Garrity, R. B. (1993). Total quality management: An opportunity for high performance in federal organizations. *Public Administration Quarterly, 16*(4), 430.

Gates, S. (1999, October). *Aligning strategic performance measures & results: Report R-1261-99-RR.* New York: Conference Board.

Goldstein, H. (1993, August). *The new policing: Confronting complexity.* Paper presented at Conference on Community Policing. Washington, DC: U.S. Department of Justice, National Institute of Justice.

Gore, A. (1993). *Creating a government that works better and costs less: A report of the National Performance Review.* New York: London House.

Hatry, H. P. (1999). *Performance measurement: Getting results.* Washington, DC: Urban Institute Press.

Hoover, L. T. (1996). Translating total quality management from the private sector to policing. In L. T. Hoover (Ed.), *Quantifying quality in policing* (pp. 1–22). Washington, DC: PERF.

Kaydos, W. (1999). *Operational performance measurement: Increasing total productivity.* Boca Raton, FL: St. Lucie Press.

Keehley, P. (1993). Does TQM spell "time to quit merit"? *Public Productivity & Management Review, 16*(4), 387.

Kelling, G. L. (1999, October). *"Broken windows" and police discretion.* Washington, DC: U.S. Department of Justice, National Institute of Justice.

Kelling, G. L., & Moore, M. H. (1998, November). *"The evolving strategy of policing." Perspectives on policing,* no. 4. Washington, DC: National Institute of Justice & Harvard University.

Kennedy, D. M., & Moore, M. H. (1997). Underwriting the risky investment in community policing: What social science should be doing to evaluate community policing. In R. G. Dunham & G. P. Alpert (Eds.), *Critical issues in policing: Contemporary readings* (3d ed., pp. 469–488). Prospect Heights, IL: Waveland.

Lawler, E. E., III (1992). *The ultimate advantage: Creating the high involvement organization.* San Francisco: Jossey-Bass.

Leishman, F., Loveday, B., & Savage. S. P. (2000). Introduction: Core issues in policing revisited. In F. Leishman, B. Loveday, & S. Savage (Eds.), *Core issues in policing,* 2d ed. Harlow, UK: Pearson Education.

Lovelock, C. H., Lewin, G., Day, G. S., & Bateson, J. E. G. (1987). *Marketing public transit.* New York: Praeger.

MacDonald, J. (1994). *But we are different: Quality for the service sector*. Didcot, UK: Management Books.

Maguire, E. R., & Uchida, C. D. (2000). Measurement & explanation in the comparative study of American police organizations. In *Measurement & analysis of crime and justice* (vol. 4, pp. 491–557). Washington, DC: U.S. Department of Justice, National Institute of Justice. Office of Justice Programs.

Martin, L. L. (1993). *Total quality management in human service organizations*. London, UK: Sage.

Moore, M. H., & Poethig, M. (1999). The police as an agency of municipal government: Implications for measuring police effectiveness. In R. H. Langworthy (Ed.), *Measuring what matters: Proceedings from the Policing Research Institute Meetings* (pp. 151–167). Washington, DC: U.S. Department of Justice, National Institute of Justice.

Moore, M., Thacher, D., Dodge A., & Moore, T. (2002). *Recognizing value in policing: The challenge of measuring police performance*. Washington, DC: PERF.

Moore, M. H., & Trojanowicz, R. C. (1988). *Corporate strategies for policing. Perspectives on Policing, No. 6*. Washington, DC: Harvard University & National Institute of Justice.

Morley, E., Bryant, S. P., & Hatry, H. P. (2001). *Comparative performance measurement*. Washington, DC: Urban Institute Press.

Nyhan, R. C., & Marlowe, H. A., Jr. (1995). Performance measurement in the public sector: Challenges & opportunities. *Public Productivity and Management Review, 18*(4), 333–348.

Osborne, D., & Gaebler, T. (1992). *Reinventing government: How the entrepreneurial spirit is transforming the public sector*. Don Mills, ON: Addison-Wesley.

Peak, K. J., & Glensor, R. W. (1999). *Community policing & problem solving: Strategies & practices*. Upper Saddle River, NJ: Prentice Hall.

Peters, T. J., & Waterman, R. H., Jr. (1982). *In search of excellence: Lessons from America's best run companies*. New York: Harper & Row.

Poister, T. H., & Henry, G. T. (1994). Citizen ratings of public and private service quality: A comparative perspective. *Public Administration Review, 54*(2), 155–160.

Police Resources in Canada, 2004. (2004). Ottawa: Statistics Canada—Canadian Centre for Statistics.

Porter, M. E. (1996, November–December). What is strategy? *Harvard Business Review. HBR ON—Point No 413, 74*(6), 61–78.

Posner, B. G., & Rothstein, L. R. (1994, May-June). Re-inventing the business of government: An interview with change catalyst David Osborne. *Harvard Business Review, 72*(3), 132–143.

Report of the Auditor General of Canada. Moving toward managing for results. Chapter 11.(1997, October). Auditor General of Canada. Retrieved April 2008 from http://www.oag-bvg.gc.ca/domino/reports.nsf/html/ch9711e.html

Rohm, H. (1996, December). *Public sector performance management in the USA. The Foundation for Performance Measurement*. Retrieved September 2007 from http://www.fpm.com/script/UK/Dec96/961206.htm

Stephens, D. W. (1996). Community problem-oriented policing: Measuring impacts. In L. T. Hoover (Ed.), *Quantifying quality in policing* (pp. 95–129). Washington, DC: PERF.

Swanson, C. R., Territo L., & Taylor, R. W. (1998). *Police administration—Structures, processes, and behaviour.* Toronto, ON: Prentice Hall.
Trojanowicz, R., & Bucqueroux, B. (1990). *Community policing: A contemporary perspective.* Cincinnati, OH: Anderson.
Vinzant, J. C., & Vinzant, D. H. (1999). Strategic management spin-offs of the Deming approach. *Journal of Management History, 5*(8), 516.
What works: Management applications of performance measurement in local government. (2001). Washington, DC: ICMA (International City/County Management Association) Centre for Performance Measurement.
Wholey, J. S., & Hatry, H. P. (1992). The case for performance monitoring. *Public Administration Review, 52*(6), 604–610.
Wisniewski, M., & Dickson, A. (2001). *Hello, hello, hello! What's going on here then? Measuring performance in Dumfries & Galloway Constabulary. Research Paper No. 2001/5. Management science: Theory, method and practice.* Glasgow, Scotland: Strathclyde Business School.

Notes

1. The Calgary Police Department became the Calgary Police Service in 1973 when it was the first Canadian police organization to implement community policing.
2. This study uses the term *traditional policing* to collectively describe the *professional*, the *reform*, and the *bureaucratic* eras of policing, which preceded *community policing.*
3. Community policing and contemporary policing are used interchangeably in this study. It is the author's experience that the term *contemporary policing* removes some of the misunderstanding associated with the term *community policing.*
4. While some police organizations are still called police departments or police forces, since the advent of community policing Canadian and British police organizations have increasingly called themselves police services to reflect the emphasis on service rather than identifying themselves as a bureaucratic department of government.
5. *Public sector reform* is also known as *new public management* (NPM), the *reinvention of government,* and *managerialism.*
6. Since the 1980s, the thrust of the value-for-money movement in British policing has been to "energize the principles of NPM and institutionalize the performance culture [of police services]" (Leishman, Loveday, & Savage, 2000, p. 1).
7. The terms *customer* and *client* are used interchangeably in this paper.
8. This paper uses TQ for all strategic initiatives focused on quality and valued service delivery, such as, but not limited to, total quality management, total quality leadership, total quality, total quality service, total and continuous improvement (MacDonald, 1994), and the initiatives found in high-involvement organizations (Lawler, 1992).
9. Measurement is about quantifying, counting, and assigning meaningful scores to variations in some phenomenon using valid and reliable methods (Maguire & Uchida, 2000, p. 497).

10. A performance indicator, also known as a performance metric, is "a specific numerical measurement for each aspect of performance (i.e., an output or outcome) that is under consideration" (Morley, Bryant, & Hatry, 2001, p. 35).
11. In a TQ environment, a customer or client is anyone, internally or externally, who receives or uses a service or product (Keehley, 1993).
12. Sometimes called quality of service (QS) surveys.
13. Some aspects of social disorder may be difficult to categorize and thus measure, because, for example, what is an annoyance to some may be music to others.
14. A copy of the survey is available from the author at tcoleman@sasktel.net.
15. The RCMP and the provincial police organizations of Ontario and Quebec were each considered as one police agency. That is, individual detachments of these organizations were not classified as separate police agencies for the purpose of this study.
16. The author of this study was a police officer from 1969 to 2007. From 1997 to 2007, he was a chief of police.
17. Required by the Canadian Centre for Justice Statistics.
18. There are 10 provinces in Canada.
19. Canada has two official languages—English and French.
20. Some authorities on policing have considered the outcome of policing to be the equivalent of the bottom line found in the private sector.
21. Further inquiry is necessary to determine if any of these organizations conduct surveys only to comply with standards compliance such as those of the Commission on Accreditation for Law Enforcement Agencies (CALEA).

2

Responding to Transnational Crimes and Emerging Law Enforcement Issues

The War on Drugs in Chicago
Thinking Locally, Acting Globally

4

GAD J. BENSINGER
Loyola University Chicago

THOMAS J. LEMMER
Chicago Police Department

ARTHUR J. LURIGIO
Loyola University Chicago

Contents

Introduction

Chicago is the third largest city in the United States, with a population of 2.9 million people. Located in America's heartland, Chicago is one of the nation's most important transportation centers with one of the world's busiest airports, O'Hare International Airport. Seven interstate highways run through the city, allowing thousands of trucks to flow into Chicago's 200 truck terminals each day. Chicago is also known for its ethnic diversity. Less than 50% of the city's residents are Caucasians; the rest are African Americans, Hispanics (primarily of Mexican origin), and a growing South Asian population (the third largest in the United States after New York and San Francisco). Chicago's greater metropolitan area, known as Chicago land, boasts a population of between 8 and 10 million people.

Chicago's reputation for crime and corruption has been long-standing. Whether deserved, Al Capone's legacy has been hard to shed. Chicago, like many other American cities, during the past 30 years experienced a major rise in violent crime, which has gradually been declining since the mid-1990s. In 2005 Chicago recorded 448 homicides, the lowest total in 40 years. Still, the city's location makes it a hub for drug trade with an uninterrupted supply of opiates from four global sources: Mexico, South America, Southeast Asia, and Southwest Asia. According to the Drug Enforcement Administration (DEA), drugs are trafficked into the city by commercial trucks, package delivery services, couriers, railways, and cars (DEA, 2005).

This chapter traces Chicago's drug problem from the mid-1970s to the present time, examines the scope and nature of the city's current drug problem, and describes, in some detail, the latest strategies and tactics deployed by law enforcement agencies to reduce the supply and demand for drugs. Because of the global nature of drug trafficking, attention is also paid to ongoing efforts to disrupt the production and trafficking of drugs destined for Chicago.

Chicago's Drug Problem: A 30-Year Perspective

The Mexican Connection: "From the Farm to the Arm"

By the mid-1970s Chicago had become the major distribution hub for Mexican heroin in the United States. The impetus for Chicago becoming a center of illegal drug distribution for heroin smuggled from Mexico into the United States was the collapse of the "French Connection" in 1972, which ended the New York based *la Cosa Nostra's* monopoly in the heroin trade (President's Commission on Organized Crime, 1986). With the availability of "white heroin" trafficked from Europe sharply reduced, one of Mexico's major drug trafficking clans, the Herrera family, took advantage of the opportunity to fill the void by establishing almost exclusive dominance over the heroin trade east of the Mississippi River.

The Herrera clan, made up of some 15 families related through marriage and totaling some 3,000–4,000 members though not all going by the same name, were based in Durango, Mexico, some 260 miles south of Guadalajara. Described by the deputy chief of the DEA as a "social phenomenon" (Wiedrich, 1984), they are believed to have started their smuggling activities in the early 1960s. Some Herreras are said to have come to Chicago seeking employment in the 1950s. However, the first encounter the Chicago Police Department (CPD) had with the Herreras was in 1973, when a beat police officer observed drug dealings by 17-year-olds in one of the city's neighborhoods. According to the commander of the CPD's Gang Crimes Section at that time, "This was unheard of… .kids dealing like that" (O'Brien, January 8, 1978). Merely 5 years after that first encounter, one of Chicago's leading newspapers, the *Chicago Tribune*, branded the city with a new title: "Heroin City, USA" (O'Brien and Koziol, 1978). By that time the Herreras controlled the entire drug operation, beginning with the cultivation of opium poppies in the mountains northwest of Durango and the extraction of the opium to its transformation into heroin, the trafficking to Chicago, its sale on Chicago's streets, and distribution throughout the eastern half of the United States, including New York.

In 1977, the DEA in Chicago estimated that as much as 11 tons of Mexican heroin were being illegally trafficked from Mexico to Chicago. Although the reported figures for seized heroin at that time conflict and are not wholly reliable, seizures of heroin by the CPD and the DEA in Chicago reportedly increased from 32 pounds in 1973 to 411 pounds in 1977 (O'Brien and Koziol, 1978). In 1977, according to the CPD, of the 400 known dealers of Mexican heroin in the city, 99% belonged to the Herrera family.

The lifestyle of the Herreras, however, did not distinguish them from their neighbors and did not reveal their illegal activities. They continued residing in dilapidated houses and driving beat-up, used cars. But they used their neighborhood currency exchanges to transfer the profits they were making via money orders to Mexico. As CPD arrests of the Herreras increased, the family's monopoly began to be dented. Newspaper accounts during the late 1970s and early 1980s relate the arrest of numerous Herreras including clan members such as Jose Herrera, Jesus Herrera, Dias Jose Ramon-Herrera, Angel "Papo" Herrera, Asencion Herrera, and Rodolfo Herrera-Medina. Rodolfo Herrera-Medina, for example, was among 120 suspects arrested in what at the time was dubbed by law enforcement officials as the "biggest drug bust of all time." Coming after a 2-year undercover investigation code-named Operation Durango, between 400 and 500 federal and local law enforcement agents arrested the 120 suspects and seized 10 pounds of heroin, properties in excess of $1 million, and very large amounts of cash. Operation Durango also netted 13 pounds of cocaine, which by then started to gain popularity (Possley and O'Brien, 1985).

Although Mexican authorities at the time were accused by their American counterparts of complicity in the drug trade, the Mexican police, from time to time, acted against the Herreras. Thus, for instance, in fall 1978 seven major Herrera heroin dealers were imprisoned in Mexico, and two were killed in a shootout with police. Even the so-called godfather of the organization, Jaime Herrera-Nevarez, was arrested and held in custody for 6 months after two members of his organization implicated him as the owner of 13 pounds of heroin bound for Chicago (O'Brien, October 12, 1978). Jaime Herrera-Nevarez was again arrested on drug charges in August 1988 and imprisoned in Mexico City (DEA, n.d.a). By then, however, as discussed herein, the drug scene in Chicago was beginning to change, with new players, especially Colombians, trafficking cocaine to Chicago. Moreover, by the early 1990s the heroin trade in Chicago was being taken over by new smugglers, including Nigerians, Pakistanis, Thais, and Chinese (Blau, 1992).

The Southeast Asia Connection: China White Heroin

The DEA's Domestic Monitor Program (DMP) reported that beginning in 1991 the supply of Southeast Asian heroin reaching Chicago shifted the consumers' demand from the low-purity Mexican heroin (brown) to the high-purity China white heroin (ICJIA, 1997). By 1994, heroin purity levels in Chicago had reached 28%, which was high for Chicago standards but still lower than the national average (ICJIA, 1997). Law enforcement officials and drug-treatment providers were speculating at the time that the demand for higher-purity heroin was linked to the desire of new and younger heroin users, leery of the growing danger of HIV infection, to snort the drug rather than inject it with syringes (Blau, 1992).

Over the years, the purity level of heroin in Chicago continued to increase. The traditional $10 "dime bag" in 2003 was almost 10 times more potent than it had been in the mid-1980s. Dr. Westley Clark, director of the Federal Center for Substance Abuse Treatment in Washington, D.C., was quoted in the *Chicago Tribune* saying, "From a heroin consumer's point of view, it's as good as it's ever been" (Bebow, 2004).

The Colombian Connection: Chicago's Crack "Epidemic"

The most notorious Colombian drug organizations operating out of Colombia in the 1980s and 1990s were the Medellin and Cali cartels. Traffickers from

Medellin started their illegal activities trading marijuana. After switching to cocaine in the mid-1970s they quickly established a monopoly over the drug's distribution, which lasted until the death of the organization's major leader, Pablo Escobar, in December 1993 (DEA, n.d.b). The Medellin cartel's success prompted a competing cartel in Cali also to engage in drug trafficking. Unlike the Medellin cartel, the Cali group limited its violent activities and assumed a pretense of legitimacy. The violent battles waged between the Colombian government and the Medellin cartel provided the Cali cartel the opportunity to gain supremacy in the mid-1990s. At the height of its power, the Cali organization had at its disposal 727 aircraft with which to traffic drugs to Mexico and from there to the United States (Constantine, 1997). Having gained much prominence and power, the cartel planned to exercise control over the government. However, its attempt to influence Colombia's 1994 presidential elections backfired badly. Colombia's president, Ernesto Samper, having received campaign funding from the cartel, came under intense American pressure to crack down on the cartel's leaders. Consequently, the Colombian government mounted a fierce military campaign against the organization, arresting the cartel's leader in June 1995 (Luft, 1995). By the end of 1996, the entire top echelon of the organization was either dead or behind bars (Constantine, 1998). The imprisonment of the Cali cartel's leadership by no means ended the trafficking of drugs from Colombia. As is discussed later in this chapter, new organizations reactivated the trade to such an extent that they became the world's leading traffickers of cocaine as well as a major source for the supply of heroin (Constantine, 1997).

Large quantities of cocaine began reaching Chicago in the mid-1980s. Before 1985, cocaine in Chicago was very expensive, costing as much as $80,000 a kilo and not widely used. By 1988, however, the price of a kilo of cocaine was estimated at only $15,000 with an estimated street value of $140,000 (Risley, 1998). Such a sharp drop in cost was a clear indication that drug dealers were encountering few obstacles trafficking cocaine to Chicago. Indeed, as the CPD's deputy chief of detectives later noted, such extraordinary high profits gave the traffickers the impetus to seek an efficient delivery system to carve out an ever larger share of the market. Enter Chicago's notorious criminal street gangs (Risley, 1998). With street gangs taking over the sale of cocaine in the city, competition among the street dealers depressed the price of a dose of cocaine even further, fights over gang turfs escalated violence attributed to gangs, and arrests of people under the age of 18 rose sharply. According to Risley (1998), in 1985 the CPD arrested about 3,000 youths for narcotics offenses. By 1994, the number of youths arrested on drug charges had risen to 11,000. The introduction of crack cocaine (cocaine that is 75–90% pure and is formed into small pellets, or rocks, that can be smoked) in 1989 (several years after Los Angeles and New York) further aggravated the situation. The cheap price of cocaine, coupled with the fact that it could be snorted or smoked rather than injected with a hypodermic needle, increased the drug's popularity in the early 1990s to such an extent that the new phenomenon started to be termed an epidemic. The increasing popularity of cocaine was first officially documented when a 1991 survey, conducted by the National Institute of Drug Abuse (NIDA), revealed that 144,000 people living in the Chicago metropolitan area had tried cocaine in 1990. The number of heroin users at the same time was estimated to be only 36,000 (Blau, 1992). Admissions to publicly funded drug treatment centers in Illinois for persons addicted to cocaine, measured by the University of Illinois School of Public Health, also rose sharply.

As previously noted by the authors in an earlier article (Lemmer, Bensinger, & Lurigio, 2006), the central role played by Chicago's gangs in the city's illegal drug trade has significantly affected Chicago's homicide rate, especially since gang members are much more likely to kill, not intimidate, their rivals. In fact, some of the enormous profits generated by street sales were used by gangs to purchase firearms of increasing lethality, leading to the rise of gang-motivated homicides. Consequently, it is not surprising that a statistical analysis of Chicago's homicide rates reveals that from 1970 through 1990, Chicago's homicide rate was only tangentially related to gang violence and that a new trend that began in 1991 unmistakably shows a correlation between the number of gang-motivated homicides and the city's homicide totals (Lemmer et al., 2006). Another analysis conducted by the Illinois Criminal Justice Information Authority (ICJIA, 1997) indicates that in Chicago street gang-related homicides between 1987 and 1994 increased from 51 to 243. In 1994, street gang-motivated homicide for the first time became the most common type of homicide in Chicago, accounting for 243 of that year's total of 931 homicides (a record high, not seen since then).

Chicago's high homicide rate put increasing pressure on the CPD to reduce crime in the city. Beginning in the late 1980s, the CPD's Narcotics Section deployed a two-pronged strategy to reduce the drug use in the city. The first strategy involved traditional police tactics aimed at reducing the supply of drugs by seizing contraband and arresting drug traffickers and street dealers. For instance, the Narcotics Section in 1991 seized 3,430 grams of crack cocaine compared with just 100 grams seized in 1988 (Silverman & Martin, 1993). And, primarily due to drug arrests in Chicago, between 1991 and 1994 the number of felony cases filed in the Circuit Court of Cook County (Chicago and suburbs) increased from 13, 318 to 18,233 (ICJIA, 1997). (County figures do not include federally prosecuted cases in Chicago. Though federal prosecutions in the 1990s accounted only for 2% of the drug prosecutions in the city, they usually involved large-scale investigations and prosecution in Chicago's federal courts of notorious gang leaders such as the Latin Kings' leader Gustavo Colon and the highest-ranking leader of the Gangster Disciples Larry Hoover.)

The CPD's second strategy was aimed at creating an environment that discouraged narcotics transactions through the initiation of demand-reduction tactics. This strategy was based on the assumption that increasing the risk of arrest would deter consumers from buying illegal drugs. One such tactic, code-named Operation Risky Business, was initiated by the Narcotics Section in 1989. According to Raymond Risley, the section's commander, the section deployed two to three police officers to pose as low-level street dealers in a particular area or street corner known for drug dealing. The officers would sell a packet of 1% cocaine or .5% heroin to any individual who approached them soliciting drugs. These packets were produced by the CPD's crime laboratory. The transaction was videotaped by an officer in an unmarked police vehicle, and the offender was then arrested. If a vehicle was involved, it was seized. In 1989, Operation Risky Business netted the arrest of 388 offenders (Risley, 1990). Another related tactic employed at that time involved using undercover police officers to make controlled purchases of narcotics from low-level dealers on city streets. These dealers were subsequently arrested and charged with the delivery of a controlled substance (Risley, 1990).

In 1993, just as Chicago's homicide rate was peaking and pressure for reform was mounting, the CPD decided to reinvent itself by adopting a new and ambitious strategic plan that emphasized a proactive rather than the traditional reactive approach to crime fighting (Rodriguez, 1993). The Chicago Alternative Policing Strategy (CAPS), Chicago's own version of community policing and problem-oriented policing, began as a pilot project in 1994 and was implemented citywide by spring 1995. Advocates of this new strategy have been encouraged by the fact that, following the implementation of CAPS, homicides in Chicago declined to a 40-year low.

The Mexican–Colombian Connection: More Cocaine and Purer Heroin

Geographically, Mexico provides a natural land bridge between the drug-producing countries of South America, specifically Colombia, and drug consumers in the United States. Seeing a need to secure their distribution routes to the U.S. markets, the Cali cartel allied itself with traffickers from Mexico to transfer and deliver Colombian-produced cocaine to the American markets. The collapse of the Cali cartel in 1995–1996 provided these Mexican traffickers an opportunity to increase their own control over the cocaine trade. Consequently, Colombians remained in control of the sources of supply, the processing and manufacturing of the drugs, and their transport to Mexico. The Mexicans, on the other hand, gained complete control over the distribution of cocaine in the western half of the United States and the Midwest, including Chicago. Commenting on this development in late 1997, the then administrator of the DEA described this new situation as "the most significant change in the wholesale US cocaine trade in the last two decades" (Constantine, 1997).

It is important to note here that Colombian cartels originally obtained unrefined cocaine from Peru and Bolivia and that the planting of coca in Colombia began only in the early 1990s. Likewise, opium poppy cultivation and heroin production in Colombia did not start until drug traffickers in the 1990s were encouraged to do so by leftist guerrillas, especially the Revolutionary Armed Forces of Colombia (FARC) in the territories they controlled. This arrangement provided the traffickers with a secure (secured by the FARC) supply of drugs, and by taxing the shipments the guerillas obtained money to finance the war. Coca continues to be grown in FARC-controlled areas, and the group has been accused of involvement in both drug production and transit. At the present time, however, right-wing paramilitary groups, such as the United Self Defense Forces of Colombia (AUC), have seized much of the territory controlled previously by the FARC and control most of the illegal drug production and export to the United States. Both the FARC and the AUC were named by the U.S. government as Specially Designated Global Terrorists in October 2001, thus subjecting them to economic sanctions. In May 2003, they were further designated as Significant Foreign Narcotics Traffickers.

Large amounts of Colombian-grown cocaine and heroin have been reaching Chicago's neighborhoods and suburbs in recent years to meet the strong demand for narcotics (Keilman, 2006; Main, 2004). A study by the Office of National Drug Control Policy in Washington, D.C., in 1997 reportedly estimated that 333,000 people in Chicago and its suburbs are hard-core users of cocaine and heroin (Bendavid, 1997). A more recent study, describing the availability of drugs in Chicago as "bountiful," reported that Chicago ranked second in the United States in the number of heroin-related deaths (628 within a 2-year period) and that the Chicago metropolitan area for 5 consecutive years recorded the largest number of heroin-related emergency room visits in the nation (Bebow, 2004). This grave situation prompted one of the area's most powerful members of Congress, Representative Henry Hyde, chair of the International Relations Committee, to propose a five-point plan to eradicate opium in Colombia (Main & Sweet, 2003) and to organize a fact-finding mission to Colombia for Chicago and suburban police officials (Main, 2004). Interviewed by the authors for the purpose of this chapter, John Risley, an official CPD delegate on the mission and now deputy superintendent in charge of the CPD's Bureau of Strategic Deployment, related that the trip achieved two main objectives. First, the Colombian hosts and the American delegates acquainted each other with their respective law enforcement priorities relative to the drug trade as well as its impact on the daily lives of ordinary citizens in Colombia and Chicago. Second, the trip provided the Americans with an opportunity to express appreciation for the Colombian efforts in combating that nation's major drug cartels. Risley specifically noted the difficulties faced by the Colombian police, including a paramilitary barracks life away from family and the heightened risk of injury and death. Although Colombian law enforcement officials have reciprocated by visiting Chicago, no joint counternarcotics initiatives of any kind have been directly undertaken by the two law enforcement entities. The DEA remains the CPD's sole official conduit for sensitive intelligence regarding drug trafficking to Chicago (Risley, personal communication, Chicago, March 14, 2006).

The Drug Problem in Chicago

The most widely available and used illegal drugs in Chicago include marijuana, cocaine, heroin, and methamphetamines. While Chicago may be a methamphetamine transit point to other locations, its effects in Chicago appear to be minimal.

Marijuana

Marijuana is the drug of choice for 18- to 20-year-olds in Chicago and, therefore, is the most widely available illicit drug in the city. Bulk marijuana shipments are transported to Chicago by the same Mexican-based traffickers who smuggle cocaine and heroin. Criminal street gangs control the distribution and retail sale of the drug in the city (DEA, 2005). In a single seizure by the CPD in August 2005, 355 pounds of marijuana, with an estimated street value of just under $1 million, was recovered from an Arizona resident of Mexican descent following a traffic stop in an area of Chicago long known as a Latin King street gang stronghold (Noel, 2006). In May 2003, CPD officers had made an even larger marijuana seizure from four Chicago residents of Mexican descent when they recovered a total of 4,941 pounds of marijuana with an estimated street value of $13.5 million (CPD, May 8, 2003).

Additionally, drug case submissions to the Illinois State Police (ISP) crime laboratory in Chicago also support the conclusion that marijuana leads in availability among the city's drug markets. During the 8-year period from 1998 through 2005, an average of 26,151 marijuana cases per year were submitted by police in Chicago to the ISP laboratory for analysis (Bauer, 2006). This represents an apparent fluctuation in drug preferences in Chicago, as in 1998 cocaine case submissions outnumbered those of marijuana cases. By 2000, the submission levels for these two substances were roughly equal, and beginning in 2001 marijuana cases outnumbered cocaine cases. Overall, during the 8-year period, marijuana cases comprised 42.9% of all drug case submissions to the crime laboratory, rising from 35.66% of all case submissions in 1998 to 48.4% in 2005.

Cocaine

The Drug Abuse Warning Network (DAWN) has reported that there are more estimated cocaine-related emergency room visits in Chicago than in any other city it monitors (DEA, 2005). As already noted, Mexican traffickers dominate the cocaine distribution network into and out of Chicago (as far east as New York City). In Chicago, local cells and gang members distribute and sell the drug (DEA, 2005). As noted, while cocaine use in Chicago remains high, ISP crime laboratory submissions data suggest that its use may have diminished somewhat from 1998 to 2005. During the 8-year period, on average 23,056 cocaine cases per year were submitted by police in Chicago for analysis by the state laboratory (Bauer, 2006). Overall during this period, cocaine cases comprised 37.8% of all drug case submissions, dropping from 45.5% of all drug cases sent to the state laboratory in 1998 to 33.1% in 2005.

While typically the quantities of cocaine seized by police in any single case fell in the "personal use" or small-quantity street-dealer level, during the period, large seizures of several kilograms of cocaine occurred with some frequency and were regularly reported by Chicago media outlets. For example, following a narcotics surveillance in August 2005, CPD officers recovered five bricks of cocaine with a combined weight of more than 12 pounds or about 5.45 kilograms (Noel, 2006). Other accounts more specifically contained references to the international connection to the city's gang-operated drug markets. Acting on a tip in September 2003, CPD and suburban police officers arrested two Chicagoans and two Mexican nationals in a Chicago suburb and seized 312 kilograms of cocaine with an estimated street value of $39 million. The cocaine had been hidden in 760 five-gallon pails of green avocado dip (CPD, September 22, 2003). In September 2005, CPD officials announced the seizure of 88 kilograms of cocaine with an estimated street value of $11.3 million brought to Chicago via the Mexican pipeline (*Chicago Tribune*, September 14, 2005). Then in another example, following a 2-year investigation into a Four Corner Hustler street gang narcotics operation, CPD officers arrested both a high-ranking gang member and a Nigerian national who was identified by police officials as a major drug supplier. At the time of the suspect roundup in this case, police recovered 50 grams of crack cocaine, 11 pounds of powder cocaine, and 2.2 pounds of heroin (Bush & Heinzmann, 2005).

Heroin

ISP crime laboratory submissions data for the years 1998 through 2005 indicate that despite the enforcement efforts from police heroin availability has apparently remained fairly stable in Chicago. During 1998, there were 11,387 heroin submissions, and in 2005 there were 11,124 heroin cases submitted from Chicago to the ISP laboratory. On average during the 8-year period, 11,393 heroin cases were submitted per year, and overall heroin accounted for 18.7% of all drug cases from the city (Bauer, 2006). Chicago's hunger for heroin, noted earlier in this chapter, continues to be satisfied by large supplies of heroin trafficked by Mexican-based organizations, independent Colombian traffickers, and Nigerian and other West African groups that smuggle Southeast and Southwest Asian heroin to the city (DEA, 2005). The Chicago heroin market is characterized by high quantities of the drug, high purity levels, and low prices. At the retail level, the drug is sold by gang members at so-called open-air markets.

Beginning in June 2003, combating the city's gang-controlled open-air markets has been an increased priority for CPD officials. Since that time, CPD officials have regularly reported on their efforts in this area, frequently conducting full press conferences announcing the results of their investigations. As heroin is sold via the same gang-controlled drug markets, as noted already, significant heroin seizures often occurred during investigations recovering large quantities of cocaine. However, significant heroin-specific investigations have also been conducted, resulting in some disruption to several highly lucrative narcotics operations. In March 2004, 30 individuals were arrested in a series of raids conducted in Chicago, Indiana, and Ohio relative to a Chicago-based heroin trafficking network (*Chicago Tribune,* 2004). The April 2005 arrests by CPD officers of 13 members of the Unknown Vice Lords street gang further identified this interjurisdictional reach of Chicago's drug-dealing gangs. Operating from the Douglas Park area of Chicago's Westside, gang members were selling 13-dose tin-foil packets of heroin, known as "jabs." These multidose packets were sold for $100 to buyers from communities as far as 95 miles from the city. By reselling the individual doses from the jab at $20 per dose, suburban and rural user–sellers could offset the cost of their own drug use through the sale of a portion of the heroin jab to buyers in their own communities (*Chicago Tribune,* April 7, 2005).

Methamphetamines

For many communities in the United States, the methamphetamine problem has emerged as a larger problem than marijuana, cocaine, and heroin

(Leinwand, 2005). The problem has largely affected rural or nonurban areas in the United States. While methamphetamine is often produced in local laboratories, according to the DEA the drug is also trafficked from Mexico and California to Chicago for distribution in the Midwestern part of the country. At the present time, however, there is no evidence that Mexican-produced methamphetamine is distributed in Chicago (DEA, 2005). Based on the number of drug seizure cases submitted for analysis to the ISP crime laboratory in Chicago from 1998 through 2005, methamphetamine seizures represent only a small fraction, roughly 1%, of the narcotics cases uncovered by police within the city (Bauer, 2006).

The Law Enforcement Effort in Chicago: A Closer Look

The current law enforcement efforts in Chicago targeting the city's drug problems can be easily traced back to Operation Headache, which commenced in 1990. This investigation targeted Chicago's Gangster Disciples street gang and its then already imprisoned leader Larry Hoover. Investigators from the Chicago Office of the DEA and the CPD's Gang Investigation Section discovered a level of organizational sophistication within the Gangster Disciples that rivaled that of traditional organized crime groups. Originally formed in Chicago's Southside Engelwood community during the 1960s, by the 1990s the Gangster Disciples had grown into Chicago's largest street gang. Not only did the gang control large turf areas across Chicago, but factions of the gang also had been identified throughout the United States. The gang's criminal activities were documented as including narcotic sales, murder, aggravated batteries, drive-by shootings, ambush-type shootings, robberies, burglaries, theft, weapons violations, gang intimidations, and assaults (Guzman, 1998). Some estimates placed the gang's membership in Chicago alone at 30,000, with thousands of additional members belonging to the gang's various factions in at least 35 states (Knox, 2001). Illinois prison officials placed the number of Gangster Disciples in the Illinois Department of Corrections at 5,100 members, including Hoover (Parsons & Gibson, 1995). Hoover, then age 44, was already serving a 150–200-year prison sentence for a 1973 gang-related murder over drug profits (Martin, 1996).

Based on the gang's considerable size, developing the sophistication of the gang became a key objective of its leadership. In addition to increasingly hierarchical organizational structure, the gang adopted formal rules and attempted to emulate a corporate-style management approach, which included a board of directors with Hoover as its chair. Under Hoover's directions, the Gangster Disciples not only operated extensive narcotics trafficking operations but also began to engage in an elaborate series of public relations actions intended to shield the gang from law enforcement scrutiny. These included the creation of a political action committee known as 21 Century Vote, a rap concert company, and a prisoner rights advocacy group (O'Brien, O'Connor, & Papajohn, 1995). Moreover, these efforts were met with at least some success. Hoover achieved support for his own parole from many prominent individuals, including a former Chicago mayor and numerous additional elected officials and leaders within the African American community. Additionally, under the guise of a community activist, Hoover operative and gang member Wallace "Gator" Bradley was successful in being included in an Oval Office visit with an unsuspecting President Bill Clinton (Knox, 2001).

The 5-year investigation conducted under Operation Headache disclosed that Hoover, with the assistance of at least 38 major coconspirators, was able to direct a massive cocaine and heroin trafficking network from his Illinois prison cell. Federal prosecutors identified this drug network as having amassed $10 million in drug profits during the course of the investigation. While individual gang members sold drugs for personal profit, "street taxes" were passed up the gang hierarchy, and a portion of the weekly drugs sold were to include drugs purchased from and sold for the profit of gang leaders. Investigators were able to secure the key evidence necessary to gain indictments and ultimately convictions for Hoover and his accomplices through the use of eavesdropping devices. Tiny wireless microphones were hidden in official visitor ID tags, which were then unknowingly worn by gang lieutenants as they met with Hoover in the Vienna, Illinois, Correctional Center (O'Brien et al., 1995).

Operation Headache is also remembered for a key statement regarding the significance of the investigation made by then U.S. Attorney James Burnes when he announced the indictments of Hoover and his coconspirators. On August 31, 1995, Burns declared, "We ripped off the head of the snake" (Lehmann & McNamee, 1995). Implied in the declaration was that the Gangster Disciples as a criminal organization would die as a result of the removal of the gang's top leaders to federal prison and their corresponding isolation from the gang's day-to-day activities. Initial reaction to the declaration can best be summarized as an overstatement from an overoptimistic prosecutor (Martin, 1996). However, with the distance of time, senior CPD officials have indicated that Operation Headache and subsequent investigations have altered Chicago's gang landscape more than many critics initially anticipated. Clearly, the Gangster Disciples remain Chicago's largest single street gang, with affiliated factions present in communities across the country. However, the gang is more loosely organized, with more internal strife, 10 years after Operation Headache than when the investigation commenced, and the ability of gang leaders to tightly control the drug markets operated by its various factions and members has been significantly diminished (Risley, personal communication, Chicago, March 14, 2006; Cronin, personal communication, Chicago, March 24, 2006).

Currently, major drug enforcement operations in the Chicago metropolitan area are coordinated through a program called the High Intensity Drug Trafficking Area (HIDTA). Established by the U.S. Congress and implemented in Chicago in 1995, HIDTA coordinates all drug control efforts among local, state, and federal law enforcement agencies. One important benefit of the program is that it reduces the risks to police officers engaged in undercover work or surveillance from being targeted by fellow police officers who otherwise could be unaware of an ongoing operation.

The DEA has been engaged in numerous counternarcotics operations in Chicago. The following is just one such example. Code-named Operation Money Clip, the DEA targeted a Mexican-based organization that trafficked cocaine, heroin, and marijuana and allegedly laundered as much as $200 million from its operations in the United States. Begun as a routine traffic stop in Texas, the operation evolved into a multijurisdictional investigation involving DEA agents in 25 cities including Chicago. The CPD, the Illinois State Police, and several suburban police departments participated in uprooting the Chicago branch of the organization (DEA, 2004).

However, given the scope of the drug problem in the United States, on a key level the capacity of the DEA to affect the day-to-day drug problem in Chicago, or any local jurisdiction, is extremely limited. Survey data collected as part of the evaluation of Chicago's community policing effort CAPS indicated significant concerns among residents in many Chicago communities. In 2003, 26% of all Chicagoans surveyed listed street-corner drug dealing as a "big problem" in their neighborhood (the highest of the three possible levels of concern). The community's acknowledgment of the drug problem's connection to the city's gang problem can also be seen in these data. Gang violence was identified as a big problem by 21% of the city's surveyed residents (Chicago Community Policing Evaluation Consortium, 2004). In fact, rising gang violence connected to Chicago's drug markets, which began during 2000, had caused an end to a 6-year decline in the city's overall yearly murder total in 2001. This increased gang violence coincided with unprecedented reductions in violence in New York City. These two factors allowed New York City, despite having well more than twice the population, to end the year with fewer murders than Chicago (Lemmer et al., 2006).

Chicago's experience in 2001 highlights a key reality. Thomas P. "Tip" O'Neill, Jr., the former speaker of the U.S. House of Representatives, once noted that no matter how expansive a particular issue may be, in the end all politics is local. Given the design of American federalism, the delivery of key governmental services, including water, sanitation, public education, and fire protection, is considered first and foremost to be a function of state and local government. Law enforcement is among the "local" governmental concerns, and as such O'Neill's axiom would be only somewhat overstated if it were applied to law enforcement as "all policing is local." While collaborative efforts with law enforcement agencies operating at the national level are critical for forming truly effective responses to global threats such as terrorism and narcotics trade, unlike in many other countries in the United States thousand of local police agencies remain central to day-to-day street-level narcotics enforcement. As such, when the nexus between Chicago's gang and drug problems spurred a spike in the city's murder total, it was not the DEA that felt the political heat—responding to the concerns of elected officials and the community fell almost exclusively on the CPD.

Key to the CPD's effort to reduce the levels of gang violence in Chicago was the direct targeting of the city's open-air drug markets. From 1998 through November 2003, the CPD conducted more than 50 drug conspiracy investigations, arresting some 1,700 suspects, of which 97% were convicted on criminal drug conspiracy charges. At a November 2003 press conference held by Chicago mayor Richard M. Daley and police superintendent Philip J. Cline, the CPD continued to highlight its strategy to reduce violence levels through a reenergized and enhanced focus on gang suppression and the closure of gang-controlled drug markets (CPD, November 18, 2003). Beyond its earlier community policing efforts, beginning in June 2003 the CPD intensified and implemented numerous elements of this strategy. These included reintroduction of a centralized gang intelligence unit, creation of a deployment operations center, creation of new rapid deployment units, expanded measures to identify and intervene in retaliatory gang violence through the rapid deployment of gang violence suppression units, significant increase of use of street-corner drug conspiracy investigative techniques, and increased use of drug buyer sting operations (Lemmer et al., 2006).

In short, addressing the nexus between the city's gang and drug problems was central to the CPD drive to reduce the city's violence levels. These efforts first resulted in increased arrest activity on drug-related charges. In 2004, CPD officers affected 59,051 drug arrests, which comprised a 5.8% increase from 2003 (CPD, 2005). Police officials also noted that the number of conspiracy investigations conducted had increased significantly, and as a result, compared to 10 years earlier, there were fewer open-air drug markets in the areas of the city where the prevalence had previously been the greatest. Additionally, in those places where the open-air markets remained in operation, they were less profitable than in prior years (Risley, personal communication, Chicago, March 14, 2006). Of larger significance, violence levels had dropped sharply in Chicago, even as the number of murders in many other American cities began to rise again (Zernike, 2006). Compared with 2001, when Chicago's murders totaled 666, in 2004 the number of Chicago murders was down 32.7% to 448. In 2005, the number of murders remained stable at 447, allowing CPD officials to declare that the historically low murder level, which had not been seen in Chicago since 1965, was not an anomaly. In maintaining the lower homicide level, the CPD took note of the 753 drug conspiracy arrests the agency made during its 2005 efforts to close yet another 53 open-air drug markets (CPD, 2006). However, while police officials noted that violence levels were down significantly and the CPD had impacted the drug trade, they noted as well that the city's gangs had previously demonstrated a capacity to adapt, and the demand for drugs in the city had not been eliminated. As such, the CPD's antidrug and antigang efforts would need to continue and adapt, when necessary, as well (Risley, personal communication, Chicago, March 14, 2006; Cronin, personal communication, Chicago, March 24, 2006).

Acting Globally

According to the U.S. government, the drugs that most threaten the United States are cocaine, heroin, marijuana, and amphetamine-type stimulants (Department of State, 2006). As already discussed in this chapter, these are the very drugs that also threaten Chicago the most. Consequently, since Colombia and Mexico are the main source countries for the trafficking of cocaine, heroin, and marijuana to Chicago, the ensuing discussion regarding global drug control strategies and tactics undertaken by the United States in cooperation with foreign governments is limited to these two countries.

Colombia

A full 90% of the cocaine trafficked to Chicago originates in Colombia. Likewise, most of the heroin that is smuggled to Chicago is processed from poppies grown in Colombia. Not surprisingly, such tactics as eradication of crops, elimination or disruption of means of production, and interdiction, underwritten or undertaken by the United States in Colombia, are supported and encouraged by law enforcement officials in Chicago (Risley, personal communication, Chicago, March 14, 2006).

Interdiction

Interdiction by the Colombian National Police, Army, Navy, and Air Force resulted in record seizures of cocaine in 2005—more seizures than by any other country (Department of State, 2006). Notwithstanding the success of Colombian interdiction efforts, cocaine and heroin continue to be trafficked from Colombia north through Central America and the Caribbean. At the present time, seven Central American countries are used by major drug traffickers to transit drugs from Colombia to Mexico. In fact, U.S. government-affiliated agencies, such as the Consolidated Counterdrug Database, report that 90% of the cocaine intended for the U.S. market was trafficked through the so-called Central American corridor to Mexico during the first half of 2005 (Braun, 2005).

Colombian cocaine is smuggled by land, air, and water. Most of the cocaine is transited by traffickers taking advantage of Central America's long coastlines. Since 2004, there seems to have been a significant increase in night air smuggling to hundreds of airstrips scattered around Central America. U.S. air reconnaissance, for instance, reported the discovery of an "aircraft graveyard" in Guatemala, close to the Mexican border, with scores of damaged or abandoned airplanes that had been used by drug traffickers (Braun, 2005). Drug traffickers also use the Pan-American Highway as an additional smuggling route for cocaine and heroin. To counter these activities, the United States has entered into numerous bilateral agreements with the countries of the Central American corridor to conduct counternarcotics operations aimed at seizing contraband. According to the United States, such cooperative operations have recently yielded unprecedented amounts of seized cocaine (Braun, 2005). The DEA, the Department of Justice, and the Department of Homeland Security and the Department of Defense are the U.S. agencies most frequently involved in interdiction. The DEA has been involved in hundreds of such operations. One recent new initiative undertaken by the DEA to disrupt the transit of drugs and money between Colombia and the United States is the multiagency International Drug Flow Prevention Strategy (IDFPS). The first IDFPS operation, called All Inclusive 1-2005, was started on August 5, 2005, and continued through October 8, 2005. Called "All Inclusive" because it targeted land, maritime, and air smuggling, it resulted in the seizure of large quantities of cocaine and illegal currency in Nicaragua, Belize, Panama, and Mexico (Braun, 2005).

Crop Eradication

Crop eradication in Colombia is carried out manually by U.S. government-supported Colombian police units and military forces and through aerial spraying. It is estimated that more than 170,000 hectares of coca were eradicated by these means in 2005, thus eliminating a potential yield of more than 150 metric tons of cocaine with a street value estimated at $15 billion. In addition to the elimination of coca plants, the program is said to have resulted in the eradication of 2,000 hectares of opium poppy in 2005 (Department of State, 2006).

Disruption of Production and Networks

From a U.S. viewpoint, an important deterrent for international drug traffickers is their fear of being captured and extradited to the United States. Consequently, an important U.S. strategy targets the leadership within the hierarchy of major trafficking organizations. In recent years, especially under the administration of Colombia's former president, Alvaro Uribe, there have been as many as 315 extraditions from Colombia to the United States. With U.S. assistance, the upper echelons (kingpins) of the Colombian trafficking organizations are being targeted by special police teams that, together with air mobile commandos (known as the Jungle Commandos), carry out special operations aimed at capturing targeted leaders (Department of State, 2006).

Institutional Support and Economic Assistance

The United States has been engaged in strengthening and professionalizing such institutions as the police and the prosecution and Colombia's judicial and financial systems. To that end, the United States has provided these institutions with technical assistance, training, and equipment. At the same time, the United States has intensified its efforts to prod the Colombian government to fight corruption to weaken the drug organizations' ability to bribe and intimidate government officials (Department of State, 2006). In recent years, the United States has granted close to $5 billion to Colombia in economic assistance, making that country the fifth largest recipient of American foreign aid. One of the more successful programs, initiated with this aid, entices Colombian farmers to stop cultivating coca and opium poppies by accepting "Alternative Development." One such alternative has been the ever expanding cut-flower business, which has turned into an annual $600 million enterprise (PBS, 2006).

Efforts by the U.S. government aimed at strengthening former President Alvaro Uribe's administration showed signs of success. The recent congressional elections in Colombia evidenced public support for the right-of-center coalition and apparently provided the president sufficient political power to win reelection in May 2006 (Forero, March 14, 2006). In a show of support for President Uribe and his policies, shortly after the congressional elections a federal grand jury in the United States indicted 50 commanders of the FARC, charging them with trafficking and being responsible for manufacturing and exporting "devastating amounts of cocaine" as well as using violence and intimidation to enforce their activities (Forero, March 23, 2006). In the meantime, Colombia's military forces continue their successful offensive (Plan Patriota) against the FARC while the government attempts to entice the right-wing paramilitary militias to demobilize with certain legal immunities. The government also has established an interagency organization to reestablish its control over areas of the country previously held by the FARC and other militias. By the end of 2005, the Colombian police reestablished their presence in all of the country's municipalities, thus helping pacify the nation. Limiting the reach of the war into large cities has stabilized Colombia's economy and significantly reduced the country's unemployment.

Mexico

Mexico continues to be the principal transit country for cocaine trafficked to the United States, including Chicago. As a source country, Mexico is a major supplier of heroin and marijuana for Chicago (Risley, personal communication, Chicago, March 14, 2006). And Mexican-based criminal organizations continue to use the city as one of their major drug distribution centers. The U.S. government's expressed goal in Mexico is for both governments to exchange intelligence and information on illicit drug-related activities and work as a team against the Mexican drug organizations (Department of State, 2006).

Interdiction and Disruption of the Drug Trade

In 2005, Mexican authorities mounted 28 separate major operations arresting drug traffickers, violent kidnappers, and corrupt officials linked to drug trafficking. During the first 11 months of 2005, close to 15,000 individuals were arrested on drug-related charges, large quantities of illegal drugs were seized, and cars, boats, and airplanes were confiscated (Department of State, 2006).

Mexican–American bilateral cooperation in the war on drugs is based on numerous agreements and treaties signed by both countries over the years. For instance, Mexico is a signatory to the 1990 Ixtapa Declaration, under which it is committed to undertake counternarcotics actions and prevent money laundering. U.S. law enforcement agencies, such as the DEA and Federal Bureau of Investigation (FBI), maintain offices in Mexico and work with Mexican law enforcement agencies on a regular basis. Mexico City is the DEA Country Office in Mexico. Other DEA offices are located in Guadalajara, Hermosillo, Mazaltan, and Monterrey. The DEA assists the Mexican government primarily in interdiction and crop eradication efforts. Special units of the Mexican Federal Investigations Agency (FIA) and the DEA meet regularly to share intelligence and plan and execute investigations (Embassy of the United States–Mexico, 2006). The United States and Mexico have agreed on a plan that targets the leadership of major drug trafficking organizations. Under terms of the U.S.–Mexico Extradition Treaty of 1980, more than 40 Mexican citizens and defendants accused of narcotics trafficking, money laundering, and related serious crimes were extradited to the

United States in 2005 (Department of State, 2006). One example of many that illustrates interagency cooperation involving U.S. and Mexican law enforcement agencies was the recent arrest of Arriola-Marquez, a major Mexican drug trafficker and head of an international distribution network reaching into the United States. The arrest was carried out by an elite drug enforcement unit of the FIA following an extensive investigation assisted by the DEA. Other law enforcement agencies involved in this operation included the FBI, the Mexican Office of the Attorney General (PGR), as well as several other Mexican and American law enforcement agencies (DEA, 2006). Another sphere of Mexican–American bilateral cooperation is border security. Joint border security projects along the borders and airports include U.S.-assisted and -financed training, technical assistance, and procurement of equipment to detect contraband. In 2005, the U.S. government provided Mexico with eight helicopters equipped with infrared radar and refurbished another eight helicopters to enhance police and border surveillance (Department of State, 2006).

Crop Eradication

Eradication of opium poppies and cannabis grown in Mexico is a difficult task. Military forces are dispatched to the remote Sierra Madre Mountains to destroy these crops manually, and helicopters spraying herbicides are also used in the eradication program. According to the Mexican government, during the first 11 months of 2005 eradication of marijuana totaled close to 31,000 hectares, and the eradication of opium poppy approximated 20,500 hectares (Department of State, 2006).

Institutional Support and Economic Assistance

The United States has been assisting the government of Mexico to professionalize and upgrade its criminal justice system by providing training and donating equipment, especially to the Mexican police and prosecutors. For example, the U.S. Embassy's Law Enforcement Professionalization and Training Program in 2005 sponsored training for 2,800 law enforcement personnel.

The PGR, a major player in the war on drugs, received new tools to improve the capabilities of the office to conduct investigations and was provided with special training for its information technology engineers. In the meantime, according to a U.S. assessment, the FIA was evolving into one of the most professional and effective law enforcement agencies in Mexico (Department of State, 2006).

There have been many allegations of corruption in Mexico's antidrug efforts over the years. Under the presidency of Vicente Fox from 2000 to 2006 the administration instituted a number of anticorruption measures affecting all government institutions, including the Mexican military (Department of State, 2006). The Fox administration's effort to fight the drug cartels by decapitating their leadership, however, only intensified the rivalry between the drug gangs and led to even greater violence. Since taking office on December 1, 2006, President Felipe Calderón has shown unprecedented determination to defeat the drug trafficking cartels by dispatching more than 25,000 troops and federal police into areas where the local police forces are perceived to be corrupt. At the same time, he has authorized the extradition of a greater number of cartel members to the United States and has increased the level of intelligence sharing on drug shipments with the United States, leading to ever greater seizures of trafficked drugs.

Conclusion

The federal and state laws that control the manufacture, sale, and distribution of illegal drugs in the United States are quite recent. One of the first antidrug laws in the United States was a 1905 New York state law, which targeted cocaine, morphine, and opium. More important for present-day drug policy, however, was the Harrison Narcotic Drug Act of 1914. Applied to opium and its derivatives and to coca leaves and their derivatives, the new law was the first of a series of federal laws that attempted to stop drug trafficking. Still, it took the federal government another 60 years before creating the DEA and launching the official War on Drugs. Established in 1973, the DEA consolidated all other federal drug enforcement agencies and became responsible for controlling the use and distribution of narcotics and other dangerous drugs.

This chapter has demonstrated the extent to which Chicago, primarily because of its geographic location and diverse population, has become an important market and distribution hub for illegal drugs trafficked mainly from Mexico and Colombia. At the present time, the most widely available illegal drugs in Chicago include marijuana, cocaine, and heroin. Marijuana has been smuggled from Mexico to Chicago since the 1950s. By the mid-1970s, Chicago had become the major distribution hub for Mexican heroin in the United States, and large quantities of cocaine began reaching Chicago in the mid-1980s.

The global war on drugs has not reduced the availability of either heroin or cocaine in Chicago. A full 90% of the cocaine trafficked to Chicago originates in Colombia, and Mexico continues to be the city's major supplier of heroin and marijuana. It can, of course, be argued that without the global war on drugs the problem in Chicago would be even worse. Still, as noted in this chapter, the capacity of the federal effort to affect the day-to-day drug problem in Chicago is extremely limited. Constitutionally, in the United States, the responsibility for public safety is vested locally. Thus, while collaborative efforts with such federal agencies as the DEA are important, in the final analysis it is the responsibility of the CPD to respond to the concerns of the city's citizens and elected officials. Consequently, as discussed previously, it is the strategies and tactics deployed by the CPD in recent years that have reduced violence to a level not seen in Chicago since 1965. Senior police officials in Chicago admit that the war on drugs cannot be won by law enforcement alone. They believe, however, that their antidrug and antigang efforts have indeed impacted the local drug trade and that they now have the strategic and technological advantage to prevail and adapt to changing conditions and new challenges.

References

Bauer, R. (2006). *Number of Chicago drug case submissions to the Illinois State Police Labs for years 1998–2005.* Illinois Criminal Justice Information Authority.

Bebow, J. (2004, January 30). Flood of heroin ravaging city. *Chicago Tribune.*

Blau, R. (1992, July 23). Shifting heroin may be city's next drug plague. *Chicago Tribune.*

Bendavid, N. (1997, December 12). Survey of drugs in Cook County: 333,000 labeled hard-core users. *Chicago Tribune.*

Braun, M. (2005, November 9). Statement of Michael A. Braun, chief of operations, Drug Enforcement Administration, before the House International Relations Committee, Subcommittee on Western Hemisphere. Retrieved February 28, 2006 from http://www.dea.gov/pubs/cngrtest/ct110905p.html

Bush, R., & Heinzmann, D. (2005, July 20). Drug sting nets 19 arrests; 2-year operation considered big blow to Chicago-area gang. *Chicago Tribune.*

Chicago Community Policing Evaluation Consortium. (2004, April). *Community policing Chicago, year 10.* Illinois Criminal Justice Information Authority.

Chicago Police Department. (CPD). (2003, May 8). News release: Chicago police seize more than two tons of marijuana, charge four men in Southside drug bust. Retrieved March 28, 2006 from http://www.cityofchicago.org/police

Chicago Police Department. (CPD). (2003, September 22). News release: Chicago police seize $39 million in cocaine secreted in Mexico guacamole shipment. Retrieved March 28, 2006 from http://www.cityofchicago.org/police

Chicago Police Department. (CPD). (2003, November 18). News release: Chicago police to target open-air drug markets. Retrieved March 28, 2006 from http://www.cityofchicago.org/police

Chicago Police Department. (CPD). (2005). *2004 annual report.* Chicago, IL.

Chicago Police Department. (CPD). (2006, January 24). News release: Chicago police credit innovative strategies, community partnerships for driving down crime in 2005. Retrieved March 28, 2006 from http://www.cityofchicago.org/police

Chicago Tribune. (2004, March 18). Police bust tri-state heroin trafficking.

Chicago Tribune. (2005, April 7). 13 arrested in drug bust of Douglas Park gang.

Chicago Tribune. (2005, September 14). 3 men charged in $11 M cocaine bust.

Constantine, T. (1997, March 12). Statement by Thomas A. Constantine, administrator, Drug Enforcement Administration, U.S. Department of Justice, before the Senate Foreign Relations Committee regarding Mexico and Southwest Border Initiative. Retrieved March 14, 2006 from http://www.usdoj.gov/dea/pubs/congrtest/ct970312.htm

Department of State. (2006). International Narcotics Control Strategy Report—2006. Retrieved March 2006 from http://www.state.gov/p/inl/rls/nrcrpt/2006/voll/html/62106.htm

Drug Enforcement Administration. (DEA). (n.d.a). Jaime Herrera-Nevares. *DEA History Book, 1975–1980.* Retrieved March 2, 2006 from http://www.dea.gov/pubs/history/1975-1980.html

Drug Enforcement Administration. (DEA). (n.d.b). The origins of the Medellin Cartel. *DEA History Book, 1975–1980.* Retrieved March 2, 2006 from http://www.dea.gov/ Pubs/history/1975-1980.html

Drug Enforcement Administration. (DEA). (2004, October 19). News release: Operation Money Clip dismantles major money laundering and drug operation. Retrieved from http://www.dea.gov/

Drug Enforcement Administration. (DEA). (2005). Briefs & background, drugs and drug abuse, State Factsheets, Illinois. Retrieved February 28, 2006 from http://www.dea.gov/pubs/states/illinoiisp.html

Drug Enforcement Administration. (DEA). (2006, February 3). News release: Joint U.S.-Mexico operation nets head of international drug cartel. Retrieved March 15, 2006 from http://www.dea.gov/pubs/pressrel/pr020306p.html

Embassy of the United States–Mexico. DEA Mexico City Country Office web page. Retrieved March 16, 2006 from http://mexico.usembassy.gov/mexico/edea.html

Forero, J. (2006, March 14). Elections reflecting rightward course buoy Colombian leaders. *New York Times.*

Forero, J. (2006, March 23). U.S. indicts 50 leaders of Colombian rebels in cocaine trafficking. *New York Times.*

Guzman, J. (1998). *Gang Reference Book: 1998.* Chicago: Chicago Police Department.

Illinois Criminal Justice Information Authority. (ICJIA). (1997). *Trends and issues. State of Illinois.*

Keilman, J. (2006, February 26). Outmost bliss. *Chicago Tribune Magazine.*

Knox, G. (2001). *The gangster disciples: A gang profile.* Chicago: National Gang Crime Research Center.

Lehmann, D., & McNamee T. (1995, September 1). Gangster disciples leader, 38 alleged members indicted. *Chicago Sun-Times.*

Leinwand, D. (2005, July 6). Meth is top drug problem, survey says. *Chicago Sun-Times.*

Lemmer, J., Bensinger, G., & Lurigio, J. (2006). Revisiting the new/old problem of gangs in Chicago: A historical analysis of police responses. Unpublished.

Luft, K. (1995, June 11). With arrest Colombia dents Cali drug cartel. *Chicago Tribune.*

Main, F. (2004, June 6). Colombia's killing fields claiming lives in Chicago. *Chicago Sun-Times.*

Main, F., & Sweet, L. (2003, November 6). High heroin death rate leads Hyde to demand action. *Chicago Sun-Times.*

Martin, A. (1996, January 29). Even with leaders in jail gang's drug business is flourishing. *Chicago Tribune.*

Noel, J. (2006, August 8). Huge stores of marijuana, cocaine found in 3 arrests; $1.7 million worth of drugs off streets, authorities estimate. *Chicago Tribune.*

O'Brien, J. (1978, January 8). Herraras: Family firm with a low profile. *Chicago Tribune.*

O'Brien, J. (1978, October 12). Heroin kingpin seized. *Chicago Tribune.*

O'Brien, J., & Koziol, R. (1978, January 8). Heroin city USA—Chicago new title. *Chicago Tribune.*

O'Brien, J., O'Connor, M., & Papajohn, G. (1995, September 1). U.S. goes behind bars to indict 39 gang leaders. Hoover taped by wires worn by visitors. *Chicago Tribune.*

Parsons, C., & Gibson, R. (1995, September 1). Peace in prison means relying on gang leaders. *Chicago Tribune.*

Possley, M., & O'Brien, J. (1985, July 24). Midwest drug blitz racks up 120 arrests. *Chicago Tribune.*

President's Commission on Organized Crime. (1986). *America's habit: Drug abuse, drug trafficking, and organized crime.* Washington, DC: Government Printing Office.

Public Broadcasting Service. (PBS). (2006). *Wide angle—Colombia.* Retrieved April 11, 2011 from http://www.pbs.org/wnet/wideangle/tag/colombia/

Risley, R. (1990). Chapter II: Demand reduction in large urban areas. In M. Seng & G. Bensinger (Eds.), Reducing *the demand for drugs: The role of law enforcement.* Chicago: Loyola University.

Risley, R. (1998, Fall). A police officer's perspective on gangs, drugs, guns on the streets of Chicago. *The Compiler,* Illinois Criminal Justice Information Authority.

Rodriguez, M. (1993). *Together we can.* Chicago: Chicago Police Department.

Silverman, D., & Martin, A., (1993, August, 15). Crack takes hold here. Drug plagues city, suburbs. *Chicago Tribune.*

Wiedrich, B. (1984, April 1). Agents in Chicago tie heroin to Mexican "godfather." *Chicago Tribune.*

Zernike, K. (2006, February 12). Violent crime rising sharply in some cities. *New York Times.*

Recruitment Activities of Terrorist Groups

5

An Analysis of PKK/KONGRA-GEL Terrorist Organization

MUTLU KOSELI
Turkish National Police

Contents

Introduction

Understanding terrorist groups' recruitment strategies is the initial step for blocking terrorists' activities. Thus, it is necessary to learn where terrorists recruit, how they approach their targets, what tools they use, whom they target, and the reasons that an individual would choose to join the organization. According to Gerwehr and Daly (2006), once governments clearly recognize the recruitment process, tactics could be developed to counteract the ability of terrorist groups to increase their membership. To be more successful in the fight against terrorism, officials should become aware of recruitment strategies that can serve to prevent or even eliminate the conditions under which people join terrorist organizations.

Due to the lack of available data sets on terrorism issues, researchers have not dealt with this antiterrorism topic in depth (Silke, 2001). For example, to produce studies that reveal the facts surrounding terrorism, researchers must have access to a global range of biographical data of different terrorist groups. According to Hudson and Majeska (1999), having possession of these important data sources would enable terrorism experts and academicians to analyze the various characteristics common to terrorists (e.g., their educational, occupational and socioeconomic backgrounds, social and family status, methods and places of recruitment, physical appearance, and gender). Although some researchers have taken such an approach, studies remain insufficient. Because there is no standardized recruitment process directly related to specific regions and the people with which the group operates, the topic of recruitment processes becomes a difficult topic to investigate. Certainly there are overlapping topics regarding the recruitment activities of different terrorist groups. Nevertheless, significant differences remain. Thus, each group should be studied independently to understand the facts surrounding recruitment tactics.

This study is designed to fill these gaps. A number of studies related to terrorism have dealt mostly with a single form of contemporary terrorism generally referred to as *global jihad* rather than including secular or nationalist terrorist groups such as Ireland's Irish Republican Army (IRA), Spain's Euskadi Ta Askatasuana (ETA), or Turkey's Kurdistan Worker's Party (PKK/KONGRA-GEL). In short, few researchers have focused on terrorism from the perspective of this study that will fill the gap through an examination of PKK's recruitment patterns. By focusing on the PKK's recruitment patterns, this study is designed to improve on policies that will prevent individuals from joining terrorist groups.

Insights From the Literature

To better understand who the terrorist groups recruit and what types of individuals are attracted to join, the social-psychological and sociological literature regarding extremist and totalistic organizations are examined. Through a review of works in different disciplines including political science, sociology, and criminal justice (Brubaker & Laitin, 1998), the first step in this study addresses the recruitment strategies of terrorist groups.

Initially, the literature is examined to identify the recruitment patterns of terrorist groups in general, followed by an evaluation of the motivational factors that affect recruitment activities. The socioeconomic characteristics of the targeted persons and how terrorist groups approach their targets are investigated to understand the factors that contribute to easier achievement of recruitment.

Terrorist groups consider their potential recruits' cultural, social, and historical background into their recruitment activities. Primarily, class structure is used to determine whether the youth was reared in an elite class or was from a socially disadvantaged family. More importantly, terrorist groups consider those who might envision joining the organization as an act of self-discovery (Gerwehr & Daly, 2006). Considering these conditions, recruitment activities depend on the group's audience and environments. Given these considerations, numerous recruitment activities are carried out among opposition groups. Furthermore, terrorist groups attempt to adapt themselves to such conditions by changing their appearances and names or restructuring the organization. Understandably, there is no one single form of recruitment methods imposed, but rather the patterns vary according to the regions and society in which the group operates (Gerwehr & Daly, 2006).

Conditions That Breed Terrorism

According to Behron, Blimes, and Mewhinney (2005), recruitment factors that contribute to the spread of terrorism can be classified under two categories: (1) internal effects and (2) external effects. Internal effects explain what the terrorist groups themselves can do to motivate potential followers, and external effects refer to outside factors wherein the groups have little or no control.

Internal Factors

Quality and Quantity of Terrorist Attacks The quality and quantity of terrorist attacks are important factors given that potential terrorists are more likely to join a more popular organization that is also likely to be successful (Behron, et al., 2005).

Ideology According to Fradkin, Haqqani, and Brown (2005), ideology plays an important role in shaping a terrorist group's organizational structure, leadership and membership motivation, recruitment, support, and strategies and tactics. While terrorists with no ideological motivation can be referred to as ordinary criminals (Ackerman et al., 2007), experts have pointed out the importance of reducing ideological appeal to counter the posed threat by terrorist organizations (Gunaratna, 2005). Ideology also provides a motive and framework for terrorists to justify their actions (Borum & Tilby, 2005) and defend their violence by placing the blame on their victims or other actors through motivation derived from their ideology (Brynjar & Katja, 2004; Drake, 1998).

Politically motivated terrorism involves a deeply held sense of grievance over some form of social or economic injustice. For example, modern terrorist organizations justify their actions through stated political aims as well as by appeals to a higher universal truth and the demand for political transformation (Simonsen & Spindlove, 2000). Unquestionably, radical ideology is a fundamental element in the emergence of terrorism. From this point of view, Brynjar and Katja (2004) argued that explanations should focus on the terrorists' social framework of *ideologies* and *beliefs*. This approach might clarify why writers in the late 1800s provided an ideological groundwork to the terrorist movement.

An ideology is defined as the beliefs, values, principles, and objectives by which a group identifies with its distinctive political identity and aims. Importantly, ideology provides a motive and framework for action (Drake, 1998). One of the well-known key influences was introduced by Karl Marx and Friedrich Engels whose ideas included, in general, the ideology concept with force or violence. For example, a motive for violence by extremist leftist groups could be explained by Marx: "Revolutionary terrorism was the only solution to shorten the 'agonies of the old society and the birth pangs of the new'" (as cited in Hübschle, 2006, p. 3).

Many radical leftist groups represent a mixture of nationalism as illustrated by Mao Zedong and Fidel Castro as well as Latin American groups of the Castro period. In addition, numerous leftist groups of the 1970s had nationalist anti-American thoughts in which the United States was depicted as a hostile imperialist power. Radical left ideology was also found as the bases for nationalist organizations such as Italy's Mazzini, Algeria's National Liberation (FLN), the Popular Front for the Liberation of Palestine (PFLP), Turkey's PKK, and the religiously motivated Egyptian Muslim Brothers (Sedgwick, 2007).

Ideology also plays a critical role in target selection by terrorist groups. For example, ideology is an initial motive for action and provides a point of view to be able to understand the other's perception: "The ideology of a terrorist group identifies the 'enemies' of the group by providing a measure against which to assess the 'innocence' or 'guilt' of people and institutions" (Drake, 1998, p. 23). Terrorist groups consider legitimate targets as individuals who disobey the terrorists' beliefs or who block their aim. Through motivation derived from ideology, terrorists justify their violence by placing the responsibility on their victims or other actors and take initial steps to determine who or what will be attacked. The role of ideology is important because it identifies how the group's members perceive the world around them or how they justify that certain people or things are legitimate targets. In reality, ideology is not the only factor that determines a terrorist group's decision; however, it provides a view in which terrorists can justify their attacks (Borum & Tilby, 2005).

Terrorists have various objectives when selecting their targets. For example, Drake (1998) alleged that a rational terrorist's behavior would be to select an attack target that would present the greatest cause–benefit. According to Drake, ideology is seen as a crucial factor that affects the decision to select a target. Of course, there is no single source that can effectively explain a terrorist group's target selection given that other factors including strategies, society's reaction to the actions, and the security environment within which the terrorists operate are all taken into consideration (Sedgwick, 2007).

Sedgwick (2007, p. 99) explained the common points of all radical ideologies in three stages: (1) all condemn the current system as illegitimate; (2) a system must be developed to replace the current one; and (3) the current system must be overthrown in order for a new one to be built. Further, Sedgwick explained that all ideologies stand against "apathy (which might be defined as a failure to support the radical group in question), the existing regime, and a collaborating elite, usually the bourgeoisie." Apparently, ideology also determines what a group stands against that has been found to be more important than what the group stands for. However, the type of attack is a tactical decision that is even less determined by ideology. Perhaps the opportunity and effectiveness of an attack is more important than ideology although ideology's effect on a target selection cannot be disregarded (Ackerman et al., 2007).

External Factors

Physical Environment Some location settings supply an extra opportunity for terrorist recruitment activities given that more potential targets are available that have a high possibility of responding positively and that terrorist groups can operate more freely. Specifically, schools, prisons, and sanctuaries (chapels) are considered by terrorists to be places where they can employ higher recruitment tactics.

According to the International Crisis Group (2002), schools or colleges represent important terrorist recruitment targets because students between the ages of 15 and 25 typically possess the needed energy, ambition, and identity-seeking characteristics in addition to being clustered together where they are ready for motivational terrorist group activities. For many terrorist groups, prisons are used as a means to recruit new members while providing advanced training to existing members. Commonly, terrorists are aware that prison cellblocks typically play the role of a hidden campus where offenders are housed due to nonserious crimes but can become graduates of organized crime. Considering this to be a serious problem, some states have brought reforms to the policy agenda to prevent prisons from becoming recruitment grounds for terrorist organizations (Cuthbertson, 2004). Jails and prisons are major recruitment sites for extremist groups, because inmates who feel alienated, restricted, and rebellious might find the antisocietal passion and language to be attractive as well as a possible source of support and purpose (Broom & Tilby, 2005).

Prisons, Opposition Institutions, and Groups Borum and Tilby (2005) argued that people are often drawn into terrorist groups through various forms of opposition activities. For example, radical movements that protest certain dissatisfying government policies may later evolve into larger activities including terrorism. College campuses, often referred to as fertile breeding grounds for extremists, represent one such example where some students may participate in opposition groups. In numerous countries around the world, student opposition groups can create great governmental problems. To meet this goal, some political parties may also have the ideology or mentality that opposes the government or advocates for an ethnicity group's ideas. Thus, they may serve as a gathering point for people who share the same ethnicity that makes it easy for terrorist groups to locate target groups. As opposed to autocratic states, democracy is an advantage for these structural types, because this system of government is more prone to becoming a target of terror attacks given its greater tendency to be the site and producer of domestic terror activity. Open societies allow terrorist groups to grow and limit the government's ability to eliminate terrorism once it begins. In other words, terrorist groups may form their own political parties that further make democracies more vulnerable to terrorism. According to Forsberg (2006), political parties may have an effect on the emergence of terrorist group conflict paths that may also lack moderates, which causes them to be more violent. Thus, terrorist groups target these kinds of places and institutions as recruitment sources. For example, many terrorist group members were previously enrolled in student associations, workers' unions, and peasant cooperatives in which they were motivated to join the terrorist groups while participating in these institutions (Brynjar & Katja, 2004).

Individuals who actively perform inside of these opposition groups might also be involved in demonstrations. Due to prohibited behaviors during these activities, they might also perhaps be taken into custody or even arrested. As a result, being in this situation may encourage these individuals to join the armed part of a terrorist group. Individuals who have been previously arrested or taken into custody are more likely to join terrorist groups.

Migration Immigration is another important factor that has created a condition that increases the chances of joining a terrorist group. For example, newcomers to Europe sometimes experience confusion regarding their new surroundings. Being removed from their community of origin and unable to understand their new country's way of life may lead to social isolation and an identity crisis. According to Taarnby (2005), people who migrate for different reasons are familiar with these situations; however, a few become overwhelmed by the experience.

A study conducted in the Netherlands identified three main categories of immigrants who are accepted by the Dutch domestic intelligence service. The first group includes so-called new immigrants, who consist of students or economic refugees reared in Middle Eastern and North African countries and traveled to Europe having no prior involvement with a radical group. The second category is described as second- or third-generation immigrants whose parents or grandparents migrated to European countries as guest workers. People in these groups are citizens of European countries, and they speak the language fluently. Finally, the third category consists of a growing number of people who recently converted to Islam.

Although these groups are not connected by any socioeconomic indicators, they typically experience tension in their personal lives and are faced with deep and sustained identity crises that might result in searching for healing by joining terrorist groups. New generation migrants also find themselves in a dilemma caught between the traditional values of their parents and the demands and promises of a Western society. While on one hand they typically reject their parents' traditions, it is very difficult for them to access into European societies on the other hand. According to Neumann (2007), high numbers of the migrated young population have increased radicalization and recruitment activities of terrorist groups.

Effects of Family Members or Peers to Join the Group Numerous studies have revealed that people learn deviant behavior from others, namely, family members, peers, and individuals who are around them. For example, families who were guerrilla sympathizers also urged their children to join the armed struggle.

According to Florez-Morris (2007), the role that the media plays can further be a source of inspiration for joining a terrorist group. A good example is found in Bandura's (1973, 1977) social learning theory based on the idea that people learn from one another by means of observation, imitation, and modeling. Bandura explained that individuals, especially children, learn aggressive behavior by observing how others behave and suggested that violence follows when an observed hostile model is copied. This also can explain terrorist behaviors. For instance, teenagers who live in breeding grounds of political conflict may directly witness violent behaviors and seek to imitate the actions or even exert more violence. Victoroff (2005) also used Bandura's (1973) theory to explain the learned behavior in certain school-like structures where people can be taught about an extremist form of jihad or any other type of violence ideology. This kind of education also affects nonattendees through cultural diffusion. In today's time, boundaries are widened and didactic learning of violent or terrorist behavior also occurs via audiovisual tapes, compact disks, books, other forms of publications, and the Internet. Thus, especially young people can easily be influenced by didactic teaching or social learning, and they may act toward terrorism; subsequently, social learning theory can express some part of terrorist behavior (Victoroff, 2005).

According to social learning theory, deviant behaviors are a product of learning the values and aggressive behaviors linked with criminality. As such, deviant behavior is learned through observed condition, and aggression is acquired through direct conditioning and modeling the actions of others. This can also explain some terrorist behaviors. For example, Ryan, Vanderlick, and Matthews (2007) stated that "terrorism is a learned behavior that is specifically taught through the various mechanisms that are common to any and all learned behaviors" (p. 1). In this sense, terrorism can be learned just as any other criminal behavior (Akers & Silverman, 2002). Researchers have also suggested that necessary abilities for terrorist activities are learned primarily in terrorist camps lecturing ideological or paramilitary trainings that carry out hate and determination to inflict harm on others (Hudson, 1999; White, 2003). Thus, learned ideological values are simply the result of terrorist behavior (Gaynor, 2002; Nacos, 2004).

Characteristics of Individuals Targeted for Recruitment

An individual's vulnerability for becoming targeted by terrorist groups should also be considered when addressing recruitment activities, given that many people are known to join the organization out of their own desire to do so. However, even if a person would like to join, he or she may be unable to contact the terrorist group due to its secret nature. On the other hand, terrorist groups may not accept the person because of security reasons. In reality, terrorist groups find people to be recruited (Alkan, 2002).

Through a review of the literature, there have been few scientific studies regarding the vulnerability of individuals to be recruited by terrorist groups. For example, many empirical studies have focused on demographic variables primarily because they are the easiest to collect (Gerwehr & Daly, 2006). Researchers have found numerous reasons individuals join terrorist groups, such as age, economic inequalities, poverty, previous involvement in government opposing organizations, political climate of the country, media effect, use of excessive police force, peer influence, family attitudes, and an individual's feeling of restlessness, ineffective police, and ideology. Other factors that may possibly be related to terrorism have also been studied. For example, Köseli (2006) considered the effect of education, unemployment, and population size. According to Hudson and Majeska (1999), these are effective issues that may encourage individuals to drop out of society, and they are related to joining a terrorist group; however, they are not enough without proper motivation.

Age

Age represents one of the factors related to recruitment by terrorist groups given that young people are more prone to become involved in violent actions. According to several researchers, different proportions of young people in a city's population contribute to crime rates (Baron & Straus, 1988; Cohen & Land, 1987; Land, McCall, & Cohen, 1990; Messner & Tardiff, 1986; Patterson, 1991). Ellis (1991) also found the age structure of a population to be the most important single factor in criminal violence. In a multivariate regression analysis of U.S. cities between 1970 and 1980, Jacson (1991) found that young age groups are most likely to participate in gangs. Similarly, Florez-Morris (2007) interviewed a number of terrorist group members and found that many were leftist teenagers and young adults when they joined the group. Some groups prefer to recruit younger members due to the advantages; for example, youngsters are less likely to question instructions and are less likely to attract attention (Hudson & Majeska, 1999). Terrorist groups may also attempt to recruit children and raise them according to the group's ideology. Although some terrorist groups are opposed to recruiting children, others have no rules because they aim to expand their military activities and therefore focus on all available recruits (Hunter, 2006). Finally, young people are targeted for recruitment purposes because they represent the easiest group to find support, and they have specific features that include a lack of self-esteem and a need to strengthen their identities (Victoroff, 2005).

Family

According to Taylor and Quayle (1994), many people become involved in political violence because they seek a sense of purpose that will contribute to a meaning in their lives. Erikson (1959) suggested that identity formation occurs during the adolescence period in which ideologies play a role in shaping one's identity. Böllinger alleged that overly controlling parents prevent their children from building their own independence that may result in an identity crisis that could possibly lead to violent behaviors (Wolfgang & Ferracuti, 1982). For example, young people may turn to political violence in a desperate search to find their identity and may also be willing to join terrorist groups. According to Tajfel and Turner (1986), social identity theory offers an excellent explanation concerning this youth issue. The social psychological theory addresses group behavior to explain the role that identity plays in a person's search for his or her place in the infinite world. In short, individuals define themselves through their identity which is seen as an important part of their personality. Schwartz (2005) described identity as a hook in the sea of endless possibilities that allows a person to define himself or herself as being someone in particular. In discussing the role of identity in global conflicts, Huntington (1996) stated that identity is at the core of world conflicts, because a group's self-definition might be the source of disagreement. Finally, identity develops in groups that take the critical issues of culture and social environment seriously according to social identity theory. Thus, individuals who cannot find their identity through familial ties may possibly search for a solution by seeking out a group where they can feel confident rather than dejected. This might be an explanation as to why some people join terrorist organizations.

Educational Level

Kepel (1984) defined the ideology and objectives of extremists in Egyptian movement and argued that the causes for this trend were due primarily to macrolevel social failures by the Egyptian government, including economic policies and strategies wherein poverty, unemployment, and demoralization were rampant. Kepel outlined the poor conditions of education, health care, substandard housing, and local services that made Egypt a fertile breeding ground for extremism. Similarly, Sambanis (2004) focused on the relationship between political violence and education as well as its relationship to poverty and inequality. Results of multiple regression analysis revealed that educational level was related to political violence. Sambanis concluded that education encourages political participation and directs people to solve their problems through institutional pathways rather than violence.

Ethnicity

Ethnicity is also an important factor in the decision to join terrorist groups (Glenny, 1992; Woodward, 1995). In studies related to ethnicity, ethnic conflict, and nationalism, researchers have theorized between ethnicity and nationalist violence. For example, Lemarchand's (1996) work on Burundi and Tambiah's (1996) and Brass's (1997) works on ethnic riots focused on the effect of ethnicity on violence. In other studies of violence, ethnicity was rarely examined as only incidentally and peripherally (e.g., Gurr, 1970; Tilly, 1978). Although researchers have recognized the significance of ethnicity (Brubaker & Laitin, 1998), there have been no analytical distinctions made as to the theoretical significance concerning ethnic violence. Brubaker and Laitin (1998) suggested that violence should be taken more seriously in studies that address ethnic and nationalist conflicts.

Socioeconomic Problems

Studies have revealed that socioeconomic problems have a significant impact on the recruitment process of terrorists. Most ethnic leaders of terrorist groups or guerrilla armies are well educated and come from middle-class backgrounds; however, members of these ethnic violence organizations are more often poorly educated and come from lower- or working-class backgrounds (Waldmann, 1985, 1989). For example, the following problems suffered throughout the 1990s in Algeria were related to joining violence groups: high unemployment and underemployment rates; inadequate housing, health services, and education; an eroding infrastructure; inequality of income distribution; and government corruption (Connor, 1972).

Researchers generally agree that most targets recruited for terrorist activities are composed of very large groups; however, the majority who join these groups tend to reside in a country's poorest part or come from poverty-stricken families (Stern, 2000). Researchers who have conducted cross-country studies reached the same conclusion that poverty level and economic development is significantly related to political violence. For example, in MacCulloch's (2004) study from 1975 to 1995 and including over 60 countries, revolutionary activities were found to be related to income, and countries with a higher gross domestic product (GDP) had fewer revolutionary activities. As an explanation, Brynjar and Katja (2004) concluded that governments of wealthy countries have the ability to build strong law enforcement and intelligence structures against revolutionary threats and are thus able to deter armed insurgencies. On the other hand, poverty-stricken countries do not have these capabilities; consequently, their intelligence and police forces are usually ill-equipped, ill-trained, underpaid, and corrupt. Due to these issues, efforts by these countries against terrorist or insurgent groups are ineffective or too violent and corrupt to overcome armed insurgents. Findings of

Florez-Morris's (2007) study also supported this statement and concluded that ineffective police organizations indirectly contribute to the joining of terrorist groups by being unable to apprehend these groups and curb their activities. Fearon and Laitin (2003) found that countries with upper poverty levels and weak organizational structures are high-risk groups for political conflicts as opposed to factors such as ethnic-religious diversity or socioeconomic inequality and a lack of democracy.

As a result of interviews conducted with terrorist group members, Florez-Morris (2007) found that the most popular motivation for joining a radical leftist group involved the concern regarding socioeconomic injustice and inequality. Although there were numerous statements made by reputable people, Florez-Morris's finding is important given that there is a lack of empirical research in this field. As an expert on terrorism, Laqueur (1999) alleged that terrorism occurs as a response to injustice and further stated that political, economic, and social arena inequalities increase its likelihood. Another explanation related to inequality–terrorism is that lower-class people often experience higher levels of subjective feelings of powerlessness and, in turn, are more prone then others to engage in delinquency (Braithwaite, 1979; Messner & Golden, 1992; Shaw & McKay, 1942).

Brynjar and Katja (2004) also claimed that income inequality is a contributing factor to political violence in developed countries as well as in less developed countries. By examining the statements made by leftist terrorist groups, all accused the current system as being unequal. Thus, they promised their sympathizers that they would bring equality to all with the new system they would establish after overthrowing the old one. Although researchers have found a relationship between violent crime and socioeconomic inequalities (Bourguignon, 2001; Chiu & Madden, 1998; Demombaynes & Ozler, 2002; Ehrlich, 1973; Lederman, Loayza, & Menéndez, 2000; Wilson & Daly, 1997), there are not enough studies in terms of political violence. Some found a trend for countries with a higher level of internal inequality to be more exposed to internal armed conflicts. Brynjar and Katja accepted that although socioeconomic inequalities play an important role there should be other contributing factors as well. In another study conducted by Köseli (2006) regarding the relationship between terrorism and inequality in Turkey, findings indicated that there is a significant relationship between the two phenomena. Although Köseli did not focus on any one specific group but rather on the general problem of terrorism and terrorist activities of all groups, this study centers on only the separatist group.

Some individuals join terrorist groups due to monetary benefits they can gain. For example, Jemaah Islamiyah, a Southeast Asian militant Islamic organization, was the beneficiary of generous funding in which each member reportedly received a monthly stipend of 300 Pakistani rupees, or approximately Rp. 30,000 at the 1987 exchange rate equivalent to $15 in U.S. currency.

According to the International Crisis Group (2003), this was sufficient for living expenses given that room and board were already covered.

Gender

When addressing terrorism, males are typically perceived as joining terrorist organizations; however, women have always played a very important role in recruitment sources, and historically they have participated side by side with men in terrorist group activities. In many cultures, women are typically portrayed as being more peaceful and loving as opposed to hatred and are more likely to be moderate, compromising, and tolerant; therefore, women are excluded from and protected against any form of combat activities in many countries. Nevertheless, women do operate in numerous terrorist groups in different parts of the world, and their role is expanding (Berko & Erez, 2009). For example, females inside a terrorist group vary from being collaborators, informers, human shields, recruiters, and perpetrators involved in acts of destruction and death.

According to Bloom (2005), there are various reasons for the increased participation of women in terrorist groups; namely, they operate more freely because they are less likely to arouse suspicion. Existence of women inside a terrorist organization also triggers the male activities given that men would not allow themselves to stand behind women. In addition, women have different feelings that men do not, which can contribute more to the group's activities. However, women's motive to join a group, their roles in the group, and their attitudes are unlike those of men (Bloom, 2005). Many terrorist groups set up specific sections to recruit and motivate women such as arms or organized activities specific to women associations (Berko & Erez, 2009).

Employment

Another significant issue that affects one's decision to join a terrorist group is unemployment. According to Majeska and Hudson (1999), individuals who are socially alienated or have dropped out of society are more likely to join terrorist organizations. In exploring the role of unemployment in illegal activities, Machin and Meghir (2004) found a significant relationship and concluded that declining labor market opportunities are likely to increase illegitimate (criminal) activities, while participation in legitimate (labor market) activities is decreasing. In a study regarding the Maoist insurgency in Nepal, Murshed and Gates (2003) determined that the lack of employment opportunities is an important factor that assisted Maoist recruitment and retention thus making life in Maoist cadres a relatively attractive option. Similarly, Heskin (1984) found that a possible source of motivation for paramilitary participation in Northern Ireland was the result of high levels of unemployment coupled with substandard housing standards, high prices, and low incomes that were characteristic of the province when compared with areas of the United Kingdom.

Finally, in a study conducted by Smith and Morgan (1994) that focused on left- and right-wing America in the 1980s, they stated that contrary to right-wing terrorists, many of whom were unemployed, left-wing terrorists were employed primarily in professional occupations.

Effects From Use of Excessive Police Force

According to Florez-Morris (2007), use of excessive police force in response to legal demonstrations was found to be related to motivations of joining leftist groups. Florez-Morris also asserted that people who join leftist terrorist groups are somehow affected by the use of excessive police force. In addition, some members join terrorist groups due to their desire to gain social acceptance in a clique. Crenshaw (2001) explained that an individual who is searching for his or her own identity may find respect by joining a terrorist group as an opportunity for self-improvement.

Although the aforementioned issues may result in people dropping out of society, this is not enough to persuade them to join terrorist groups. In other words, motivation by a terrorist group is necessary. Conversely, Majeska and Hudson (1999) claimed that motivation is not sufficient; rather, there should be an existing opportunity for the potential member as well as acceptance of him or her by the terrorist group. For many terrorist organizations, recruits must be accepted by the group, and they must possess certain skills that will benefit the organization.

Importantly, recruitment models used by terrorist groups to infiltrate target populations and to coerce crowds must be examined. In the following section, an evaluation of recruitment strategies employed by terrorist groups is presented.

Recruitment Approaches

Another important point for those who deal with terrorists is that often they alter or adapt their own shape and patterns of activity to facilitate recruitment in accordance to the situation at hand. For example, if a government prohibits the activities of these or affiliated groups, they may develop a variety of measures against government tactics, namely, changing their names and meeting places, communication methods, types of activities, and a timetable to avoid interference from authorities. Essentially, terrorist groups may maintain access to a target population and still continue their recruitment activities (Gerwehr & Daly, 2006).

There are many kinds of recruitment activities that vary according to the group's structure and societies' specifications. Because there is no uniform recruitment method, there is also no solution that fits all terrorist groups. Thus, different recruitment methods may be required for various terrorist activities (Gerwehr & Daly, 2006).

Recruitment models represent the paths or methods used by terrorist groups. For example, Gerwehr and Daly (2006) examined recruitment approaches by dividing them into two groups. First are direct efforts or face-to-face invitations to participate, and second are indirect efforts such as propaganda activities posted on web pages, newspapers, radio, or television wherein no face-to-face interactions exist (Gerwehr & Daly, 2006). Here, the important distinctive issues to make are whether the source of the recruitment effort is physically close to the target audience and whether integration occurs in or out of the public. From this perspective, variations of recruitment can be observed (Gerwehr & Daly, 2006).

Gerwehr and Daly (2006) referred to "public and proximate" recruitment as efforts consisting of activities that are made through face-to-face interactions in small groups, which also include activities that can be seen by the public. Examples are used in prisons, refugee camps, legal associations, political parties, and similar places that offer better results and are viewed as being more amenable from the perspective of terrorists. Social and cultural activities can be considered under this approach. Alkan (2002) claimed that terrorist groups also organize social activities such as picnics, concerts, sporting events, tea parties, meetings, and youth camps under legal organizations, namely, political parties and associations.

Another approach to recruitment that is used for broader target groups is referred to as public and mediated activities (Gerwehr & Daly, 2006) that include efforts through the mass media. Both legal and illegal means of propaganda can be examined in this group. Currently, the Internet is one of the favorite methods used in mass propaganda activities. In this approach, specific populations who have common characteristics are targeted. Although personal contact is not possible, terrorist groups have unrestricted communication. For example, the Internet has many advantages, namely, easy access, lack of regulations, vast potential audiences, and fast information flow. According to Weimann (2004), the Internet can target a variety of audiences such as current and potential supporters, international public opinion, and the public enemy. From the same perspective, other publications of terrorist groups can be considered because they serve the same purpose.

Terrorist groups also use the mass media approach with intimacy or clandestinely for recruitment purposes. This private and mediation approach includes some illegal printings that are published and distributed either covertly or through Internet web pages that are password protected or underground propagation of digital videos. In this model, there is a population that is already prepared to accept the terrorist group's message, and a large number of people can be affected all at once. In addition, the environment can be controlled and outside interventions can be prevented.

As previously mentioned, terrorist groups also use private and proximate recruitment strategies in which communication activities are out of the public's eyes. Target populations may consist of individuals attending a paramilitary training program or receiving tutorial vocational instruction. This effort is used in situations where there is a specific targeted group or small groups. Here, peers and relatives of prospective recruits are used to give sales pitches. This technique can be used on an individual basis where terrorists can directly approach and manipulate new recruits. Alkan's (2002) social methods of terrorist recruitment is a good explanation. In this classification, the influence of friendship and relatives has an important effect on targeted recruits. Alkan explained that friendships developed in high schools, universities, work environments, and neighborhoods are so important in this perspective given that younger generations find their identity in these close companionships; therefore, it might be easier for terrorist groups to find the right recruits and then motivate them according to the group's ideology.

Methodology

Data Collection

Data were collected and coded from statements provided by newly recruited militants when they were taken into custody. Of significance to this data source, all members were captured moments before they passed the border toward Northern Iraq to join the illegal terrorist camps and receive military and ideological training. Statements used in this study contain the initial process involved in joining the terrorist organization, propaganda obtained through different means, and why persons decide to join. Importantly, the confiscated information serves to enlighten terrorism scholars and officials in correctly identifying the reasons why people join the group, the qualifications required to enlist, and the motivations behind becoming a member.

Because all statements were collected from specific questions, they contain sufficient evidence to answer the needs of the study. In addition, statements were left blank if they could not be adequately answered. Thus, some variables resulted in a high number of missing values.

Data Analysis

Due to the nature of the data set and to enable a better understanding of terrorist group recruitment techniques, basic statistical analysis was used in this study. Results are interpreted according to these findings.

Limitations

This study is limited to data provided by 244 individuals who were captured while in the process of joining the illegal camps of the PKK/KONGRA-GEL terrorist group. Therefore, these results cannot be generalized to other terrorist groups. In addition, self-proclaimed statements were given to law enforcement officials. In other words, different types of data collection methods would have afforded more detailed information regarding the variables used. Finally, because some individuals were under the age of 15, they gave their statements directly to the prosecutor and law enforcement officers who were no longer in possession of them; therefore, some variables in the data set have a high number of missing values.

Results

Role of Opposition Institutions, Associations, and Political Parties

Political party can be seen as having an effect on joining a terrorist group. According to the statements of the detained group members, 25.3% indicated that they were affected by political party propaganda activities known to be affiliated with the PKK. Indeed, this is a very high percentage when compared with the other given answers to the question, "What made you join the group?" The results revealed that propaganda activities made in the political party was one of the most effective factors that played a role in recruiting new members for the terrorist group.

Effect of Previous Arrests or Detention

Results revealed that among the valid 50% of the data the new recruits had previous arrests or detention, and 50% did not have any previous arrests or detention. This reveals that former conviction records had an effect on the decision to join terrorist groups; however, recruits who did not have previous arrest records had as much possibility of joining a terrorist group. Thus, decision makers should consider this issue when developing new policies to prevent the joining of terrorist groups. Briefly, officials' target populations would not be only the people who were previously arrested but also those who had never been detained.

Educational Level

From the results of the frequency analysis test, a high number of illiterate militants had a valid test score (11.7), followed by primary school graduates

(24.5%) and secondary school graduates (18.1%). Table 5.1 shows the summary of frequency analysis. These figures reveal that a large percentage of recruited individuals have very low or no educational profiles. There weren't any university graduates among the individuals in the data set, and only 16% of them were currently university students when they were apprehended. High school graduates made up 29.8%, thus revealing that the educational level of those joining the terrorist group was extremely low.

Gender

The results of the frequency analysis test indicated that a large percentage of recruits were men (82.4%), whereas women made up only 17.6%. Although the percentage of women appears to be low compared with men, it can also be considered as high when their roles in society and their interest in activities related to combat are taken into consideration. On the other hand, men are the main source of recruits into terrorist groups.

Migration

This variable was examined to determine the effect that migration had on joining the terrorist group. However, the percentage of recruits who migrated from their homes to another location is very difficult to determine. For the purpose of this study, recruits were therefore assumed to have migrated if their birthplace and where they were coming from to join the terrorist group were different. In other words, they were assumed to have not migrated if their birthplace and where they were coming from were similar. According to the findings, 44.2% had migrated, whereas 55.8% had not. Still, the percentage of migrated recruits can be considered high given that it is almost half of the valid percentage.

Family Members or Peer Influences

Frequency analysis showed that 82.1% of valid data indicated that individuals who decided to join the terrorist group did not have family members or relatives acting in the group, whereas only 17.9% did.

Apparently, friends tended to be more effective than having relatives in the terrorist group. For example, 30.1% of the newly recruited militants who gave statements indicated that they joined the group as a result of propaganda provided by their friends. This percentage was the highest among the stated reasons for being recruited into the group. Thus, peers were perceived to have a significant effect in one's decision to join terrorist groups.

Number of Siblings

According to the results of the frequency analysis test, recruited militants came from very crowded families. Only 9.2% of the valid cases had four or less siblings. Conversely, 44.7% had five to eight siblings, followed by 46.1% who had nine or more. This might possibly be an important factor that policy makers should focus on.

Socioeconomic Problems

From the data set, it was difficult to determine the income levels of militants who were recruited into the terrorist group. However, when they were asked, "What was your reason for joining the terrorist group?" 8.4% stated that they joined due to "bad economic conditions," which may indicate that negative economic conditions are not the initial factor in deciding to join the group. However, a lack of data was the real issue in understanding the effects that socioeconomic problems play in recruitment efforts.

Employment Status

Data indicated that 64.6% of the new recruits were unemployed and only 34.6% had jobs. From these results, a great number of unemployed individuals constituted the recruitment targets.

Age

Apparently, most of the recruits were under 21 years of age (Table 5.1). For example, 8.8% were under 15, and 60.8% were between the ages of 15 and 21. Only 26.2% were between the ages of 21 to 29, while only 4.2% were over 30 years of age. As revealed by these percentages, the PKK focuses on young people to recruit new members.

Escape From Family Pressure

Among the 244 recorded cases, 166 missing statements could either not be found or the answer as to why the individual joined the group was left blank. From the remaining 78 usable statements, 15.7% of the newly recruited members decided to join the terrorist group to escape family pressures. Although the percentages were low, they still represented a considerable amount. Because all answers were coded, "escaping from family pressures" was one of the most frequently repeated reasons for joining the terrorist group. As stated in the literature review, controlling parents who over pressure their children may result in an identity crisis that could result in some youths choosing to join terrorist groups.

Table 5.1 Frequencies and Percentages of Respondents' Demographic Information and Reasons for Joining a Terrorist Organization (n = 244)

Variables		Frequency	Percent
Previous Arrest Rate	Do not have previous arrest	36	50.0
	Have previous arrest	36	50.0
Education Level	Illiterate	11	11.7
	Primary school	23	24.5
	Secondary school	17	18.1
	High school	28	29.8
	University	15	16.0
Gender	Man	201	82.4
	Woman	43	17.6
Migration Pattern of the Individuals	Migrated	84	44.2
	Not migrated	106	55.8
Relatives Inside the Terrorist Group	No family members in the group	46	82.1
	Have family members in the group	10	17.9
Number of Siblings	1 to 4 siblings	7	9.2
	5 to 8 siblings	34	44.7
	9 and more siblings	35	46.1
Reasons for Joining the Terrorist Group	Propaganda in the political party	21	25.3
	Affected from the propaganda of the press	1	1.2
	Affected from the propaganda of his or her friends	25	30.1
	Bad economic conditions	7	8.4
	Pressure of security forces	8	9.6
	Propaganda activities of the terrorist group members (not friends)	8	9.6
	Freedom from family pressures	13	15.7

Table 5.1 (Continued) Frequencies and Percentages of Respondents' Demographic Information and Reasons for Joining a Terrorist Organization (n = 244)

Variables		Frequency	Percent
Employment Status	Do not have a job	82	64.6
	Have a job	44	34.6
Age Distribution of the Individuals	Less than 15 years old	21	8.8
	15–21 Years Old	146	60.8
	21–29 Years Old	63	26.3
	30 and up	10	4.2

Excessive Police Force

According to the frequency analysis of "What made you decide to join the group?" 9.6% of the newly recruited militants stated that they joined as a reaction to pressure of security forces. Although this number looks small, it should be considered as an important issue that affects people's decision to join terrorist groups. From this statement it can be inferred that this specific issue should be further researched to determine whether or not it has a significant effect on individuals who decide to join a terrorist group.

Recruitment Approaches

According to the results, propaganda activities of friends was the most frequently cited reason (30.1%) that newly recruited militants decided to join the terrorist group, followed by propaganda activities conducted by a political party (25.9%) affiliated with the PKK. This reveals that the terrorist group uses private and proximate recruitment approaches.

Public Policy Implications

Through this study, the recruitment activities used by terrorist groups, specifically the PKK, were revealed. The goal was to examine the characteristics common to individuals that terrorist groups frequently target for recruitment and to determine if those who respond to terrorist group propaganda activities exist. In addition, internal and external factors that affect recruitment activities and approaches used by terrorist groups were analyzed.

Frequency analysis was used to test the self-reported statements obtained from 244 newly recruited militants who were captured shortly before they joined the illegal terrorist group camps. The valuable information gathered from these statements should enable policy makers and officials to initiate new policies designed to prevent or eliminate terrorist group recruitment activities. In other words, it is a well-known fact that public policy often changes when a particular occurrence becomes public knowledge that can be open to questions.

The results of the frequency analysis revealed that numerous individuals who join the terrorist groups are undereducated as well as more prone to becoming members. Thus, it is recommended that policies should be developed to increase the educational level as well as educational opportunities for the youth population. Although primary and secondary education has been emphasized, the need for teaching skills that will enable youth to continue their higher education or enter the labor force is an important policy consideration. Besides classroom curricula, how education socializes youth should be taught, and educators should be provided with materials to instruct youth on how to avoid terrorist recruiters. This might be another recommended policy issue in terms of education (Koseli, 2006).

Athough young men make up the majority of recruited terrorist group members, there is a growing number of women who have also been recruited. Thus, it is recommended that policy makers develop specific programs geared toward women in an effort to prevent them from joining terrorist organizations.

In this study, approximately one-half of the 244 cases were considered to be migrants. This reveals that migration is also an issue that policy makers should consider. Newly recruited militants who migrated from their hometowns were found to be more likely to respond to propaganda activities of terrorist groups. Therefore, policy makers should also focus on this issue. Despite the motive for those who migrated, policy implications can decrease migration as well as implement rehabilitation studies.

Individuals who had been detained for any reason also had a significant effect on the decision to join illegal terrorist group camps. Thus, officials should exercise caution regarding those who were detained and released for minor offenses. Related government institutions should also keep an eye on these individuals. It is recommended that rehabilitation or training programs be made available that may deter detainees from joining terrorist groups.

From the coded statements made by the captured terrorist recruits, the most common reason for joining the group was the influence of friends. This shows that terrorist group members typically use private and proximate recruitment methods to convince individuals to join their terrorist group. Young people might be warned and made aware of these tactics. The second most important reason that recruits joined the terrorist group was through their affiliated political party propaganda. In this case, the political party works as a base for terrorists to earn new recruits, spread propaganda, and convince them to transfer to the illegal terrorist group camps. Although it is extremely difficult and problematic for policy makers to prevent these kinds of political activities since anything that they may do can be considered as interruption to the democracy and thus used as counterpropaganda material by terrorist supporters. To prevent these illegal activities, knowing that a legal political party promoted terrorism and encouraged the use of violence or joining a violent terrorist group is an issue that policy makers should consider.

Data indicated that policy makers should place particular importance to socioeconomic factors. Although a low percentage of newly recruited militants stated that they joined the group due to poor economic conditions, other indicators show that almost all the recruits had economic problems. According to the UNDP Report (2006), other negative factors that might persuade individuals to engage in terrorism include their significantly low employment status and insufficient opportunities for young people to earn a living. Policies also should consider creating job opportunities for young people and educating them to be able to develop their skills to join the workforce (Koseli, 2006). According to the UNDP Report (2006), youth are seen as a possible threat to security, and a largely young population combined with unemployment, urbanization, and other factors can lead to violence. The report further warned that as the young population increases and they have fewer educational and employment opportunities, there is an increasing concern that these conditions may encourage their participation in violence. The report also stated:

> The issue of "youth and violent conflict" concerns more than youth: it is a reflection—and at the same time a further aggravation—of a broader societal crisis. Trying to understand the intersection between youth and violent conflict is a way of re-examining societies and development processes. (p. 12)

It has also been argued that including youth in the decision-making process would help them to not become involved in violent acts. Other than the traditional way of being in the youth division of a political party, creating youth councils and forums in which young people can meet together to discuss issues relating to their communities might help encourage more youth to become involved in decision making that might prevent them from participating in violence (Matthews & Limb, 2003; UNDP, 2006).

Individuals who join terrorism organizations typically live in crowded families that result in limited parental attention. Often, the parents cannot deal with their child's problems as they should. Because prospective recruits usually come from low-income families, they can also feel poverty more strongly. This might explain why some of the recruited militants in this study stated that they decided to join the terrorist group "to be free from family pressure." To prevent disadvantaged youth from joining terrorist organizations, it is recommended that programs and polices be developed to help these individuals.

Conclusion

This researcher accepts that counterrecruitment interference should correspond to the patterns and recruitment activities of terrorist groups. For example, what kinds of patterns are there? How much variety is there in the overall pattern? Of course, there is a wide variety; however, a review of the literature related to recruitment tactics used by terrorist groups reveals a few common structures. From this perspective, recruitment patterns of the PKK/KONGRA-GEL terrorist organization were revealed. Policy makers can gain much benefit from these types of studies and use them as a road map to produce appropriate policies that will prevent people from joining terrorist groups. According to Faria and Arce (2005), the level of terrorist activity is determined by four parameter values: (1) deterrence policy; (2) terrorist militancy; (3) political opinion; and (4) the effectiveness of terrorism in influencing recruitment.

In addressing recruitment issues in this study, the data set was obtained from 244 self-reported statements of newly recruited militants who were captured while joining an illegal terrorist camp. These data provided important information that described the reasons individuals join terrorist groups, their family and economic backgrounds, and the recruitment strategies and approaches used by terrorist groups. Preventing recruitment activities should take high priority, because this one factor can diminish the ability of all terrorist groups. For example, manpower for carrying out attacks and sustaining operations is a critical resource for terrorist organizations; therefore, obstructing recruitment activities can dismantle their ability to function.

Because recruitment plays a vital role, terrorist groups have developed a variety of strategies for enlisting new members. Realizing that these strategies will help officials to prevent terrorist activities will also enable them to more effectively cope with terrorist groups. To alter terrorist groups, the results of this study clearly show that states must take proactive steps to stop all terrorist threats rather than just responding to attacks. Thus, a multidisciplinary approach was used in this study to offer possible solutions to the problems associated with terrorism.

According to the results of frequency analysis, physical environment was found to be extremely important. For example, many of the newly recruited militants shared similar backgrounds such as being a member of the political party that is known to be affiliated with the PKK. In addition, those who migrated from their homes were more likely to join the terrorist group. Most importantly, the results revealed that terrorist groups tend to target the young population. In numerous cases, recruits obtained initial propaganda from their peers that convinced them to join the terrorist group. Others stated that joining a terrorist group would relieve them from being pressured by their families. Because the majority of recruits were extremely undereducated, they did not continue their education, they had poor economic situations, and they did not have a decent job. These conditions made them feel hopeless and without any life expectations. Therefore, they joined the terrorist group as an escape from situations that created hopelessness.

Once newly recruited militants contact the terrorist organization, the group's solidarity, peer pressure, and group dynamics serve as a type of pressure that entices individuals to remain with the organization. According to Post (1986), terrorists tend to unite recruits with the group, and a collective mentality emerges. In other words, a need of belonging convinces recruits to stay inside the group. For example, terrorist groups become a family for new recruits, and it is important for the group members to generate an organizational culture in which individuals can sense a feeling of family relations.

The whole picture portrays the idea that terrorist groups adjust their recruitment activities according to their targets and environment. In addition, terrorist groups attempt to adapt themselves to the conditions to recruit new members (Gerwehr & Daly, 2006). Considering the specifications of the PKK/KONGRA-GEL recruitment activities that were revealed in this study, there is no single form. In other words, recruitment activities of terrorist groups vary according to the conditions and the target groups. Therefore, one may expect to observe different findings according to the society in which the groups operate, and further recruitment patterns might be imposed.

However, observing the whole picture will give policy makers and officials who are developing policies an idea of how to solve the problem. If policy makers can implement better polices to prevent individuals from joining terrorist groups, the problem of terrorism throughout the country will finally come to an end. Finally, police measures to combat recruitment activities are not enough; therefore, innovative governmental policies should be considered in an effort to prevent the recruitment of terrorism.

References

Ackerman, G., Abhayaratne, P., Bale, J., Bhattacharjee, A., Blair, C., Hansell, L., Jayne, A., et al. (2007). *Assessing terrorist motivations for attacking critical infrastructure*. Retrieved from https://e-reports-ext.llnl.gov/pdf/341566.pdf

Akers, R. L., & Silverman, A. (2002, December 10–11). *Toward a social learning model of violence and terrorism*. Presentation at the National Institute of Justice Conference on Violence and Terrorism, Washington, DC.

Alkan, N. (2002). *Gençlik ve terörizm. Emniyet Genel Müdürlüğü Basımevi*. Ankara, Turkey.

Bandura, A. (1973). *Aggression: A social learning analysis*. Englewood Cliffs, NJ: Prentice-Hall.

Bandura, A. (1977). *Social learning theory*. New York: General Learning Press.

Baron, L., & Straus, M. A. (1988). Cultural and economic sources of homicide in the United States. *Sociological Quarterly, 29,* 371–390.

Berko, A., & Erez, E. (2009). *Gender, Palestinian women, and terrorism: Women's liberation or oppression?* Retrieved from http://www.sullivan-county.com/x/converts.htm

Behron, J., Blimes, R. J., & Mewhinney, & E. C. (2005). *Slaying the hydra: Recruitment and terrorist group duration.* Paper presented at the annual meeting of the Midwest Political Science Association, Palmer House Hilton, Chicago, Illinois. Retrieved from http://www.allacademic.com/meta/p84971_index.html

Blomberg, S., Brock, G., Hess, D., & Orphanides, A. (2004). *The macroeconomic consequences of terrorism.* Seoul, Korea: Korea Institute for International Economic Policy.

Bloom, M. M. (2005). *Dying to kill: The allure of suicide terror.* New York: Columbia University Press.

Borum, R., & Tilby, C. (2005). Anarchist direct actions: A challenge for law enforcement. *Studies in Conflict & Terrorism, 28,* 201–223.

Bourguignon, F. (2001). Crime as a social cost of poverty and inequality: A review focusing on developing countries. In S. Yusuf, S. Evenett, & J. Wui (Eds.), *On facets of globalization* (p. 171). City, WA: World Bank.

Braithwaite, J. (1979). *Inequality, crime, and public policy.* London, UK: Routledge and Kegan Paul.

Brass, P. R. (1997). *Theft of an idol: Text and context in the representation of collective violence.* Princeton, NJ: Princeton University Press.

Brubaker, R., & Laitin, D. D. (1998). Ethnic and nationalist violence. *Annual Review of Sociology, 24,* 423–452.

Brynjar, L., & Katja, S. (2004). *Causes of terrorism: An expanded and updated review of the literature.* Retrieved from http://rapporter.ffi.no/rapporter/2004/04307.pdf

Burr, J. M., & Collins, R. O. (2006). *Alms for jihad: Charity and terrorism in the Islamic world.* New York: Cambridge University Press.

Chiu, W. H., & Madden, P. (1998). Burglary and income inequality. *Journal of Public Economics, 69,* 123–141.

Chua, A. (2003). *World on fire: How exporting free market democracy breeds ethnic hatred and global instability.* New York: Anchor Books.

Crenshaw, M. (2001). *Terrorism in context.* University Park: Pennsylvania State University Press.

Cohen, L. E., & Land, K. C. (1987). Age structure and crime; symmetry vs. asymmetry, and the projection of the crime rate through the 1990s. *American Sociological Review, 52,* 170–183.

Connor, W. D. (1972). The manufacture of deviance: The case of the Soviet purge, 1936–1938. *American Sociological Review, 37*(4), 403–413.

Cuthbertson, I. M. (2004, Fall). Prisons and the education of terrorists. *World Policy Journal, 21,* 3.

Demombaynes, G., & Ozler, B. (2002). *Crime and local inequalities in South Africa.* Retrieved from http://wdsbeta.worldbank.org/external/default/WDSContentServer/IW3P/IB/2002/12/14/000094946_02120504013794/Rendered/PDF/multi0page.pdf

Drake, C. J. M. (1998, Summer). The role of ideology in terrorists' target selection. *Terrorism and Political Violence, 10*(2), 53–85.

Ellis, H. (1991). *Identifying crime correlated in a developing society: A study of socio-economic and sociodemographic contributions to crime in Jamaica, 1950–1984.* New York: Peter Lang Publishing.
Ehrlich, I. (1973). Participation in illegitimate activities: A theoretical and empirical investigation. *Journal of Political Economy, 81*(3), 521–565.
Erikson, E. H. (1959). Late adolescence. In D. H. Funkenstein (Ed.), *The Student and Mental Health*. Cambridge, MA: Riverside Press. 66–106.
Eubank, W., & Weinberg, L. (1994). Does democracy encourage terrorism? *Terrorism and Political Violence, 6*(4), 417–443.
Faria, J. R., Daniel, G., & Arce M. (2005). *Terror support and recruitment*. Retrieved from http://www.aeaweb.org/annual_mtg_papers/2005/0109_1300_0403.pdf
Fearon, J. D., & Laitin, D. D. (2003, February). Ethnicity, insurgency, and civil war. *American Political Science Review, 97*(1), 88.
Florez-Morris, M. (2007). Joining guerrilla groups in Colombia: Individual motivations and processes for entering a violent organization. *Studies in Conflict & Terrorism, 30*, 615–634.
Forsberg, O. J. (2006, March 22). *Political parties and terrorism: Another reason democracies are more prone to domestic terrorism*. Paper presented at the annual meeting of the International Studies Association, Town & Country Resort and Convention Center, San Diego, CA.
Fradkin, H., Haqqani, H., & Brown, E. (2005). Islamism and terrorism: The ideological dimension. In H. Fradkin, H. Haqqani, & E. Brown (Eds.), *Current trends in Islamist ideology* (Vol. 1). Washington, DC: Hudson Institute.
Gaynor, B. (2002). *Terror as a strategy of psychological warfare*. Retrieved from http://www.ict.org.il/articles/articledet.cfm?articleid=443
Gerwehr, S., & Daly, S. (2006). *Al-Qaida and global jihad*. Retrieved from http://www. rand.org/pubs/reprints/RP1214/
Glenny, M. (1992). *The fall of Yugoslavia: The third Balkan war.* London, UK: Penguin.
Gurr, T. R. (1970). *Why men rebel.* Princeton, NJ: Princeton University Press.
Gunaratna, R. (2005). The ideology of Al-Jama'ah Al-Islamiya. In H. Fradkin, H. Haqqani, & E. Brown (Eds.), *Current trends in Islamist ideology* (Vol. 1). Washington, DC: Hudson Institute.
Heskin, K. (1984). The psychology of terrorism in Northern Ireland. In Y. Alexander & A. O'Day (Eds.), *Terrorism in Ireland* (pp. 88–105). Kent, UK: Croom Helm.
Hübschle, A. (2006). The T-word: Conceptualising terrorism. *African Security Review, 15*, 3.
Hudson, R. A., & Majeska, M. (1999, September). *The sociology and psychology of terrorism: Who becomes a terrorist and why?* Report prepared under an Interagency Agreement by the Federal Research Division, Library of Congress, Washington, DC.
Hunter, C. (2006, July 4–7). *Occupied Palestinian territories: Palestinian children and Hamas*. Forum presented at the Coalition to Stop the Use of Child Soldiers, Chateau de Bossey, Switzerland.
Huntington, S. P. (1996). *The clash of civilizations and the remaking of world order.* New York: Simon & Schuster.
International Crisis Group. (2002, December 11). *Indonesia backgrounder: How the Jemaah Islamiyah terrorist network operates*. Jakarta/Brussels.

International Crisis Group (2003, August 26). *Jemaah Islamiyah in South East Asia: Damaged but still dangerous*. Executive Summary Report No. 63. Jakarta/Brussels.
Jacson, P. I. (1991). Crime, youth, gangs, and urban transition: The social disclosure of postindustrial economic development. *Justice Quarterly, 8*(3), 379–397.
Kepel, G. (1984). *Muslims extremisms in Egypt*. Los Angeles: University of California.
Kurrild-Klitgaard, P., Justesen, M. K., & Klemmensen, R. (2006). The political economy of freedom, democracy and transnational terrorism. *Public Choice, 128*, 289–315.
Kohlmann, E. F. (2006). *The role of Islamic charities in international terrorist recruitment and financing*. Copenhagen, Denmark: Danish Institute for International Studies.
Koseli, M. (2006). *Poverty, inequality & terrorism relationship in Turkey*. Doctoral dissertation. Retrieved from http://etd.vcu.edu/theses/available/etd-08102006-134519/unrestricted/koselim.phd.pdf
Land, K. C., McCall, P. L., & Cohen, L. E. (1990). Structural covariates of homicide rates: Is there any invariance across time and social space? *American Journal of Sociology, 95*(4), 922–963.
Laqueur, W. (1999). *The new terrorist*. New York: Oxford University Press.
Lederman, D., Loayza, N., & Menéndez, A. M. (2000). *Violent crime: Does social capital matter?* Retrieved from http://wbln0018.worldbank.org/LAC/LACInfoClient.nsf/d29684951174975c85256735007fef12/f37a845e8a6d211185256801 005504b1?
Lemarchand, R. (1996). *Burundi: Ethnic conflict and genocide?* New York: Woodrow Wilson Center Press.
Lichbach, M. I. (1987). Deterrence and escalation: The puzzle of aggregate studies of repression and distress. *Journal of Conflict Resolution, 31*(2), 266.
MacCulloch, R. (2004). The impact of income on the taste for revolt. *American Journal of Political Science, 48*(4), 830–848.
Machin, S., & Meghir, C. (2004). Crime and economic incentives. *Journal of Human Resources, 39*, 959–982.
Matthews, M. and Limb, M. (2003). Another white elephant? Youth councils as democratic structures. *Space and Polity, 7*(2), 173–192.
Messner, S. F., & Golden, R. M. (1992). Racial inequality and racially disaggregated homicide rates: An assessment of alternative theoretical explanations. *Criminology, 30*, 421–447.
Messner, S. F., & Tardiff, K. (1986). Economic inequality and levels of homicide: An analysis of urban neighborhoods. *Criminology, 24*(2), 297–314.
Murshed, S. M., & Gates, S. (2003, March 28–29). *Spatial-horizontal inequality and the Maoist insurgency in Nepal*. Paper presented at the Project Conference on Spatial Inequality in Asia, United Nations University Centre, Tokyo.
Nacos, B. (2004). The terrorist calculus behind 9/11: A model for future terrorism? In G. Martin (Ed.), *The new era of terrorism: Selected readings*. Thousand Oaks, CA: Sage Publications.
Neumann, P. R. (2007). Europe's jihadist dilemma. *Survival, 48*(2), 71–84. Retrieved from http://dx.doi.org/10.1080/00396330600765518
Pape, R. A. (2003). The strategic logic of suicide terrorism. *American Political Science Review, 97*(3), 343–361.
Patterson, E. B. (1991). Poverty, income inequality and community crime rates. *Criminology, 29*(4), 755–776.

Post, J. M. (1986). "Hostilité, conformité, fraternité": The group dynamics of terrorist behavior, *International Journal of Group Psychotherapy, 36*(2), 211–24.
Priest, D., & White, J. (2005, February 17). War helps recruit terrorists, Hill told. *Washington Post*, p. A01.
Rosendor P., & Sandler, T. (2004). *Too much of a good thing? The proactive response dilemma.* Retrieved from http://www-rcf.usc.edu/~bpeter/papers/TerrorRecruit.pdf
Ryan, C., Vanderlick, J., & Matthews, W. (2007). *A paradoxical analysis of social learning theory as applied to the potential reform of terrorist offenders.* Retrieved from http://www.picj.org/docs/issue3/A%20Paradoxical%20 Analysis%20 of%20Social%20Learning%20Theory%20as%20Applied%20to%20The%20 Potential%20Reform%20of%20Terrorist%20Offenders.pdf
Sambanis, N. (2004). Poverty and the organization of political violence. *Brookings Trade Forum 2004*, 165–211.
Schwartz, S. J. (2005). New identity for identity research: Recommendations for expanding and refocusing the identity literature. *Journal of Adolescent Research, 20*(3), 293–308.
Sedgwick, M. (2007). Inspiration and the origins of global waves of terrorism. *Studies in Conflict & Terrorism, 30*, 97–112.
Shaw, C. R., & McKay, H. D. (1942). *Juvenile delinquency and urban areas.* Chicago: University of Chicago Press.
Silke, A. (2001). The devil you know: Continuing problems with research on terrorism. *Terrorism and Political Violence, 13*(4), 1–14.
Simonsen, C. E., & Spindlove, J. R. (2000). *Terrorism today: The past, the players, the future.* Upper Saddle River, NJ: Prentice Hall.
Smith, B. L., & Morgan, K. D. (1994). Terrorists right and left: Empirical issues in profiling American terrorists. *Studies in Conflict and Terrorism, 17*(1), 39–57.
Stern, J. (2000, December 7). *Countering terrorism effectively* (Press Release). Cambridge, MA: Harvard University Belfer Center for Science and International Affairs.
Taarnby, M. (2005). *Recruitment of Islamist terrorists in Europe. Trends and perspectives.* Centre for Cultural Research, University of Aarhus.
Tajfel, H., & Turner, J. C. (1986). The social identity theory of intergroup behavior. In S. Worchel & W. G. Austin (Eds.), *Psychology of intergroup relations* (pp. 7–24). Chicago: Nelson Hall.
Tambiah, S. J. (1996). *Leveling crowds: Ethno nationalist conflicts and collective violence in South Asia.* Berkeley: University California Press.
Taylor, M., & Quayle, E. (1994). *Terrorist lives.* London: Brassey's.
Tedeschi, J. T., & Felson, R. B. (1994) Violence, aggression, and coercive actions. Washington, DC: American Psychological Association.
Tilly, C. (1978). *From mobilization to revolution.* Reading, MA: Addison-Wesley.
Victoroff, J. (2005). The mind of the terrorist: A review and critique of psychological approaches. *Journal of Conflict Resolution, 49*, 3.
Waldmann, P. (1985). Gewaltsamer Separatismus. Am Beispiel der Basken, Franko-Kanadier und Nordiren. *Kiilner Z. Soziol. Sozialpsychol, 37*(2), 203–29.
Waldmann, P. (1989). *Ethnischer Radikalism, Ursachen zmd Foigen gewaltsamer Minderheitmkonflikte am Beispiel des Baskmlandes, Nordirlands und Qzrebecs.* Opladen, Germany: Wesdeutscher.
Weimann, G. (2004). How modern terrorism uses the Internet. Retrieved from http://www.terror.net

White, R. W. (1993). *Provisional Irish republicans: An oral and interpretive history.* Westport, CT: Greenwood.

Wilson, M., & Daly, M. (1997). Life expectancy, economic inequality, homicide, and reproductive timing in Chicago neighborhoods. *British Medical Journal, 314*, 1271–1287.

Wolfgang, M. E., & Ferracuti, F. (1982). *The subculture of violence: Towards an integrated theory in criminology*. Beverly Hills, CA: Sage Publications.

Woodward, S. L. (1995). *Balkan tragedy: Chaos and dissolution after the cold war.* Washington, DC: Brookings Institute.

Policing and the Mentally Ill
Local Policing and International Standards

6

DUNCAN CHAPPELL
University of Sydney, New South Wales, Australia
Simon Fraser University, BC, Canada

Contents

Introduction

The way people with a mental illness are treated is often regarded as one of the important measures of a nation's commitment to human rights and respect for individual freedom. Over recent decades, in many parts of the world, major advances have been made in the protection of the mentally ill from abusive practices, including their release from indeterminate detention in mental institutions and provision for their treatment in the community.

Despite these reforms, the impact and stigma of mental illness continues to present a challenge in many societies, including those societies' criminal justice systems. Police, in particular, are confronted with difficult law enforcement decisions as they encounter the mentally ill in their daily activities. It is the police who are most frequently a point of first contact for mentally ill persons on the street. It is also police who are most likely to be called for assistance in dealing with persons who, because of their mental illness, are believed to be a threat to themselves or others.

Policing experts acknowledge that encounters with people who are believed to be either mentally ill or mentally disordered are among the most sensitive of all police interactions. In the United States, for example, such interactions with emotionally disturbed persons (EDP), as they are often termed, have been referred to in the following way:

> EDP calls are difficult as well as frequent. What and whom you will find when you respond to them is likely to vary enormously.... [Sometimes] officers who respond to EDP calls find that the people involved have already left or are in the care of other responsible people. More often officers find people who are acting in a manner that seems irrational. Most EDP calls turn out to involve people who are neither a danger to themselves or others. Nevertheless police are called to respond to a large number of cases that are dangerous or that, if improperly handled, could quickly become dangerous. As police, we are responsible for getting such people to mental health professionals, but we also have other responsibilities. We must protect the lives and safety of EDPs as well as the lives and safety of other innocent people, including ourselves. We also have an obligation to protect EDPs' rights and dignity. (NYPD, 2003, p. i)

For many police executives, the setting of guidelines in regard to the handling of persons with a mental illness, together with appropriate training for officers, is becoming a matter of high priority. At the same time police leaders often face wider problems associated with the inadequacy of public health services for mentally ill persons. As a result the mentally ill tend to go through a repetitive cycle of admissions to hospital, while many come into conflict with the law and are incarcerated.

This chapter examines contemporary policing issues affecting the mentally ill both in Australia and in an international context. Particular attention is devoted to the way police exercise their powers of apprehension and detention within the framework of the UN Code of Conduct for Law Enforcement Officials (1979), the UN Basic Principles on the Use of Force and Firearms by Law Enforcement Officials (1990), and the UN Principles for the Protection of Persons with a Mental Illness and the Improvement of Mental Health Care (the UN Principles; 1991) (see in general UN Blue Book Series, 1995).

In compiling this chapter three principal sources of information have been relied upon. First, material has been obtained from the records of the New South Wales (NSW) Mental Health Review Tribunal (MHRT). The MHRT is an independent quasi judicial body constituted under the NSW Mental Health Act of 1990 (hereafter referred to as the Act). The MHRT has some 33 heads of jurisdiction including considering the disposition and release of persons acquitted of crimes by reasons of mental illness, determining matters concerning persons found unfit to be tried and prisoners transferred to hospital for treatment, and reviewing the cases of detained forensic patients (see Boyd-Caine & Chappell, 2005).

A second source of material is that of the proceedings of the NSW Legislative Council Select Committee on Mental Health (2002). The NSW Select Committee conducted an extensive inquiry into mental health services in NSW, including examining issues affecting the police.

The third reference source relied upon is that of another parliamentary inquiry into mental health undertaken at the federal level of government in Australia by a Senate Select Committee (Australian Senate, 2006). The Senate Committee, which has conducted widely publicized hearings across the nation, has done much to heighten community awareness and concern about the paucity of services available to those suffering from a mental illness. Australian law enforcement agencies have been prominent among the witnesses appearing before the Senate Committee in detailing their involvement with mentally ill people. In addition, the witnesses have outlined the problems that agencies confront in ensuring appropriate respect for and protection of the human rights of this group in Australia.

Dilemmas of First Contact

> Law Enforcement officers throughout the country regularly respond to calls for service that involve people with a mental illness—often without needed support, resources, or specialized training. These encounters can have significant consequences for the officers, people with a mental illness and their loved ones, the community, and the criminal justice system. (Bureau of Justice Assistance, 2008, p. vii)

This recent statement by justice officials in the United States emphasizes the nature of the dilemma that confronts front-line police in jurisdictions across the globe. It is a dilemma that has intensified in most contemporary law enforcement settings due to the deinstitutionalization movement, which has seen most persons with a mental illness residing in the community rather than in secure hospitals. Recent research data suggest that behaviors that seem to be the result of a mental illness represent a factor in about 3–7% of all law enforcement requests for service (Bureau of Justice Assistance, 2008).

In the United States, police are involved annually in millions of encounters with persons of all types, many of whom may be detained on a short-term basis in jails or, if convicted, in state and federal prisons. The rate of serious mental illness for all of these more than 6 million persons currently either in custody or under correctional supervision in the community in the

United States is about three to four times that of the general U.S. population. As the U.S. president's New Freedom Commission on Mental Health (2004) stated:

> The people with serious mental illnesses who come in contact with the criminal justice system are typically poor and uninsured, are disproportionately members of minority groups and often are homeless and have co-occurring substance abuse and mental disorders. They cycle in and out of homeless shelters, hospitals and jails, occasionally receiving mental health, substance abuse services, but most likely receiving no services at all (APA, 2000). The majority of these individuals has committed misdemeanour crimes and do not belong in the criminal justice system. The problem is inescapable in almost every urban community. It has frustrated judges, prosecutors, criminal justice system administrators, families, and consumers alike. Advocates from across the spectrum are united in recognizing the need for reform (New Freedom Commission on Mental Health, 2004, p. 1).

Undoubtedly, the substance of the situation described in the United States regarding the plight of the mentally ill and their involvement with the criminal justice system can be translated across national boundaries to most parts of the world. Certainly it is a situation all too familiar in an Australian context as both the NSW Legislative Council Select Committee on Mental Health (2002) and Australian Senate (2006) have documented.

Exercising Discretion and the Use of Force

Despite the problems identified for police in responding to EDP, the general consensus seems to be that in most cases law enforcement officers do a difficult and stressful job in a professional and humane manner. In NSW, for instance, the NSW Select Committee noted that the NSW Police Service, a statewide agency, with about 14,000 sworn officers, was held in high regard for the way it dealt with interactions with mentally ill people (NSW Legislative Council Select Committee on Mental Health, 2002, p. 223). The NSW Select Committee recognized that the police consider this aspect of their work as often demanding, time-consuming, and frustrating. Sometimes it is also dangerous, as a contemporary Australian case illustrates.

Early in January 2006 neighbors and mental health workers in a town near Sydney, NSW, called for police to assist with a man who was acting aggressively. Four officers responded and found the man armed with a pitchfork and knives. Despite being asked to put these weapons down, the man advanced toward the officers, who retreated while emptying their capsicum spray cans at him. The man kept advancing and was eventually subdued by the officers. Three of the officers suffered injuries requiring hospital treatment (Totaro, 2006).

This incident prompted a strong statement from the NSW police commissioner warning that Australia was in the grip of a mental health crisis and that police officers could not bear the brunt of inadequate mental health services and would defend themselves against attacks. In a media interview after the incident, the commissioner stressed how police had only an extremely limited time to react and would have to live with the consequences of their decisions for the rest of their lives:

> They have to make huge judgment calls. These officers are being required to react in split seconds and can mean the difference between the person losing their life—either the officer or the mentally ill person. (Totaro, 2006)

The use of force, including deadly force, against mentally ill or disturbed individuals is an area fraught with controversy in Australia, just as it is in other jurisdictions. The way police manage situations like the "pitchfork" attacker, collectively and individually, can reveal much about their commitment to the upholding of the civil liberties of the citizens they are required to protect. International norms of conduct for law enforcement officials stress that in carrying out their duties police should use nonviolent means before resorting to the use of force or firearms. The norms state that an officer may use force and firearms "only if other means remain ineffective or without any promise of achieving the intended result" (UN Basic Principles on the Use of Force and Firearms, 1990, Principle 4).

Police may only use firearms in strictly limited circumstances:

> 9. Law enforcement officials shall not use firearms against persons except in self-defence or defence of others against the imminent threat of death, or serious injury, to prevent the perpetration of a particularly serious crime involving grave threat to life, to arrest a person presenting such a danger and resisting their authority, or to prevent his or her escape, and only when less extreme means are insufficient to achieve these objectives. In any event, intentional lethal use of firearms may only be made when strictly unavoidable in order to protect life.
>
> 10. In the circumstances provided for under principle 9, law enforcement officials shall identify themselves as such and give a clear warning of their intent to use firearms, with sufficient time for the warning to be observed, unless to do so would unduly place the law enforcement officials at risk or would create a risk of death or serious harm to other persons, or would be clearly inappropriate or pointless in the circumstances of the incident. (UN Basic Principles on the Use of Force and Firearms, 1990)

Regarding these international principles, it is apparent that the four NSW police officers who apprehended the pitchfork attacker acted in an extremely courageous and appropriate way, even though their own lives were at significant risk and they might well have resorted to the use of lethal force. However, in Australia as in many other nations, police have on occasion been the subject of substantial criticism as a result of their mishandling of cases involving mentally ill or mentally disordered persons. In NSW, for example, the shooting of Roni Levi, a mentally disturbed person and a French citizen, on Bondi Beach in June 1997 resulted in a public outcry that reached well beyond Australian shores. The circumstances surrounding this shooting are described in the following account of the incident drawn from a subsequent investigation by the NSW Police Integrity Commission (PIC, 2001):

> Roni Levi was 35 years old at the time of his death. On the evening before the shooting Mr Levi, with the assistance of some friends, voluntarily admitted himself to St Vincent's Hospital suffering from borderline delusional thought processes. Sometime during the night, Mr Levi left the hospital and went home to his flat in Bondi. Mr Levi was observed by his flatmate as being uncommunicative and in a confused and distressed state. Mr Levi obtained a knife from the kitchen and left the flat, his flatmate following him for a short while before running to nearby Bondi Police Station and informing police of the situation. Mr Levi was spotted a short time later on Bondi Beach still in possession of the kitchen knife. He was pursued by six police officers, four from Bondi Police Station and two from Paddington Police Station. The six officers partially surrounded Mr Levi, who was still holding the knife, and remained in a semi circle position around him as he moved up Bondi Beach towards the esplanade. After about twenty five minutes, at approximately 7.30 am (Constables) Podestra and Dilorenzo each fired two shots fatally wounding Mr Levi. Mr Levi was pronounced dead approximately one hour later at St Vincent's Hospital.
>
> The shooting of Mr Levi was the subject of a coronial inquiry, however the inquiry was terminated on 6 March 1998 and the matter was referred to the DPP. On 30 June 1998 the DPP determined that there was no reasonable prospect of conviction against either Podesta or Dilorenzo and decided not to prosecute the officers in relation to the shooting of Roni Levi.
>
> The Commission's investigation did not re-investigate the circumstances of the shooting of Roni Levi on 28 June 1997, other than in the context of the scope and purpose of the hearing, namely to examine allegations that one or both officers involved in the shooting were affected by drugs and/or alcohol at the time of the shooting and to examine allegations of police misconduct with respect to the investigation of the shooting. (PCI, 2000, paras. 1.20–1.22)

Fortunately, the evidence suggests that police shootings of this nature remain relatively rare occurrences in NSW although in other Australian jurisdictions, and especially in Victoria in the past their prevalence has aroused considerable public disquiet. A review undertaken by the Australian Institute of Criminology (AIC) has revealed that during the period 1990–1997 a total of 41 persons were shot by police. The greatest number of these shootings (21, or 52%) occurred in Victoria, 8 in NSW and the balance among the remaining Australian jurisdictions. All but one of these deaths occurred while police were in the process of detaining or attempting to detain a person. In more than one-third of the cases the AIC noted that the persons who were shot were either mentally ill or psychologically disturbed at the time of the incident. The report concluded:

> Police must be provided with the necessary defence and negotiation skills and weapons training necessary for dealing with irrational, armed and violent offenders who may also be psychologically disturbed, mentally ill, or drug/alcohol affected. (Dalton, 1998, p. 6)

The AIC's own report suggests that better training and allied practices and procedures among Australian police forces has resulted in a diminution of the number of police shootings and in the application of more appropriate nonlethal methods of restraining and apprehending mentally ill or mentally disordered persons. Some examples of these more appropriate police practices can be found among two contemporary cases of forensic patients dealt with by the MHRT. These are cases that also illustrate the reality that on occasions emotionally disturbed persons seek to place themselves in situations in which they hope to be killed by the police.

Case Studies

Case 1

Forensic patient A suffered from chronic paranoid schizophrenia for which he had received spasmodic treatment. Following a series of violent incidents and while on bail and failing to take his antipsychotic medication, he formed an elaborate though psychotic plan to have himself killed by the police. As part of this plan he went to an airport and tried to light a fire, believing that he would be shot. He was unsuccessful in lighting the fire but took out a knife and threatened police and airport security personnel. A security guard was subsequently stabbed and seriously wounded while seeking to disarm and apprehend A. A was eventually acquitted of a range of charges on the basis of his mental illness.

Case 2

Forensic patient B, who also suffered from severe chronic paranoid schizophrenia, entered a café in a metropolitan area while experiencing delusional beliefs that he was being pursued by people who were out to harm him. Armed with a knife, the patient then took hostage a number of the customers in the café in hopes that the police, when they responded, would kill him. The police emergency response team did come to the scene of the hostage taking. A lengthy period of negotiation then took place with the forensic patient, who eventually released all of the hostages and then surrendered himself. He too was ultimately found to be not guilty of a range of charges associated with the hostage taking, on the grounds of his mental illness.

Lessons Learned

In these two cases very considerable skill and bravery on the part of the police and other persons resulted in the disturbed mentally ill individuals being apprehended alive. As a result of the mentally ill individuals' subsequent successful treatment using anti-psychotic drugs, both of these forensic patients have now been allowed to return to live in the community on conditional release programs supervised by local community mental health teams. These cases suggest that the protection of the human rights of the mentally ill has been enhanced by a range of measures introduced by Australian police.

The Scheduling Process

Another challenging area for police arises from their involvement in the civil justice process, which applies in many societies to the scheduling of mentally ill persons. In each Australian jurisdiction police are given wide-ranging legal powers to intervene in the lives of the mentally ill and disordered. In NSW, for example, under the current mental health legislation:

> If a member of the Police Force finds a person in any place who
>
> 1. appears to be mentally disturbed and the member of the Police Force has reasonable grounds for believing:
>   a. that the person is committing or has recently committed an offence and that it would be beneficial to the welfare of the person that the person be dealt with in accordance of this Act rather than otherwise in accordance with law, or
>   b. that the person has recently attempted to kill himself or herself or that it is probable that the person will attempt to kill himself or herself or attempt to cause serious bodily harm to himself or herself, the member of the Police Force may apprehend the person and take the person to a hospital (other than an authorised hospital).
> 2. A member of the Police Force may apprehend any such person without a warrant of a justice. (NSW Mental Health Act, 1990, section 24)

Australian police have expressed strong views about the way these powers apply in practice. First, they indicate frustration at being requested to intervene and apprehend persons believed to be mentally ill and dangerous who should in reality be dealt with by health professionals in the community. Police have accused these health professionals of "abdicating their responsibilities" and thrusting them upon law enforcement officers because no one else wants to or can manage difficult situations like these (Police Federation of Australia, 2005, p. 3).

Second, police also express their frustration about the legal definitions of mental illness or mental disorder, indicating that health professionals often refuse to schedule people apprehended by law enforcement officers because they fail to meet the requisite legal criteria. In a joint submission made to the Senate Committee, Australian police associations recommended that all mental health legislation should contain definitions of mental illness and mental disorder in a sufficiently broad manner to allow scheduling of persons in need of assistance but who, at present, fell into a gap in such legislation (Police Federation of Australia, 2005, p. 4).

A third area of police concern relates to the sheer amount of time and resources required to be committed by law enforcement to the scheduling process. Australian police are replete with horror stories of shuffling persons they believed to be mentally ill around emergency departments at a number of hospitals, seeking an authoritative ruling regarding their scheduling and admission to a secure ward as an involuntary patient. As the Australian police associations stated to the Senate Committee:

> What are police to do with a person who has been reported to them due to their behaviour that may not constitute a criminal offence but is sufficient for police to convey them to a hospital or institution for assessment when following that assessment police are told the person will not be scheduled? Should the person be taken home, or back to the streets, often to the volatile environment from which they have just been removed? Or should they be taken to the police station for charging as police have no general power to simply hold them for their own safety and well being? The decision is the police officers' and they can only hope that the choice they make for the individual is the best one for their well-being and care. There have been many instances of where police have then had complaints lodged against them by members of the public for the decision they have made. These complaints often take years to be investigated before the officer is cleared of any wrongdoing.
>
> Police are often frustrated and angered by mental health professionals, who are fully aware of a police officer's duty of care. Duty of care essentially dictates that a police officer must do all within their power to take a person to a place of safety. Mental health professionals abuse the fact that once police bring in a person to be assessed for scheduling, they cannot simply leave due to their duty of care to the individual concerned. Hence, whilst the decision is

> being made on whether or not to schedule a patient, police continue to remain with the patient, their role in effect changing from a policing role to a mental health role. (Police Federation of Australia, 2005, p. 10)

These issues are clearly both controversial and not readily resolved. It remains a core function of democratic policing that law enforcement officers provide protection and support for the community they serve, and in particular "to those members of the community who by reason of personal, economic, social or other exigencies are in need of immediate aid" (UN Code of Conduct for Law Enforcement Officers, 1979, article 2). It is difficult to see how any other social agency, including health departments, can assume basic responsibilities for the interventions required to bring mentally ill or disordered persons into treatment venues. It is also a matter of considerable debate whether the definitions of mental illness and mental disorder, which can trigger enormous intrusions into the personal lives of individuals, albeit for their perceived benefit, should be further extended. Recent experience in the United Kingdom with attempts to broaden the scope of mental health legislation to capture personality disorders proves just how controversial and contentious proposals like these can be. It would appear that concerted opposition to these proposed reforms by many influential groups, including professorial bodies like the British Medical Association (BMA), has resulted in their removal from draft legislation tabled in the British Parliament (see Kmietowicz, 2005).

More promising prospects for change may well be found in the way the police and mental health agencies interact during the scheduling process. It does appear highly wasteful of scarce and costly law enforcement resources to require police officers to spend lengthy periods waiting for decisions about a person's diagnosis and treatment. Much could probably be achieved in reaching agreement about resource allocation and time tables through greater dialogue between health and law enforcement bodies. In a number of Australian jurisdictions, dialogue of this type has already led to the development of comprehensive Memorandums of Understanding (MOUs) between such bodies, which has eased tension and led to much better management of the entire scheduling process.

Transportation of Mentally Ill Persons

A further problem for police, and one often closely related to the scheduling process, is the need for their assistance in transporting persons, either believed or established to be mentally ill, to and between a range of mental health facilities. For mental health workers, the police provide a source of frequent aid in managing the safe and secure transportation of people who present a perceived or actual risk of harm to themselves and others. For police, on the other hand, this role is often viewed as an inappropriate task imposed upon them by health systems reluctant or incapable of dealing with difficult clients.

In an Australian context, as recent evidence presented to the Senate Committee has illustrated, the transportation problem has become the focus of major attention by law enforcement agencies. In their submission to the Senate Committee Australian Police Associations indicated that the preferred option to transport mentally ill persons was by trained medical staff in their own rather than police vehicles (Police Federation of Australia, 2005, pp. 10–11). Where this was not possible and the risks to staff were low, the use of regular ambulance services would be appropriate. The associations contended:

> The use of police to transport mentally ill persons should only occur during any initial apprehension by police when the person has been apprehended by police or when the risk to staff is high and mental health staff trained in the management of challenging behaviour are unable to manage the situation without police involvement. Police vehicles should only be used in extreme circumstances. (Police Federation of Australia, 2005, pp. 10–11)

There is much to be said for this suggested approach to transporting the mentally ill. The use of police vehicles for this purpose raises the prospect of mentally ill persons being perceived as criminals rather than patients and adds to the already extensive stigma associated with mental illness in many parts of society. Police vehicles are also not designed for such a purpose, raising a further risk of injury occurring to either the person being transported or the police themselves.

This risk is exacerbated when, as is often the case, in rural areas of Australia police may have to drive many hours to transport a mentally ill person from a remote part of the country to the nearest secure mental health facility where treatment can be provided. While alternative transportation by air may be a possibility, most Australian airlines including the Royal Flying Doctor Service (RFDS), which provides the sole medical link for many rural communities, have stringent requirements relating to the carriage of dangerous or disturbed individuals. In the case of the RFDS these requirements include sedation and the accompanying of the patient by trained medical staff as well as police. Such sedation carries risks of its own, and especially so when the flight in a small aircraft may take a number of hours as well.

In a number of Australian jurisdictions, discussions are ongoing regarding how best to respond to these various transportation issues. Much of the discussion and the likely response are centered on the allocation of resources between law enforcement and health agencies. From the health agencies perspective, if greater responsibility is to be assumed by health professionals in this aspect of the management of mentally ill persons, more specialized and secure ambulance services seem destined to be developed. Ambulance officers are already often in the front line when they respond to calls for assistance from police at crime scenes and accidents. Recent research shows that these officers also experience the highest risk of occupational violence, both physical and psychological, among all groups of health professionals (Mayhew & Chappell, 2003). These risks often extend to health staff in the emergency departments to which the ambulance staff subsequently deliver their patients, many of whom are under the influence of drugs as well as mentally ill on occasion.

Detention in Police Custody

This chapter is not intended to deal at any length with the vexed issue for all custodians of the mentally ill of ensuring the maximum protection of their human rights while they are detained. For the police, this function is a constant challenge since they detain numerous persons, many of whom may be mentally ill, for varying periods of time through their general participation in the criminal justice system. Because of the relatively short duration of most forms of police custody, the types of screening that identify those detainees most likely to be suffering from a mental illness are often less available at this stage of the criminal justice process, even though the risks of self-harm may well be at their highest. For this reason most Australian law enforcement agencies, prompted in part by a far-reaching national inquiry into deaths in custody, have in recent years done much to improve the physical facilities in which persons are detained by police as well as developing comprehensive guidelines for the safe management of all persons held in custody, in accord with international standards (Royal Commission into Aboriginal Deaths in Custody, 1991; Williams, 2001).

Training

Many law enforcement agencies are now including the handling of interactions with mentally ill persons as part of their basic recruit education training programs as well as in refresher courses for operational officers. These curriculum changes recognize the frequency and sensitivity of police encounters with mentally ill persons. However, few research studies have been conducted to evaluate the effectiveness of such training or its relevance to police working in different cultures and across international boundaries. All too often training may also only occur after some critical incident has taken place involving a mentally ill person, as in the case of a police shooting. In NSW, for example, the separate shooting deaths by police of mentally ill persons, one in 1998 and the other in 2002, prompted coronial inquiries and the following recommendation:

> The NSW Police Service urgently provides comprehensive training to all NSW Police Academy students and operational police officers in the appropriate dealing with the mentally ill. Such issues should include issues such as the

> recognition of common and significant psychiatric problems techniques for dealing with mentally ill persons and legal issues associated therewith. (Police Federation of Australia, 2005, p. 14)

Training of this type is now provided in NSW, apparently with good results as demonstrated by the pitchfork case. Officers seem to favor their training on this aspect of their daily work. However, they are apprehensive about being perceived incorrectly by the public as now becoming mental health experts even if they do acknowledge the benefits of understanding more about a form of illness that afflicts a significant number of the people they encounter in their daily work.

Conclusion

Despite raising awareness among many police of the nature of mental illness and its impact upon those who suffer from it, there still remains in most societies a deep-seated stigma associated with this type of ailment and unwillingness to recognize or deal with the discrimination that flows from such stigma. The police typically share the values and norms, whether good or bad, of their fellow citizens. Much of the educative effort now being devoted to train police better to understand and deal with mentally ill people could therefore be applied with equal benefit to the communities in which they reside. Only when a broad segment of a society has such knowledge can it be anticipated that the prejudice and discrimination exhibited toward the mentally ill will truly dissipate.

In this chapter principal attention has been given to developments occurring in democratic and developed nations. In less affluent nations as well as in those having scant respect for human rights, the general plight of the mentally ill can be quite dire. Human rights groups like Amnesty International have drawn attention to the arbitrary detention and ill treatment of people with mental disabilities in a number of countries. For instance, Amnesty reported recently the following conditions prevailing in a group home visited in Bulgaria:

> Residents in the Samuil social care home for adults with mental disabilities endure systematic abuse, gross neglect and ghastly living conditions in violation of international human rights standards. Samuil is a mixed institution, housing both men and women over age 18.... Conditions in social care homes for adults are often cruel, inhuman and degrading. The high numbers of deaths testify to medical neglect and a lack of food and warmth. Residents may be physically restrained with belts or straitjackets or secluded in a small room with no windows or a cage for indefinite amounts of time. Medication is widely administered, often solely to control behavior. (Amnesty International, 2002)

In a comprehensive and controversial cover story first published in November 2003, *Time Asia* gave a graphic account of the conditions experienced by the mentally ill in many Asian nations (Beech, 2003). *Time Asia* reported that most Asian nations spent very small amounts on mental health care. In Pakistan, for example, so little was provided from government coffers that private donors had to try to meet the shortfall. In China, according to the Global Burden of Disease Study conducted jointly by the World Health Organization (WHO) and Harvard University for the World Bank, only 2% of the nation's health budget was spent on mental health while psychiatric disorders accounted for 20% of that nation's health burden (WHO, 2005, p. 135). The same study suggested that the situation was especially acute for serious mental illnesses with, for instance, 90% of schizophrenics being kept at home without access to medication or therapy. The continuing stigma of mental illness in China, as elsewhere in much of Asia, meant that people were not prepared to admit a relative had a mental disease (WHO, 2005).

Situations like these clearly present huge challenges for the governments and citizens of a significant number of the world's nations. They must also be challenges, largely undocumented, for the police working in these nations. It is to be hoped that in the future more can be learned about the local situation confronting police in their interactions with mentally ill persons in nations still struggling with social, economic, political, and allied reform. Through enhanced knowledge it may be possible to begin dialogue and discussion about how to assist police in such nations to join in the movement to give effect to internationally accepted principles for the protection and treatment of persons with a mental illness. These principles emphasize, among other things, that "all persons with a mental illness, or who are being treated as such persons, shall be treated with humanity and respect for the inherent dignity of the human person" (UN Principles for the Protection of Persons with a Mental Illness and the Improvement of Mental Health Care, 1991, principle 1). Globally, much still remains to be done in law enforcement to make principles like these a part of accepted practice in operational policing at the community level.

References

American Psychiatric Association (2000). Psychiatric agencies in jail and prisons: A task force report of the American Psychiatric association. Washington, DC.

Amnesty International. (2002) *Bulgaria. Arbitrary detention and ill treatment of people with mental disabilities. Appeals cases: Samuil social care home for men and women*, London: Amnesty International. Retrieved March 6, 2010 from http://www.amnesty.org/en/library/info/EUR15/010/2002/en

Australian Senate. (2006). *Final Report of the Review of the Select Committee on Mental Health. A national approach to mental health—From crisis to community.* Canberra: Australian Senate.

Beech, H. (2003) Hidden away. *Time Asia, 162*(18). Retrieved March 6, 2010 from http://www.time.com/time/magazine/asia/0,9263,501031110,00.html

Boyd-Caine, T., & Chappell, D. (2005). The forensic population in New South Wales. *Current Issues in Criminal Justice, 17*(1), 5–29.

Bureau of Justice Assistance. (2008). *Improving responses to people with mental illness. The essential elements of a specialized law enforcement-based program.* New York: Council of State Governments Justice Center.

Dalton, V. (1998). Police shootings 1990–97. *Trends and Issues in Crime and Criminal Justice, 89*, 1–6.

Kmietowicz, Z. (2005). Rip up Draft Mental Health Bill and start again says BMA. *British Medical Journal*, 330, 326.

Mayhew, C., & Chappell, D. (2003). The occupational violence experiences of 400 Australian health workers: An exploratory study. *Australia and New Zealand Journal of Occupational Health and Safety*, *19*(6), 5–43.

New Freedom Commission on Mental Health. (2004). *Sub Committee on Criminal Justice: Background paper. DHHS Pub No. SMA-04-3880.* Rockville, MD: New Freedom Commission on Mental Health.

New York City Police Department. (NYPD). (2003). *Policing student guide. Policing the emotionally disturbed.* New York: Author.

New South Wales Legislative Council Select Committee on Mental Health. (2002). *Inquiry into mental health service in New South Wales. Final report.* Sydney: NSW Parliament Legislative Council.

New South Wales Mental Health Act. (1990).

New South Wales Police Integrity Commission. (PIC). (2001). *Report to Parliament: Operation Saigon,* Sydney: Author.

Police Federation of Australia. (2005). *Submission to the Senate Select Committee on Mental Health.* Canberra: Australian Senate.

Royal Commission into Aboriginal Deaths in Custody. (1991). *Final report.* Canberra: Australian Government Publishing Service.

Totaro, P. (2006, January 5). Pitchfork attack last straw for Moroney. *Sydney Morning Herald*, p. 3.

United Nations (UN) Code of Conduct for Law Enforcement Officers. (1979).

United Nations (UN) Basic Principles on the Use of Force and Firearms. (1990).

United Nations (UN). Principles for the Protection of Persons with a Mental Illness and the Improvement of Mental Health Care. (1991).

United Nations (1995). United Nations Blue Book Series, Vol. II. The United Nations and human rights. New York: Department of Public Information, United Nations.

Williams, P. (2001). Deaths in custody: 10 years on from the Royal Commission. *Trends and Issues in Crime and Criminal Justice*, 203, 1–6.

World Health Organization. (WHO). (2005). *Mental health atlas 2005.* Geneva: WHO.

7

Policing Mental Illness
The Need for Specialized Police Training Program in Dealing With Mentally Ill Persons

AVDI S. AVDIJA
Indiana State University

Contents

Introduction

The police response involving individuals with mental illness has long been an issue in policing (Ratansi, 2004). Lately, the police encounters with mentally ill people have become exponentially noticeable when the number of mentally ill cases is on the rise (Laberge & Morin, 1995; Teplin, 1983). In any society, a police officer's duty is to deal with and respond to all cases involving violence. A new role has been added to their service, however, as the problems of dealing with mentally ill persons have become transparent. This is primarily as a result of insufficient community-based mental health care in dealing with mentally ill persons (Ratansi, 2004). Bonovitz and Bonovitz (1981), for example, found that between 1975 and 1979 there was a 227% increase in the number of police encounters with mentally ill persons in the United States. Thus, in many ways, as many researcher have argued, the street problems of mentally ill people have become the burden of the police officers, acting the role of "street-corner psychiatrist" (Ratansin, 2004; Steadman, Deane, Borum, & Morrissey, 2000; Teplin & Pruett, 1992).

Dealing with mentally ill persons is a challenge even for the mental health professionals, let alone the police. On many levels, the police officers are inadequately trained on issues related to mental illness. Thus, most police officers do not have the appropriate training or are not fully prepared to effectively use verbal (i.e., psychological) techniques to assess and deescalate encounters involving people with mental illness. Consequently, the mentally ill people then become targeted and disproportionately arrested by the police as a means of resolving the situations at hand (Ratansin, 2004). Thus, a proper police training program that is evidence based and that has been shown to be effective is a necessary component of policing.

Theoretical Perspectives

The relationship between mental illness and criminal behavior is more often explained by factors other than mental illness (Hiday, 1995). Research that is focused on the propensity of violence by persons with mental illness shows that, in general, mentally ill persons are no more prone to criminal activity than other segments of the general population (Florez, Holley, & Crisanti, 1996; Hodgins & Cote, 1993; see also Cohen & Freeman, 1945; Talbott, 1979). In other words, the relationship between criminal behavior and mental illness is weak. This means that mentally ill persons, when excluding factors (e.g., socioeconomic status, substance abuse, gender, marital status) that affect the general population, are unlikely to commit more crimes than non-mentally ill people. They are just more visible to the general public (their behavior, respectively) and thus are disproportionately arrested and institutionalized, consequently making the quantity of arrests more pronounced compared with the general population (Durbin, Pasewark, & Albers, 1977). Research shows that the majority of offenses that are specifically related to persons with mental disorders tend to be a nuisance, and only a small portion of persons with mental illness become violent (Chaiklin, 2004).

Some research indicates that mentally ill persons are more likely to engage in criminal behaviors only when certain influential conditions are present. That is, they are more likely than normal people to engage in criminal behaviors when they possess one or more of the following personal and social characteristics: prior criminal record leading to institutionalization, being victimized, problems with marital status, being homeless, or exposure to addiction through substance abuse (which is an example of frequent cases involving domestic violence; Ratansin, 2004; Teplin, 1985). However, this correlation with crime is more administrative than etiological. The correlation between crime and mental illness is a by-product of failures in the social system to properly deal with mentally ill persons, which creates the conditions that result in a disproportionate arrest rate involving persons with mental illness. Reiteratively, the propensity to get involved in criminal behavior for mentally ill persons is about the same as that of the general population (Talbott, 1979; Teplin, 1990; see also Gottredson & Hirschi, 1990). Some researchers who have studied the relationship between mental illness and criminal behavior have used arrest rates (police records) as the dependent variable. This way, they have introduced some misconception about the true figure of criminal behavior involving mentally ill persons (Lurgio & Swartz, 2002). As mentioned earlier, in the United States mentally ill persons are inappropriately and disproportionably processed through the criminal justice system. In this context, an increased arrest rate does not depict the true and accurate picture of the actual propensities of mentally ill persons for criminal behaviors compared with the general population, it tells us only that the police are more likely to arrest them because of the stigma that society has attached to them (Becker, 1963; Lemert, 1972; Paternoster & Iovanni, 1989).

Mental Illness in the Public Agenda

Based on the available empirical evidence on police responses to calls involving mentally ill persons, three main factors have brought about the issue of mental illness in the public agenda: (1) deinstitutionalization of mentally ill persons; (2) criminalization of mentally ill persons; and (3) well-publicized incidents involving the police and persons with mental illness.

Deinstitutionalization

The term *deinstitutionalization* makes reference to two parallel processes: one is the transfer of mentally ill patients from institutional settings into the community, and the second is the development of a system that can provide special care for mentally ill persons while they live in the community (Hunt, 2008). In the United States, the deinstitutionalization of mentally ill patients did not occur until the 1950s. Thus, "fifty years ago, public mental health care was based largely on national care. In 1955, there were 560,000 patients in state mental hospitals.... By 1998 the number of patients in state mental hospitals had dropped down to 72,000" (Ratansin, 2004, p. 17). This translates that deinstitutionalization of the mentally ill persons resulted in many of them being abandoned. Many of the mentally ill individuals were left on the streets to fend for themselves. In many instances, they victimized others and quite often became victims themselves. The system that was supposed to be put in place in the community, and that would offer a more personalized care for individuals with mental illness, was not readily available to respond to this newly created problem (Erickson & Erickson, 2008).

Initially, deinstitutionalization was meant to solve the problem of inadequate treatment that mentally ill patients were receiving in mental health hospitals. Consequently, this inadequate treatment of these persons became the central criticism of mental health reformers, and, in fact, they began to voice their opinions against this treatment that mentally ill persons were experiencing (Lamb & Weinberger, 1998; Ratansin, 2004). They argued that mental health hospitals were simply "warehousing" patients and that advancements in psychotropic medication were a better and less stigmatizing means for improving the well-being of individuals with mental illness (Lamb, 2000; Lamb & Weinberger, 1998; Ratansin, 2004). That is, keeping mentally ill persons isolated in mental health hospitals was considered inhumane when the advent of new medications would allow them to live within mainstream society. Accordingly, "the replacement of long-stay psychiatric hospitals with smaller, less isolated community-based alternatives for the care of mentally ill people became known as deinstitutionalization movement" (Ratansin, 2004, p. 18).

Unfortunately, the deinstitutionalization movement was not fully funded by the federal government and fell short of realizing its objectives. The inability to establish treatment centers (due to lack of federal funding) in all communities resulted in inadequate treatment options and lack of services (e.g., food, clothes, shelter) for mentally ill persons and thus forced many of them into a state of homelessness (Tyson & Carroll, 2001). Statistically, approximately 25% of the homeless population in the United States has had previous psychiatric hospitalization, and 25 to 50% are mentally ill (Sullivan, Burnam, & Koegel, 2000). And as mentioned at the beginning of this research chapter, the problem of mental illness has shifted from being a mental health institutions' problem to becoming the problem of the police on the streets. As a result, the arrest rates among former mental patients compared with the general population started to increase overwhelmingly (Hiday, 1999; Monahan, 1992; Robkin, 1979).

Criminalization

Mental illness is a disease, not a crime. Needless to say, the criminal justice system in America has failed to recognize that mentally ill persons have been misplaced across many different institutions, and that has made many of them vulnerable and involuntarily exposed to criminality.

Abramson (1972) was one of the first researchers to notice a disproportionate increase of arrest rates involving mentally ill persons. Thus, according to Abramson, in many cases the police used arrest as a response to controlling violence where in fact arrest was not mandated, and the individuals in question appeared to be suffering from some form of mental illness (Ratansin, 2004).

In this context, many researchers argued and still argue that criminalization of mentally ill people came about as a result of deinstitutionalization (see Dodge & Schreiber, 2009; Hiday, 1995; Teplin, 1990). That is, the changes in mental health policies were responsible for an increase in the number of contacts between persons with mental illness and the police. In the previous section, the argument was that the government failed to fund the deinstitutionalization of mentally ill persons. This implies that deinstitutionalization introduced new problems in the world of mental health. Thus, many mentally ill persons were left to survive on their own; as a result, a great number of them become homeless. Obviously, homeless people have frequent contact with law enforcement. More often than not, police–mentally ill encounters have a tendency to result in arrests and thus cause a disproportionate representation of mentally ill people in the criminal justice system. Individuals with mental health problems who became homeless, and whom medical institutions failed, soon became part of criminal justice institutions since their behavior on the street conflicted with the norms of society; as such, they became the problem of the police (Talbot, 1979). Unfortunately, society to this day has attached a stigma to persons with mental illness and demands that the police response accordingly.

In summation, the argument that focused on what causes criminalization of mentally ill persons is twofold. On one hand, some researchers argue that failure of the deinstitutionalization movement is a direct cause for an increase in the number of police contacts with mentally ill persons (Lamb, 2000; Lamb & Weinberger, 1998; Sullivan, Burnam, & Koegel, 2000). On the other hand, failure of mental health hospitals to adequately house mentally ill persons resulted in further stigmatization of mentally ill persons (Talbot, 1979; Sellers, Sullivan, Veysey, & Shane, 2005). More research is needed, however, to determine the true cause of criminalization of mentally ill persons, and that now is affecting the criminal justice system, the police in particular.

Well-Publicized Incidents

The third factor that has significantly contributed to putting mental illness on the public agenda relates to police incidents involving persons with mental illness where the outcomes were fatal. As noted already, the deinstitutionalization appeared to have some relationship with criminalization. In fact, deinstitutionalization largely contributed to the mentally ill persons being abandoned; that is, a significant number of them became homeless or not properly taken care of. And for mentally ill persons who became homeless, the frequency of contacts with the police increased. Yet the police were not well prepared or properly trained to handle cases involving mentally ill persons; thus, some serious incidents reached the public through mass media.

According to Amnesty International USA (1999), the problem of the mentally ill entered the public agenda when the police were noted using excessive force, including deadly force, against mentally ill people who could have been subdued though less extreme measures. Amnesty International USA reported several cases that caught media attention. For instance, Ricardo Clos was reported to have died after being shot 38 times by Los Angeles sheriff's deputies, who had responded to a call for help from his wife in February 1999. When the police responded to this case, Clos was holding a kitchen knife; in response, the police reportedly opened fire on Clos, leaving him dead. In April 1999, a mentally challenged man who had stabbed himself in the stomach was shot to death by the police in San Jose, California. This case was similar to the previous one. The man in question was shot by the police because he had refused to put down the knife. In August 1999, 31-year-old Gidone Busch, a mentally ill man armed with a hammer, died after New York City Police Department (NYPD) officers shot him 12 times in Borough Park, Brooklyn, New York. After this case was publicized by the local media, it led to a protest in the local community (Amnesty International USA, 1999; Kifner, 1999). On June 13, 2001, San Francisco Police shot and killed 23-year-old Idriss Stelley as he stood alone in Metreon Theater holding a knife. Stelley was a college student who had a history of mental illness (Stolen Lives Project, 2004).

Many cases involving police and mentally ill persons have resulted in fatal shootings. A small number of those cases are known as "suicide by cop," while the majority of them are purely incidental, resulting from police mishandling. In suicidal cases, suicidal individuals usually provoke the police into shooting them. In mishandled cases, on the other hand, the responsibility falls to the police and their lack of proper training to adequately deal with cases involving mentally ill persons. Most of the previously mentioned fatal incidents could have been prevented if the police departments had offered special training to their police officers for properly handling cases involving mentally ill persons or if the police departments had special crisis intervention teams ready to respond to those cases.

Crisis Intervention Team Program

Frequently, the police officers are the first source of contact with the criminal justice system for most cases involving mentally ill persons (Teller, Munetz, & Ritter, 2006). Thus, how the police respond to these cases can have a tremendous impact on the resolution of the encounters and the future well-being of individuals with mental illness. Given the importance of the role police play in dealing with mentally ill persons, a number of specialized police response programs have been developed to assist officers in better handling and resolving encounters that involve persons with mental illness, such as crisis intervention team (CIT), mobile crisis team (MCT), and hostage negotiation team (HNT) programs, just to name a few. However, for the purpose of this chapter, the focus will be directed to CIT program and its success in addressing the issue of mental illness as it implicates the police.

The CIT was first established in Memphis, Tennessee, in 1988 after an individual with a history of mental disorder was shot dead by a police officer. The CIT program is a specialized unit that is staffed by police officers with special training in mental health issues. The CIT units usually receive about 40 hours of intensive educational training provided by local mental health professionals, family advocates, and mental health consumer groups (Teller et al., 2006; Vickers, 2000). Additionally, the CIT program support partnerships between the psychiatric emergency departments and police departments, thus, increasing the likelihood that mentally ill persons are taken to medical facilities rather than jails (Compton, Esterberg, McGee, Kotwicki, & Oliva, 2006). In other words, persons who suffer from a mental illness are recognized as being mentally ill and not as criminals. By recognizing the fact that mental illness is a disease and not a crime, the police will be able to treat the mentally ill persons in a way that will minimize the use of force or in many instances the use of deadly force.

Evidently, CIT has been shown to be quite successful in dealing with mentally ill persons. Several empirical studies have focused on the evaluation of the effectiveness of CIT programs. Bower and Pettit's (2001) study, for example, shows that in New Mexico in 1999 the CIT officers responded to 3,257 calls, an average of 271 calls per month. Almost half of the calls (45%) resulted in transporting individuals to a local mental health facility rather than jails. Furthermore, this study shows that injuries to citizens (with mental problems) during the CIT contacts occurred in only a little over 1% of the calls. Compton et al. (2006) noted that CIT programs are rapidly expanding across the nation. In fact, because of the evidence that shows the effectiveness of CIT program, some police departments seek to train approximately 20% of their police forces.

Teller et al. (2006) evaluated the effectiveness of a CIT program that was implemented by the Arkon Police Department in Ohio. In their study, they found that after the implementation of the CIT program the overall rates of transporting persons with mental illness to jail decreased significantly. In other words, the officers who had received the CIT training were more likely to transport persons with mental illness to the treatment facilities rather than jails (Teller et al., 2006, pp. 232–235). According to Hails and Borum (2003), CIT program identifies the officers with the greatest interest, most amendable attitudes, and best interpersonal skills and then provides them with intensive training and deploys them specifically as a first-line response to those specialized calls. Thus, according to Hails and Borum, programs such as CIT have the potential to reduce unnecessary arrest and the use of force; rather, in collaboration with mental health services, the police transport mentally ill offenders to designated facilities where they can get the proper treatment rather than punishment.

In summation, special police training programs such as CIT have several objectives and the outcome measures showing that those police departments that have implemented programs such as CIT are more effective in dealing with mentally ill people. As a result, they have minimized police use of force, resulting in reduction of injuries to the police and the mentally ill persons alike, have established proactive intervention to deter crisis-related events from possible undesirable outcomes, and, most importantly, have created partnerships between mental health agencies and the police.

Criminal Justice and Mental Health Services Partnerships

Now that we are aware of the fact that the problem of mentally ill persons has inevitably become part of policing, it is necessary to find avenues to effectively deal with it. In the previous section I argued that the positive outcome of having the police forces trained in dealing with mentally ill persons is promising. Furthermore, if the police officers receive some type of training that is specifically designed to prepare them in dealing with the mentally ill, it will prevent the escalation of the use of force and, in many cases, the use of deadly force. As discussed earlier, in the past, because of lack of police training, a number of cases have resulted in tragedies. Programs such as CIT have been purposefully design to prevent problems that may unnecessarily result in tragedies. Moreover, many individuals with mental illness unnecessarily enter the criminal justice, a system that is not well prepared or designed to handle cases involving mentally ill persons or give them the appropriate treatment (Oliva & Compton, 2008). Individuals with mental illness who unnecessarily enter the criminal justice system need psychiatric treatment, and this requires a partnership between the police departments, mental health systems, and consumers of mental health services, namely, the mentally ill people and their families. Fortunately, the need to act—by developing programs that involve more than just criminal justice agencies—has not fallen on deaf ears. Since 1988 when the CIT was developed in Memphis, many law enforcement agencies have followed this lead and have developed programs that are specifically designed to better handle persons with mental illness.

Reiteratively, the CIT is a police-based specialized response team that deals with persons who have some mental illness and act out violently. The general idea of the CIT program is to improve the nature of the response to those individuals while ensuring the correct nature of their decisions (Seller et al., 2005). Based on the findings of the research studies presented here, it appears, at least in principle, that CIT is effective and a necessary tool in dealing with mentally ill persons (Bower & Pettit, 2001; Compton et al., 2006; Hails & Borum, 2003; Teller et al., 2006). However, it largely depends on the resources that (the stakeholders) the mental health system (since they are largely responsible for shifting the problem of mental illness from being a problem of mental health institutions to becoming a problem of the police) and the criminal justice system are willing to allocate in further developing this program. Needless to say, a healthy collaboration between the criminal justice system—the police in particular—and the mental health system is for the well-being of the mentally ill persons and the community itself, for a healthier and civilized society. Furthermore, with the investment of and partnership among each community's stakeholder, the objectives of programs such as CIT will be feasible.

The society is responsible for creating or inflating the problem of police–mentally ill encounters. Therefore, it follows that the society is responsible for taking responsibilities to ensure that mentally ill people are treated humanely.

References

Abramson, M. F. (1972). The criminalization of mentally disordered behavior: Possible side-effects of a new mental health law. *Hospital and Community Psychiatry, 23*, 101–105.

Amnesty International USA. (1999). *Mentally ill or homeless: Vulnerable to police abuse*. Retrieved December 20, 2008 from http://www.amnesty.org/en/library/asset/AMR51/147/1999/en/735f2b8c-e038-11dd-865a-d728958ca30a/amr511471999en.pdf

Becker, H. (1963). *Outsiders: Studies in the sociology of deviance*. New York: Free Press.

Bonovitz, J. C., & Bonovitz, J. S. (1981). Diversion of the mentally ill into the criminal justice system: The police intervention perspective. *American Journal of Psychiatry, 138*(7), 973–976.

Bower, D. L., & Pettit, G. W. (2001). The Albuquerque police department's crisis intervention team: A report card. *FBI Law Enforcement Bulletin, 70*(2), 1–60.

Chaiklin, H. (2004). Current and prior mental health treatment of jail inmates: The use of the jail as an alternative shelter. *Journal of Social Distress and Homeless, 10*(3), 255–268.

Cohen, L., & Freeman, H. (1945). How dangerous to the community are State hospital patients? *Connecticut State Medical Journal, 9*, 697–700.

Compton, M. T., Esterberg, M. L., McGee, R., Kotwicki, R. J., & Oliva, J. R. (2006). Crisis intervention team training: Changes in knowledge, attitudes, and stigma related to schizophrenia. *Psychiatric Services, 57*(8), 1199–1202.

Compton, M. T., Bahora, M., Watson, A. C., & Oliva, J. R. (2008). A comprehensive review of extant research on crisis intervention team (CIT) programs. *Journal of American Academy of Psychiatry and Law, 36*, 47–55.

Dodge, M., & Shreiber, T. (2009). The challenges of policing the mentally ill: An exploration of gendered and ungendered perspectives. In R. L. Gido & L. Dalley (Eds.), *Women's mental health issues across the criminal justice system* (pp. 71–83). Prentice Hall.

Durbin, J. R., Pasewark, R. A., & Albers, D. (1977). Criminality and mental illness: A study of arrest rates in a rural state. *American Journal of Psychiatry, 134,* 80–84.

Erickson, P. E., & Erickson, S. K. (2008). *Crime, punishment, and mental illness: Law and behavioral sciences in conflict.* New Brunswick, NJ: Rutgers University Press.

Florez, J. A., Holley, H. L., & Crisanti, A. (1996). *Mental illness and violence: Proof or Stereotype?* Ontario: Public Health Agency of Canada.

Gottfredson, M. R., & Hirschi, T. (1990). *A general theory of crime.* Stanford, CA: Stanford University Press.

Hails, J., & Borum, R. (2003). Police training and specialized approaches to respond to people with mental illnesses. *Crime & Delinquency, 49,* 52–61.

Hiday, V. A. (1995). The social context of mental illness and violence. *Journal of Health and Social Behavior, 36,* 122–137.

Hodgins, S., & Cote, G. (1993). The criminality of mentally disordered offenders. *Criminal Justice and Behavior, 20*(2), 115–129.

Hunt, R. (2008). *Introduction to community-based nursing.* New York: Lippincott Williams and Wilkins.

Kifner, J. (1999 November 2). No charges against officers in fatal Brooklyn shooting. *New York Times,* p. 1, B1.

Laberge, D., & Morin, D. (1995). The overuse of criminal justice dispositions: Failure of diversionary policies in the management of mental health problems. *International Journal of Law and Psychiatry, 18*(4), 389–414.

Lamb, H. R. (2000). The 1978 APA conference on the chronic mental patient: A defining moment. *Psychiatric Services, 51,* 874–878.

Lamb, H. R., & Bachrach, L. L. (2001). Some perspectives on deinstitutionalization, *Psychiatric Services, 52,* 1039–1045.

Lamb, H. R., & Weinberger, L. E. (1998). Persons with severe mental illness in jails and prisons. *Psychiatric Services, 49,* 483–492.

Lemert, E. M. (1972). *Human deviance, social problems, and social control,* 2nd ed. Englewood Cliffs, NJ: Prentice-Hall.

Lurgio, A. J., & Swartz, J. A. (2002). Changing the contours of the criminal justice system to meet the needs of persons with serious mental illness. *Policies, Processes, and Decisions of the Criminal Justice System, 3,* 45–108.

Monahan, J. (1992). Mental disorder and violent behavior: Perceptions and evidence. *American Psychologist 47*(4), 511–521.

Oliva, J. R., & Compton, M. T. (2008). A statewide crisis intervention team (CIT) initiative: Evaluation of the Georgia CIT program. *Journal of the American Academy of Psychiatry and the Law, 36,* 38–46.

Paternoster, R., & Iovanni, L. (1989). The labeling perspective and delinquency: An elaboration of the theory and an assessment of the evidence. *Justice Quarterly, 6*(3), 359–393.

Robkin, J. G. (1979). Criminal behavior of discharged mental patients: A critical appraisal of the research. *Psychological Bulletin, 86*(1), 1–27.

Ratansi, S. (2004). *Specialized response programs: Police handling of encounters involving persons with mental disorders.* Unpublished dissertation, University of Cincinnati.

Sellers, C. L., Sullivan, C. J., Veysey, B. M., & Shane, J. M. (2005). Responding to persons with mental illnesses: Police perspectives on specialized and traditional practices. *Behavioral Sciences and the Law, 23,* 647–657.
Steadman, H. J., Deane, M. W., Borum, R., & Morrissey, J. P. (2000). Comparing outcomes of major models of police responses to mental health emergencies. *Psychiatric Services, 51*(5), 645–649.
Stolen Lives Project. (2004). Retrieved January 20, 2009 from http://www.reclaiming-quarterly.org/web/metreon/index.html
Sullivan, G., Burnam, A., & Koegel, P. (2000). Pathways to homelessness among the mentally ill. *Social Psychiatry and Psychiatric Epidemiology, 35*(10), 444–450.
Talbott, J. A. (1979). Deinstitutionalization: Avoiding the disaster of the past. *Hospital and Community Psychiatry, 30*(9), 621–624.
Teller, J. L., Munetz, M. R., & Ritter, C. (2006). Crisis intervention team training for police officers responding to mental disturbance calls. *Psychiatric Services, 57*(2), 232–237.
Teplin, L. A. (1983). The criminalization of mentally ill: Speculation in search of data. *Psychological Bulletin, 94,* 54–69.
Teplin, L. A. (1985). The criminality of the mentally ill: A dangerous misconception. *American Journal of Psychiatry, 142,* 593–599.
Teplin, L. A. (1990). The prevalence of severe mental disorder among mail urban jail detainees: Comparison with the epidemiologic catchments area program. *American Journal of Public Health, 15,* 139–156.
Teplin, L. A., & Pruett, N. S. (1992). Police as street-corner psychiatrist: Managing the mentally ill. *International Journal of Law and Psychiatry, 15,* 139–156.
Tyson, K., & Carroll, E. (2001). Innovative therapeutic care for homeless, mentally ill clients: Intrapsychic humanitarian in a residential setting. *Journal of Contemporary Human Services, 8*(6), 591–603.
Vickers, B. (2000). *Memphis, Tennessee, police department's crisis intervention team.* Washington, DC: Bureau of Justice Assistance.

8 Protecting Vulnerable Young People in Cyberspace From Sexual Abuse

Raising Awareness and Responding Globally[1]

JULIA C. DAVIDSON
University of Westminster

ELENA MARTELLOZZO
University of Westminster

Contents

The Context of Online Abuse

Internet use has grown considerably over the last 5 years, and information technology (IT) now forms a core part of the formal education system in many

[1] Reprinted with permission from Taylor & Francis, Ltd.

countries, ensuring that each new generation of Internet users is more adept than the last. Research conducted in the United Kingdom by Livingstone and Bober (2004) suggested that the majority of young people aged 9–19 accessed the Internet at least once a day. The Internet provides the opportunity to interact with friends on social networking sites such as MySpace and Bebo and enables young people to access information in a way that previous generations would not have thought possible. It also allows users to post detailed personal information, which may be accessed by any site visitor and provides a platform for peer communication hitherto unknown. There is however, increasing evidence that the Internet is used by some adults to access children and young people to "groom" them for the purposes of sexual abuse; MySpace expelled 29,000 convicted sex offenders and is being sued in the United States by parents who claim that their children were contacted by sex offenders on the site and consequently abused (BBC Online, 2007). The Internet also plays a role in facilitating the production and distribution of indecent illegal images of children (Davidson & Martellozzo, 2005; Quayle & Taylor, 2003).

Internet sex offender behavior can include the construction of sites to be used for the exchange of information, experiences, and indecent images of children; the organization of criminal activities that seek to use children for prostitution purposes and that produce indecent images of children at a professional level; and the organization of criminal activities that promote sexual tourism. Indecent images of children are frequently shared by sex offenders using the Internet, and the industry in such images is becoming increasingly large and lucrative (Wyre, 2003). Taylor, Holland, and Quayle (2001) suggest that some online sex offenders are "collectors" of indecent images of children who routinely swap images with other collectors. It is also suggested that these images come from photographs taken by people known to the children such as members of their family (interview, Metropolitan Police HTCU; interview, Quayle, 2006) although at present there is little empirical evidence to support this claim and more research is needed. Quayle and Taylor (2003) comment on the possible motivations of online child sex abusers. It is suggested that sex offenders perceive the Internet as a means of generating an immediate solution to their fantasies. Factors including presumed anonymity, disinhibition, and ready accessibility undoubtedly encourage offenders to go online. Quayle and Taylor also acknowledge, however, that the unique structure of the Internet may play a major role in facilitating online child abuse. Recent research conducted with practitioners from the National Probation Service suggests that sex offenders' Internet use is frequently not limited to abuse and that the Internet often plays a significant role in other areas of their lives, including networking with other adults and online shopping, for example (Davidson, 2007).

Legislation and Protecting Children Online

Recent legislation has sought to protect young people from Internet abuse through the introduction of a *grooming* clause. This new offense category was introduced in the Sexual Offences Act of 2003 in England and Wales (this section of the act also applies to Northern Ireland):[2] Section 15 makes "meeting a child following sexual grooming" an offense and applies to the Internet, other technologies such as mobile phones, and the real world. Grooming involves a process of socialization during which an offender seeks to interact with a child (a young person under 18 in Scotland, England, and Wales), possibly sharing their hobbies and interests in an attempt to gain trust to prepare them for sexual abuse. Several countries are beginning to follow the United Kingdom in legislating against grooming behavior. Sexual grooming has also recently been added to the Crimes Amendment Act of 2005 in New Zealand. In the United States it is an offense to electronically transmit information about a child aged 16 or under for the purpose of committing a sexual offense (US Code Title 18, Part 1, Chapter 117, AS 2425). The Australian Criminal Code (s218A) makes similar restrictions as does the Canadian Criminal Code (s172.1). The legislation in the United Kingdom differs in that the sexual grooming offense applies both to the Internet and to the real world; legislation in other countries addresses only electronic grooming via the Internet and mobile phones.

The concept of sexual grooming has been drawn from the sex offender literature, where it is well documented (Finkelhor, 1984), into legislation and is now filtering into policy and crime detection and prevention initiatives. Considerable efforts have already been made to increase online child protection internationally. The G8 countries[3] have agreed to a strategy to protect children from sexual abuse on the Internet. Key aims include the development of an international database of offenders and victims to aid victim identification and offender monitoring and the targeting of those profiting from the sale of indecent images of children. Internet service providers and credit card companies, such as the UK's Association for Payment Clearing Services, have also joined the international movement against the production and distribution of sexually abusive images of children online.

[2] The Sexual Offences Act of 2003 (England and Wales) is currently under review in Northern Ireland. Some concerns have been raised regarding a lack of clarity around the age of consent and informed consent. Currently the age of consent is 17 in Northern Ireland (it was raised from 16 to 17 under the Children and Young Persons Act of 1950). NI Office, July 2006.

[3] The G8 Countries are the seven most developed economies in the world (plus Russia): America, Britain, Canada, France, Germany, Italy, Japan, and Russia.

Their efforts have focused primarily on attempting to trace individuals who use credit cards to access illegal sites containing indecent images of children. There has also been an attempt to put mechanisms into place that would prevent online payment for illegal sites hosted outside the United Kingdom.

Organizations like the Virtual Global Taskforce (VGT), the Internet Watch Foundation (IWF),[4] and the Centre Exploitation and Online Protection Centre (CEOP) in the United Kingdom are making some headway in attempting to protect children online. VGT is an organization that comprises several international law enforcement agencies from Australia, Canada, the United States, the United Kingdom, and Interpol. Through the provision of advice and support to children, VGT aims to protect children online and has recently set up a bogus website to attract online groomers. Many police forces in the European Union, Canada, and the United States are working to trace Internet sex offenders and their victims. In the United Kingdom, National and local high-technology crime units currently investigate the grooming of children on the Internet and indecent online images of children. Successful prosecutions have been brought under the acts in the United Kingdom, both for grooming online and for the possession of indecent Internet images on the Internet following Operation Ore. This operation was launched following information provided to the UK police by the Federal Bureau of Investigation (FBI) in the United States regarding peer-to-peer technology in sharing indecent images of children. The National Crime Squad has made several thousand convictions since 2002 under Operation Ore.

Educational Context of Internet Safety

Police–School Partnerships

Children and young people make extensive use of the Internet using interactive services such as games, chat rooms, and instant messages. Calder (2003) emphasizes the importance of encouraging appropriate and safe use of the Internet by assisting children and young people to

[4] Recent statistics produced by the IWF suggest that 615 reports of Internet abuse were received during their first year of operation (1996), compared to 27,750 reports in 2006 (85% of which related to suspected child abuse websites). During the 10 year period, 31,000 websites have been found to contain potentially illegal child abuse images. It is claimed that the number of reported websites containing illegal child abuse images has fallen in the UK from 18% in 1996 to 0.2% in 2006. A breakdown of countries where websites containing child abuse images appear to have been hosted during the period 1996-2006 is provided by the IWF who suggest that: 51% of sites were hosted in the United States, 20% in Russia, 5% in Japan, 7% in Spain, and 1.6% in the United Kingdom (Internet Watch Foundation, October 2006).

feel comfortable navigating the information highway. Technology, it is suggested, should be combined with education to raise awareness among children, parents, and teachers and to promote effective interagency partnership working.

Some researchers have suggested that all children should undertake life skills education programs at school on appropriate and inappropriate sexual behavior (Anderson, 2003) that could incorporate Internet safety. This study suggests that not enough is currently being done in the United Kingdom to educate children about sexual abuse or to safeguard them from the dangers of the Internet. Indeed, the Institute for Public Policy Research (2004) suggests that there is a need for greater cooperation among the government, the police, and schools in properly protecting children from sexual abuse. With the explosion of illegal child abuse images over the Internet and the increased and inherent difficulty from a legislative point of view in identifying and successfully prosecuting offenders it becomes imperative that a strong educational focus on safety-proofing children against such images, as much as possible, is where governments should place emphasis. In other words, the focal point should be the management of the "online environment" in which children can potentially be "trapped" and become victims through risk of being exposed to abusive images or to being groomed.

The field of knowledge management (KM; Prusak, 2001; Wiig, 2000) has much to offer in this regard. KM by its very nature is a field made up of many disciplines from information technology, information science, and artificial intelligence through to business, management, and organizational studies to social, group, educational, cognitive psychology, and some areas of philosophy (Barclay & Murray, 2000).

For our purposes here what is important from a KM perspective is the view that knowledge cannot be managed (Anderson, 2003; Brown & Duguid, 2001; Chia, 2003; Tsoukas & Mylonopoulos, 2003; Tsoukas and Vladimirou, 2001) in the mechanistic way envisioned by IT hardware and software systems and by the addition of parental control techniques to software and hardware. Rather, the only thing that can be managed is the context in which knowledge occurs (Dean & Gottschalk, 2007). It is suggested that it is preferable to raise awareness among young people about the potential dangers they may encounter online than to attempt to monitor their online behavior. This point is particularly relevant for teenage users who may resent any such action and who may well have sufficient computing knowledge to disable any such controls.

Hence, a strategic partnership between police and educational agencies like schools and parent groups forms part of the online environmental context that must be managed well through establishing quality safety programs for children and young people. Therefore, this study sought to explore the extent to which the first interactive Internet UK safety program designed by the Metropolitan Police was effective in raising children's knowledge about Internet safety.

The Metropolitan Police Safer Surfing Program

The Metropolitan Police program differs from other educational Internet programs in that it is interactive and delivered directly to children in schools. The program was designed in 2002 for use with 12–14-year-old[5] children as this age group has been identified as active, independent users of the Internet (O'Connell, 1993). The program has the following aims:

- Encourage safe use of Internet chat rooms and interactive games among school children
- Outline the potential dangers of talking online to virtual friends via an interactive session
- Educate children about strategies for safe use of the Internet via an interactive session using a mnemonic (S, Secrets don't keep them; A, Attachments don't open them; F, False don't believe them; E, Exit don't stay there; R, Remember public chat rooms and no personal details)
- Educate children about the dangers of opening attachments coming from unreliable sources as they may be containing illegal and damaging material
- Educate parents about safety issues and strategies via educational information and presentations.

The program is interactive and delivered by two Safer Schools Officers to small groups of children in classrooms.[6] The session begins with a short introduction where children are encouraged to discuss their use of the Internet. This is followed by a chat room exercise involving a live link to a Safer Schools Officer in an adjacent room. Children believe they are talking online (via a laptop computer controlled by the Safer Schools Officer) to a 13-year-old child (Nadia). Children are asked to provide questions to put to the fictitious child in the chat room. A link is provided to a website containing information about the fictitious child and the children are asked if they would like to meet her. The children are later introduced to the police officer who played the role of the child.

[5] The program was, however, used with children aged 10-plus.
[6] The program was delivered by Police Safer Schools Officers as part of their routine work and was not therefore labor intensive.

Research Methods

This section of the chapter briefly describes the purposive sample used as well as the nature of the semistructured interviews. The first stage of the research sought to explore the context in which the police and schools work to educate children about sexual abuse and Internet safety. This issue was explored via a literature review and semistructured interviews with a small sample of Safer Schools Police Officers, teachers, and head teachers in London schools ($n = 18$). Findings from this element of the research are clearly limited given the small sample size. The second stage of the research sought to explore children's experiences on the Internet and to evaluate the effectiveness of the Metropolitan Police Safer Surfing Program. A nonrandom, convenience sample of 188 children aged 10–14 participated in observations of program delivery. The observational data provided a valuable insight into program delivery, children's response, and children's Internet use. The research was conducted in nine schools in three London boroughs from March to December 2004. A stratified, convenience sample of children was used to reflect the diversity of the boroughs and the schools. The sample is representative by gender (although boys outnumber girls as one of the participating schools was single sex): 89 (45%) of the children were female, and 111 (55%) were male; in terms of ethnicity, 58 (29%) of the children were Black or Black British, 62 (31%) were White or White British, 39 (20%) were Asian or Asian British, 25 (13%) were of mixed ethnicity, and 16 (8%) were Chinese or other ethnic group.

A total of 200 children were interviewed, 98 not having received the police program and 102 having received the program. Every effort was made to ensure that the children in the preprogram group had not received other Internet safety programs or been instructed about Internet safety by their teachers. It was not possible to ensure that children had similar experience of Internet use in both groups, given that assignment to groups was by necessity largely nonrandom and purposive with the vast majority of children in the age group regularly accessing the Internet on a weekly basis.

The research undertaken with parents is more limited as only one group of 35 parents had received the program during the research period. The 35 parents receiving the program were interviewed regarding its effectiveness. This extent to which children discussed the program with their parents was explored in focus groups with children.

The British Society of Criminology Ethical Code of Conduct in Research (2004) informed the research conduct. Ethical clearance was gained from the University of Westminster Ethics Committee. Informed consent was gained from respondents; assurances about anonymity and confidentiality were given. Written consent for children to participate in the research was gained from their parent or guardian via head teachers before focus group interviews were undertaken.[7]

Results

This section reports on the findings in relation to children's Internet use, their experiences in chat rooms, as well as their views about gender and risk of sexual abuse. Further more, the impact of the Safer Surfing Police Program is also noted.

Children's Internet Use

Children use the Internet a great deal, and this has been well documented in other research (Livingstone, 2004, 2005; O'Connell, 2003). According to ICAC (2000) more than 30 million children in the United States alone use the Internet. A report on the Nation's Youth (2004) suggests that 1 in 4 children on the Internet had an unwanted exposure to sexually explicit pictures that were inappropriate for children to view. Approximately 1 in 5 received a sexual solicitation or approach; 1 in 17 was threatened or harassed; 1 in 33 received an aggressive sexual solicitation (from someone who asked to meet them somewhere, called them on the telephone, sent them regular mail, money, or gifts).

The children interviewed in this research were enthusiastic Internet users and enjoyed discussing the topic. Older children in the sample (12+) tended to use chat rooms and interactive games and chat facilities such as MySpace and MSN Messenger. Younger children (10–11) tended to play secure games on websites such as Disney's Toontown and were much less familiar with peer-to-peer networks. All of the children used the Internet for research and homework and were actively encouraged to do so at school. Given that some of the younger children (10–11) had no experience with chat rooms and did not understand how they function, it may be better to target educational programs addressing Internet safety with the 12-plus age group, whose members are actively involved in chatting online, or to adapt such programs for younger children. There is some research evidence to suggest that older

[7] None of the children interviewed disclosed sexual abuse; this would have given rise to difficulty with the notion of absolute confidentiality, due to concerns over child protection. In past work with adult offenders, respondents have been informed at the outset of any research interview that such disclosure would be reported, which is good research practice. But it was decided here that such a statement would alarm the children. Had any such disclosures been made they would have been reported to the head teacher, and this would have been discussed with the child in private at the end of the focus group.

children retain such information more effectively and are more able to act upon it (Tutty, 1997).

The majority of children (130, or 65%) had access to at least one computer at home, and 97 (49%) had computers in their bedrooms. Other children did not have a computer at home but had access to a computer at relatives' or friends' houses, and 30 (15%) used Internet cafes on a regular basis (more than once per week). The findings suggest that almost all of the children had access to the Internet outside school. A total of 120 (60%) accessed the Internet more than four times per week; this was particularly true of the 12–14 age group. Of those children accessing the Internet, 91(76%) were largely unsupervised and spent long periods of time on their computer particularly during school holidays and on weekends. The children's comments illustrate this point:

"I use the Internet a lot when I'm on holiday" (FGl).
"My mum and dad do not know anything about computers so I can do pretty much what I want" (FG2).
"My parents trust me; I'm not silly and I know what to do on there" (FG20).
"I don't want them [parents] watching me; I can do what I want" (FG3).

A total of 71 (36%) said that their parents knew little about computers:

"My mum is so bad at computers I can do what I like" (FG15).
"We know much more than they [parents] do about computing" (FG3).

Generally the children had a great deal of knowledge about computing, and the majority of 12–14-year-olds were extremely confident Internet users.

Children's Experiences in Chat Rooms

Children were questioned about their interactions in chat rooms, and 25 (13%) reported occasions where they believed they or a friend or relative had been talking to an adult posing as a child. On several occasions this was clear as the person's Internet profile revealed their real age. A small number of the children (10, or 5%) had been approached in a chat room regarding sex and had told their parents; they reported feeling uncomfortable and uncertain about to whom they were talking. The children made the following comments:

"I met a pervert in a chat room and told my mum" (FG3).
"I met someone who wasn't what they said they were." Q. What did they say? "They pretended to be a kid; I didn't think they were" (FG4).
"Someone asked me if I did sex; I exited and told my mum" (FG6).

The majority of children (140, or 70%) claimed that they would always know if they were talking to a child as children use a unique computer slang online that adults would not be able to understand and would not use:

> "Children use words that aren't formal, like slang. So you'd be able to tell if someone was lying" (FG4).
> "Teenagers always talk a certain way; I'd be able to tell if it's an adult" (FG13).
> "They [children] use texting words; they shorten them because it's easier" (FG14).
> "I would be able to tell unless they said something odd" (FG24).

The children having received the police program did appear to have a greater amount of awareness about this issue:

> "They could have learned how to talk in this way" (FG2).
> "Some people pretend to be your friends" (FG15).
> "People on the Internet may not be what they seem" (FG2).

Children's Views About Gender and Risk of Sexual Abuse

A question about risk of sexual abuse and gender was added to the interview schedule after it had been raised on several occasions and was clearly an emergent theme. The vast majority (140, or 70%)[8] believed that girls were much more at risk. The children's comments illustrate this point:

> "Those people pick on girls, and boys can handle themselves better" (FG3).
> "Boys have more self-defense, and they [sex offenders] prefer girls" (FG4).
> "Most boys are big and can look after themselves; boys will fight and run away" (FG10).
> "Those men like girls not boys" (FG10).
> "Boys are rough and strong and know how to defend themselves" (FG13).
> "Boys are much stronger than girls; they know how to run away and avoid risk" (FG14).

The children seemed to use gender stereotypes in explaining why girls are more at risk of sexual abuse. Girls were described as weaker and boys as stronger and more able to defend themselves. The quotes demonstrate that the children often noted that men seem to perpetrate this type of offense and would therefore target girls. Several children also noted that most cases

[8] Children in the postprogram group were less likely to believe this, with 50% (51) agreeing that girls are more at risk compared to 91% (89) in the preprogram group.

covered by the media involve the sexual abuse of girls. While it is the case that males perpetrate the vast majority of sexual abuse[9] against female victims,[10] it seems important to reinforce the point with children that boys are also at risk.

Impact of the Safer Surfing Police Program

Some of the children not having received the police program had a basic understanding about the dangers of chat rooms (38, or 34%). This knowledge is, however, very limited, and when the children were questioned further it was clear that some of them would be willing to provide personal information and on some occasions meet with an online acquaintance:

> "I would trust people after speaking online with them for a while, perhaps after 2 weeks, and then I'd know they were OK and would meet them" (FG24).
>
> "It would be alright if you met them out where there were lots of other people around" (FG20).
>
> "If they tell you to meet in a busy place then they are friends; if they ask you to meet at the back somewhere then that's scary and you shouldn't go" (FG23).

This finding is confirmed by Livingstone's (2005) survey of a large sample of children, where 46% were willing to provide personal information to online acquaintances, and this percentage increased considerably when children were asked if they would provide personal details when entering an online competition for a prize.

Although children in the postprogram group did not always recall the safer mnemonic, they did appear to be much more knowledgeable about safety strategies (80% mentioned safety strategies during interviews compared with 34% in the preprogram group). The postprogram group also appeared much more knowledgeable about the dangers of private chat rooms. Some of these children mentioned the benefits of staying in public chat areas:

> "You could be in a public chat room and they might suggest going into a private chat room; this is all right if you'd met." Q. Why not if you haven't met? "Because they might not be telling the truth" (FG9).

[9] A study of 60,991 sexual assault victims conducted in the United States suggests that male sex offenders were the perpetrators in 96% of cases (Snyder, 2000, p. 8).

[10] Rennison (2002) suggests in her analysis of U.S. crime statistics that females were the victims of 89% of all reported sexual assaults between 1992 and 2000.

> "In private chat rooms they can say what they like, but other people listen in public chat rooms" (FG11).

Children in this group also raised an important point about using a false personal identity online in order to protect themselves:

> "We go into chat rooms to meet different children who we don't know, but I don't tell who I really am" (FG11).

The preprogram group did not raise these issues.

Children having received the program appeared much more knowledgeable about Internet dangers, and the majority of the children had clearly learned the key program messages and were able to discuss safety strategies. It would seem that children have some basic knowledge about the possible dangers of chatting online gained from peers and from news coverage:

> "It's just what you hear on the news" (FG11).
> "You know about Jessica and Holly[11]; we saw what happened on TV" (FG29) (reference to the Soham Case).

The police program served to reinforce this and to educate the children about safety strategies. It is however of concern that the children in this study did not appear to have discussed the program with their parents. Only 32 (31%) of the postprogram group children had informed their parents about the police program, and few had given the leaflet to their parents. Parents and careers form an important part of the safety loop, and they must be included if the program is to have any lasting impact upon the children.

Discussion

This study explored the impact of a police program designed to educate children about online safety and the extent to which teachers informally and formally educate secondary and primary school children about sexual abuse both in the real world and in cyberspace. The research demonstrates that teachers felt untrained in this sensitive area, which is more usually addressed by Safer Schools Police Officers. UNICEF (2005) suggests that teachers should be educating children about sexual abuse as part of their general sexuality education. However, this is a sensitive area, and the delivery of such education

[11] The respondent's reference to "Jessica & Holly" refers to a widely publicized case in the UK involving the abduction and murder of two children in Soham in August 2002 by a known sex offender working as a school caretaker.

is dependent upon building teachers' confidence and understanding through effective training in collaboration with the police. While there are some difficult areas to confront given that much sexual abuse is perpetrated by people known to children and often from within their immediate families, this is an important aspect of crime prevention. There are clearly enormous benefits to be gained from systematically informing parents about their children's sex education and strategies for safety.

Some teachers believed that sexual abuse and Internet safety should be covered in the national curriculum. However, it is possible that the Department for Education and Skills (DFES), which leads government work to ensure that all children and young people stay healthy and safe, receive an education, and the highest possible standards of achievement and live a safe and healthy childhood (http://www.dfes.gov.uk), may issue such guidance in future.

Teachers welcomed the involvement of Safer Schools Police Officers on this topic, suggesting that presentations on sensitive issues such as sexual abuse delivered by the police had a greater impact upon the children than those given by teachers:

> "If we try and teach them about abuse and staying safe on the Internet they probably will not listen, I'm not saying we shouldn't, but we need training really and we need the police to support us with this sort of program. I think we need to be working with the police on this one" (R9).

The Safer Schools Police Officers were largely very positive about their role in educating children about sexual abuse but saw it as rather limited to short classroom-based sessions. Police officers particularly liked the interactive nature of the Safer Surfing program and thought this element had a real impact upon the children.

Teachers emphasized the importance of taking the social and cultural context into account when educating children about sexual abuse and safety. It was suggested that police officers working in this context would have to consider the possibility that they may be working with vulnerable children, who are sexually aware and sexually experienced and who may have been sexually abused. This would presumably also apply to any teacher raising issues about sexual abuse in the context of lessons.

Intervention programs operate successfully in the context of the formal education system in other countries. For example, in New Zealand the Keeping Ourselves Safe (KOS) program was developed by the police and the Department of Education and is delivered to all children in schools by trained teachers, and the police also have a significant input to this program. Other similar programs are operating in the United States; the Safe-T program, for example, operates in middle and junior schools in Vermont and aims to prevent sexual victimization and to promote healthy relationships in young people (http://www.pcavt.org). Some research suggests that such programs are successful in raising knowledge levels among children (Briggs, 1991). Others have suggested that older children (8+) are better able to act on such knowledge (Tutty, 1997).

In the United States, the Internet Crime Against Children (ICAC) Task Force has created a program to help both children and parents to understand the importance of the Internet but also the danger that may be encountered while using it. The program has been developed by NetSmartz Workshop. NetSmartz is an interactive, educational safety resource from the National Center for Missing and Exploited Children and Boys & Girls Clubs of America (BGCA) that uses age-appropriate, 3-D activities to teach children and teens how to be safer when using the Internet. NetSmartz has been implemented in more than 3,000 BGCA Clubs nationally, serving more than 3.3 million young people.

The program provides parents, children, and teachers with an overview of online risks. More recently the CEOP has designed an Internet safety presentation that is delivered to children in the United Kingdom. The *Getting It Right* presentation was evaluated by Wishart et al. (2005), who found that children's awareness of key safety issues rose following the presentation. No follow-up work has been conducted but is planned.

Parental controls and firewalls can also be set up on home computers, but a degree of technical knowledge is needed to do so. This research and O'Connell's (2003) work demonstrates that parents do not necessarily have this knowledge. While children are well protected on the Internet at school given the knowledge of computing staff and technological advancement in this area, they are most vulnerable at home, and ensuring that parents have some basic knowledge about Internet protection is of paramount importance. This issue could be addressed via a simple leaflet when a home computer is purchased; it could be argued that the dissemination of this information is the responsibility of Internet service providers and companies responsible for the production, sale, and distribution of computing equipment.

The police have worked in primary and secondary schools in the past to educate children about safety and sexual abuse, but it is clear from this study that the challenge is for education providers, Internet service providers, and the police to work together in systematically informing children and their parents about sexual abuse and safety strategies both in cyberspace and in the real world. The findings from this research also suggest that there is a need for governments to provide clear guidance and possibly training for teachers on educating children about sexual abuse; the police and social services should be also involved in this process.

Conclusion

Recent research (Livingstone, 2004, 2005; O'Connell, 2004) has played a key role in raising awareness about children's use of the Internet and online risks as have organizations such as the Virtual Global Taskforce. However, this research suggests that children are not routinely educated about sexual abuse in the context of formal education and are infrequently educated about basic safety online at school in the United Kingdom. The issue is really much wider than online safety; teachers participating in this work have suggested that it seems pointless to warn children about the dangers they may encounter in cyberspace unless this information is imparted in the context of wider education about sexual abuse. Along with the police, schools should play an active role in educating children about sexual abuse and safety strategies in the context of the national curriculum. To do this effectively, training and guidance should be provided for teachers, and such work should involve parents and careers. This research has demonstrated that children who received the Metropolitan Police Safer Surfing program appeared to be more knowledgeable about the dangers they might encounter when online.

This research highlights that the Met Safer Surfing program designed by police is a useful and relatively effective addition to managing the knowledge that children need to know about the online environment to remain safe from prolonged exposure to illegal child abuse imagery on the web.

This police initiative in the United Kingdom to work systematically with schools to educate children about sexual abuse in the real world and in cyberspace has potential to evolve into communities of practice internationally (Alavari & Leidner, 2001).

In the KM literature these communities are made of members who have a professional interest in some area and seek out others with similar interests; hence, a self-organizing type of group evolves over time. This professional interest is largely based on the tacit knowledge of individuals and hence resides in the head (Gottschalk, 2005) and is consequently rarely made explicit or documented to the degree that such tacit knowledge requires to be of value. Such practice links often begin in an informal manner as in working together on a project like the Safer Surfing program and may become formalized at some point. However, the really key point is that what form such a community of practice may take in reality is the richness and depth of the knowledge sharing that takes place in them which is the essential element (Dean & Gottschalk, 2007).

John Carr (2006) in the United Kingdom suggests that international efforts to protect children online are largely failing as the number of indecent images of children on the Internet continues to increase and the images become ever more disturbing, involving a greater degree of violence and increasingly younger children. It is suggested that governments are failing to make the growing trade in indecent images of children a high enough political priority and that the hidden nature of online grooming and lack of public awareness makes this possible. Indeed, other recent research conducted in the United Kingdom suggests that child victimization and protection issues are not a high priority for the criminal justice agencies involved in the investigative process (Davidson, Bifulco, Thomas, & Ramsay, 2006). Carr advocates a global initiative, and key areas are identified where action should be taken. Carr is correct in suggesting that the key issue is one of effective leadership and that a "global leadership mechanism" (p. 1) should be developed. This mechanism, it is suggested, should take the form of a new nongovernmental organization (NGO) or a network that draws on existing NGOs. This central body would act to scrutinize and advise governments, law enforcement agencies, and the industry. It would also provide a hitherto absent degree of IT industry public accountability. This is undeniably an essential move as at present attempts to protect children online are ad hoc, and some international police forces have only just begun to recognize the scale of the problem. Given the way police networks function across international boundaries then the knowledge value of having such an informal network that is supportive of educational awareness programs can only act to enhance the establishment of a more formal international central mechanism as noted to effectively intervene to protect vulnerable children and young people from sex offenders in cyberspace.

References

Alavari, M., & Leidner, D. E. (2001). Knowledge management and knowledge management systems: Conceptual foundations and research issues, *MIS Quarterly, 25*(1), 107–136.

Association of Chief Police Officers. (2004, January 30). Media Literacy and Internet safety report arising from the seminar Internet safety.

Anderson, M. L. (2003). Embodied cognition: A field guide. *Artificial Intelligence, 149*(1), 91–130.

Anderson, W. (2003). Child safety—child sexual abuse—does it affect your child? Retrieved from http://www.health24.w.za(news)child_safety/1-943.23020.asp

Barclay, R., & Murray, P. (2000). What is knowledge management? *Knowledge Praxis.* Retrieved from http://www.media-access.com/whatis.html

BBC Online. (2004). Internet chat danger for children. Retrieved from http://news.bbc.co.uk/1/hi/uk/1222257.stm

BBC Online. (2005). Police research & Internet grooming case. Retrieved from http://news.bbc.co.uk/1/hi/england/london/3177010.stm

BBC Online. (2007). Myspace bars 29,000 sex offenders. Retrieved from http://news.bbc.co.uk/2/hi/technology/6914870.stm

Briggs, F. (1991). Child Protection Programmes: Can they protect young children? *Early Child Development and Care, 67*, 61–72.
Brown, J., & Duguid, P. (2001). Knowledge and organization: A social-practice perspective. *Organization Science, 12*(2), 198–213.
Calder, M. (2003). *Child sexual abuse and the Internet: Tackling new frontiers.* London: Russell House Publishing.
Carr, J. (2006). *Out of sight, out of mind: Tackling child sexual abuse images on the Internet—a global challenge.* NCH, the Children's Charity.
Chia, R. (2003). From knowledge-creation to the perfection of action: Tao, Basho and pure experience as the ultimate ground of knowing. *Human Relations, 56*(8), 953–981.
Children's Charities Coalition for Internet Safety. (2004). *Child safety online: Digital manifesto summary.* NCH. Retrieved from http://www.nch.org.uk/chis
Chase, E., & Statham, J. (2005). Commercial and sexual exploitation of children and young people in the UK—A review. *Child Abuse Review*, 14, 4–25.
Cobley, C. (2005). The legislative framework. In A. Matravers (Ed.), *Sex offenders in the community: Managing and reducing the risks.* Cambridge, UK: Willan Publishing.
Davidson, J. (2004, October 6–9). Child sexual abuse prevention programmes: The role of schools. In O. Giotakos, R. Eher, & F. Pfafflin (Eds.), *Sex offending is everybody's business, 8th International Conference of the International Association for the Treatment of Sexual Offenders.* Pabst: Lengerich House Publishing.
Davidson, J. (2006). Current practice and research into Internet sex offending. Risk Management Authority Scotland (to be published 12/06).
Davidson J., Bifulco, A., Thomas, G., & Ramsay, M. (2006). *Child victims of sexual abuse: Children's experience of the investigative process in the criminal justice system.*
Davidson, J., & Martellozzo, E. (2004). Educating children about sexual abuse and evaluating the Metropolitan Police Safer Surfing Programme. Retrieved from http://www.saferschoolpartnerships.org/ssp-topics/evaluations/documents/ssfindingsreport.pdf
Dean, G., & Gottschalk, P. (2007). *Knowledge management in policing and law enforcement: Foundations, structures, applications.* Oxford, UK: Oxford University Press.
Department for Children Schools and Families. (XXXX). Retrieved from http://www.dfes.gov.uk
Feather, M. (1999). Internet and child victimisation. In J. Stanley (2001) Child abuse and the Internet. *Child Abuse Prevention Issues* Number 15 Summer 2001. (National Child Protection Clearinghouse).
Gallagher, B., Fraser, C., Christmann, K., & Hodgson, B. (2006). *International and Internet child sexual abuse and exploitation.* Centre of Applied Childhood Studies, University of Huddersfield.
Gamble, J. (2006). Retrieved from http://www.ceop.gov.uk/who_is_ceo.html
Gottschalk, P. (2005). *Strategic knowledge management technology*, Hershey, PA: Idea Group Publishing.
Home Office Task Force on Child Protection on the Internet. (2003). Good practice models and guidance for the Internet industry on chat services; instant messages; web based services.
Internet Watch Foundation (2003). Impeding the abuse of credit card services to pay for illegal images online. Retrieved November 30, 2007 from http://www.iwf.org.uk/media/news.archive-2004.15.htm

Internet Watch Foundation. (2006, October 24). *Remove online images of child abuse.* Press release and conference, Central Hall, Westminster, London.
Jewkes, Y. (2006). *Crime on line.* Cambridge, UK: Willan Publishing.
Krone, T. (2005). Combating online child pornography in Australia. In E. Quayle & M. Taylor (Eds.), *Viewing child pornography on the Internet. Understanding the offence, managing the offender, helping the victims.* Dorset, UK: Russell House Publishing.
Livingstone, S. (2005). *UK children go online: Emerging opportunities and dangers.* London School of Economics.
Livingstone, S., & Bober, M. (2004). *UK children go online: Surveying the experiences of young people and their parents.* LSE Academic Publishing.
Livingstone, S., & Bober, M. (2005). *Internet literacy among children and young people.* London School of Economics.
Martellozzo, E. (2004, October 6–9). *Child pornography on the Internet: Police strategies.* In O. Giotakos, R. Eher, & F. Pfafflin (Eds.), *Sex offending is everybody's business, 8th International Conference of the International Association for the Treatment of Sexual Offenders.* Pabst: Lengerich.
O'Connell, R. (2002). Be somebody else but be yourself at all times: Degrees of identity deception in chatrooms. Retrieved from http://www.once.uclan.ac.uk/print/deception_print.htm
Prusak, L. (2001). Where did knowledge management come from? *IBM Systems Journal, 40*(4), 1–5.
Quayle, E., & Taylor, M. (2001). Child seduction and self-representation on the Internet. *Cyberpsychology and Behaviour, 4*(5), 597–607.
Quayle, E., & Taylor, M. (2002). Paedophiles, pornography and the Internet: Assessment issues. *British Journal of Social Work, 32*, 863–75.
Quayle, E., & Taylor, M. (2003) *'Model of problematic Internet use in people with a sexual interest in children.' Cyberpsychology and Behaviour, 6*(1), 93–106.
Readfern, G. (2004, September 29–October 5). Who is she talking to? *Children Now.*
Rennison, C. M. (2002). Rape and sexual assault: Reporting to police and medical attention, 1992–2000. US Department of Justice, Bureau of Justice Statistics. Retrieved from http://www.ojp.usdoj.gov/bjs/abstract/rsarp00.htm Accessed 27/11/2007
Robbins, P., & Darlington, R. (2003). The role of the industry and the Internet Watch Foundation. In MacVean & Spindler (Eds.), *Policing paedophiles on the Internet.* New Police Bookshop.
Snyder, H. (2000). *Sexual assault of young children as reported to law enforcement: Victim, incident, and offender characteristics.* American Bureau of Justice Statistics Clearinghouse.
Tsoukas, H., & Mylonopoulos, N. (2003). Part special issue introduction: Modelling organisational knowledge. *Journal of the Operational Research Society, 54*, 911–913.
Tsoukas, H., & Vladimirou, E. (2001). What is organisational knowledge? *Journal of Management Studies, 38*(7), 973–993.
Tutty, L. M. (1997). Child sexual abuse prevention programmes: Evaluation, what do they tell? *Child Abuse & Neglect, 18*, 179–192.
UNICEF. (2005). Information for teachers: Sexual education. Retrieved from http://www.unicef.org/teachers/protection/prevention.htm

Wiig, K. (2000). Knowledge management: An emerging discipline rooted in a long history. In C. Despres & D. Chauvel (Eds.), *Knowledge horizons: The present and the promise of knowledge management*. Boston: Butterworth-Heinemann.

Wishart et al. (2005). Evaluation of "Getting to know IT all" presentation as delivered in UK schools during November 2005. University of Bristol.

Woolley, C. C. M., & Gabriel, T. C. (1999). Children's concepts of some child sexual abuse prevention concepts. *Australian Journal of Disaster and Trauma Studies, 18*, 16–36.

3

Knowledge Management: Capturing, Sharing, and Sustaining

Patrol Police Officers' Professional Knowledge

An Empirical Study of Knowledge Types in Law Enforcement*

9

STEFAN HOLGERSSON
Linköpings University

PETTER GOTTSCHALK
Norwegian School of Management

Contents

Introduction

The amount of research on police officers' professional knowledge is very limited. Remarks on this subject made by Sweden's only police professor, Leif G. W. Persson,[1] can easily give the impression that professional knowledge is not required, or even present, within the part of the police force that serves in uniform: "It's no bloody intellectual profession. It's basically: 'Get out on

* Reprinted with permission from Taylor & Francis, Ltd.

the streets, get some names and kick some ass.'" This view on the uniformed police is enhanced in detective stories. In these novels, often the work of the uniformed police, this view of the patrol officer is peripheral, as opposed to the work of the detectives, and is more or less ridiculed.

Uniformed patrol police officers need a range of different forms of knowledge together with a flexible intellect to be able to function in a satisfying manner. This chapter argues for the need to classify patrolling police officers' professional knowledge. The contribution of the research is to illustrate the wide range of knowledge of police officers.

The Literature on Patrol Officers

Kirkham (1974), an American criminologist who worked as a uniformed police officer during a period of time, writes in an article titled "From Professor to Patrolman" that as a criminology professor he always enjoyed the luxury of having great amounts of time in which to make difficult decisions. As a police officer, however, he found himself forced to make the most critical choices in a time frame of seconds rather than a day. He found himself progressively awed by the complexity of tasks faced by individuals whose work he once thought was fairly simple and straightforward (Kirkham, 1974). Another American professor, Goldstein (1967), emphasized that a police officer must be able to make highly sophisticated judgments that have a great impact on the lives of the involved persons. These kinds of judgments are not made mechanically and are at least as difficult to make as, for example, those a researcher in social sciences has to deal with. Often, a police officer's decisions are more difficult than, for example, those made by a prosecutor or a judge, as a police officer must make decisions under the pressure of the immediate circumstances (Goldstein, 1967).

Norwegian criminology professor Finstad (2000) stated that police work involves criminality control (intervene against criminal actions, carry out controls in case of suspicions), physical work (help injured persons out of car wrecks and burning houses, take care of drunk persons), social work (help exposed children and teenagers, support persons with psychological problems), transportation work (drive prisoners to their cell, deliver documents), service work (open locked car doors), information work (describe the shortest route to the pharmacy, inform tourists about which expositions can be seen at the museum, inform about the opening hours of the passport office), cultural and assignment work (role plays and lectures at schools about traffic safety and drugs), hotel and restaurant work (make sure that prisoners and witnesses have something to eat and drink), office work (write reports), and acting (act in front of the general public in order to create security, law, and order). According to Finstad (2000), the profession of police officer is indeed an intellectual and analyzing occupation, as it involves analyzing different situations and environments as well as making decisions using a broad repertoire of interpretations and actions. Finstad (2000) considered the police profession to be a handicraft—not in the sense of mass production but rather as a form of art handicraft (see also Waddington, 1999). According to Brown (1988), this handicraft is largely based on experience and intuition. Bittner (1972) pointed out that the worrying issue is that police work is not seen as the heavy handicraft it is and that it often is assumed that those who work as police officers do so because they would have problems finding work elsewhere. Bittner believes that police work needs to be addressed and judged in a more serious and analyzing manner.

Bayley (1994) believed that police officers acquire a large knowledge bank. This is especially true for front-line police officers, whose knowledge has been the subject of research on a far too small scale. Practical knowledge is underrated as it usually consists of intuitive, experience-based, inexplicit, and nonsystematized knowledge. By trying to formulate this knowledge it becomes available for persons from outside and possible to develop and spread in words.

Similarly, McElroy (1998) emphasized that police officers must be able to function in different roles. They must be able to plan, solve problems, spread, and gather information, organize cooperations, and coordinate working efforts within a certain area (McElroy, 1998). Last, Broderick (1977) believed that police work in addition contains a large amount of abstract knowledge that shall be applied on specific problems. To be able to do so, according to Broderick, police officers need both theoretical and practical knowledge.

Professional Knowledge

Göranzon (1990, 1998) divides professional knowledge into three different types:

1. Statement knowledge/theoretical knowledge, which refers to principles, theories, methods, and regulations.
2. Skill knowledge/practical knowledge, which refers to knowledge that is acquired as well as used during the practice of the craft or profession.
3. Familiarity knowledge, which refers to the knowledge attained by being part of a tradition. Göranzon considered the interaction with others within the same profession as crucial for this type of knowledge to emerge.

Several researchers have made similar classifications. Nordenstam (1983), for example, used Wittgenstein's (1953) division of knowledge into three types of groups:

1. Theoretical/scientific knowledge
2. Practical/productive knowledge
3. Knowledge as practical wisdom

Gustavsson (2000) divides knowledge in the same manner. He points out, as does Göranzon (1990, 1998), that during a long period of time theoretical-scientific knowledge was considered the only form of knowledge. This type of knowledge has a long tradition with roots in the Greek antique (see Aristotle). An important principle is the distinction between knowing something with full certainty on one hand and believing and guessing on the other. The second type of knowledge as defined by Gustavsson is practical-productive knowledge. This kind of knowledge stands in close relation to skills and practical abilities, knowledge in practice. Practical wisdom is the third form of knowledge described by Gustavsson. Characteristic for this knowledge type is that the goal of an action at the same time is part of the action. This form of knowledge has a political and ethical dimension, of which the purpose is people's well-being. For example, when building a house, the manufacturing process is separated from the fact that we will live in the house and want it to be designed in a way that gives us a high living standard (Gustavsson, 2000).

Josefson (1991) used another classification of knowledge. She presented different aspects of knowledge instead of different knowledge types. The first aspect consists of statement knowledge and the other of familiarity knowledge. Josefson wrote that these aspects of knowledge are closely related and that the borders are shifting. Familiarity knowledge gives life to the abstract terminology of the statement knowledge. She emphasized that professional knowledge consists of these two aspects, because most people tend to consider knowledge equal to statement knowledge (Josefson 1991).

Rolf (1995) pointed out that researchers like to divide reality into classes, types, and categories. He criticized researchers such as Nordenstam (1983) and Göranzon (1990, 1998) for doing so. He stated that researchers such as Nordenstam (1983) who referred to Wittgenstein's (1953) writings misinterpreted his ideas. Wittgenstein did not try to sort knowledge into different categories, according to Rolf. Wittgenstein's entire philosophy was opposed to the idea of categorizations and classifications. Instead, he wanted to illustrate that knowing something and saying something sometimes overlap with each other and sometimes not.

Research Methodology

The study was mainly qualitative, as it is based on participative observation and interviews with police officers (Holgersson, 2005). This study involved more than 6,000 hours of participant observation and 2,000 interviews, involving all (21) police districts in Sweden, from interviews with police officers in the biggest city in Sweden, Stockholm, with 1.5 million citizens, to snow scooter patrolling in the mountains in the North. The interviews with police officers and participative observation started in the beginning of 1998 and ended in April 2005. Police officers' working performance and varying opportunities of acting in different types of situations was the focus of the study. One of the authors (Holgersson) is, in addition to being a researcher, also an active police officer, which provided good possibilities of getting a close insight in the knowledge need for a police officer.

The approach applied in this research was not strictly inductive, as it contained some deductive elements. Goldkuhl and Cronholm (2003) define a method called multigrounded theory (MGT), which is inspired by grounded theory (see Strauss & Corbin, 1990), but their method also contained deductive elements (see also Cronholm, 2004, 2005; Goldkuhl, 2004).

In addition to studying a number of different types of places, this research also included various types of police officers: new recruits, experienced officers, officers with a special interest in some kind of activity, officers known by other police officers as lazy/high performing, and officers known as "normal" (Patton, 1990).

Most interviews had an informal structure (Patton, 1990), where the interviewed person had ample opportunity to talk freely about the work and explain what he or she thought was important knowledge for being a good officer. Bryman (1997) found that unstructured interviews are effective to use in combination with participative observations because then it is possible to obtain a deeper understanding of a phenomenon.

The study also included participant observation techniques in combination with interviews for a period of 6 months with the same police officers. The intention was to test different types of knowledge and see how it worked, for example, if it was possible to catch more drunk drivers when acting in a special way (Holgersson, 2005).

Results

Police officers' knowledge is an important factor to take in consideration. It's otherwise difficult to get police officers with satisfied performance. A description and definition of this knowledge is essential. This article can be seen as a first step in trying to identify the knowledge of patrolling police officers. Carlström (1999) studied police investigators in the city center of Stockholm and believed that their knowledge is transitory, that is, perishable. It is impermanent and needs to be filled up constantly. When investigators described the process that leads to a suspicion, they used the word *intuition.* A deviation can give them the feeling that something is not right. Their professional knowledge is specific and cannot be generalized or used in other contexts than where it belongs. It is related to place and time and cannot be applied elsewhere. It concerns a specific surrounding, time and context, specific persons, cars, addresses, and crimes. Among patrol or local police officers,[2] there is knowledge that is perishable as well as knowledge that is more or less constant and not as dependent on time and place.[3] The present study confirm this conclusions.

It is normal for knowledge within organizations to be divided into silent (tacit) and explicit knowledge (Goldkuhl, Röstlinger, & Braf, 2001). Nonaka and Takeuchi (1995) and Zack (1999) made such a classification. Schön (1983, 1987) argued that there is a difference between espoused knowledge and knowledge in use. The professional knowledge described in this section consists of different types of knowledge but is always knowledge in use (skill/ability).[4] Often it is not explicit and consists of so-called silent knowledge (see, e.g., Polanyi, 1962; Rolf, 1995). Police officers have different skills and knowledge (Figure 9.1).

Usually there is more than one way to solve a situation (see, e.g., Broderick, 1977), and to reach the best possible solution police officers can use different knowledge areas. A strength within one area can compensate for a weakness in another. When, for example, a police patrol comes across a group of teenagers smoking in the subway, a police officer with good argumentative abilities but not as much authority can use his argumentation skills to persuade them to stop smoking. However, a minimum level of most knowledge areas is required for front-line patrol and local police officers to be able to function in a satisfying manner. If, for example, a police officer has difficulties dealing with his own feelings and therefore becomes too nervous to perform a task or too angry to control himself, advanced skills in other areas become

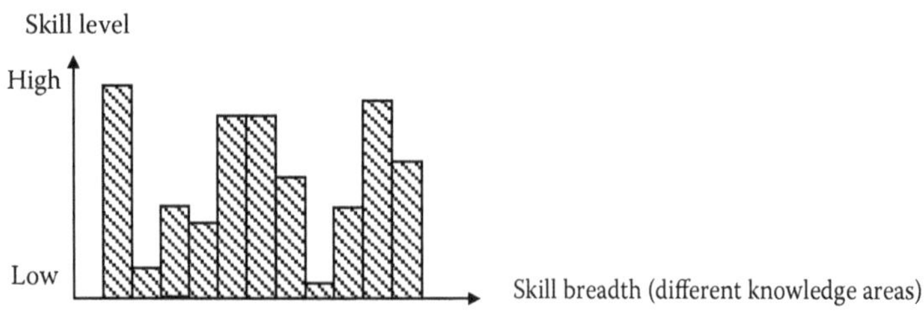

Figure 9.1 Skill levels of police officers.

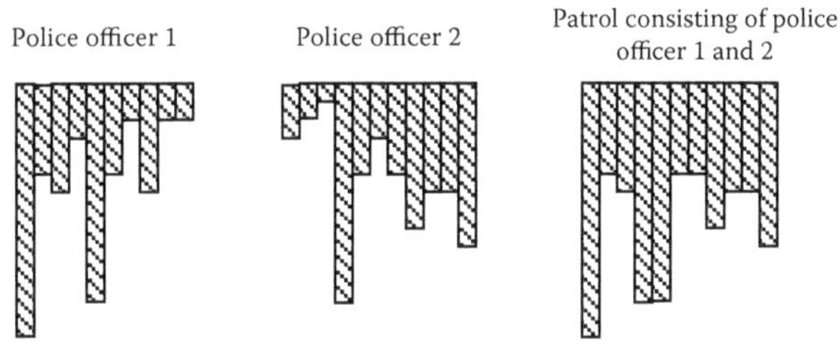

Figure 9.2 Knowledge levels of patrol officers.

irrelevant. When tasks shall be performed, police officers usually are part of a patrol.[5] The patrol has its own knowledge profile (Figure 9.2).

Carlström (1999) wrote that she could observe police officers develop a collective memory, a type of common knowledge bank. Argyris and Schön (1996) use the term collective maps to describe an understanding pattern that several persons develop together and emphasize the importance of this organizational learning (see also Berger & Luckmann, 1979).

Patrol Police Officers´ Professional Knowledge

Holgersson (2005) tries to classify knowledge in use in the police practice. He found there are at least 30 categories of knowledge:

1. Using the skills of other police officers
2. Showing empathy toward a victim
3. Prioritizing cases and using available resources effectively
4. Distinguishing deviations and categorizing individuals, objects, and events
5. Forming a suspicion
6. Communicating with individuals and groups
7. Getting an informant and interacting with an informant
8. Using and understanding different social language variations
9. Dealing with mentally ill and unstable persons
10. Saving lives and minimizing the proportions of injuries
11. Preparing mentally and communicating with colleagues
12. Mediating peace and solving problems
13. Performing in-house investigation and using information in, among others, computer systems
14. Acting preventive
15. Showing authority and inspiring with respect
16. Conveying a serious message
17. Acting in case of an attack
18. Thinking safety

19. Taking investigation measures at the crime scene
20. Keeping feelings under control and supporting each other
21. Debriefing an event
22. Planning measures based on a certain problem picture and existing legislation
23. Showing consideration and humbleness
24. Using different communication aids
25. Conducting a technical investigation
26. Giving advice and instructions
27. Balancing between common sense, ethics, and legislation
28. Using imagination and adapting, among others, driving techniques to increase the chances of catching an offender
29. Finding an offender
30. Presenting a case to decision makers

To make it more communicable and understandable Holgersson (2005) first presented the knowledge type in the form of a novel and made afterward an analysis of the defined knowledge type. Here is one example:

> They had just left Advokatbacken and only driven a short bit over Tingsvägen when Fredrik Påhlsson shouted: "There we have something!" and made a fast U-turn. The old red Opel started to drive faster but had no chance against the police car's 250 hp engine. The driver did not even reach the cycle lane that he intended to drive into in order to avoid the police patrol. Instead, the driver stopped the car and jumped in between the two passengers on the backseat. Both Fredrik Påhlsson and Anna Ekeroth were quickly out of the police car and approached the Opel. They knew exactly who had been driving the car.

Skolnick (1966) pointed out that police officers automatically notice people's way of walking, their clothes, and their car to be able to distinguish deviations. Rubenstein (1973) believed that these routine controls of the environment help make police work more efficiently. Finstad (2000) emphasized police officers' ability to notice deviations. She believed that one of the most important things in the working day of police officers is how they examine the environment and what they do on their own initiative. However, it is easy to believe that being active, for example stopping and carrying out a control, is the same as being efficient. Believing that being active and being efficient is the same thing is at best debatable but can lead to overcontrol, according to Finstad. That police officers sort the impressions they get, usually consisting of meager and superficial information, is a prerequisite for police work, according to Holmberg (1999). Police officers can recognize suspect persons from a long distance.

Carlström (1999) observed that police officers can begin to form suspicions based on a detail that does not fit in the picture they are used to. When she was out on the street with the investigators, it was clear that they saw and observed things that she did not notice. They could, for example, hear somebody whistle, which could be a signal between thieves before breaking into a car (Carlström, 1999).

Knutsson and Partanen (1986) discovered that police officers point out hidden occurrences and meaningful or interesting situations, using different signs that ordinary people do not notice or are unaware of. Knutsson and Partanen write that police officers often have an amazing ability to discover cars that contain "mischief" or to find drug addicts—even when the cars or persons do not send out any particular distinguishing signs. Something is there that the police officers use as a starting point. Following are some factors that Knutsson and Partanen say influence whether a car is stopped or not:

- The looks of the car. Does it look like a car with mischief, or is it a brand that is easy to steal?
- The looks of the driver and the passengers. Are they old or young; do they have long hair or appear nervous?
- Driving behavior. Does the driver drive particularly fast or slow, turn as soon as the police are within sight, or behave strangely in another way?
- Time of the day. Cars that are out driving in the middle of the night are suspect.
- Place. Cars that are parked in a hidden place or are badly parked are suspect.
- Time and place combined. If a car is parked or is driving near a bank or industrial area, this is suspect.

Knutsson and Partanen (1986) experienced that the reasons for controls vary. Sometimes the grounds are so vague that police officers, when asked, cannot say exactly why they examined a certain car or area.

Wahlin (1999) observed that criminals can learn how to behave to avoid drawing the attention of the police. This becomes a struggle between a police officer's knowledge about how to interpret his surroundings and a professional criminal's knowledge about how to blend into his surroundings:

> You learn how to use psychology; you become a little bit a psychologist. When you behave in one way, not so many persons will notice you. It's the same thing; I have escaped from the police several times. When you walk over the street with some bags or whatever in your hands, they'll soon have stopped with their windows down. When you look guilty or suspect, of course they will look what you have with you. But then all you can do is go on, put your head in their police car and talk to them. Then you'll make it.... That's how they think as well. They look for signals.... In the beginning you become

> tensed of course, but you learn how to control your feelings. You show nothing. You've just got to make the best out of the situation.... It's an instinct of self-preservation. You learn all these tricks, how to behave. It's the same when you meet people in the stairs or something like that. Usually you say hi and continue down. You've got to be a bit social. You try to get as little attention as possible, but at the same time not too little, because then you'll draw too much attention anyway. (Wahlin, 1999, p. 37)

A police officer observes his surroundings and judges what he sees. Different behaviors, individuals, and objects make the police officer form suspicions of different degrees. Does somebody walk too fast? Does somebody walk too slowly? Does somebody look around too much? Does somebody look around too little? Does somebody seem to be nervous? Is this a person the police know from before? How does a person behave when he looks at a police officer—does he look too long, too short, or avoid looking at all? The environment and the persons who accompany somebody also go into forming judgments. A broken headlamp, an expired tax control sticker, the driver not using a safety belt, and the looks of the driver in combination with the state of the car can all factor into a possible intervention. An ex-police officer states, "I remember that when I just started I was impressed with the older police officers who could notice everything at once when a car approached."

Other statements during the observations illustrate these behaviors:

> I was standing outside a bar together with a younger colleague. It was closing time and full of people outside the bar. I looked at my colleague. He was looking out over the crowd but seemed to have a 'thousand miles look'. He looked into the crowd without focusing on the individuals to be able to see what state they were in. I asked him: "What are you looking at?" He answered, a little surprised, that he did not look at anything in particular and wondered why I asked that. I continued to ask: "Do you see that guy in a white sweater, do you see that his eyes are 'dark' of anger and that he is staring at the guy standing in front of him?" "Oh, yeah, I think you're right," my colleague answered curious. We went to the man in the white sweater and talked to him. He turned out to be angry but our conversation with him calmed him down. When we were back on our spot on the sidewalk I asked my colleague: "Look, is there anything in particular you see right now?" "Well, perhaps he in the blue sweater?" he answered wondering.... We continued to stand there and observe and spoke to a number of persons in order to prevent fights. It hit me that one has to learn things that I considered obvious. My young colleague was not tired or unmotivated. That was not the reason why he did not see when there was reason to talk to certain individuals. He needed guidance in what to focus on. He also needed to learn that one does not need to wait for a decision of a coercive measure to just talk to a person.
>
> At another occasion I was standing at a railing in a newly opened department store together with an older colleague. The store had several open floors and there were many persons walking around. I saw that my colleague switched focus constantly, all the time examining new people. I asked him: "Maybe you think my question is strange, but what is it you're looking at when you stand here looking out over the crowd of people?" My colleague answered, after having thought it over: "I look if

there is something that isn't right, if someone is looking around too much, or too little, if someone walks too fast or too slow...." We compared our judgments and saw that we roughly made the same conclusions about which individuals were divergent. We realized that this is a form of knowledge one acquires by working as a police officer. That you react to what is different.

Holgersson's (2005) experience was that part of the categorizing that can be used in, for example, Stockholm was not at all functional on the countryside. This is mainly the case when deciding which cars to control. Holgersson noticed several times that cars that draw attention when he works in the countryside are driven by young persons from a small village who have an interest in cars. These cars and drivers pass controls almost always without any remarks. Other police officers who come from a big city to a small town have observed the same. In smaller towns, personal knowledge seems to be more important than in a big city. Police officers in a small village are usually very well informed about the criminals and the cars they drive. Still, the ability to notice what is deviant is important even in small towns.

The ability to distinguish the deviant and to find reasons to act against an individual or a vehicle is developed as an experience-based knowledge. This ability consists partly of being able to discover the deviant, as already described, and partly of being able to consider different factors once something deviant has been discovered. When, for example, a police officer starts to suspect a case of drunken driving as the driver of a car makes a "pear"[6] or "truck"[7] turn, brakes without reason, drives too slow or too staggering, only one of these signs, if clear enough this may be enough motivation to stop the car. It is probable that a drunk driver behaves in a certain way but not at all certain.

Other variables can raise or lower the degree of suspicion of an ongoing drunken driving case. If it is a Friday afternoon and the car belongs to a construction or plumbing company, only small unclear indications can be enough motivation to stop the car.[8] If, on the other hand, the driver of the car is an old man with a hat or a woman staring forward who seems to be a bad driver, the suspicion degree may become lower. The looks of the driver, possible passengers, and the environment in which the car is observed influence the decision. If the suspected driver is seen outside a liquor store on a Saturday morning with a bag from that store in his car, the suspicions will be stronger than when the driver stops outside a church on a Sunday morning. The degree of suspicion also rises when the driver already is known to the police from similar crimes.

Even when a police officer discovers something illegal, he must constantly make the decision (see previous section) if it is an errand that is suitable to be engaged in at that moment. Shall a patrol, for example, stop and make a report about someone for not using a bicycle lamp or for illegal bill posting?

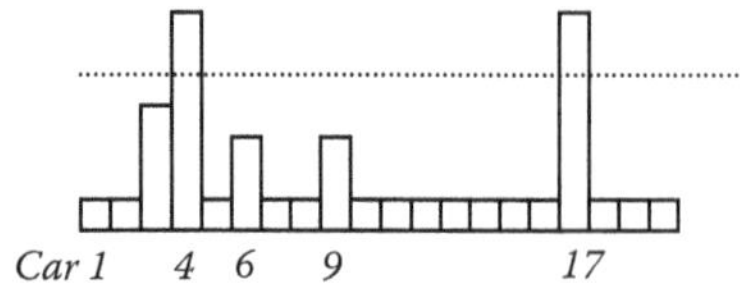

Figure 9.3 Police officer reactions and conclusions.

The police officer asks himself two things: Is the degree of suspicion high enough to motivate an intervention; and does the gravity of the suspected crime justify an intervention?

In Figure 9.3, the patrol meets 20 cars:

- Car 3 looked shabby, but the patrol made the judgment that the driver in combination with the looks of the car did not make the suspicion strong enough to motivate stopping the vehicle.
- Car 4 was stopped as the patrol suspected that the driver might be lacking a driving license. Nothing could be objected to the car or the driver.
- In cars 6 and 9 the driver was not wearing a safety belt. However, the patrol did not turn to stop these vehicles because of the traffic intensity. The patrol thought it would take too long a time to turn around and catch up with the cars that should be stopped, considering the crime that was committed.
- Car 17 drew the patrol's interest. The patrol had to wait for three vehicles to pass before they could turn and follow car 17. None of these three cars drew more attention than car 17. The patrol caught up with the car and made it pull over. It turned out that a driving ban had been imposed on the car. However, it was not the owner who was driving the car, and the driver stated that he did not know about the driving ban. As a result no report was written. While the patrol was standing outside car 17 talking to the driver, they discovered another car that drew their attention. They followed after and stopped the car. The driver turned out to lack a driving license, which resulted in a primary report for aggravated unlawful driving.

It is important that a police officer makes a balanced decision and finds a suitable level for when to investigate something further. In that way he can avoid controlling too many vehicles or individuals. An experienced police officer states, "When you're young you tend to see things more in black and white. You haven't developed an instinctive feeling. The older ones use a more grayish scale."

A university student who came along with police officers during a few shifts learned:

> There was a difference between the younger and older police officers. The older ones were calm, observed the surrounding and saw when something wasn't right. It seemed as if the older police officers stopped the right cars. Often something was wrong when they stopped a car. I asked them: "How do you know which cars to stop?" They answered: "We just look." The younger ones panicked a little; when 500 cars had passed they seemed to think: "Something must happen! Let's take one, maybe we're lucky."

The Value Shop to Categorize Professional Knowledge

It is possible to use a theoretical model as the "value shop"[9] to categorize professional knowledge. A value shop is characterized by five primary activities: (1) problem finding and acquisition; (2) problem solving; (3) choice; (4) execution; and (5) control and evaluation (Stabell & Fjeldstad, 1998), as illustrated in Figure 9.2. Problem finding and acquisition involve initial crime scene assessment (Smith & Flanagan, 2000). Problem solving is the actual generation of ideas and action (or treatment) plans based on an assessment of incoming information.

Choice represents the decision of choosing between alternatives. While it is the least important primary activity of the value shop in terms of time and effort, it is also the most important in terms of value as it is selecting an appropriate line of inquiry. Execution as case development represents communicating, organizing, and implementing the decision or performing the treatment. Control and evaluation activities involve monitoring and measurement of how well the solution solved the original problem or met the original need in terms of postcharge case management.

This may feed back into the first activity, problem finding and acquisition, for two reasons. First, if the proposed solution is inadequate or did not work, it feeds back into learning why it was inadequate and begins the problem-solving phase anew. Second, if the problem solution was successful, the firm might enlarge the scope of the problem-solving process to solve a bigger problem related to or dependent upon the first problem being solved.

In police investigations, the process begins with an initial crime scene assessment where sources of potential evidence are identified (Figure 9.4). The information derived from the process then has to be evaluated to gauge its relevance to the investigation. During the next stage, the information is interpreted to develop inferences and initial hypotheses. As more information is collected, this is then fed back into the process until the objectives of the investigation are achieved. Providing a suspect is identified and charged, the investigation then enters the postcharge stage, where case papers are compiled for the prosecution. Subsequently, the court process begins.

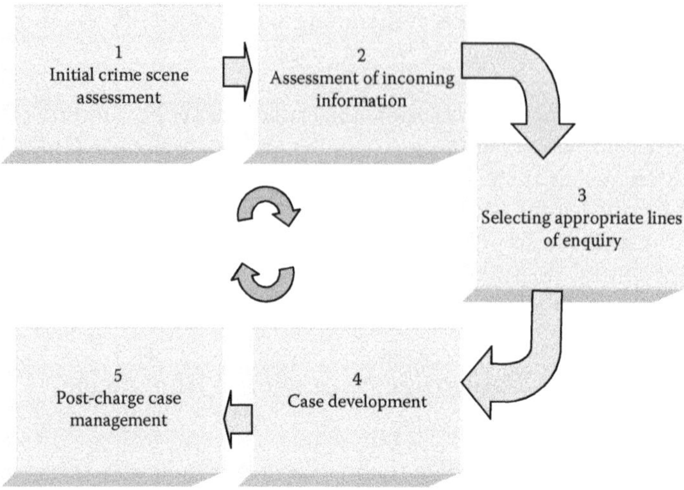

Figure 9.4 Identifying sources of evidence.

A total of 30 types of knowledge are presented in this chapter. These knowledge types might be critical, important, or useful in the five primary activities of a value shop. We define a scale including very important (critical), important, and not important (useful) in this research to be able to classify knowledge types. We apply critical, important, and useful to each knowledge type as listed in Table 9.1.

Not surprisingly, we found that most types of knowledge were applied in case development. By this stage of the investigative process, information has been integrated into the investigation and interpreted accordingly. Options for gathering additional information have been reviewed. If sufficient information has been gathered, it may be possible to move to the postcharge element of the investigative process. Where additional information is required, the investigative cycle continues to iterate. If more information is required, it is important to consider where this information is likely to reside.

Discussion

In some countries the length of the education to become a police officer is up to 3 years, whereas other countries require less than a year. How will that affect the chances of training a reflective practitioner? Is the education too theoretical in some countries? Is it too short in others? It's not possible to answer such questions without knowing which type of professional knowledge a police officer needs to have. Therefore, it is surprising how little research has been done in this area. Maybe this is one reason that the work of a police officer is seen simply as not needing many skills beyond shooting

Table 9.1 Importance of Knowledge Types in Value Shop Activities

	1 Initial Crime Scene Assessment	2 Assessing Incoming Information	3 Selecting Appropriate Lines of Inquiry	4 Case Development	5 Postcharge Case Development
I Using the Skills of Other Police Officers			C	I	U
II Showing Empathy Toward a Victim	I	U		C	
III Prioritizing Cases and Using Resources	I		C	U	
IV Distinguishing Deviations and Categorizing	I		C		U
V Forming a Suspicion	I	C		U	
VI Communicating With Individuals and Groups	I	U		C	
VII Getting an Informant and Interacting		I	U	C	
VIII Using and Understanding Variations	I	U		C	
IX Dealing with Mentally Ill and Unstable Persons	I	U		C	
X Saving Lives and Minimizing Injuries	U		C	I	
XI Preparing Mentally and Communicating	I			C	U
XII Mediating Peace and Solving Problems		C	I	U	
XIII Performing In-House Investigation	C	I	U		
XIV Acting Preventive		C	U	I	
XV Showing Authority	I		U	C	
XVI Conveying a Serious Message	I	U		C	
XVII Acting in Case of an Attack		U	I	C	
XVIII Thinking Safety	C		U	I	
XIX Taking Measures at the Crime Scene	C	I		U	
XX Keeping Feelings Under Control	I	U		C	

(*Continued*)

Table 9.1 (Continued) Importance of Knowledge Types in Value Shop Activities

	1 Initial Crime Scene Assessment	2 Assessing Incoming Information	3 Selecting Appropriate Lines of Inquiry	4 Case Development	5 Postcharge Case Development
XXI Debriefing an Event			U	I	C
XXII Planning Measures Based on Legislation		I	U	C	
XXIII Showing Consideration and Humbleness		U		C	I
XXIV Using Different Communication Aids	U		I	C	
XXV Conducting a Technical Investigation	U	C		I	
XXVI Giving Advice and Instructions		C	U	I	
XXVII Balancing Common Sense and Ethics	I		C	U	
XXVIII Using Imagination and Adapting	U		C	I	
XXIX Finding an Offender	C		I	U	
XXX Presenting a Case to Decision Makers			U	C	I

Notes: C, critical. I, importance. U, useful.

and self-protection. This article pointed out that the work of the police officer is far more complex. Is there a need to change philosophies surrounding the way we look at police work? A lot of researchers have shown that police organizations have a problem adapting new methods and acting in an efficient way. Could one reason be that the difficulties to work as a police officer had been too much neglected?

Conclusion

A patrolling police officer should have a lot of professional knowledge to be able to act in an appropriate way. A lot of the professional knowledge is so-called tacit knowledge and can be hard to describe in such a way that a new recruit can adapt the knowledge only by reading a text. In nursing the importance of the reflective practitioner has been observed through the research (see, e.g., Burns & Bulman, 2000). It is important to try to describe and identify professional knowledge because it's then easier to discuss and reflect on different knowledge (see Josefson, 1991). To get police officers with a high level of skills it's important to help the officers become reflective and able to develop and share knowledge. To identify and describe professional knowledge it's therefore very central. One way to describe and identify the professional knowledge is to use a theoretical model as the value shop.

References

Argyris, C., & Schön, D. A. (1996). *Organizational learning: A theory of action perspective.* Massachusetts: Addison-Wesley, Reading.

Bayley, D. (1994). *Police for the future.* New York: Oxford University Press.

Berger, P. L., & Luckmann, T. (1979). *Kunskapssociologi—Hur individen uppfattar och formar sin social verklighet.* Stockholm: Wahlström & Widstrand.

Bittner, E. (1972). *The function of the police in modern society.* National Institute of Mental Health. Rockville, MD: Center for Studies of Crime and Delinquence.

Broderick, J. (1977). *Police in a time of change.* Morristown, NJ: General Learning Press.

Brodeur, J.-P. (1998). *How to recognize good policing—Problems and issues.* Washington, DC: Sage.

Brown, M. (1988). *Working the street, police discretion and the dilemmas of reform.* New York: Russel Sage Foundation.

Bryman, A. (1997). *Kvantitet och kvalitet i samhällsvetenskaplig forskning* (*Quantity and quality in social research*). Lund: Studentlitteratur.

Burns, S., & Bulman, C. (2000). *Reflective practice in nursing—The growth of the professional practitioner.* London: Blackwell Science.

Carlström, A.-K. (1999), *På spaning i Stockholm. Institutet förfolklivsforskning—etnologiska institutionen.* Stockholm: Stockholm University.

Cronholm, S. (2005, November 23–25). *Multi-grounded theory in practice—A review of experiences from use.* Presented at QUALIT, Brisbane, Australia.

Cronholm, S. (2004, April 29–30). Illustrating multi-grounded theory. In A. Brown & D. Remenyi (Eds.), *Proceedings of the 3rd European Conference on Research Methodology for Business and Management Studies* (ECRM 2004). Reading, UK: Reading University.

Finstad, L. (2000). *Politiblikket* (*Policing Lenses*). Oslo, Norway: Pax Förlag A/S.

Goldkuhl, G. (2004). Conceptual determination when developing a multi-grounded theory—Example: Defining ISD method. Accepted to the 3rd European Conference on Research Methods in Business and Management (ECRM 2004). Reading, UK.

Goldkuhl, G. (2005). Work practice theory—What it is and why we need it. In *Proceedings of the 3rd Intl Conf on Action in Language, Organizations and Information Systems* (ALOIS), University of Limerick.

Goldkuhl, G., & Braf, E. (2001). Contextual knowledge analysis—understanding knowledge and its relations to action and communication. In *Proceedings of 2nd European Conference on Knowledge Management* (ECKM 2001), Bled, Slovenia.

Goldkuhl, G., Röstlinger, A., & Braf, E. (2001). Organisations as practice systems—integrating knowledge, signs, artifacts and action I Proceedings of Organisations Semiotics, IFIP 8.1 Conference, Montreal, Canada.

Goldkuhl, G., & Cronholm, S. (2003). Multi-grounded theory—Adding theoretical grounding to grounded theory. *Accepted to the 2nd European Conference on Research Methods in Business* (2ECRM). Reading, UK.

Goldstein, H. (1967). Police policy formulation: a proposal for improving police performance. *Michigan Law Review, 65.*

Gottschalk, P. (2006). *Knowledge management systems in law enforcement: Technologies and techniques.* Hershey, PA: Idea Group Publishing.

Gustavsson, B. (2000). *Kunskapsfilosifi. Tre kunskapsformer i historisk belysning* (*Knowledge philosophy. Tre knowledge forms in historical context*). Stockholm, Sweden: Wahlström & Widstrand.

Göranzon, B. (1990). *Det pratiktiska intellektet—Datoranvändning och yrkeskunnande* (*The practical intellect—Computer application and occupational knowledge*). Stockholm, Sweden: Carlsson Bokförlag.

Göranzon, B. (1998). En mötesplats för reflektion (A meeting point for reflection). In C. Hoberg (Ed.), *Precision och improvisation—Om systemutvecklarens yrkeskunnande* (*Precision and improvisation—About the system designers occupational knowledge*). Stockholm, Sweden: Dialoger.

Holgersson, S. (2005). Yrke: POLIS Yrkeskunskap, motivation, IT-system och andra förutsättningar för polisarbete (Profession: Police—Occupational knowledge, motivation, IT system and other requirements for police work). PhD doctoral dissertation. Linköping: Institutionen för datavetenskap, Linköping University, Sweden.

Holmberg, L. (1999). Within the frame work of the law: The police work method and discretion. Kobenhaven: Gyldendal.

Josefson, I. (1991). *Kunskapens former, Det reflekterande yrkeskunnandet.* Stockholm: Carlssons.

Kirkham, G. (1974, June 2). From professor to patrolman: A fresh perspective on the police. *Journal of Police Science and Administration.*

Knutsson, J., & Partanen, P. (1986). Vad gör polisen? En jämförelse mellan kvarterspolistjänst och ordningspolistjänst. BRÅ, 1986:2. Stockholm: Brottsförebyggande rådet.
McElroy, J. E. (1998). Service delivery of police agencies i Brodeur, J.-P. (red) How to recognize good policing. Problems and Issues. Washington DC: Sage.
Molander, B. (1996). *Kunskap i handling* (*Practical knowledge*). Göteborg: Daidalos AB.
Nonaka, I., & Takeuchi, H. (1995). *The knowledge-creating company. How Japanese companies create the dynamics of innovation.* New York: Oxford University Press.
Nordenstam, T. (1983). Ett pragmatiskt perspektiv på datautveckling (A pragmatic perspective on data evolution). In B. Göranzon (Ed.), *Datautvecklingens filosofi* (*Philosophy of the computer evolution*). Stockholm, Sweden: Carlsson och Jönsson.
Patton, M. Q. (1990). *Qualitative evaluation and research methods.* Newbury Park, CA: Sage Publications.
Polanyi, M. (1962). *Personal knowledge—Towards a post-critical philosophy.* London: Routledge.
Rolf, B. (1995). *Profession, tradition och tyst kunskap: En studie i Michael Polanyis teori om den professionella kunskapens tysta dimension* (*Profession, tradition and tacit knowledge - A study in Michael Polanyi's theory of the professional knowledge's implicit dimension*). Nora, Sweden: Nya Doxa.
Rubenstein, J. (1973). *City police. Farrar.* New York: Straus and Grioux.
Sheehan, N. T. (2005). Why old tools won't work in the "new" knowledge economy. *Journal of Business Strategy, 26*(4), 53–60.
Schön, D. (1983). *The reflective practitioner: How professionals think in action.* England: Basic Books.
Schön, D. (1987). *Education the reflective practitioner.* San Francisco: Jossey-Bass.
Skolnick, J. (1966). Justice without trial: Law enforcement in a democratic society. New York: John Wiley.
Smith, N., & Flanagan, C. (2000). The effective detective: Identifying the skills of an effective SIO, Police Research Series Paper 122. London: Policing and Reducing Crime Unit.
Stabell, C. B., & Fjeldstad, Ø. D. (1998). Configuring value for competitive advantage: On chains, shops, and networks. *Strategic Management Journal, 19*, 413–437.
Strauss, A. L., & Corbin, J. (1990). *Basics of qualitative research, grounded theory procedures and techniques.* Newbury Park, CA: Sage Publications.
Waddington, P. A. J. (1999). *Policing citizens.* London: UCL Press.
Wahlin, L. (1999). Den rationella inbrottstjuven? En studie om rationalitet och rationellt handlande i brott. Lund: Sociologiska institutionen, Lunds Universitet.
Wittgenstein, L. (1953). *Philosophische Untersuchungen.* Oxford: Blackwell.
Zack, M. H. (1999). Managing codified knowledge. *Sloan Management Review, 40*(4), 45–58.

Notes

1. Lecture in Folkes hus, Stockholm, October 16, 2002.
2. Holgersson (2005) does not agree with Carlström's statement that police investigators' knowledge only is perishable. Part of their knowledge is tied to persons, place, and time, but they also make use of knowledge that is more constant over time.

3. See Goldkuhl and Braf (2001). They make a distinction between knowledge of typical and knowledge of specific matters.
4. See Molander (1996).
5. The same is true when police officers are part of a group that shall solve certain tasks.
6. Steering movements come too late, become too big and need to be corrected (shape of a pear).
7. The driver makes a turn as if he were driving a truck with a long trailer behind him.
8. A police officer who is known to be good in catching drunk drivers has stated that construction workers, electricians, plumbers etc., who drive a company car to and from work like to drink a couple of beers after work at the beginning of the weekend. During participating observation, I have discovered several drunk drivers with this type of car on Friday evenings.
9. A term from the business management literature. The value shop is an organization that creates value by solving unique problems. Knowledge is the most important resource (Sheehan, 2005).

Relevant Laws and Empirical Research on Profiling in Law Enforcement in the United States

10

KATRINA W. BERGER
Department of Homeland Security

DEE WOOD HARPER, JR.
Loyola University

Contents

Introduction

Profiling is a process in which law enforcement officers make judgments about a person relative to possible criminal activity being committed based on various factors; these factors may include such things as the person's race, manner of dress and grooming, behavioral characteristics, when and where the observation is made, and the circumstances under which the officer makes the observation and in relation to other information that the officer may already possess (Fredrickson & Siljander, 2002). Profiling is a normal aspect of law enforcement and if used properly can be a highly effective investigative tool.

Unfortunately, the term *profiling* is often used interchangeably and incorrectly with the term *racial profiling.* Racial profiling occurs when a law enforcement officer stops, questions, arrests, searches, or otherwise investigates an individual because that officer believes that members of that person's racial or ethnic group are more likely to commit the sort of crime the officer is investigating than are those of other racial or ethnic groups or the population as a whole. In this instance, the officer is making a prejudgment about the individual based on their race or ethnicity. This is an inappropriate form of profiling that no law enforcement agency should condone or promote.

History of Profiling

In the 1970s, profiling developed as an investigative technique for law enforcement (O'Connor, 2006). In the mid-1970s, the Drug Enforcement Administration (DEA) began to compile common traits and characteristics, or a profile, of individuals engaging in drug trafficking and distribution. The profile itself is not a single, concise list of characteristics; instead it is a list of often contradictory characteristics used to identify drug smugglers and traffickers (Trende, 2000). In addition, many local law enforcement agencies have developed their own modified versions of the drug courier profile based on the local practices of narcotics violators in their respective geographic areas (Cogan, 1992).

The drug courier profile was first used by law enforcement in the airport environment. From 1977 until 1982, the drug courier profile enjoyed widespread use by law enforcement in airports to aid in the identification of those involved in drug trafficking and drug distribution. With the development of the drug courier profile, law enforcement officers were able to identify patterns of common characteristics of drug couriers that distinguished them from ordinary or innocent airline passengers (Wilson, 1996). As a result, law enforcement officers could more readily identify narcotics violators, even without tips or other prior information (Wilson, 1996).

In the airport environment, plainclothes law enforcement officers will typically position themselves in various areas, such as airline ticket counters and airport deplaning gates, and observe those traveling between "source" and "use" cities. The officers will quietly observe travelers to determine if any are exhibiting characteristics matching the drug courier profile characteristics or are otherwise acting in a suspicious manner. If so, it may be likely that the individual is carrying narcotics. The law enforcement officer will then approach the person and question him or her.

Law enforcement officers, as well as the courts, have found some characteristics and behaviors very indicative of criminal activity. The use of an alias is an inherently suspicious behavior to which the courts and law enforcement officers give great weight as an indicator of criminal activity (Wilson, 1996). In addition, lies, discrepancies, and otherwise suspicious answers to a law enforcement officer's questions also are good indicators of criminal activity. If two suspects are traveling together, it is common for them to deny knowing each other or otherwise attempt to deny that they are traveling together; when interviewed they frequently give contradictory statements, which only adds to law enforcement's suspicion that they are involved in criminal activity (Wilson, 1996).

The war on drugs in the 1980s had a significant impact on policymaking and law enforcement practices. Major changes were implemented in policing strategies on a national level. These changes included very aggressive policing procedures and the aggressive targeting of drug offenders. The use of the drug courier profile to aid in targeting drug offenders was firmly established in law enforcement agencies, both on the federal and state and local levels. There were substantial financial benefits for law enforcement departments, especially at the state and local levels, that were "tough" on drug offenders; from the 1980s continuing into the 1990s, the federal government dramatically increased expenditures for law enforcement to aid in the war on drugs (Engel & Calnon, 2004). As part of the war on drugs, financial resources for law enforcement shifted from the federal level to the local level (Engel & Calnon, 2004). This was achieved primarily through the creation of joint task forces that included DEA, the U.S. Customs Service (USCS), and other federal law enforcement agencies working cooperatively with state and local agencies to eradicate illegal narcotics (Engel & Calnon, 2004). The total DEA budget for state and local task forces increased from $45.7 million in 1991 to $105.5 million by 1999 (U.S. GAO/GGD-99-108, 1999).

In 1984, DEA initiated Operation Pipeline, a nationwide highway drug interdiction program focusing on private motor vehicles. This was an intensified enforcement interdiction, the purpose of which was to find illegal drugs being transported on the nation's highways and interstate system (Gross & Barnes, 2002). This goal was to be achieved by generating a high volume of legal traffic enforcement stops to screen for criminal activity, especially drug trafficking (Gross & Barnes, 2002). As it would be impossible to stop and search every vehicle, profiling was used pervasively by law enforcement to indicate those most likely to be involved in drug trafficking activity.

Profiling on the interstates basically works as follows. Once a vehicle is stopped for a traffic violation, the law enforcement officer is trained to look for indicators that the person may be involved in transporting narcotics. During the 1980s, large late-model vehicles with large trunks were popular with drug traffickers to be used in transporting narcotics on the interstates. A vehicle bearing Florida tags was another potential indicator. Drug traffickers also commonly used rental vehicles. Interior indicators could include the odor of marijuana or the strong odor of coffee, perfumes, or air fresheners, which are commonly used to mask the smell of marijuana, and signs of concealed compartments in the vehicle that could be evidenced by loose or missing screws in side panels or door panels and duct-taped or riveted panels. Law enforcement officers are trained to question the driver and passengers regarding such things as their vehicle registration, their itinerary, the purpose of their trip, and the names and addresses of the people they are going to see (Gross & Barnes, 2002). Officers are trained to question the driver separately from the passengers and look for nervousness or behavioral indicators such as the failure to maintain eye contact or inconsistencies in statements. The more characteristics and indicators that matched the drug courier profile, the greater the chance the individual was involved in transporting narcotics.

By the mid 1990s, the entire practice of profiling had come under stark criticism as it appeared to show patterns of discrimination against minorities. One widely publicized case, *Wilkins v. Maryland State Police* (1993), revealed that the law enforcement agency was blatantly targeting Black drivers; just 1 week prior to the offending vehicle stop and search that was the basis of the lawsuit, the Maryland State Police had circulated an internal memo alerting officers to be on the lookout for drug couriers, the majority of whom would be Black (Trende, 2000). As a result of instances such as this, many state legislators proposed and passed legislation banning racial profiling and setting up stringent policies regarding the collection of data on drivers' race and ethnicity in all vehicle stops conducted by law enforcement (Engel & Calnon, 2004).

Court Cases

The courts in the United States have laid down several landmark jurisprudences on profiling. This section discusses these major cases.

United States v. Elmore: The Elmore Profile

In *United States v. Elmore* (1980), the Court in the 5th Federal Circuit set forth what it considered to be the acceptable characteristics of the drug courier profile. These characteristics became known as the Elmore Profile and gained wide popularity with law enforcement agencies across the United States for use in the airport environment (Cogan, 1992). The seven primary characteristics of the Elmore profile are as follows: (1) arriving or departing from a known drug source city; (2) traveling with a large quantity of empty luggage or traveling with little or no luggage; (3) having an unusual itinerary; (4) traveling under a false name or alias; (5) carrying large amounts of cash; (6) purchasing airline tickets with cash, especially with small currency denominations; and (7) exhibiting nervous or hurried behavior (Cogan, 1992).

Florida v. Royer: The Reasonableness Test

Many critics have argued that the factors in a drug courier profile are too varied and contradictory. In addition, the profiles are so fluid that law enforcement has virtually unlimited discretion and can claim almost any characteristics fit the "profile." These critics argue for a firm set of established and consistent factors that would constitute the drug courier profile. However, in *Florida v. Royer* (1983), the Supreme Court expressed its preference for a reasonableness test over such rigid guidelines. The court found that too many different observations amount to a drug courier profile and that it would be impossible to consolidate these myriad possibilities into one rigid and finite formula (Dunderdale, 2000).

United States v. Montoya de Hernandez: Profiling and Rights at the International Border

In *United States v. Montoya de Hernandez* (1985), the Supreme Court provided a lengthy discussion of rights at an international border and in particular, an individual's 4th Amendment rights regarding a lengthy and nonroutine detention after having been profiled as an alimentary canal smuggler. These types of drug couriers smuggle narcotics into the United States by swallowing a large number of balloons or condoms filled with either cocaine or heroin. Generally after the alimentary canal smugglers have cleared inspection by USCS, they leave the airport and go to a prearranged location, often a hotel, where they are met by other coconspirators. Over the course of the next several days, the smugglers pass the drug-filled balloons or condoms during their bowel movements. This is a very effective, albeit dangerous, smuggling method; alimentary canal smugglers can usually ingest a kilogram or more of cocaine or heroin and are often able to smuggle the narcotics into the United States undetected.

In the case at hand, USCS agents suspected Montoya of being an alimentary drug smuggler. Customs officials detained Montoya in a locked room for 16 hours for a monitored bowel movement to determine if she was in fact smuggling narcotics into the United States. The Supreme Court upheld Montoya's lengthy detention and stated that the Customs officials, upon questioning Montoya, had developed a reasonable suspicion that she was smuggling narcotics internally, in large part because she fit the profile of an alimentary drug smuggler: Montoya had arrived in the United States from Bogotá, Colombia, a known source city and country for cocaine and heroin; she spoke no English and stated that she had no friends or family in the United States; she had no hotel reservations, very little luggage, and could not explain how her ticket was purchased; and she was in possession of $5,000 cash, which was an amount typically paid to these types of drug couriers (Gregory, 1994). Montoya refused a voluntary x-ray, which would have provided conclusive evidence whether she was carrying illegal narcotics internally. After 16 hours, Customs officials requested a court-ordered x-ray and body cavity search. The request was granted, and the ensuing x-ray and search revealed the presence of contraband concealed inside Montoya's body (Johnson, 2002).

United States v. Sokolow: Approval of the Use of Profiling by Law Enforcement

In 1989, the U.S. Supreme Court definitively spoke on the use of profiling by law enforcement in the landmark case *United States v. Sokolow.* In that case the Supreme Court generally approved the use of profiling and provided guidelines on the acceptable use of drug courier profiles. The Court held that it is necessary for profiling cases to be decided using a "totality of the circumstances" approach and consider all the facts known to the law enforcement officer at the time of the stop. The Court went on to state that common sense conclusions regarding human behavior are allowed. Critics of the drug courier profile argued that the factors comprising the profile are circumstantial and if taken separately are all innocent behaviors. The Court in *Sokolow* said this approach was incorrect and that these factors should be considered in the totality of the circumstances to validate a proper search or seizure. The Court held that the relevant issue is not whether the type of conduct is innocent or guilty but instead the degree of suspicion that attaches to certain kinds of noncriminal behavior.

Whren v. United States: Pretext Stops Allowed

In *Whren v. United States* (1996), the Supreme Court held that using a traffic stop as a pretext for a narcotics investigatory stop was constitutional. The officer's motivation for the stop is immaterial. In essence, if a law enforcement officer has probable cause to believe that a traffic violation has occurred, then the officer has a legal basis to stop the car even if his or her real intention is to question the driver and make observations that may lead to probable cause to search the vehicle for the presence of narcotics (Gross & Barnes, 2002). This ruling gave law enforcement a solid basis to use profiling on the highways to interdict illegal narcotics.

Profiling Studies

Few empirical studies on profiling have evaluated the difference in the rates of stops and searches of minorities to determine if profiling is discriminatory or truly an effective policing technique. Most studies have merely stated that the rates are different for minority groups than the population at large and conclude that this difference is due to racial profiling and racial discrimination by law enforcement (Engel & Calnon, 2004).

One study of particular relevance addressed the various types of statistical methods used to evaluate profiling (Becker, 2004). The researchers in this study argue that the proper method to use in evaluating profiling is to focus on the "find rate," which is the percentages of individuals who are stopped and searched and who are found to be engaging in criminal activity, for example, being in possession of narcotics. By focusing on the find rate, one is much more able to accurately evaluate how profiling enables law enforcement to detect criminal activity. The higher the find rate, the lower the number of innocent people who are stopped and searched. If the find rate among a particular group is low relative to other groups, then a disproportionate number of innocent people of that group are being stopped and searched. On the other hand, if the find rates are the same regardless of racial group, then profiling is being used appropriately even though more people of one particular group, for example Hispanics, are stopped and searched (Becker, 2004).

Identifying the factors that influence a law enforcement officer's decision whether to search a vehicle or make an arrest following a traffic stop is another issue in the profiling research literature (Engel & Calnon, 2004). While this study does not deal exclusively with profiling, it does emphasize that to determine if profiling is racially discriminatory or ineffective, it is important to take into account the factors relating to the driver that influence the officer's decisions to stop or search and also the fact that different racial groups exhibit different rates of law-violating behaviors.

Minority perceptions regarding profiling have also been the subject of some limited research in the field (Reitzel, Rice, & Piquero, 2004). Findings from this research indicate that Hispanics are more likely than non-Hispanics to believe that racial profiling is widespread and that they personally have been racially profiled. Additionally, the data showed that Hispanics' perceptions regarding the disrespect of law enforcement toward them or other negative experiences with respect to law enforcement appeared to be more on an individual and personal level and was not perceived to be a more global problem with all Hispanics (Reitzel et al., 2004). Despite the limitations of this survey, its findings are important in that this group of minority citizens believed that racial profiling was taking place regardless of whether it was or not. Additionally, many of them perceived that they personally had been racially profiled by law enforcement. These types of perceptions can likely lead to poor police–minority relations.

In response to a request from the chair of the Congressional Black Caucus, the U.S. Government Accountability Office (GAO) prepared a report compiling information on both the findings and the research methodologies of several analyses that had been conducted regarding the racial profiling of motorists. In brief, the GAO found that no comprehensive source of data existed on a nationwide basis that could be used to determine whether race was a predominant factor in motor vehicle stops. The GAO identified five quantitative analyses of racial profiling that included data on vehicle stops. These analyses included studies conducted involving vehicle stops on I-95 in Maryland and Volusia County, Florida, and on the New Jersey Turnpike as well as an audit conducted by the American Civil Liberties Union (ACLU) regarding an analysis of stops of motorists and pedestrians made by the Philadelphia Police Department's Narcotics Strike Force (GAO, 2000a).

After an examination of these five quantitative analyses, the GAO concluded that while each of these analyses claimed that racial profiling had occurred, each one had made invalid comparisons with their data. Simply comparing the race of motorists stopped with the racial percentages in the larger population was not a valid comparison. This type of analysis or comparison did not address whether different groups of the population (e.g., different races) are at the same or differing levels of risk for being stopped by law enforcement because of possible differences in their rates or severity of committing traffic violations (GAO, 2000a).

The GAO further noted that high-quality data from multiple sources was needed to build a stronger and more complete original database from which further empirical research could be conducted on racial profiling. Various sources of acceptable data included law enforcement records, motorist surveys, law enforcement surveys, and other empirical research and studies. The best possible data for research on racial profiling would include complete, accurate, and consistent information on the characteristics of vehicle stops as well as the characteristics or the people involved in the stops and comparisons with the characteristics of those individuals who were not stopped (GAO, 2000a).

In conclusion, the GAO found that due to a very limited number of empirical studies and due to the methodological limitations in the analyses that were reviewed, the available data did not allow solid conclusions to be drawn regarding racial profiling. Specifically, a pervasive issue the GAO had with all of these analyses is that there is questionable validity with research that merely compares the racial composition of one group of motorists who are stopped on a particular roadway in a particular location with the racial composition of a greater population whose racial composition is very different.

U.S. Customs Service's Response to Racial Profiling

Prior to its merger with the Immigration and Naturalization Service (INS) in 2003 as part of the creation of the new Department of Homeland Security, the USCS was one of the oldest federal law enforcement agencies in the United States. USCS, one of the agencies under the Treasury Department, was responsible for collecting revenue and duties from international trade. Its mission was also to ensure that merchandise and people entering and exiting the United States did so in compliance with the laws and regulations of the United States.

To carry out its missions, USCS was vested with very broad search authority and could conduct searches of individuals entering the United States without a warrant and without probable cause. The Supreme Court has held that routine border searches conducted by USCS personnel are reasonable and therefore do not violate the 4th Amendment of the U.S. Constitution simply because they occur at the border. These types of searches require law enforcement to have a very low level of suspicion of criminal activity before conducting a search.

USCS policy dictates that its inspectors should never use race, gender, color, or ethnicity as a factor in the determination of level of suspicion for a border search or detention. Instead, inspectors must be able to articulate specific facts and reasons that are race, gender, and ethnically neutral to justify a border search (GAO, 2000b). As part of their training, USCS inspectors are taught to closely scrutinize passengers who are arriving into the United States at international airports or other ports of entry, especially those arriving from known source countries for illegal narcotics, such as Colombia and Jamaica. USCS inspectors are trained to look for signs of nervousness, suspicious behavior, and conflicting statements to develop a reasonable suspicion to conduct a further examination or search of an arriving passenger (Gregory, 1994). In addition to their own observations, USCS inspectors also receive information from their passenger analysis units (PAUs), which aids them in targeting arriving passengers for search or further examination (GAO, 2000b). The PAUs are located in international airports in the United States and are composed of senior inspectors who have been granted access to various law enforcement databases to assist them in identifying the potential risk of incoming passengers; for purposes of this discussion, the focus is on the potential risk that the incoming passenger is attempting to smuggle narcotics or other contraband into the United States.

Lawsuits Lead to GAO Study

In the late 1990s a rash of lawsuits was filed against USCS by airline passengers who alleged that they had been targeted and singled out for examination by USCS inspectors through discriminatory practices and were therefore inappropriately and illegally subjected to searches, especially strip searches. The U.S. Senate requested that the GAO conduct a review of USCS policies and procedures for conducting personal searches to determine what controls were in place to ensure that USCS inspectors were not inappropriately (i.e., racially) selecting passengers for personal searches (GAO, 2000b).

The GAO responded to the request by analyzing USCS personal search reports for airline passengers subjected to personal searches for fiscal years 1997 and 1998. The GAO found that, in general, airline passengers of certain races were in fact more likely than other passengers to be selected for more intensive and intrusive searches, such as x-rays or strip searches (GAO, 2000b). However, these passengers were not more likely, or even as likely, to be found smuggling illegal narcotics or other contraband into the United States. The most flagrant difference involved U.S. citizen Black females. Based on fiscal year 1998 data, the GAO found that they were nine times more likely than U.S. citizen White females to be subjected to an x-ray after having been frisked or patted down; however, based on the x-ray results, the U.S. citizen Black females were less than half as likely to be found smuggling illegal narcotics or other contraband than were U.S. citizen White females (GAO, 2000b).

The GAO study found from survey responses that USCS inspectors generally relied on more than one factor in deciding whether to conduct a pat down or other type of search and that the majority of inspectors' search reports provided three or more articulated reasons for conducting a personal search (GAO, 2000b). While these factors identified as the reasons individual passengers were selected for intrusive searches were seemingly race and gender neutral, the fact remained that based on established profiles that described the types of people who were most likely to be smuggling illegal narcotics, Black women were stopped and strip searched twice as often as White men and women and three times as likely as Black men (Davies, 2003).

USCS Response: Self-Initiated Assessment and Reforms

Due to the media coverage and intense Congressional interest in USCS based on the allegations that had been made in lawsuits regarding the targeting of minorities for intrusive searches at international airports and other ports of entry, USCS responded quickly to address these issues (Cogan, 1992). Raymond Kelly, the commissioner of USCS at the time, appointed a special commission to address these issues and prepare a report on personal searches conducted by USCS (Cogan, 1992). In fact, USCS was already addressing the allegations lodged against it regarding racial profiling and was in the process of reforming its policies and procedures at the time the GAO was doing its report for the U.S. Senate.

In 1999, USCS conducted a review of its personal search policies and procedures for the purpose of ensuring that its practices did not discriminate on the basis of gender, race, color, or ethnicity (GAO, 2000b). Based on its review, USCS implemented a number of changes in its existing policies and procedures. USCS began its reforms by revising its search policies. Race was removed as a factor that could be considered in targeting. Instead, USCS inspectors were to select individuals to stop and search using observational techniques focusing on specific behaviors exhibited by a subject (Ramirez, Hoopes, & Quinlan, 2003).

Under the new personal search policy, supervisory approval was required for all pat down searches with the exception of an immediate pat down or frisk for weapons (GAO, 2000b). Supervisors were also required to complete check sheets for all negative personal searches ("Kelly Acts on Personal Searches: Fairness Key to Reforms," 1999). In addition, port directors' approval was required for any search involving an individual being taken to a medical facility for an exam, such as an x-ray (GAO, 2000b). Other reforms included that mandatory notification be made to a federal magistrate when USCS officers detained a subject for more than 4 hours ("Kelly Acts on Personal Searches," 1999).

Part of the USCS reforms included a new data collection system; inspectors were required to collect data regarding the race, age, gender, and citizenship of those individuals detained for a personal search ("Kelly Acts on Personal Searches," 1999). The data analysis unit (DAU) created at the headquarters level was responsible for reviewing and analyzing all collected data for, among other things, determining the effectiveness of the inspectors' activity and also to ensure that racial profiling was not occurring.

Reforms also included new signs at international airports to better inform travelers and a new system to help accommodate travelers who may have been delayed by a personal search ("Kelly Acts on Personal Searches," 1999). Such reforms were an attempt to improve not only race relations but also the agency's relations with the public as a whole. Further, as part of the complaint process, USCS assigned passenger service representatives at 17 of the country's largest international airports. These passenger service representatives were responsible for handling passenger complaints, interacting with travelers, and attempting to improve passenger relations. In March 1999, USCS established the Customer Satisfaction Unit at USCS Headquarters to aid in the centralization and standardization of the passenger complaint process. A passenger complaint tracking system was also implemented to facilitate the tracking and review of passenger complaints (GAO, 2000b).

In all, the GAO was complimentary of the reforms made by USCS and noted that "... [U.S. Customs] new policies and controls will better safeguard rights of U.S. citizens and the traveling public" (GAO, 2000b, p. 10). In the year following these reforms, USCS reported 75% fewer personal searches but a 226% improvement in the rates of positive searches (i.e., those resulting in the discovery of contraband; Johnson, 2002). In essence, the self-initiated reforms resulted in a much more effective and efficient law enforcement process. The lesson learned from the USCS experience was that limiting officers' discretion does not necessarily have an adverse impact on a law enforcement agency's mission (Johnson, 2002). Instead, the self-imposed regulation can actually result in improvements and more efficient performance. Also, by implementing reforms that ensure that the officers are acting in a nondiscriminatory manner, the public's perception of the agency improved.

The Arab and Muslim Experience Post September 11, 2001

In the aftermath of the terrorist attacks of September 11, 2001 (9/11), blatant racial profiling of Arabs and Muslims occurred. They were disproportionately targeted for in-depth screening and searches at airports. Some were even denied the right to board and travel on their ticketed flights. They were also targeted for vehicle stops and for investigative interviews by law enforcement. The terrorist attacks of 9/11 had a tremendous impact on the American public's attitudes toward racial profiling. Prior to 9/11, public sentiment had been adamantly opposed to racial profiling. After 9/11, the American public was overwhelmingly in favor of racial profiling and much more likely to condone it if the purpose was to deter terrorism or in furtherance of some other national security goal (Johnson, 2004).

Profiling of Arabs and Muslims after 9/11 is significantly different from previous forms of profiling. First, based on the terrorist attacks of 9/11, the intelligence and law enforcement communities identified a specific criminal and terrorist organization composed almost entirely of Muslims. Second, this organization posed a much greater potential national security threat—future terrorist attacks—than does narcotics (Ramirez et al., 2003). Even other minority groups who had previously been targeted under alleged racial profiling policies seemed to be in agreement that although many innocent people would also be targeted under such a policy, the prevention of future terrorist attacks and enhancement of national security justified the use of racial profiling with respect to Arabs and Muslims (Davies, 2003).

In June 2003, the Civil Rights Division of the Department of Justice (DOJ) issued guidelines regarding the proper consideration of race in the law enforcement arena. Adhering to previous pre-9/11 sentiment regarding racial profiling, the DOJ stated that in the realm of traditional law enforcement activities (e.g., drug enforcement), race should not be considered unless a witness to a crime has identified the perpetrator as being of a particular race (Johnson, 2004). In contrast, the DOJ describes race may be a justifiable basis when dealing with a national security issue or what DOJ described as a border integrity issue (Johnson, 2004). The DOJ noted that the distinction was justified on the basis of national security.

It has been over 10 years since the terrorist attacks of 9/11 and public sentiment is not as wholeheartedly in favor of the racial profiling of Arabs and Muslims as it had been in the immediate aftermath of 9/11. Reportedly, that there are currently over 3.5 million people of Arab ancestry residing in the United States. With a group of people that large, ethnicity alone is not going to be a useful indicator in determining possible terrorist activity (Davies, 2003). For this reason, an Arab appearance by itself should not be allowed as a legitimate basis for suspicion by law enforcement personnel. Furthermore, intelligence sources indicate that there are a relatively small number of individuals involved in planning terrorist activities. Because of this fact, critics argue that even using multiple criteria, any terrorist profile will likely yield many false-positives. As a result, many innocent people would be stopped and searched but not many terrorists would be detected (Colb, 2001).

In January 2010, the Transportation Security Administration (TSA) issued a new security directive mandating enhanced security screening for all individuals flying into the United States from anywhere in the world who has a passport issued by, or who is flying from or through a country that is a state sponsor of terrorism or is otherwise a country of interest with regard to national security (TSA, 2010). Again, many innocent people will be subjected to enhanced security screening, but since national security is at issue the targeting of these individuals is allowed solely on the basis of their association to a suspect country.

As an alternative to the racial profiling of Arabs and Muslims, law enforcement could increase their investigations of those Arab and Muslim individuals who are already suspected of criminal activity; consensual or criminal predicate stops and searches can be used by law enforcement to further investigations regarding these suspects. In addition, law enforcement officials should strive to develop positive relationships with those in the Arab and Muslim communities through consensual encounters. If the Arab and Muslim communities develop a trusting relationship with law enforcement, they are much more likely to voluntarily provide information and intelligence regarding possible terrorist activities (Ramirez et al., 2003).

Immigration Enforcement and Profiling

It is impossible to determine the exact number of illegal aliens present in the United States. While many illegal aliens come to the United States seeking only to work and earn better wages, it has been argued that their sheer numbers are putting a severe financial strain on the country. For example, illegal aliens take advantage of many of the same services the United States routinely provides to its poor citizens, such as free medical care. In addition, many illegal aliens are convicted felons. Of every 12 aliens apprehended by Border Patrol, 1 has a criminal record often containing convictions for felonies and other crimes (Buchanan, 2006). The majority of illegal aliens present in the United States are from Mexico. It is therefore not surprising that aliens of Mexican or other Hispanic origin comprise the majority of those apprehended and deported. This naturally gives rise to allegations that U.S. immigration officials use racial profiling to target Mexicans and other Hispanics in their day-to-day law enforcement activities.

Operation Wetback

Allegations against U.S. immigration officials regarding the use of racial profiling to aid in the apprehension of illegal aliens is not a new concept. INS was roundly criticized for its profiling techniques used during Operation Wetback in 1954. Thousands of illegal aliens were apprehended as law enforcement officers swarmed through Mexican barrio communities in the Southwestern United States. Blatant racial and ethnic profiling was used during this operation with officers stopping people on the street simply because they looked Mexican and demanding identification and proof of U.S. citizenship (PBS, 2006). By fall 1954, apprehensions and deportations under this operation dwindled as INS funding for the operation ran out and opponents of the operation, in Mexico as well as in the United States, complained that the program was xenophobic and used police-state tactics (Koestler, 2006).

Court Decisions

The courts have been more liberal in allowing race or ethnicity to be considered in profiling in immigration enforcement than they have generally been in criminal law enforcement. This liberalism is primarily due to the fact that race or ethnicity is more directly related to illegal alienage. In 1975, the Supreme Court held in the case of *United States v. Brignoni-Ponce* that Mexican appearance could be one factor to be considered in an immigration stop as long as it was not the only factor that law enforcement considered (Johnson, 2004). In that case, the court found a Border Patrol stop to be invalid because it was based exclusively on the subject's Mexican appearance.

However, the Court noted that the likelihood of any given person of Mexican ancestry being an illegal alien was high enough that Mexican appearance could be a relevant factor for law enforcement officers to consider in determining whether to make an immigration stop. It is unlikely that a court today would find Mexican appearance to be as strong a proxy for immigration status as it did in the mid-1970s (Johnson, 2004).

In 1985, the U.S. Court of Appeals for the Ninth Circuit in *Nicacio v. INS* held that an illegal alien profile used by the INS and Border Patrol was invalid because it focused almost exclusively on race in immigration stops (Johnson, 2002). Agents testified in that case that factors in the illegal alien profile they used included Hispanic appearance, dirty or unkempt appearance, and the fact that the person wore work clothing. The court noted in the *Nicacio* case that these are all characteristics shared by U.S. citizens as well as illegal aliens who lived and worked in the area. In addition, extensive testimony from INS and Border Patrol agents indicated that these officers relied too heavily on this invalid illegal alien profile and their subjective intuitions and failed to articulate specific factors and rational inferences they drew from these factors suggesting that the subjects they stopped were indeed illegal aliens.

287(g) Cross-Designation Program

The Illegal Immigration Reform and Immigrant Responsibility Act of 1996 (IIRAIRA) Public Law 104-208 enacted on September 30, 1996, amended the Immigration and Nationality Act (INA) by adding Section 287(g), 8 U.S.C. Section 1357(g) to the Act. Section 287(g) of the INA authorized the attorney general of the United States (later amended to the Secretary for the Department of Homeland Security) to enter into written agreements to delegate the authority of enforcing federal immigration laws to state and local law enforcement agencies. The agreements allow designated officers within the state and local agencies to perform immigration law enforcement functions, pursuant to a Memorandum of Understanding, provided that the state or local law enforcement officers receive the requisite training and act under the supervision of sworn U.S. Immigration and Customs Enforcement (ICE) agents (U.S. Immigration and Customs Enforcement, 2006).

This cross-designation of officers between ICE and state and local law enforcement agencies is beneficial in that it increases immigration enforcement resources and support in more remote geographical locations where ICE may not have an established presence, thereby allowing for better enforcement coverage throughout the United States. While not yet extensively used, these 287(g) initiatives have been somewhat successful where implemented and have generated numerous investigative leads, arrests, and convictions for a variety of both state and federal charges (U.S. Immigration and Customs Enforcement, 2006).

However, these 287(g) initiatives have generated an outcry from Hispanic activists that these cross-designation programs lead to racial profiling by state and local law enforcement who act under the cover of their immigration authority to target Hispanics. To ensure that these programs do not promote racial profiling, in jurisdictions where the 287(g) initiative is implemented, the program should be closely monitored and supervised to ensure that state and local law enforcement officers are using only their immigration authorities incidental to their normal law enforcement duties, such as during a normal traffic stop for a moving violation or when responding to a crime scene.

Conclusion and Policy Recommendations

Despite many criticisms, the fact remains that profiling is an effective and essential law enforcement tool. Law enforcement resources will always be limited; profiling, if used correctly, allows law enforcement officers to narrow their focus and concentrate their investigative efforts on those subjects who have certain characteristics or fit a profile of those more likely to be committing a certain type of criminal activity. Profiling will grow increasingly controversial as long as issues such as terrorism and illegal immigration remain in the political spotlight. Due to the ethnic element often inherently present in these activities, any type of enforcement against certain ethnic groups engaging in illegal immigration or terrorist activities will likely raise allegations of racial profiling. Both the legislature and the judicial system will continue to review the use of profiling to insure that it is being used in a race-neutral manner.

In light of this heightened scrutiny, law enforcement agencies would be well advised to initiate internal assessments of their profiling practices to ensure that their officers are acting in a nondiscriminatory manner. As seen by the reforms implemented by USCS, using a narrower profile and limiting officers' discretion can actually result in more efficient performance by the agency. If law enforcement agencies do not engage in self-policing and allow profiling abuses to continue, it is likely that the legislature and judiciary will act to further limit the use of profiling.

There is a crying need for well-designed research that accurately assesses whether or not racial and ethnic profiling occurs in a discriminatory manner. That is, an automobile stop, an airport secondary search, and so forth occur only because of a person's race or ethnicity and without considering other behaviors. This will be exceptionally difficult to measure because in those circumstances where discrimination is likely to occur the decision maker can "manipulate the data" by making additional stops or searches of nontargeted groups to provide cover for active racial and ethnic profiling.

While many law enforcement agencies may voluntarily collect various types of information regarding their stops, searches, and arrests, there is no nationwide mandate that they do so. Additionally, the data collected are likely to be flawed if it is not done by an independent oversight agency. If the collection of specific information were mandatory, the result would be a much more complete and comprehensive original database allowing more thorough empirical research to address the effectiveness of profiling. The federal government should consider implementing such practices.

Despite all the criticism, profiling is an effective law enforcement technique. In the first 6 years of profiling use at the Miami International Airport, over 1,000 arrests were made, and more than $1 billion in narcotics was seized (Wilson, 1996). Profiling results in successful arrests and seizures more often than would random targeting of individuals (Trende, 2000). The key to using profiling appropriately is to be able to articulate indicators of criminal behavior that are both race neutral and nondiscriminatory.

References

Becker, S. (2004). Assessing the use of profiling in searches by law enforcement personnel. *Journal of Criminal Justice*, 23, 183–193.

Buchanan, P. J. (2006). *State of emergency: The third world invasion and conquest of America*. New York: St. Martin's Press.

Cogan, M. R. (1992). The Drug Enforcement Agency's use of drug courier profiles: One size fits all. *Catholic University Law Review*, *41*, 943–978.

Colb, S. F. (2001, October 10). The new faces of racial profiling: How terrorism affects the debate. FindLaw.Com Legal News & Commentary. Retrieved from http://writ.news.findlaw.com/scripts/printer_friendly.pl?page=/colb/20011010.html

Davies, S. L. (2003). Reflections on the criminal justice system after September 11, 2001: Profiling terror. *Ohio State Journal of Criminal Law*, 1, 45–101.

Dunderdale, M. W. (2000). Totality of the suspicious circumstances: Airport drug courier profile use in Massachusetts since *Commonwealth v. Torres*. *Suffolk Journal of Trial & Appellate Advocacy*, *5*, 125–148.

Engel, R. S., & Calnon, J. M. (2004). Examining the influence of drivers' characteristics during traffic stops with police: Results from a national survey. *Justice Quarterly*, *21*(1), 49–90.

Florida v. Royer. (1983). 460 U.S. 491.

Fredrickson, D. D., & Siljander, R. P. (2002). *Racial profiling*. Springfield, IL: Charles Thomas Publisher, Ltd.

Gregory, A. M. (1994). Smugglers who swallow: The constitutional issues posed by drug swallowers and their treatment. *University of Pittsburgh Law Review*, *56*, 323–365.

Gross, S. R., & Barnes, K. Y. (2002). Road work: Racial profiling and drug interdiction on the highway. *Michigan Law Review*, *101*, 651–754.

Hall, S. E. (1993). A balancing approach to the constitutionality of drug courier profiles. *University of Illinois Law Review*, 1993, 1007–1036.

Johnson, K. R. (2002). New voices on the war on drugs: U.S. border enforcement: Drugs, migrants, and the rule of law. *Villanova Law Review*, 47, 897–919.
Johnson, K. R. (2004). Racial profiling after September 11: The Department of Justice's 2003 guidelines. *Loyola Law Review*, 50, 67–87.
"Kelly acts on personal searches: Fairness key to reforms." (1999, October). *U.S. Customs Today.* Retrieved from http://www.cbp.gov/custoday/oct1999 /perserch.htm
Koestler, F. (2006). Operation Wetback. *The Handbook of Texas Online.* Retrieved from http://www.tsha.utexas.edu/handbook/online/articles/00/pqol_print.html
Nicacio v. INS, (1985). 797 F.2d 700.
O'Connor, T. (2006). History of profiling. Retrieved from http://faculty.ncwc.edu/toconnor/428/4281ect01.htm
Public Broadcasting System. (PBS). (2006). "Operation Wetback." *The Border.* Retrieved from http://www. pbs.org/kpbs/theborder/history/timeline/20.html
Ramirez, D. A., Hoopes, J., & Quinlan, T. L. (2003). Defining racial profiling in a post-September 11 world. *American Criminal Law Review, 40*(3), 1195–1233.
Reitzel, J. D., Rice S. K., & Piquero, A. R. (2004). Lines and shadows: Perceptions of racial profiling and the Hispanic experience. *Journal of Criminal Justice, 32*, 607–616.
Trende, S. P. (2000). Why modest proposals offer the best solution for combating racial profiling. *Duke Law Journal, 50*, 331–380.
Transportation Security Administration. (TSA). (2010). TSA Statement on New Security Measures for International Flights to the U.S. Retrieved from http://www.tsa.gov/press/happenings/010210_statement.shtm
United States v. Brignoni-Ponce. (1975). 422 U.S. 873; 95 S.Ct. 2574.
United States v. Elmore. (1980). 595 F.2d 1036 (5th Cir. 1979), *cert. denied*, 447 U.S. 910.
United States v. Montoya de Hernandez. (1985). 473 U.S. 531.
United States v. Sokolow. (1989). 490 U.S. 1.
U.S. Government Accountability Office. (GAO). (1999, July). *Report to congressional requesters, drug control: DEA's strategies and operations in the 1990's*. GAO/GGD-99-108. Washington, DC: Author.
U.S. Government Accountability Office. (GAO). (2000a, March). *Report to the Hon. James E. Clyburn, chairman, Congressional Black Caucus, racial profiling: Limited data available on motorist stops*, GAO/GGD-00-41. Washington, DC: Author.
U.S. Government Accountability Office. (GAO). (2000b, March). *Report to the Hon. Richard J. Durbin, U.S. sen., U.S. searches could produce better results*, GAO/GGD-00-38. Washington, DC: Author.
U.S. Immigration and Customs Enforcement. (2006). Pamphlet: Delegation of immigration authority—Section 287(g) Immigration and Nationality Act.
Whren v. United States. (1996). 517 U.S. 806.
Wilkins v. Maryland State Police. (1993). Civil Action No. CCB93483, Maryland Federal District Court.
Wilson, B. A. (1996). The war on drugs: Evening the odds through the use of the airport drug courier profile. *Boston Public Interest Law Journal*, 6, 203–242.

Municipal Police Departments' Attention to Crime Analysis

Essential or Impractical?[1]

11

BRION SEVER
Monmouth University

VENESSA GARCIA
Kean University

ANTONIA TSIANDI
Monmouth University

Contents

[1] Reprinted with permission from Taylor & Francis, Ltd.

Introduction

The term *police innovation* is a relatively broad one that can be used to describe a number of tools employed by the police. For instance, *innovative* may be used to depict departments that require advanced education or training, have modern armor and weapons, develop new policies, or obtain the newest computer software. Regardless of the type of innovation, however, the term is generally used to describe techniques that are somewhat modern or regarded as advanced beyond the standard in the field. Though researchers do not seem to agree on a universal definition of innovation, let alone why innovation differs across departments, King (2000) noted that researchers have commonly defined police innovation as new to policing or state-of-the-art and that great debate has taken place over the ever-changing idea of what constitutes innovative in policing.

It is not the purpose of our study to add to the theoretical debate of the type of police activities that are innovative. Instead, we do argue that innovation involves strategies and practices not only that are new and modern but also that can be used to aid the efficiency, accuracy, and effectiveness of a department. Some of these strategies can be new, but some simply may consist of relatively old technology or strategies that are *unused* because of a perceived lack of need or resources. We contend that departments that attempt to use strategies that aid in exploring all the options available are also innovative in nature. This could include undertaking training on budgeting techniques, writing grants to acquire funding, expanding computer expertise in the department, reaching out in community collaborative efforts, or purchasing the newest computer software.

One popular innovative strategy of law enforcement today is found in the area of crime analysis. In the most rudimentary form of crime analysis, police departments compare the commonalities of the crimes that occur in their jurisdictions. Moreover, a primary goal of crime analysis is for police to use trends to identify potential victims and offenders as well as the probable location and time of crime (Rich, 1995). Historically, the techniques of crime analysis have included the use of standard forms, cards, and crime mapping, more notably pin maps, whereby crimes possessing similar characteristics are color-coded according to their type, time, and space of occurrence (Harries, 1999).

Pin maps were one of the first crime mapping techniques to advance crime analysis based on mapping patterns of crime (Harries, 1999). Through pin mapping, crime hot spots were discovered by color-coding pins to draw out patterns in crime types occurring in various sections of a neighborhood. Since they provide police with some guidance to where crimes may occur and to problematic areas within the jurisdiction of their patrol, pin maps provided a needed advancement of patrol based on simple word of mouth by citizens and police. Unfortunately, manual pin mapping has its limitations.

The problems caused by the outdated crime analysis technology come about when the patterns become too multidimensional for one map. For example, how does a police department map a rash of residential muggings involving violence over a period of time compared with a rash of residential burglaries not involving violence over a period of time? Within that same neighborhood how does one also trace street theft, commercial theft, and motor vehicle thefts over a period of time? Moreover, how does the crime analyst also include the background characteristics of the offender, the victim, the time of day of the crime, and other such important information? When such sophisticated analysis is desired, the pin map becomes an inadequate technology in crime analysis. Using this same example, crime mapping forms and cards become too numerous to uncover true patterns of crime.

As it has advanced many other facets of our society, modern technology has begun to deal with some of the problems of crime analysis in its raw form. As modern technology improves, law enforcement officials find themselves using more sophisticated techniques of analyzing crime. Among these techniques are computerized geographic information systems (GIS), or crime mapping systems (Eck, Chainey, Cameron, Leitner, & Wilson, 2005). Computerized crime mapping allows crime analysts to gather numerous forms of data, analyze these data, and quickly disseminate the findings. It also allows crime analysts to use internal data gathered by law enforcement officials as well as external data, such as census data, utilities information, and property assessment data (Harries, 1999; Mamalian & LaVigne, 1999; Rich, 1999). By engaging in computerized crime mapping, police can detect spatial and temporal relationships between crimes and the characteristics of the community, offenders, and victims.

Crime mapping aids in the efforts to fight and prevent crime. Departments can use crime mapping data to inform patrol efforts in crime fighting and prevention, to map calls for service, to determine resource allocation, to evaluate interventions and programs, to aid in community-oriented policing and problem-oriented policing, and to aid in more cost-effective crime fighting (Harries, 1999; Mamalian & LaVigne, 1999; Haley et al., 2001; Eck et al., 2005). Any effort to realistically expand crime mapping, however, must include an examination of the perceived need and the resources to engage in such advanced technology. Today, many departments' crime analysts are police officers who may or may not have the necessary skills to engage in computerized crime mapping. In this study, we explore the type of computer technology possessed by police departments as well as the extent and manner to which they used crime analysis.

Crime Analysis, Computerization, and Crime Mapping

Crime mapping is an important part of crime analysis, though not one and the same, so the literature on crime analysis and computerized crime mapping is abundant, particularly in the past decade. It can be separated into general studies on the benefits and complexities of crime analysis (Bennett, 1995; Cameron, 1999; Figlio, Hakim, & Rengert, 1986; Gottlieb, Arenberg, & Singh, 1994; Harris, 1985; Vellani & Nahoun, 2000; Webster and Connors, 1993) and case studies of particular departments that have implemented crime analysis (Anderson, 1990; Bellucci, 1995; Canter, 1998). Most crime mapping literature can be separated in the same manner, with similar general studies (Bibel, 2000; Block, Dabdoub, & Fregly, 1995; Eck et al., 2005; Fortner, 1998; Harries, 1999; Moore, 1995; Nulph & Mudd, 1999; Rossmo, 2000) and case studies (Bellucci, 1995; Buslik & Maltz, 1997; Clontz, 1997; Harries, 1995; Hirshfield; LaVigne & Wartell, 1998; McGuire, 2000; Rich, 1999; Weisburd & Green, 1995).

Only a few studies, however, have examined the actual use of crime analysis or computerized crime mapping on a large scale in the United States. Most recently, the U.S. Department of Justice (DOJ) Office of Community Oriented Policing Services (COPS; DOJ COPS, 2002) released findings of a national study on crime analysis. Specifically, this study was performed on all law enforcement departments employing more than 100 police officers (554 responded). They also included a sample of 777 law enforcement departments employing fewer than 100 officers, asking them many of the same survey questions. The findings revealed that among police departments employing more than 100 officers, 74% employed at least one member whose primary role was crime analysis. Interestingly, even in these large departments, there was some disagreement over who within the department should perform crime analysis. About half of these large departments were found to have centralized units that were not located in or under the authority of investigations or patrol divisions.

The study also found that 61% of the large departments surveyed used GIS mapping software and that the majority also used spreadsheets for crime analysis. Only 20% of the departments were found to use a statistical package such as SPSS or SAS. The sophistication of some of these large departments can ultimately be seen in their use of statistical analysis in crime analysis. Indeed, more than half of the departments used correlation analysis, while 36% used regression analysis.

Not surprisingly, the DOJ study (DOJ COPS, 2002) did not find crime analysis to be as popular or as sophisticated in the sample of law enforcement departments with fewer than 100 officers. Only 47% of the departments stated that they employed crime analysis, and only 23% acknowledged having a person whose primary responsibility was crime analysis. However, 45% of these departments stated that they used crime analysis for plotting crime trends and patrol strategies. Only 33% of these departments provided training for statistical analysis involved in crime analysis, and only 19% attempted to forecast crime.

Another important study in the area of crime analysis was undertaken by the Police Foundation (2000). This study placed more focus on the use of actual computerized crime mapping as a crime analysis tool. Specifically, it analyzed a convenience sample of 51 police departments that received funding from COPS, 42 of which were funded specifically to develop mapping technology. The average size of police departments in their sample was over 1,900 employees, serving an average population of over 363,000.

This study found considerable diversity in mapping approaches across the departments. Most shocking was their finding that some departments appeared to have made no plans to undertake computer crime mapping, despite having received funds from COPS specifically for this purpose. Overall, 60% indicated that they were involved in computer crime mapping, with half of these departments having three or fewer people engaged in mapping. Moreover, 77% of these departments involved in crime mapping had police officers using maps in the field. Nearly half of these departments used crime mapping to create reports on the status of crime in their cities.

Though their focus was not on crime analysis or computerized crime mapping, other studies have examined the related topic of innovations in computerization used in law enforcement. For instance, Mullen (1996) surveyed a national sample of 303 police departments concerning their use of computers. He found that having advanced computerization was correlated with departments having greater innovation in other programs and the size and budget of the department. In other words, his findings would support the notion that when it comes to innovation in policing there are haves and have nots based greatly on departmental size.

Although the present study is closely related to the studies previously reviewed, it differs from them in its sample, focus, and purpose. For instance, the focus of the DOJ study (DOJ COPS, 2002) was mostly on general crime analysis, while we analyzed crime mapping, crime analysis, and computer software. Moreover, their sample included law enforcement departments (including state and sheriff departments), while we focused mostly on smaller city police departments. The report released by the Police Foundation (2000) focused more on crime mapping and did not examine statistical packages or basic departmental needs. Additionally, their sample consisted of large departments that had received funding for the purpose of crime mapping, providing an entirely different sample than the one we explored.

The problem addressed in the present study is that most police departments within the United States tend to be small and do not have resources (i.e., budget, equipment, and trained crime analysts) to invest in such complicated technologies as GIS. We examined the resources and attention that departments placed on this technology. Therefore, the present study moved beyond the exploration of the nature of police departments' use of crime analysis and computerized crime mapping technology and examined some areas that have been largely unexplored.

Data and Methods

In fall 2002, data were collected through telephone interviews of all police departments in New Jersey that serve a population of over 15,000. This sample included cities small enough to achieve some representation of the typical police departments in New Jersey yet large enough so that the cities could have resources to devote to software and personnel. We contacted all 171 departments fitting this description by telephone. Typically, an operator directed us to the person or department in charge of crime analysis or crime mapping, and we attempted to make contact. If the contact did not return our phone calls, we attempted to make contact on two more occasions.

We were able to speak with staff members of 109 of the police departments who answered our surveys; however, we omitted 19 surveys due to incomplete data, leaving a total of 90 completed surveys, and a response rate of 53%.[2] The departments in our sample were small enough to represent typical departments in New Jersey yet large enough that they could legitimately have or at least could develop computerized crime mapping and analysis.

We were able to gather some of our data from existing sources. For instance, we gathered information on the numbers of police officers (civilian and sworn) as well as nonviolent index crime and violent index crime from the New Jersey Uniform Crime Reports (State of New Jersey, Division of State

[2] There was little difference between the 90 cities that participated in the interview and the 81 that we could not reach or that provided incomplete data. Both groups of cities were primarily urban, with the percentage of the urban population averaging 97% for those cities included and 94% for those not included. The average populations were similar, with the cities making up the data having an average population of 37,840 compared with 33,961 for the 81 cities not included in the data, and the demographic averages were also comparable. Although the possibility exists that departments with more interest in crime analysis were more likely to respond to our surveys, we believe that it was more likely the result of the personality or time availability of the particular person that we contacted. Moreover, since the theme of this study is that crime analysis and crime mapping are largely underused, any social bias present would likely suggest that these strategies are used even less than our findings indicate, ultimately strengthening our discussion.

Police, 2000). Moreover, the revenue of each city was taken from the U.S. Bureau of the Census (2000).

Most of our data were gathered via use of survey research. Specifically, telephone interviews of each department focused on the staff member who oversaw crime analysis for the department or the closest position to a crime analyst. Each department was first asked which member of their department oversaw crime analysis. If there was no specific member, we then tried to identify which member oversaw data collection efforts. Once this member was identified, we conducted the interviews, seeking information about the departments' crime analysis capabilities and the overall needs of the department.[3]

Measures

Dependent Variables

In gaining an overall picture of how departments analyzed crime data, we asked various questions describing their efforts. Five dependent variables were used in the bivariate and multivariate analyses. Departments were asked what percentage of time they devoted to crime data analysis. Second, they were asked if the department did any computerized crime mapping (1 = yes). Important to the successes of crime analysis, we asked if officers were regularly briefed on the crime data via, for example, reports (1 = yes). Departments were asked how often the department conducted crime mapping analyses (1 = daily, 2 = weekly, 3 = biweekly, 4 = monthly, 5 = as needed). Finally, we measured the leadership support given to efforts in crime analysis (leadership support index). Creating an index we combined four ordinal measures: (1) leadership financially supports crime mapping efforts; (2) accepted that mapping is a valuable tool; (3) mapping directives come from the top; and (4) employees are sent to computer crime mapping conference (1 = not accurate and 5 = very accurate). The index ranged from 0 to 20. The Cronbach's alpha for this scale was .580, which revealed moderate reliability of the index.[4]

Independent Variables

We created four rates to use in the multivariate analysis: (1) nonviolent index crime rate; (2) violent index crime rate; (3) sworn officer rate; and (4) civilian officer rate. The nonviolent index crime rate was measured by the department's total nonviolent index crimes per 100,000 people in 2000, while the

[3] Survey is available upon request.

[4] Cronbach's alpha is a coefficient of interitem reliability of a complex measure. Generally, a score of .70 is considered strong, with .60 considered acceptable. Therefore, the alphas scores of .58 and .53 are considered moderately reliable.

violent crime rate was measured by the department's total violent crimes per 100,000 people in 2000. Sworn officer rate was measured by the department's number of sworn officers per 100,000 people in 2000, and civilian officer rate was measured by the department's number of civilian officers per 100,000 people in 2000. Revenue was measured by total revenue per 100,000 people in the department's city in 2000.

From the survey we used two questions as independent variables in the multivariate analysis. We asked what formal education the crime analyst had (1 = BA/BS or above). Finally, we created an index (hurdles) to measure the hurdles faced in crime analysis efforts. This index included eight ordinal measures of department limitations with (1) computer resources, (2) financial resources, (3) time, (4) training opportunities, (5) working knowledge of how mapping is used in the field, (6) interest from administration, (7) interest from support staff, (8) difficulties with software (1 = no problem and 5 = serious problem). The index ranged from 0 to 40. The Cronbach's alpha for this scale was .530, which revealed moderate reliability of the index.

Measures of Crime Analysis Efforts

Other measures included in this analysis were used to describe the crime analysis efforts among New Jersey police departments and were collected from interview data. Among the information that we pursued in our survey were the actual person who kept crime data for the department (crime analysis staff, patrol officer, investigative staff, dispatch, other) and if the department had any type of crime mapping (1 = yes). Though crime analysis is a distinct strategy from the method of crime mapping (often crime mapping is one method by which departments analyze crime), many crime analysts mistook their use of crime mapping software as one and the same with crime analysis. As a result, we asked respondents about both in the same question, thus producing an overall amount of crime analysis and crime mapping that the department performs. In other questions concerning education and training, we used the term crime mapping and crime analysis as the same entity. This was done because the person we interviewed about crime analysis was nearly always the same person performing crime mapping.

The type of computer program, or database, used for storage by the police departments was another issue of interest in this study. It related to the renewed interest in law enforcement toward centralization and the sharing of information between departments. If departments do not have similar database programs in which data (particularly crime data) can easily be transferred from one department to another, the effort toward interdepartmental cooperation is certainly hampered. Finally, we asked each department what the greatest need was for their new recruits.

Analytic Strategy

Analysis for the data first involved a univariate description of crime analysis efforts of the police departments in the sample. We then conducted a multivariate analysis of all independent variables on each dependent variable. However, to examine the correlations between the independent variables we first examined the bivariate correlations between several city characteristics and percentage of time devoted to crime analysis (Table 11.1). Obviously, the percentage time spent on crime analysis is not necessarily indicative of the sophistication or quality of the officers' work. Time may, however, suggest how dedicated departments are to accomplishing these tasks. Looking at the table, we see that both crime rates were positively correlated to the percentage of time placed on crime analysis strategies (although only violent crime was significant), contrasting with the DOJ COPS (2002) findings, which did not find crime to have an impact on crime analysis used in large law enforcement departments.

Looking at the impact of police force size on the two strategies, we find that the number of sworn officers per 100,000 people had a significant positive impact on percentage of time devoted to crime analysis but that civilian police staff did not. The DOJ COPS (2002) found similar findings for sworn personnel in its study of large law enforcement departments, but it did not test for the effects of civilian personnel or for the impact of the number of officers on crime analysis in the sample of smaller departments. Although it may seem ideal to hire a civilian officer with the skills to analyze crime, this seldom occurs in small departments. This could result for a number of reasons, ranging from the sensitivity of the data to the lack of confidence and trust typically placed in civilian staff. The hurdles and leadership support indexes had nonsignificant impacts on the percentage of time devoted by the crime analysts, merely suggesting that leadership ideas or departmental hurdles do not necessarily limit the departments' devotion to crime analysis or the individual employees' dedication to their job.

We performed multivariate analysis on five dependent variables: (1) department computerized crime mapping; (2) officers are briefed regularly on crime; (3) crime analysis performed regularly; (4) percentage of time dedicated to crime analysis; and (5) leadership support for crime mapping index (1 = yes). The percentage of time spent on crime analysis was measured at the ratio level, as was the leadership support index. Ordinary least squares (OLS) regression analysis was used in testing these two variables, while logistic regression was used for the three dichotomous dependent variables. Tests for normality were performed on the two interval variables (percent of time spent on crime analysis and leadership support index). The percentage of time spent on crime analysis variable was found to be skewed, so its natural log was used in its place. Testing for linearity through visual analysis of bivariate scatter plots, we did not find serious linearity problems. Moreover,

Table 11.1 Pearson Correlation Coefficients Between Key Variables in the Analysis

	(1)	(2)	(3)	(4)	(5)	(6)	(7)	(8)
Civilian Officer per 100,000 pop (1)	1	(.427**)	(.114)	(.136)	(–.005)	(.109)	(.143)	(.455**)
Sworn Officers per 100,000 pop (2)		1	(.114)	(.160)	(–.245)	(.372*)	(.536**)	(.684**)
Revenue per 100,000 people (3)			1	(.169)	(–.266*)	(.044)	(–.086)	(.001)
Hurdles to Undertaking Crime Mapping (4)				1	(–.315*)	(–.212)	(–.109)	(.0547)
Leadership Support of Crime Mapping (5)					1	(–.173)	(–.098)	(–.104)
% Time Officer Devotes to Crime Analysis (6)						1	(.330*)	(.281)
Violent Index Crimes per 100,000 pop (7)							1	(.570**)
Non violent Index Crimes per 100,000 pop (8)								1

** Correlation is significant at the 0.01 level
* Correlation is significant at the 0.05 level

the existence of multicollinearity problems were tested (for all five regression models) through the use of the variance inflation factors (VIFs), and no multicollinearity problems were found. Please see Appendix A for a list of variables used in the regression analysis.

Findings

Crime Analysis Activities

Before we list our main findings in the analysis, some background information about our sample is appropriate. City populations ranged in size from 15,181 to 149,222, with the median size being 31,274. This was significantly smaller than the cities policed by the departments in the studies completed by the Police Foundation (2000) and the DOJ COPS (2002). The police force size in our cities differed along with their populations, with the smallest force employing 26 sworn officers and the largest having 441 and an overall average of 92 sworn officers for all of the cities. The civilian officers employed full time by the city also ranged widely from 0 to 440, with an average civilian force of 22. Moreover, the average city had 8 part-time civilian officers, but this group ranged from 0 to 122.

Appendix A Variables Used in the Multivariate Analysis

Dependent Variables	Description
Computerized crime mapping	Department has computer crime mapping (1 = yes, 0 = no)
Percent time on crime analysis	Percent time department crime analyst spends on analysis
Frequency of crime analysis	1 = once a day, 0 = less than once per day
Leadership support of crime mapping	Leadership supports crime mapping (Index)
Officers briefed regularly?	Officers briefed at least once a week on crime? (1 = yes, 0 = no)
Independent Variables	**Description**
Nonviolent index crime rate	Department's nonviolent index crimes per 100,000 people in 2000
Violent index crime rate	Department's violent crimes per 100,000 people in 2000
Sworn officers	Department's sworn officers per 100,000 people in 2000
Civilian officers	Department's civilian officers per 100,000 people in 2000
Formal education of crime analyst	Formal education of crime analyst (1 = BA/BS or above, 0 = less than BA/BS
Hurdles to crime mapping	Index of hurdles department faces in implementing crime mapping
Revenue rate	Revenue per 100,000 people in department's city in 2000

Table 11.2a Frequency Table of Person Who Keeps Crime Data Statistics

	Frequency	Percent
Person Who Keeps Crime Data		
Sergeant	4	4
Group effort	4	4
Patrol officer	4	4
Captain	3	3
Lieutenant	3	3
Secretary	6	7
Records bureau/central records	42	47
Other	25	28

One of the questions that we had at the beginning of this study pertained to how departments collected their crime data and who was involved in the collection process. In this study, a moderately large amount of cities had record bureaus keeping crime data for the department.[5] Coming into this study, we predicted that cities with large police departments would be more likely to have such bureaus, but our findings show this not to be the case. Specifically, the cities with record bureaus had forces that averaged 117 total officers, while those without bureaus averaged 113 officers. Thus, record bureaus seem to be in place due to reasons beyond the size and responsibilities of the police department.

Table 11.2a shows that over half of the departments (53%) did not have records bureaus, and they relied on a number of different personnel (e.g., secretaries, sergeants, patrol officers) to collect their crime data. This is predictably less than the incidence of centralized records bureaus found in large law enforcement departments in the study conducted by the DOJ COPS (2002). The education of the person most responsible for crime data collection and inputting was relatively high (45% with a bachelor's or master's degree) as shown in Table 11.2b, suggesting that departments often employ officers with formal skills gained in college to oversee their data. This also suggests that the statistics and research classes required in most college and university criminal justice departments do have relevance to the field of policing, at least in New Jersey. However, the data show that over half of the people responsible for collecting crime data possessed less than a 4-year college degree or no college education at all, and 22% had a high school diploma. Additionally, from these data we see that many of the departments did not have a technologically advanced method of data collection.

[5] We used the term *records bureau* to include a number of similar bureaus, including several departments that had a central records department.

Table 11.2b Frequency Table of Formal Education of People Who Keep Crime Data

	Frequency	Percent
Formal Education		
High school	13	22
Some college	6	10
Associate's degree	4	7
Bachelor's degree	17	29
Master's degree	9	16
Other	9	16

Examining types of software used, we found little uniformity in the database programs used across New Jersey police departments (Table 11.3).[6] Thus, our fear concerning transfer of data from department to department seems to be quite realistic. Indeed, anyone who works with data sets realizes the frustrations involved with transferring data from programs such as Excel to Lotus without data sets becoming substantially disfigured in the transport. Nevertheless, perhaps the solution to this problem may lie in better coordination and compatibility of computer software programs rather than a uniform database for all departments in a given state.

The second concern is that while many police departments lacked trained crime analysts, most college criminal justice programs train these future criminal justice professionals in only a few of the programs identified in Table 11.3 (e.g., Excel, Lotus, SPSS). Hence, while 45% of the employees engaged in crime data collection had a bachelor's or master's degree, most were not qualified to use the computer technology adopted by the police department.

Turning our attention to the more specific analysis or mapping of data, we found that crime analysis was not used every day or even weekly by most departments (Table 11.4a). In fact, nearly two-thirds (64%) performed crime analysis once a month or less often. This suggests a sizeable split of haves and have nots in regards to the innovative technique of analysis. It seems that it is predictably the larger departments with large staffs that are most dedicated to advanced computerized programs, crime collection, crime inputting, and crime analysis. Support for this idea is found in the DOJ COPS (2002) study, which found that three-fourths of large departments had a person who spent most of his or her time doing crime analysis compared with less than one-fourth for smaller departments.

[6] It should be noted that the "other" category (29%) included dozens of departments that all had unique crime database programs. We included these departments in the "other" category so that the table would not be too large.

Table 11.3 Computer Programs Used to Keep Crime Data

Program	Frequency	Percent
CAD	11	12
Excel	7	8
Unix Operating System	6	7
QED	6	7
Private Vender	4	4
Cisco	4	4
Munipole	3	3
By hand / Tally Book	3	3
Access	2	2
CPLIMS	2	2
CIS	2	2
ESRI	2	2
Lotus	2	2
E.T. Technologies	2	2
MapQuest	1	1
Oracle	1	1
SPSS	1	1
THE Program	1	1
Key Map	1	1
Larimore Associates	1	1
IMC	1	1
Alert	1	1
Other	26	29
Total	90	97

Note: Percentages do not add to 100 due to rounding.

The respondents stated that the most common reason for not engaging in crime analysis was that there was not enough crime in their cities. This justification, however, ignores two major benefits to using crime analysis. First, the use of advanced data inputting analysis for calls for service beyond crime would likely increase the efficiency of the department. Second, combining crime data collection efforts with several adjoining cities is an option for cities with minimal crime amounts. In fact, large grant solicitations often use the hook of funding to encourage smaller departments to group together and coordinate their innovative efforts.

Not reported in the findings in Table 11.4a, we also found that 80% of departments briefed their officers on crime reports on a regular basis. This may suggest that while officers do get briefed regularly about crime trends

Table 11.4a Frequency Table of Regularity of Crime Mapping/Analysis

	Frequency	Percent
Frequency of Crime Mapping/Analysis		
Daily	12	25
Weekly	4	9
Biweekly	1	2
Monthly	13	27
As needed	12	24
Other	6	13

Table 11.4b Frequency Table of Crime Mapping/Analysis Performed

	Frequency	Percent
Crime Mapping/Analysis Performed		
Run statistics on certain areas/informally discuss	24	50
Push Pins	9	19
CAD	7	15
Microsoft Map Point	2	4
Fracts	1	2
Geographical Codes	1	2
Other	4	8

in their zones of patrol, their briefings are based more on word of mouth than quantitative analysis. This can be problematic because decisions made by word of mouth do not tend to address the bigger picture, or problem, and result in departments wasting valuable resources.

Table 11.4b also shows the breakdown in type of crime mapping and analysis performed in the departments surveyed. These categories are not indicative of all the mapping or analysis being performed in the field, in that some departments may use more than one of these techniques. We simply asked departments what type of crime mapping or analysis (or closest technique to it) they performed. This table shows how broadly some departments use the term *crime mapping* or *analysis.*

Half of the departments described their crime analysis as simply running crime trends for a particular area or areas and determining hot spots or problem areas. The second most common method was the old-fashioned pin mapping, still used in a sizeable proportion (19%) of departments. Less common were the more advanced software programs of computerized crime mapping, suggesting that most departments still lag behind the group of leaders using this technology.[7] In fact, eight departments stated that they had GIS crime mapping software but that it went unused because they did not have the personnel present to put it to use. Considering that the Police Foundation's (2000) national study found that many departments receiving funding for crime mapping were not using it, these findings do not present New Jersey as the only problematic state. This being the case, however, it is surprising that only 27% of departments not having a central records department had considered hiring a full-time crime analyst or crime mapping specialist.

Multivariate Analysis

Table 11.5 presents five regression models. All independent variables were run on each of the dependent variables: (1) computerized crime mapping; (2) officers briefed regularly; (3) crime analysis performed regularly; (4) percent of time spent on crime analysis; and (5) leadership support index. As described already, the first three dependent variables were dichotomous dependent variables, so logistic regression was used, while the last two dependent variables were interval level requiring OLS regression to be used. The table presents the unstandardized regression coefficients with the standard error in brackets. The data show that few of the independent variables had significant impacts on the dependent variables, and in essence the controls that we included "washed out" the individual effects of violent crime and sworn officers found in the bivariate correlations. One commonality found was that hurdles to crime mapping had a consistent negative insignificant impact on the five dependent variables, while the revenue and crime rates consistently had a positive insignificant impact. In separate analyses not included, total violent and nonviolent crime, revenue, and police size variables (not in a rate controlling for the population) were used instead of those per population. There was little difference in the findings, as the total crime and police size did not significantly impact the dependent variables. In testing these total measures, the only impact that we found was that civilian officer size significantly increased the likelihood that officers were briefed regularly and education of officers actually decreased the time spent on crime analysis.

[7] Geographic codes are used by some departments as a form of presenting coded crime data to their officers. Fracts is an old database program that was used by one department.

Table 11.5 Multivariate Regression Analysis of City Police Size, Revenue, and Other Variables on Use of Computerized Crime Mapping

	Computerized Crime Mapping? (1 = yes, 0 = no) (Logistic)	Officers Briefed Regularly? (1 = yes, 0 = no) (Logistic)	Crime Analysis Regularly? (1 = yes, 0 = no) (Logistic)	Percent Time Spent on Crime Analysis (OLS)	Leadership Support for Crime Map (OLS)
Nonviolent index crime rate	.000	–.001	.000	.000	.000
	(.000)	(.001)	(.000)	(.000)	(.001)
Violent index crime rate	–.001	.016	.003	.002	(–.001)
	(.002)	(.012)	(.003)	(.001)	(.003)
Sworn officers rate	.014	–.002	.006	.011	–.009
	(.010)	(.014)	(.012)	(.008)	(.015)
Civilian officers rate	–.006	.166*	–.022	–.014	.034
	(.027)	(.060)	(.035)	(.021)	(.043)
Hurdles to crime mapping	–.043	–.103	.010	–.056	–.150
	(.075)	(.120)	(.093)	(.050)	(.118)
Revenue rate	.000	.000	.000	(.000)	.000
	(.000)	(.000)	(.000)	(.000)	(.000)
Education	.026	–1.321	.872	–1.097*	.207
	(.767)	(1.261)	(.963)	(.520)	(1.263)
Chi square	7.43	11.7	6.9		
2 Log linear	52.15	29.61	40.1		
R-Square				.458	.102

Unstandardized Regression Coefficients— Top figure
Standard Error—(in brackets) * – $p < .05$

Discussion and Conclusion

This study indicates that while strategies of crime analysis are used in police departments within New Jersey, there is a high level of disparity in the development of these strategies. Indeed, the most advanced methods of crime analysis are used only by a small percentage of departments, while most tend to use less modern strategies of analysis. This could be due to a lack of emphasis on obtaining external grants, whereby departments inevitably may lack the funding to pursue such technologically advanced innovation.

Questions may arise as to how much emphasis departments should place on the technological innovations and aggressive pursuit of funding to achieve them. Many may question whether small police departments really need to worry about technology and computers rather than the personal needs of their citizenship. We believe, however, that our endorsement of such innovations is not analogous to Barney Fife pleading for tear gas in Mayberry. Again, the departments examined in our study do not patrol cities with sparse populations merely in the hundreds. Thus, we believe that these technological strategies are just as essential to any moderately sized department as is added manpower, firearms, and automobiles. In essence, they are a fundamental building block of departmental strategy and should be near the top of concerns during the budgeting period.

There is no doubt that development of technological strategies takes not only an economic sacrifice from a department but also one of considerable effort and even stress. Obviously, this may cause a number of departments to avoid such change and dismiss it as unnecessary, as with any innovative practice that involves some restructuring. However, we believe that the potential impact of such innovation supersedes the temporary hurdles that exist, making it a desirable undertaking for departments of any size.

In stressing the importance of good crime analysis, in particular, we provide the analogy of the legal problem of *fruits of the poisonous tree.* Most who are familiar with the criminal justice system know that this term refers to a condition by which the original taint of an item that is discovered illegally proceeds to taint every piece of evidence found as a result. We believe that a similar situation occurs in law enforcement. In particular, the idea behind preventative patrols is that they are being dispersed in a manner that will best impede crime. The manner in which preventive patrols are dispersed is highly dependent on the department's crime analysis. The more scientific and advanced the crime analysis, the more likely preventive patrols will succeed. This also highlights the importance of placing a priority on keeping valid crime data via the assignment of qualified personnel and technology. How can a department provide strategic patrols if the crime statistics that it is using as a guide are invalid? Moreover, how can a department provide strategic patrols if it is not even basing them on crime analysis?

Technologically advanced crime analysis may have the long-term effect of increasing the efficiency of many of the police department's operations. In fact, it may in the long-term save the department money, which can be used on better technology and other departmental necessities. Specifically, good crime analysis may result in a reduction of crime, or at least more efficient coverage of target crime areas, which in turn could provide opportunities for shifts in resources. Perhaps monies used for hiring more officers (who will compete for overtime pay) can be shifted to better equipment and, hopefully, to more satisfied officers. Again, though most departments seemed to respect the importance of having advanced crime analysis techniques, few of them intended to place more emphasis on this area in the near future.

An obvious question arises from the previous discussion: What can be done to encourage departments to place more attention and resources on their crime analysis efforts? The long-term reality in crime analysis is that departments lagging behind in all forms of technology will slowly follow behind the more innovative programs. Thus, 10 years from now, the most innovative crime analysis technology at present may be found in those with the most outdated systems in the future. Today's technology will be considered outdated in 10 years, but it would still improve on techniques such as pin mapping and basic descriptive analysis. In other words, we must hope that the departments with outdated approaches today will slowly advance their crime analysis techniques, just as they have slowly implemented computers and other such technology.

Another hope is that departments will place more attention on acquiring technology through external funding, and this will aid in evening the playing field in crime analysis. Indeed, it is more likely that departments will develop crime analysis through monies not dependent on budget cuts of other departmental necessities. However, just because departments acquire advanced technology does not mean that they will necessarily put them to use. Support for this statement can be found in the eight departments in our survey that had crime mapping technology yet had no one who could put it into effect. Thus, the central issue returns to the skills pursued by the law enforcement departments and those that new employees come in with.

We were surprised to find that the data programs that college graduates were trained in were rarely used by the police departments in New Jersey. This is important to recognize as 45% of the employees who conducted the departments' crime data collection had at least a 4-year college degree. We feel that both academia and law enforcement need to coordinate their efforts to ensure that the most qualified individuals are hired. There must be some effort on the part of academia to familiarize its graduates with the technological skills needed in the field and to prepare students accordingly. On the other side of the equation, police departments might consider some level of consistency in the programs they adopt to ensure a substantial pool of qualified candidates.

Little is known of the skills and technology present in small to moderate-sized departments, because the focus has always been placed on the large programs with cutting-edge strategies. We hope that future research in criminal justice will focus more attention on these neglected departments, particularly with regards to their use of technologically advanced strategies as well as their needs. Future study in this area should move beyond the mere exploratory analysis that we have undertaken and focus on explaining the underlying causes behind technological disparities across departments. If such disparities exist because of limited resources and understaffed departments, then perhaps national funding can help remedy the situation. If they exist because of lack of concern, care, or effort by old-fashioned departments, then education on the advantages of such innovation should be stressed through a louder platform.

References

Anderson, D. (1990). Seattle, Tacoma automated crime analysis. *American City and County*, 105.

Bellucci, C. (1995). DMAP in Jersey City: Implementing a technological revolution. In C. R. Block, M. Dabdoub, & S. Fregly (Eds.), *Crime analysis through computer mapping* (pp. 195–199). Washington, DC: Police Executive Research Forum.

Bennett, T. (1995). Identifying, explaining, and targeting burglary hot spots. *European Journal on Criminal Justice Policy and Research, 3*, 113–123.

Bibel, D. (2000). Statewide crime analysis and mapping: An on-going project. *Crime Mapping News, 2*, 1–4.

Block, C., Dabdoub, M., & Fregly, S. (1995). *Crime analysis through computer mapping*. Washington, DC: Police Executive Research Forum.

Brassel, D., & Utano, J. (1979). Linking crime and census information within a crime mapping system. *Review of Public Data Use, 7*, 15–24.

Bruns, D. (1990). Special focus: Computers and communications. *Police Chief, 57*, 22–53.

Buslik, M., & Maltz, M. (1997). Power to the people: Mapping information sharing in the Chicago police department. In D. Weisburd & T. McEwen (Eds.), *Crime mapping and crime prevention* (pp. 113–130). Monsey, NY: Criminal Justice Press.

Cameron, B. (1999). Technology improves crime statistics. *Law and Order, 47*, 30–32.

Canter, P. (1998). Baltimore County's autodialer system. In N. LaVigne & J. Wartell (Eds.), *Crime mapping case studies: Successes in the field* (pp. 81–92). Washington, DC: Police Executive Research Forum.

Clontz, K. A. (1997). Spatial analysis of residential burglaries in Tallahassee, Florida: Proceedings, 1997. *Environmental Systems Research Institute International User Conference*. Retrieved on June 14, 2007 from http://www.esri.com/library/userconf/archive.html

Eck, J. E., Chainey, S., Cameron, J. G., Leitner, M., & Wilson, R. E. (2005). *Mapping crime: Understanding hot spots*. Washington, DC: U.S. Department of Justice, National Institute of Justice. Retrieved June 14, 2007 from http://www.ojp.usdoj.gov/nij/maps/

Figlio, R., Hakim, S., & Rengert, G. (1986). *Metropolitan crime patterns*. Monsey, NY: Criminal Justice Press.

Fortner, R. (1998). Computer technology: Mapping the future. *Police, 22,* 16–21.

Gottlieb, S., Arenberg, S., & Singh, R. (1994). *Crime analysis: From first report to final arrest*. Montclair, CA: Alpha Publishing.

Haarr, R. (2001). The making of a community policing officer: The impact of basic training and occupational socialization on police recruits. *Police Quarterly, 4,* 402–433.

Haley, K. N., Todd, J. C., & Stallo, M. (1998). *Crime analysis and the struggle for legitimacy.* Paper presented at the annual meeting of the Academy of Criminal Justice Sciences, Albuquerque, NM, March 10–14. Retrieved October 26, 2001 from http://www.iaca.net/Resources/FAQs/legitimacy.htm

Harries, K. (1999). *Mapping crime: Principle and practice.* Washington, DC: U.S. Department of Justice, National Institute of Justice.

Harries, K. (1995). A database for the ecological analysis of social stress and violence in small areas. In C. R. Block, M. Dabdoub, & S. Fregly (Eds.), *Crime analysis through computer crime mapping* (pp. 167–178). Washington, DC: Police Executive Research Forum.

Harris, D. (1985). Sharing crime analysis techniques and information. *Police Chief, 52,* 42–43.

Hirschfield, A., Brown, P., & Todd, P. (1995). GIS and the analysis of spatially-referenced crime data: Experiences in Merseyside, UK. *International Journal of Geographic Information Science, 9,* 191.

King, W. (2000). Measuring police innovation: Issues and measurement. *Policing: An International Journal of Police Strategies and Management, 23,* 303–317.

LaVigne, N., & Wartell, J. (Eds.). (1998). *Crime mapping case studies: Successes in the field* (vol. 1). Washington, DC: Police Executive Research Forum.

Maguire, E., & Katz, C. (2002). Community policing, loose coupling, and sensemaking in American police agencies. *Justice Quarterly, 19,* 503–536.

Mamalian, C. A., & LaVigne, N. G. (1999). *The use of computerized crime mapping by law enforcement: Survey results.* Washington, DC: U.S. Department of Justice, National Institute of Justice.

McGuire, P. G. (2000). The New York Police Department COMPSTAT process: Mapping for analysis, evaluation, and accountability. In V. Goldsmith, P. G. McGuire, J. H. Mollenkopf, & T. A. Ross (Eds.), *Analyzing crime patterns: Frontiers of practice* (pp. 11–22). Thousand Oaks, CA: Sage Publications, Inc.

Moore, M., & Sparrow, M. (1988). *Institutionalizing innovation in municipal police departments.* Paper presented at the APPAM Research Conference, Seattle, WA.

Mullen, K. (1996). *The computerization of law enforcement: A diffusion of innovation study.* Doctoral dissertation, State University of New York, Albany.

Nulph, D., & Mudd, A. (1999). *Regional crime mapping: Breaking jurisdictional barriers*. Washington, DC: U.S. Department of Justice, Criminal Division.

Nunn, S. (2001). Police information technology: Assessing the effects of computerization on urban police functions. *Public Administration Review, 61*, 221–234.

Oliver, W. (2001). Community policing in small-town and rural communities: An organizational assessment of West Virginia agencies. *Police Practice and Research, 2*, 243–271.

Police Foundation. (2000). Integrating community policing and computer mapping: Assessing issues and needs among COPS office grantees. Washington, DC.

Rich, T. (2001). Crime mapping and analysis by community organizations in Hartford, Connecticut. Washington, DC: U.S. Department of Justice, National Institute of Justice.

Rich, T. (1999, October). Mapping the path to problem solving. *National Institute of Justice Journal*, 3–9.

Rich, T. (1995). The use of computerized mapping in crime control and prevention programs. Washington, DC: U.S. Department of Justice, National Institute of Justice.

Rossmo, D. (2000). *Geographic profiling*. Boca Raton, FL: CRC Press.

Sever, B., & Coram, G. (2001, October 3–6). *Graduate programs in criminal justice: Can practitioners and future academics learn in the same departments?* Paper presented at the annual meeting of the Midwestern Criminal Justice Association, Chicago, IL.

Skolnick, J., & Bayley, D. (1986). *The new blue line: Police innovation in six American cities*. New York: Free Press.

State of New Jersey, Division of State Police. (2000). Uniform crime reports: State of New Jersey, 2000. West Trenton, NJ: Uniform Crime Reporting Unit.

Stevens, J. (1984). Computerization in law enforcement: A comparative analysis of systems applications in West Germany and the United States. *Policing Studies, 7*, 209–218.

U.S. Bureau of the Census. (2000). County and city data book 2000: A statistical abstract supplement. Washington, DC: U.S. Departments of Commerce, Economics and Statistics Administration.

U.S. Department of Justice (DOJ) Office of Community Oriented Policing (COPS). (2002). Crime analysis in America. Conducted by the Center for Public Policy, University of South Alabama.

Vellani, D., & Nahoun, J. (2000). *Applied crime analysis*. Boston: Butterworth-Heinemann.

Webster, B., & Connors, E. (1993). Police methods for identifying community problems. *American Journal of Police, 12*, 75–102.

Weisburd, D., & Green, L. (1995). Policing drug hot spots: The Jersey City DMA (Drug Market Analysis) experiment. *Justice Quarterly, 12*, 711–741.

Weisburd, D., Uchida, C., & Green, L. (Eds.). (1993). *Police innovation and control of the police: Problems of law, order, and community*. New York: Springer-Verlag.

Challenges in Contemporary Police Leadership

12

JOHN MIDDLETON-HOPE
Chief of Police (Retired), Alberta, Canada

Contents

Introduction

The police appear to have an image problem. The television, Internet, and daily news shape public perceptions about the police. In the wake of the 1991 assaults on Rodney King in Los Angeles, California, the public has become adept at videotaping, photographing, and audio taping the interactions between citizens and the police. Often capturing only portions of interactions, these videos are sold to the highest bidder and a potential scandal may emerge from these videos. These events have helped shape public perception about the police while rarely affording the opportunity for police officers and departments to exercise a do-over.

The ethical climate of a police department has often been judged by the actions and behaviors of the men and women that maintain the safety and security of communities. The majority of the contacts that police have with citizens involve a crisis or confrontation where the police see most citizens at their worst, aggressive, most vulnerable, and most stressed situations. The public is often in a situation in which the police were called to right the wrong, intervene in the family disaster, or protect the innocent. In the midst of these situations, the public expects that the police officers respond in a professional manner while observing courtesy and compassion. The awesome responsibility with which police officers are statutorily empowered necessitates that they are held to a higher standard of conduct. This interplay of emotions about public encounters, response, and expectations puts the police in a quandary—police failures have become legendary, while their successes are rarely noted with the same interest. In this regard, the public recognizes that some police officers will engage in inappropriate conduct. In turn, the public expects police executives to identify and punish these officers. In other words, the public demands the truth from the police department. The public's trust depends on this undying commitment to reveal the truth even if it damages the reputation of the department.

Not only is the public perception negatively impacted when a police officer abuses the public trust, but the relationship between the department and its city manager, city council, or police commission is often damaged as well. The perception by various oversight bodies is that the chief of police is responsible for both the actions of the officers involved in misconduct and the department's timely response to hold the officers accountable. On top of all these, the chiefs and senior leaders find most difficult to manage the challenges that attack their personal integrity and honesty. Police leaders have often built a career on these tenets (i.e., integrity and honesty), and many chiefs see their reputation embodied in these two words. In fact, when it comes to the ethical climate of a police organization, it is all about the behaviors of the chief and the messages that he or she conveys to the rest of the organization.

Due to their positional authority over their subordinates and to a degree the place they occupy in the community, chiefs must have well-developed moral or ethical reasoning skills. Conflicts arise when chiefs of police lose sight of their original vision and become obsessed with managing the various challenges to their administration. Their own behaviors can overshadow the moral justifications that have sustained them throughout their career and are then called into question. An acknowledgment that these police management problems are part of the job and separate from the personal characteristics of the chief is an important distinction to be made. Very early in their relationship, the chief and the governance body need to develop a process that would address the appropriate handling of ethical crises that might occur. Developing and agreeing on a process that will address ethical crisis is critical to the sustainability of the relationship between chief and governance.

Ethical Climate Starts at the Top

In police organizations, ethical behavior does not start with the introduction of an ethics program delivered to the officers on the street. Rather, it commences with a commitment by the chief of police to ensure there is an ethical climate established in the organization. For police departments to achieve an ethical climate in the department, chiefs of police must align their philosophy, observable behaviors, communications, and decision-making processes with ethical practices at all times. More than any rhetoric, the behaviors of the chief are observed by every member of the organization. In turn, the chief's behaviors would more clearly demonstrate the character of the organization.

Police officers are a tough crowd. They rapidly see through the haze of what they commonly refer to as *bullshit*. If the police executive demonstrates support for ethical programs, values, mission, and vision of the department and then goes about ignoring these edicts in favor of convenient responses, police officers will pick up on this quickly. As a result, future efforts to mitigate even a momentary lapse will be difficult to recover from.

Contributory Factors to Police Trouble

Virtually all media accounts about the police relate stories of poor ethical decision making not only by police officers but also by chiefs of police who are expected to know better and act accordingly. Thus, it would seem that police misconduct is at an all time high and that police officer morality is lacking if all the stories in various publications were the whole story. However, this alarming trend may be explained in part by Edward J. Tully (1999), in which he posits that there are at least six explanations for the increased number of complaints of police officer conduct. These explanations are liberally expanded herein.

First, law enforcement agencies are more alert to officer misconduct. Professional standards or internal affairs units of police organizations have developed more vigilant practices to identify and investigate accusations of inappropriate and criminal conduct by officers. Often driven by public sentiment, there is evidence that police organizations are moving to make the process of investigation more transparent, so the inappropriate behaviors of officers are more visible to the public.

Second, the numbers of opportunities for temptation are greater. Inappropriate levels of force used to subdue culprits high on illicit substances require officers to manage events they are often ill equipped to contend with. Justification for excessive force may be shrouded in a dark veil of self-deception that the culprits deserve to be treated as less than human. Exposure to large quantities of illegal drugs can be a temptation for some to cash in on the obscene profits generated by the lucrative drug trade. Providing organized crime members with information or less restrictive access to markets fuels corrupt practices where some officers benefit directly from engaging in criminal acts. Both activities reinforce a sense of entitlement that sets up officers against the community they serve.

Third, our society is producing individuals who may not exhibit strong character. Many departments struggle with the challenges of identifying quality recruits. Police entrance requirements are more stringent today than they were 25 years ago, yet young officers' involvements in inappropriate conduct are all too common. Applicants today often need only to demonstrate a departure of 3 years prior to hiring from previous inappropriate conduct. Whereas 25 years ago marijuana use may have precluded selection by some agencies, few eliminate candidates today if they have 3 years' clear conduct prior to selection. This behavior is now perceived to be minor in nature by comparison with the expectations our forefathers had of previous generations of *coppers*. In part this demonstrates that times have changed and that applications out of necessity are viewed with less jaundiced eyes. However, the majority of behavioral issues young officers are involved in are based on what they observe among senior patrol officers. Serious corruption is often a product of experience, whereas bad decisions are the outcomes of being young. Appropriate ethical decision making is still a matter of character.

Fourth, the work environment of our police officers has become more multiracial, and a greater number of women are entering the previously male-dominated occupation. These positive changes are causing organizations and chiefs to rethink the way they interact with a diverse employee population. Pinups in locker rooms that were prevalent 15 years ago no longer adorn the walls of the department. Likewise, off-color remarks about gender, sexual orientation, and race have become less tolerated in the workplace.

Fifth, the police profession currently has a well-entrenched generation of law enforcement professionals whose focus is about what is in it for them. This attitude of entitlement creates a cohort of officers determined to put self above community and the department. These behaviors jeopardize the relationship with a supportive public.

Sixth, politicians, activists, and special interest groups apply pressure on police organizations to adhere to a more inclusive ideological position that at times sacrifices the wants and needs of the community while upholding the rights of individuals. As a balanced process, there is clearly merit in engaging all sectors of the community in the decision-making process but surely not to the detriment of society as a whole. The challenge for chiefs of police is to maintain a delicate balance among each constituent.

Ethical Challenges Facing Chiefs and Senior Leaders

Chiefs face the same types of challenges as those faced by their members. However, the inappropriate actions of the chief of police are potentially more damaging than the actions of any one member of a police department. Some of the many ethical challenges that chiefs of police have been confronted with are summarized as follows:

1. Irregularities in expense account submissions such as claiming per diem or allowances that are in excess of those to which they are entitled. In their examination of police officer victimization, Gilmartin and Harris (1998) looked at the conditions that exist in which police officers justify inappropriate conduct. This exemplifies a sense of entitlement in which police officers and indeed chiefs who succumb to padding their expense account view themselves as victims in one sense or another. They feel that they deserve more than they may be entitled to. In part this psyche occurs because of the way they perceive they are treated by the organization.
2. A supplier offering perks to executives such as trips, free equipment use, or gifts. These questionable acts may be combined with inappropriate sponsorship opportunities in exchange for brand identification or exclusive status as supplier of a police or business product without the benefit of request for proposal (RFP) or other tender process.
3. Promotion favoritism or interfering in processes within the organization that provides an unfair advantage to a person or group irrespective of skills. Organizations view this controlling behavior as inappropriate and unfair. A chief's control over such activities challenges the ethical climate of the organization and may erode the relationship between chief and the membership.
4. An intimate relationship with a subordinate whether it is a contravention of policy. This activity has unseated more than one senior police executive who has failed to recognize the necessity of distance between him or her and those whom they command.
5. Discrimination or other forms of harassment based on primary grounds of gender, age, race, ethnicity, or sexual orientation. This includes permitting offensive language, behavior, and activities intended to demean a segment of the organization. To tolerate sexist or homophobic jokes or pinups in the locker room merely serves to reinforce what is tolerated within the police culture.
6. Protecting the organization from scandal by attempting to influence the outcome of an investigation, whether a criminal offense or internal disciplinary matter they both have the potential to negatively

impact the reputation of the department. Merely protecting the organization is not the issue alone. When a senior police executive interferes in an investigation, it may be construed as criminal conduct or a breach of statutory legislation. In any case, exercising undue influence strikes at the moral fabric of the organization and the integrity of the chief.

There are numerous examples in which police officers are involved in misconduct and are provided severance to leave the organization or are permitted to resign to avoid embarrassing the organization. Failure to hold officers accountable for corrupt or discreditable practices sends a message to other officers that these behaviors are acceptable. The key message is that ethical decision making and adherence to core values start at the top. They are not solely to be embraced by the officers working the street.

Strategies to Manage Ethical Challenges

Although there are numerous business decisions, the greatest challenges for police executives are decisions regarding ethical choices. The points that follow provide some strategies to manage these challenges during a chief's tenure:

1. Be actively involved in the delivery of an ethical program for your members. Ethical decision making is a top-down responsibility that requires unwavering leadership. Officers replicate behaviors that they observe in senior personnel. It is important to lead by example and to set the tone for the organization.
2. Have an ethical advisory committee of trusted advisors to whom you can turn for guidance in difficult situations. This provides the chief an opportunity to examine challenges the organization will face and provide thoughtful and considered leadership decisions that demonstrate a commitment to the core values of the police service.
3. Before making a critical decision, the chief should consider the consequences of the decision in light of public exposure and should be open to the critical opinions of everyone. By applying an ethical decision making model such as OPT (Options Project consequences Tell your story; Middleton-Hope, 2007), chiefs of police are able to apply this ethical construct to the decision-making process and arrive at a well-grounded position. Decision-making models are widely used in ethical decision-making instruction to help participants visualize and articulate how they would manage a particular dilemma.
4. Increase the transparency of your decision making by exposing the decisions and their reasons to a number of individuals among your

executives before taking action. This vetting process helps ensure that many of the possible outcomes are examined and anticipated. In addition, it enhances the chief's leadership skills by providing for an examination of the potential solutions to problems.

Political Challenges

All police leaders are affected by a number of key constituents that influence their administration. Depending on the reporting structure of the chief or department, these various constituent groups may exercise significant dominion over the chief and may affect even the day-to-day operations of the department. The challenge for police leaders is to manage effectively in a political climate. The community, including neighborhood groups, business organizations, and service clubs, has expectations of the chief that may include attending functions, meetings, and events in person. The chief, as the public face of the department, provides the vision necessary to achieve the mandate of the department. This is an opportunity to communicate the best efforts of the department to groups that look for ways to support the police. Successful chiefs monitor the pulse of the community and ensure surveys, town hall meetings, events, and functions are used to elicit inputs from the public.

There are six major political challenges facing chiefs and senior leaders. First, the chief should manage the relationship with the media. Much of the public's perception of the police is formed by the media. Police managers are expected to provide feedback to the various news outlets in their jurisdiction and, in the case of a major event, to national news teams. Developing a comprehensive, professional relationship with the media is critical. Although most departments use public information officers (PIO), it is also important to ensure that when major events occur the chief is in front of the cameras and accessible to the media.

The media often feed the interests of the public to find out what the police are up to. Well-managed media relationships can be, and, often are, these developed relationships are assets for the police. Poorly managed or a distant relationship with the media could at a minimum adversely affect the public's perception of the police and at worst could damage the department's reputation. The media are businesses and like most businesses media outlets are motivated to make profits. By working with various media outlets to reinforce positive messages and to provide timely information that meets the needs of the outlet and the police department, chiefs could be able to effectively influence outcomes. Training public information officers to represent the department will assist in optimizing the department's exposure. Whenever possible, departments should use subject matter experts who reinforce messages of public safety. Likewise, the department should ensure that accurate information is provided to the media.

A critical piece in media relations is to ensure that whatever and whenever messages are delivered to the media they are first delivered to the police department's personnel. Failure to ensure timely communication often results in misunderstanding. To support the organization, the members need to be informed of ongoing issues and the position of the department concerning these issues.

Second, the chief should manage the "political" face of the position of chief of police and the role of a public figure. The position of chief of police is a political one, and the person occupying that position is often regarded as a public figure. Events may occur that strain this relationship with other public officials. Governing bodies, such as a commission or police board, need to be considered essentially as political entities even though their members may not be elected. Most governing bodies are not likely to go down with the chief. Maintaining a business relationship that allows both the chief and the governing body to understand their individual roles will support that relationship in times of crisis and afford the governing body the opportunity to support the chief. Ensuring that the commission, city manager, or council are provided ongoing education about the operations of the police department is an effective tool in avoiding political interference and reinforces a collaborative relationship.

Third, the chief should amass a collaborative executive team that could work together. Creating an executive team that works together on the decisions that have to be made empowers the executive members to be a part of the process rather than external to it. The chief must surround himself or herself with the best people the organization has to offer. These key people must be capable of making the critical decisions needed for the organization and take effective action to advance the department's priorities. Members of the executive must also realize that not everyone in the organization will get on board with every decision and must be prepared to move ahead in spite of barriers to progress. This consensus model of leadership requires time to build and does not happen overnight. It takes time to assess input and render decisions that have a greater likelihood of acceptance.

Fourth, the chief must devise plans for times when things go wrong. A key impact on the career of chiefs of police is the failure to understand and implement prevention strategies. Failing to plan for times when things go wrong leaves the chief and ultimately the organization vulnerable. There will be occasions when members and sometimes the chief will face harassment allegations, votes of nonconfidence, and scandal due to members' conduct that attack the reputation of the department. Each assault on the integrity of the chief or the department makes the job of the chief that much harder.

If chiefs understand the fluid environment of policing and individual markets, funding changes, business challenges, and opportunities, they are able to leverage budgets in support of achieving the business priorities.

To be effective, chiefs need to understand the driving forces affecting policing such as changes in social standards, the impact of demographics on recruiting, and shifts in the organized and serious crime paradigms to a more transnational perspective. Without that understanding, senior leaders have a seriously narrow view of their role in the community.

Many governing bodies do not understand the interconnectedness of police activities in response to criminal enterprise. A chief who travels to meetings, conferences, seminars, and workshops to receive or deliver information is taking advantage of growth opportunities that will benefit the chief and the organization and not just exercising his or her globetrotting wings.

To be effective it is important to author multiple futures for the department by writing the story in advance and mentally preparing for change. This is achieved by understanding driving forces and changing social standards. Staying on top of news and the latest business strategies and providing flexible approaches that consider the best interests of the community encourages organizations to stay out in front. Looking for changing trends and drivers allows the department to respond to these challenges rather than reacting to them.

Fifth, the political authority must make provisions for a comprehensive contract for chiefs that clearly outline expectations, compensation, and tenure. By seeking legal advice and assistance in contract negotiations prior to taking the position of chief, chiefs will be clear on the relationship and what measures will be applied to their performance that will indicate success. An assessment tool to evaluate the performance of the chief against measurable outcomes will ensure that there is less room for misinterpretation. It is important to remember that the handshake deal with the chair is not worth much if a less supportive commission, city manager, or council replaces the ones who hired the chief. This can create significant distractions that may derail the relationship between the chief and the governing body.

Sixth, it is important to reinforce with the governing body that the actions of some officers are not a reflection of the chief's performance. Likewise, a crisis should not necessarily become a show stopper when there is a disagreement between the police department and governance over the handling of a contentious issue.

Providing Modern Leadership

North American policing has evolved from a command and control leadership style popularized by the professional model of policing developed in the late 1940s and lasting until the 1970s. This model to a large extent was replaced by the problem-oriented or community policing models of the 1980s and 1990s, and these latter models have been recently eclipsed by an intelligence-led policing paradigm that relies on the analysis of information synthesized as intelligence to strategically direct and deploy the department's resources. This new model requires leaders to engage an entirely new approach to decision making and managing of resources. In turn this model requires leaders with new skills and leadership styles. There remain portions of the earlier models in use today as there has not been a seamless move from one model to the next. Rather, a synergy of approaches has emerged that allowed police organizations to use portions of the various models at will.

Communities today want chiefs of police who are street-savvy business people capable of managing multimillion-dollar organizations that provide responses to meet the demands of diverse communities. Police departments certainly at the executive level are every bit as much a business as any corporate entity. The product may differ and the motivation may be public safety rather than profits, but the principles of management are similar and the business practices used to achieve success are the same.

Not everyone will agree that police organizations are businesses and chiefs are more like chief executive officers (CEOs) than cops. The truth, however, is that the current practices used in business to develop employees and establish processes that ensure fiscal accountability and strategies designed to ensure organizational effectiveness and efficiency are strikingly similar. Unfortunately, there are numerous examples of leaders today who do not lead. Instead, they simply manage. The distinction is that chiefs should lead people while managing processes. The most effective leaders believe that their job is to nurture their subordinates to become interdependent members of the organization (Anderson, 1998).

To be an effective leader in today's police organization, executives are expected to be competent, confident, articulate, and inclusive. This new leadership style requires superior critical thinking skills, decisiveness, and effective communication abilities as essential competencies. Leadership demands an understanding of generational differences, diversity opportunities, employee empowerment, collaborative decision making, and transparency of actions to be effective. Most employees, union representatives, and community members do not understand that leadership is a process and not a position. Many chiefs do not understand the difference either, making them less effective than they otherwise should be.

Leaders are expected to lead change, lead people, drive results, possess business acumen, and build coalitions and communicate effectively both internally and externally. The days of the traditional chief who rose through the ranks without the benefit of external learning has gone by the wayside. In addition, chiefs today must not only possess an understanding of the dynamics in their communities but also understand how organized and serious crime is interrelated on a national and international level. Certainly in the wake of 9/11 our world has become much smaller, and the artificial boundaries set by governments do little to deter international criminal operations.

Police organizations are and remain insulated to a degree from the changes in their environments. Traditional police leaders (i.e., police executives and union leaders) want desperately to cling to the "good old days." The community, on the other hand, demands accountability and transparency from its public institutions. This is borne out of the cultural revolution of the 1960s and 1970s. Unions seem to want greater involvement in the decision-making processes of police organizations. This involvement includes everything from being consulted or involved in shifting and deployment to discipline, promotions, and health and safety issues and includes hiring the chief of police.

The Primary Challenge

Developing Future Leaders

Taking responsibility for identifying and developing new leaders in the organization from the onset of the chief's tenure prepares the department for inevitable transition and embraces growth as a necessary step. When focusing on the top talent most likely to provide continuous leadership for the organization, it is incumbent upon police executives to provide the necessary resources to ensure that the new leadership cadre has every learning opportunity to assist in achieving success.

Engaging performance coaching programs to work with prospective candidates allows officers to plan their futures. By ensuring the development of a comprehensive leadership program, candidates could take on greater responsibilities for the direction of the organization while committing to the necessary accountability that is so critical to success. Along with coaching and leadership training, mentoring by senior police, business, and government leaders enhances new leaders' overall potential effectiveness.

Providing the organization with strategic vision is essential for leadership to grow. A critically articulated pathway will provide those being led with an understanding of the steps that are for the organization to evolve effectively and for prospective leaders to assume the responsibility of leadership. By communicating the vision of leadership broadly within the organization, emerging leaders are able to more effectively participate in the process of leadership and be more active in the legacy the chief leaves the organization.

To leave such a legacy, the leader must do the following:

1. Identify people within the organization who have high performance track records.
2. Attend to developing talent through growth and learning opportunities.
3. Foster creativity and innovation by developing a culture of risk taking and decentralized decision making that is both encouraged and rewarded.

In spite of good leadership characteristics and developing a legacy of future leaders, political issues that chiefs face have an impact on their ability to truly be effective. This challenge is played out across North America as chiefs' tenures are all too often cut short before they are able to execute a plan to leave a sustainable legacy.

Succession Management Strategy

One of the greatest legacies of leadership is to identify potential successors and commence from day one to provide them opportunities and greater responsibilities that will help them grow into senior leadership roles. Succession management is more complex than identifying a successor for the chief and the process of identification is compounded when an outside chief takes over an organization. Before the chief becomes effective, he or she needs to take time to learn about the organizational culture, strengths, challenges, opportunities, and gaps that may exist in the various processes. It may take years to properly identify leadership successors. Creating the largest pool of prospective candidates possible who are comprehensively assessed and providing organizational and learning opportunities are important in nurturing leaders in the department.

Developing competency-based assessment tools that include learning strategies that evaluate the performances of senior personnel and hold members accountable for their own outcomes advances the development of prospective candidates. Likewise, establishing learning and organizational opportunities where skills are developed and challenges are met allows contenders to demonstrate their organizational commitment and fit. At the end of the day, one of the greatest legacies a chief can leave the department is a deep bench of potential contenders. This is not easily achieved in a climate where the average tenure of a chief in the United States is 2.5 years according to the International Association of Chiefs of Police (IACP) and only slightly higher in Canada (Butterfield, 2001).

For both internal and external chiefs, the first year is frequently spent learning about the department and reorganizing and realigning people to begin the process of moving toward achieving the chief's vision. The second year by contrast greets the chief with new challenges that may require repositioning the department. This may be accomplished by developing strategic and business plans that are designed to facilitate the budget process and that will adequately position the department to achieve planning outcomes. This very limited time frame leaves little opportunity for implementing a succession strategy. In fact, succession management should not only identify prospective candidates to succeed the chief but should also examine key positions throughout the department and create a process to identify, train, and provide opportunities for officers to demonstrate the necessary attributes to compete for a broader array of leadership positions. This strategy avoids gaps that are created when experience walks out the door or when tenure is exercised and positions become vacant. Having a plan reduces the potential for random outcomes. The responsibility of developing a succession plan to replace the chief of police in Canadian law enforcement generally lies with the police commission. Although all too often they do not work with the chief to develop a strategy and are left to react when the chief retires or fulfills his or her contractual obligations and moves on.

Developing a plan that includes enhancing the strengths of senior officers in the department ensures a smoother transition from one administration to the next. A plan identifying how succession is managed, how it will be assessed, and what it will look like when it has reached the desired outcome. The process should be incorporated in the policies and procedures of the commission to ensure a commitment to process is maintained irrespective of the corporate memory of previous commissions or chiefs.

Relationship Challenges

In writing this chapter several Canadian chiefs of police were contacted and asked questions around the challenges they faced during their tenure. Without exception the chiefs agreed there were four key relationships the chief must try to maintain and that to be effective these relationships needed to be nurtured continuously. They were the relationship with the department's officers and the police union, the community, city council (or government), and the body to whom they reported (police commissions, police committees, or city management; Middleton-Hope, 2006). In each case the chiefs from small, mid-sized, and large agencies reflected that rarely were all four intact at the end of their tenures and that at best the chief could count on sustaining two or three at any time.

It has become increasingly more apparent that commission members, city managers, mayors, and council members are attending to their roles with a personal agenda. This agenda may include getting spending under control, getting the chief under control, trying to manage the department, or trying to manage hot-button issues, to name a few. There are also those chiefs who do not respond well to this kind of intrusive direction. Both outcomes often produce dysfunctional relationships. The key may be painfully obvious at the outset, that is, to establish a communications process and to work collaboratively together to arrive at a common ground that engenders mutual respect for each other's roles and responsibilities. The world of policing is generally all new to governance bodies, and it is the chief's job to provide insights into the activities of the department. Previous relationships or experiences with law enforcement may have formed the public's opinions of the police along with perceptions they develop due to the media's influences. In speaking with several chiefs of police it was more likely that a single, sometimes innocuous incident triggered events that ended the chief's tenure rather than a crisis. The fact that policing is changing is completely lost on many civic officials. Often the public's perception of a competent organization translates into how many officers they see on the street.

Opportunities to scrutinize the activities of a police department that may include zero balancing and justification of personnel and programs are often not welcomed by many police departments and officers alike. It is, however, a reality, and as chief it is important to recognize a healthy mistrust or justification of police actions exists in the public. This is all part of operating a transparent public organization that is accountable to the representatives of the citizenry. The job of policing and the activities of chiefs are inherently political as civic leaders will often use public safety and crime issues to support a particular platform. The chief's support will be solicited and even expected at times to align the business practices of the department with those of the corporation. This is a difficult tightrope to walk to ensure neutrality and a distance from the spotlight of political partisanship.

Establishing and maintaining the relationship with the city manager is a key to the overall success of the chief's tenure. The city manager may be the most trusted ally or the most feared enemy. Being mindful of whom he or she is aligned with (city treasurer, leadership team, council, city solicitor) provides the chief with the ability to leverage this relationship and enhance opportunities for the department and the chief to be more effective. Keeping the city manager well informed about major events, budget issues, and, where appropriate, discipline enables the city manager to respond to these challenges more collaboratively. More importantly, it allows the city council to be better prepared when the community wants answers. As an ally the city manager may provide a buffer against political interference (i.e., when aldermen or state representatives make requests, the chief may handle the request if appropriate and then channel the response back through the city manager). This behavior by elected officials may serve to undermine the authority or reporting relationship the city manager has with the chief or even with the elected official.

It is also important to develop and sustain relationships with other key corporate department heads that regularly interact with the police such as fire, emergency medical services (EMS), fleet, building maintenance, information technology (IT), and human resources (HR). It is also important to interact with the district attorney's office, chief crown prosecutors, other chiefs of police and agencies, and of course community groups to broaden the base of support for the chief's vision and enhance cooperative links to assist in achieving goals. Police chiefs should expect disagreements between the various departments of the city and outside agencies. One of the strongest strategies is to communicate needs and wants and to ensure that discussions are managed respectfully. There needs to be an understanding that friction will occur and an understanding that there is a mechanism to move the relationship beyond these potential barriers.

As a police leader you may be asked to question, challenge, or even discard one or more of the key tenets of your leadership approach. Leadership means having the courage to reconsider your current paradigm and the humility and self-confidence to effect change in spite of personal misgivings. These compromises do not diminish the capacity of a leader, nor will they score points with politicians. It is simply a way to express that the chief of police is flexible and willing to change (Robinson, 2001).

A point of discord is frequently the relationship between the police commission and the chief of police. This often occurs when there is a lack of understanding about roles and responsibilities and a healthy respect to ensure the lines are clearly drawn. The police commission has a clear responsibility for hiring the chief of police and for providing clear direction on policy, budget, and strategic planning. These activities are challenging and operate at a very macro level. They are not responsible for the day-to-day administration of the police department—an activity in which many commission members will want to become involved.

A clear understanding of responsibilities and duties and a process whereby the board is able to convey instructions to the chief of police will reduce the potential for disagreement. The board must clearly outline its expectations of the chief and a strategy for annual performance appraisal that is consistent with current industry standards and practices. Unless otherwise statutorily prescribed, the chief is the sole employee of the commission. All too frequently, governance is inadequately prepared to assume its responsibilities preferring instead to encroach on the domain of the chief simply because these are the activities that are most obvious to the public (deployment, duties, and functions of street-level officers).

Chiefs, on the other hand, are responsible for the effective operations of the department. Without establishing and periodically reinforcing the ground rules, commissions tend to want to accept public complaints against various officers, to try to influence investigations, and to direct other personnel within the department including but not limited to where to set up radar units. It is the desire by the police oversight bodies to control police operations for which they are not responsible. They are responsible for strategic planning and budget approval. The discussion around roles and responsibilities is important and needs to be recurring to reinforce appropriate relationship practices. It must be a conscious effort for the chief to be inclusive and communicative with his or her commission, whereas it is the commission's job to respect the chief's dominion. Agreement on jurisdictional domain and prerogatives ought to be considered and discussed whenever there is a new commission or new chief. Likewise, there needs to be an agreement on goals and outcomes and a measurement tool that fairly and equitably assesses whether the chief has been successful and to what extent.

Preparation for an inevitable crisis requires a strategy that will leverage relationships developed and nurtured in advance. By the very nature of the business, chiefs of police are confronted by crisis during their tenure. When a crisis occurs, consider the following:

1. Publicly disclose the problem and take affirmative action to deal with the issue. Tell people what you are going to do and do it.
2. Ensure that transparent investigations occur. This may require an outside agency being called in to air your department's laundry. This is a sign of strength, not one of weakness.
3. Inform your commission, city manager, or council of the investigation and reassure them you are in charge and are taking the necessary steps to thoroughly resolve the matter. Public safety is in good hands.
4. Provide open and timely information both externally and internally. Your members want to know that they can trust that you have taken command of the situation.
5. If the department is wrong, say so and what you will do to correct the situation.

Conclusion

Police leadership at the executive level is difficult at best. A lengthy and successful career leading up to appointment as chief of police is often not enough to prepare and sustain a chief during his or her tenure. It is quite candidly like few other positions in the corporate world and certainly like no other within policing.

Daily challenges will tax the strengths of even the most resilient soul. And it is becoming more apparent that the position of chief is less and less attractive. Recently, Chuck Wexler, of the Police Executive Research Forum a Washington, D.C.-based police think tank and oft used service to conduct searches for chiefs of police, and Gerry Oldani, of the executive search firm Waters-Oldani, were interviewed about the contemporary picture in executive police recruitment (Butterfield, 2001). Both suggested they were seeing a recent downturn of about 35% in qualified candidates applying for jobs as chief of police in the United States. Up until recently there were a substantial number of senior police officials who wanted to be chiefs in major centers. Not so anymore, and for some cities it is not unlike drafting a sports star. The concern is that senior police executives sought out for their leadership skills are shying away from the brass ring. This in part seems to be because deputy chiefs, as the most likely successors to outgoing chiefs, have seen the commitment to the department and the community that is required of chiefs and the toll it takes on their personal lives. The compensation does not appear to be worth it.

Unfortunately, as the gene pool for leadership candidates dwindles, commissions and city managers seem to demonstrate a lack of understanding for this reality, preferring to terminate, to fail to renew contracts, and to sever their relationship with an alarming number of existing chiefs in favor of picking a new chief. There is a mistaken belief, it would seem, that there is a leadership tree with low-hanging fruit from which to select successors. This is occurring in both Canada and the United States among small, mid-sized, and large agencies alike.

Not only is there a crisis in recruitment of new personnel and retention of potentially retiring officers, but commissions and city managers alike are also fueling a crisis in senior police leadership. Commissions and city managers share this blame with some chiefs who at the same time are reluctant to work on the relationships that keep them in office. In the end it requires a strengthening of relationships and establishing key partnerships that will assist chiefs of police in being effective at their jobs.

References

Anderson, T. D. (1998). *Transforming leadership.* Washington, DC: St. Lucie Press.

Butterfield, F. (2001). *Urban police jobs are losing their appeal.* Retrieved March 21, 2006 from http://nytimes.com

Gilmartin, K. M., & Harris, J. J. (1998, January). Law enforcement ethics: The continuum of compromise. *Police Chief Magazine,* pp. 25–28.

Middleton-Hope, J. (2007). *OPT ethical decision making model.*
Middleton-Hope, J. (2006). *Challenges in contemporary police leadership.* Unpublished original research.
Robinson, J. W. (2001). *Jack Welch and Leadership: Executive Lessons of the Master CEO.* Toronto: Random House.
Tully, E. J. (1999). Misconduct, corruption, and abuse of power: What can the chief do? *Blue Line Magazine, 11*(2), 22–25.

International Police Practices and Cultures

4

Organizational Culture in the Norwegian Counter Terrorist Unit

13

RUNE GLOMSETH
Norwegian Police University College

PETTER GOTTSCHALK
Norwegian School of Management

Contents

Introduction

The Counter Terrorist Unit belongs to Oslo Police District and is led by a police chief. It constitutes a separate police division in which all members are involved in operative activities. Administrated and organized in a staff element responsible for planning, equipment and operation, and training and exercise, the Counter Terrorist Unit comprises four divisions, which are subdivided into eight special teams.

The Norwegian Counter Terrorist Unit has two main functions: one national and one local. The former implies that it is the Norwegian Police's special unit to combat sabotage and terrorism and to deal with hostage situations, complex armed assignments, as well as organized crime. Its local function consists in reactive, uniformed policing such as around-the-clock car patrol work in Oslo Police District. Moreover, the unit is to provide assistance to other police districts whenever it is necessary. This means that the Counter Terrorist Unit accepts responsibility in demanding situations. Its members also take on a variety of assignments, which uniformed police normally are in charge of. The overall competence level within the unit is impressively high at the individual level, group level, and the organizational level. The objective of this chapter is to describe the professional culture in terms of values in the unit.

Organization Culture Values

A number of very different definitions exist of the concept organization culture (e.g., Christensen & Crank, 2001; Kiely & Peek, 2002). One of the definitions suggests organizational culture to be a set of shared norms, values, and perceptions of the world, which develop when the members of an organization interact with each other and the surroundings. Organization culture might be decisive for how the organization thinks, feels, and acts. In our opinion, the concept of culture is important to understand the nature of organizations and the behavior of its members. Organization culture has been used as an important factor in explaining the effectiveness, success, and growth of enterprises.

The emphasis in this study has been on the core element values as it is important in discussions on organization culture. Hofstede, Neuijen, Ohavy, and Sanders (1990), for example, argue that values compose the core of any culture. Being relatively lasting, values are emotional perceptions of what is appreciated and preferred in an organization. In other words, values are essential for an organization's fundamental perception of what is right and what is wrong and what is desirable and valuable in a work situation. Consequently, it is possible to claim that an organization's values dictate its behavior.

The Study

This study is based on observations, questionnaires, interviews, and examination of documents—all of which were conducted in the period between July 2001 and April 2002. The complete sample of police officers in the unit responded to the survey. Thus, the response rate in this values survey is 100%. In our presentation no distinction is made between managers and other employees, nor is information about the respondents' length of service in the Counter Terrorist Unit taken into consideration. The main argument for this decision is that the purpose of this study is to unveil the shared values, which give the unit its distinctive feature.

The aforementioned decisions were made on the basis of a preliminary analysis of the materials, which showed that there were no significant differences between managers and other employees. However, the preliminary analysis seems to indicate that minor differences (some variation) exist within the different age groups. Despite this, these differences are so small that we deem it unnecessary to focus on them in our discussion of the results. Once again, we find it necessary to point out that the responses in the survey must be interpreted with the distinction between ordinary policing and armed response in mind. Values are represented in Figure 13.1 and discussed below.

Fixed or Floating Time

Police officers in the Counter Terrorist Unit value conscious use of *time* and punctuality. Time is regarded as an important factor, both in relation to ordinary policing and training and especially when they are faced with aggravated and dangerous crime. The time factor is particularly decisive in armed responses. The tendency is confirmed clearly by the fact that more than 90% of the respondents chose the three lowest values on a scale ranging from 1 to 7. The average score is 1.83.

Time is also an important factor as service lists and job rotation lists are employed. Occasionally, changes are made to these lists to accommodate special tasks. Moreover, respondents perceive of time as part of a uniform system. This is in accordance with the findings from the interviews, which show that structure and clear objectives are considered important. As a curiosity it may be worth mentioning that watches were installed both in the offices and in the lunchroom to remind everyone that efficient use of time is vital. Consequently, a conscious, purposeful, and structured use of time is a prominent value.

Change or Tradition

Members of the Counter Terrorist Unit experience *change* as a significant factor. However, they seem to find that it must be balanced against tradition and continuity. The tendency is clear also here with more than 90% of the responses tending toward change. The average value is 3.33. On one hand, the police officers are almost continually preoccupied with self-development, team development, and development of their division. The management encourages them to frequent testing of new equipment, competence building, and further development of police methods. During the interviews, the police officers confirm that they are allowed room to influence and take part in the development of a variety of aspects of policing. On the other hand, they also value experience and thoroughly tested routines and systems. It

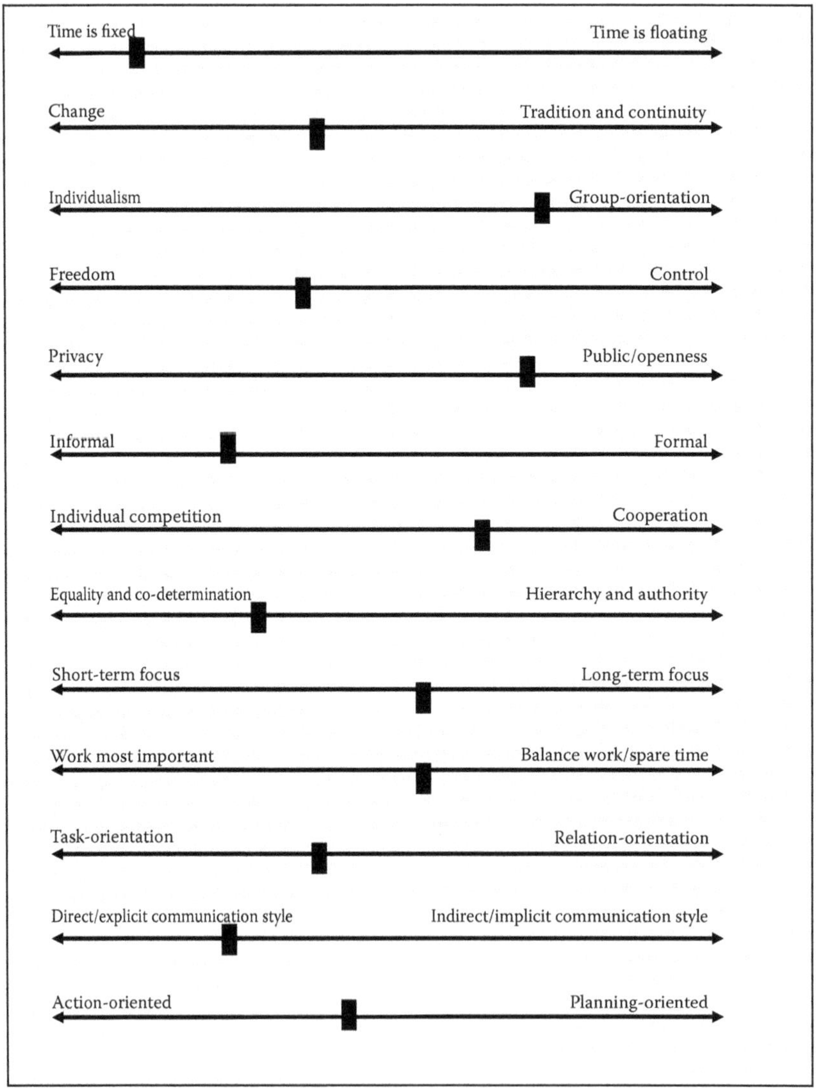

Figure 13.1 Organizational values in the police unit.

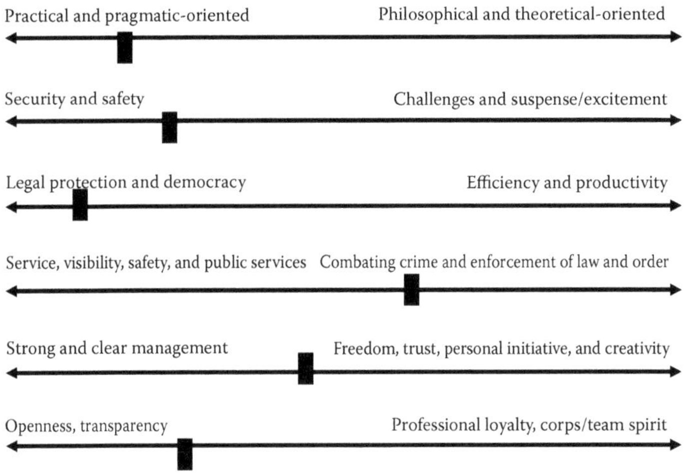

Figure 13.1 (Continued) Organizational values in the police unit.

is also appreciated that routines are thoroughly tested and have proved to work. Most organizations, in particular police organizations, view tradition and history as important. Fielding (1984) shows that police officers to a great extent tend to trust their previous experiences and arrangements that have proved to work in the past.

The principle of seniority and experience, which is important in a police context, may have influenced the responses in this section. The fact that the police are clearly governed by rules is also indicative of a preference for tradition and continuity. Nevertheless, change and development still constitute a clear value.

Individualism or Group

As for the question of *individual–group orientation*, there is a clear tendency toward the latter. More than 80% of the respondents emphasize group orientation. A typical feature of policing is team cooperation or cooperation between two partners. This is a particularly developed feature of the Norwegian Counter Terrorist Unit where regular partners go on car patrols together. Partnerships of this kind tend to last for several years. In addition, each individual member of the unit belongs to a special team. At the same time, they feel a strong sense of identity toward the unit. From the interviews we know that the ability to cooperate is highly esteemed by the members of the Counter Terrorist Unit. These findings contribute to confirm the tendency to favor group orientation.

On the other hand, police officers are described as strong individuals with distinct leader qualities. What is more, the individual member of the

Counter Terrorist Unit is responsible for his or her own actions. Attention was drawn to these contrasting values in connection with the preliminary presentation of this study for a selected number of Counter Terrorist Unit members. It was also emphasized that individual qualities have to form the basis for the unit's activities to enable it to solve complicated missions. What we see here is a healthy combination of strong individuals who stress cooperation and group orientation. This is a natural tendency, which correlates well with international police research where collectivism is clearly emphasized (see, e.g., Manning, 1977, 1979 in Bailey, Strecher, Hoover, & Dowling, 1995).

Freedom or Control

The responses along the *freedom–control* dimension also show a clear inclination toward the value freedom. Just over 86% of the responses tend in this direction, with an average score of 3.19. On one hand, the interviews and the description of the conditions in the Counter Terrorist Unit bear witness of a strong emphasis on structure, routines, and plans.

From the responses it was possible to discern that the emphasis on the aforementioned aspects was necessary to succeed, in particular in connection with armed response. As evidenced by the description given of the unit earlier in this chapter, its members emphasize that planning activities and training exercises, certifications, and routines for reporting are prominent features and are viewed as important. On the other hand, the findings show that the leader of the Counter Terrorist Unit stresses the importance of giving the individual member room to act within certain frameworks. The perspective on human life seems to be characterized by an underlying trust in the individual Moreover, police research shows that operative police work is to a great extent distinguished by autonomy. This explains that in spite of the need for an extensive use of structure and systems, the value of freedom is held in great esteem by police officers in the unit.

Privacy or Openness

The dimension *privacy–public/openness* is intended to capture how officers put into practice or value the social conditions in the unit. Which topics are being discussed and to what extent do the police officers feel that the unit is characterized by openness and intimacy? The responses leave no doubt; openness is greatly appreciated. The average value is 5.31, and approximately 75% of the responses favor the value openness. Also supporting these findings are the statements made by the respondents in the interviews concerning openness and social interaction. These values are more respected in the Counter Terrorist Unit than in other workplaces from which the respondents have experience. It is a characteristic feature of the unit that its members socialize outside work. This proves that openness among colleagues is highly treasured among the officers.

Informal or Formal

The responses made by the officers in relation to the dimension *formal–informal tone* show a clear preference for the latter, illustrated with an average value of 2.33. More than 80% of the respondents prefer an informal tone. However, some variation does exist. For example, the interviews confirm that extensive banter occurs frequently in the unit and dominates the language used by its members.

Competition or Cooperation

Cooperation is a highly appreciated value by police officers in the Counter Terrorist Unit. Just over 80% of the responses show a clear tendency toward cooperation, with an average score of 4.81. Nevertheless, the responses seem to cluster around the extreme limits of the scale. This dimension must be viewed in relation to the dimension *individualism–group orientation*, which has a similar tendency. The high value attributed to cooperation can also here be explained by the way practical work in ordinary and contingency service in pairs and teams is organized. Likewise, the attitude of applicants toward cooperation is regarded as crucial when recruitment to the unit takes place and in the socializing process for newcomers to the unit.

Nevertheless, one must bear in mind that members of the Counter Terrorist Unit are highly competitive individuals with leadership abilities and a desire to achieve. These are all factors that encourage individual competition and competition between teams and divisions. On the whole, however, this study leaves us with the main impression that cooperation is appreciated.

Equality or Hierarchy

A clear tendency can also be identified along the dimension *equality and codetermination versus hierarchy and authority*. More than 80% of the respondents are oriented toward equality, with an average value of 2.38. Very few answers cluster around the middle of the scale or around the value authority and hierarchy. The control group, which was presented with preliminary results, expressed that equality and codetermination worked in ordinary service, whereas armed response requires a clear hierarchy and commando structure to ensure an efficient and secure handling of the tasks.

The appreciation of equality is also found in the work environment of the Counter Terrorist Unit, which is characterized by equality, small distances within the layers of organization, few or no informal differences in status, a relatively tight social environment, and a welcoming reception given to new members. On the other hand, the age and experience factor appears to pull in the opposite direction. On the whole, however, the main impression left by this study is that the members of the Counter Terrorist Unit hold both equality and codetermination in great esteem.

Short-Term or Long-Term

Regarding the dimension meant to capture the focus on time among the unit's members, the responses are distributed across the entire scale with a main tendency toward the middle section. The average value is 4.38, with more than 60% of the responses showing a preference for long-term job focus. However, police work can be described as guided by incidents and fragmented. This indicates that extensive planning is not necessary and that the focus is short-term.

Consequently, this seems to indicate a preference for short-term focus, fast solutions, and quick results. Members of the Counter Terrorist Unit prefer, on the other hand, a more long-term focus, which means that they value thorough analyses where this is possible as well as decision-making processes characterized by a long-term perspective. For example, it takes 3 years to complete the training leading up to approval or certification of a specialist function such as the diving team. Likewise, Counter Terrorist Unit members have a long-term perspective on collaborative relations.

Also this dimension is situational, as evidenced by the variation in the responses. An alternative explanation to this is that the variation is an expression of individual differences. That said, there might be a correlation between the preference for a long-term perspective and the tendency to favor structure.

Schein (1990) divides the time dimension differently. He talks about assumptions about time and points to the question whether organizations have a fundamental organization directed toward the past, the present, or the future. This is a very interesting perspective from which to study the Counter Terrorist Unit. On one hand, past incidents have great significance. Likewise, members of the Counter Terrorist Unit have to focus on the present when dealing with tasks. At the same time, they are preoccupied with preparing for a potentially challenging armed response in the near future. The variation in the responses on the time dimension and Schein's understanding of this dimension can be interpreted as a confirmation that the Counter Terrorist Unit should have both a short-term and a long-term perspective, but with a main focus on the latter.

Imbalance or Balance

The responses in relation to the dimension *work is more important versus balance between work and spare time* gives an average value of 4.32. The main impression is that the majority of responses cluster around the middle of the scale. However, there is great variation with a weak tendency toward a preference for balancing work and spare time. The results indicate that the officers are very enthusiastic about their jobs, their special field, and their work environment. We have reason to infer from this that the members of the Counter Terrorist Unit show great involvement and that in return they are given a sense of work satisfaction and identity.

We believe the identity factor may be of particular importance in organizations such as the Counter Terrorist Unit. The average age of its members at the time the study was undertaken was approximately 34 years. With a few exceptions this means that the police officers are relatively early in their careers. Possible explanations for this are that they wish to give priority to their career and that to a certain extent this job develops into a lifestyle. Both factors suggest that work is considered very important.

A prominent feature of the organization culture in the police is to regard police work as more than just an ordinary job. Entering the police might mean adopting a lifestyle. On one hand, many police officers are also parents of small children—often many children, which is a factor that works contrary to the notion of police work as lifestyle. In addition, a great number of police officers actively participate in sports, outdoor life, and organizational activities as well as take on duties.

Task or Relationship

Task orientation versus relation orientation is a dimension frequently subjected to a variety of analyses of organization culture. Members of the Norwegian Counter Terrorist Unit express a clear preference for task orientation. Although more than 80% favor task orientation, the responses spread out across the scale. This tendency can be understood in the light of the officers' strong interest in professional matters and the room they are given for self-development. The emphasis on action and result orientation are likely to reinforce this tendency. During the preliminary presentation of this study, attention was given to the mortal danger the members of the Counter Terrorist Unit occasionally must expect to face. This prospect underlines the need to focus on tasks, training, and preparations. Counter Terrorist Unit officers go to work to train, build competence, and carry out assignments. All of these factors point in the same direction, so does probably the fact that the officers regard themselves as servants of the public. The vision of the Counter Terrorist Unit is very clear in this respect.

A preference for task orientation may also be reinforced by the unit's focus on routines, planning, and procedures, so efficient use of time needs to be considered.

The relaxed and informal atmosphere within the Counter Terrorist Unit, the good social environment, and the necessity to cooperate may seem to work in the opposite direction, toward relation orientation. The general impression from research on the police underlines also corps/team spirit and professional loyalty as clear features of the organization culture. These are factors that support relation orientation. We interpret the variation in the responses as an indication that both orientations are prevalent but with task orientation as the more esteemed one.

Direct or Indirect

The responses concerning *style of communication* are unambiguous. A direct style is preferred, and a clear tendency emerges that has to be seen in relation to a context involving an open and relaxed tone between the officers and the absence of conflicts. In terms of subject matter and form, the unit's regular discussions encourage a direct style. Further, the members of the unit learn to know each other very well, which makes them trust each other through training and work. This feature also points in the direction of a direct style of communication, which is always a matter of discussion among the members of the unit. We infer from this that the members of the Counter Terrorist Unit appreciate speaking one's mind.

Action or Planning

Also interesting is the dimension *action orientation–planning orientation.* This is the only dimension where it is possible to identify certain differences of some significance between managers and nonmanagers. This is a counter-intuitive result; that is, it deviates or is contrary to what is anticipated. One could expect that managers were less oriented toward operative action than young and operative police officers on the beat. Reuss-Ianni (1993) distinguishes between managers and police officers on patrol with widely different cultures of the two groups. Police officers who do not hold managerial positions display a general feeling of disdain for managers because they have lost touch with everyday practical policing.

To be fair, it should be noted that managers in the Counter Terrorist Unit are likely to possess the same qualities as their subordinates. Moreover, they have undergone the exactly same selection process, education, and training. Consequently, managers and nonmanagers share the same experiences. However, as experienced officers and managers their focus may be somewhat different. The main tendency for managers is great variation at the same time as the bulk of the answers show an inclination toward action orientation. This result may be interpreted as a confirmation that both planning and action orientation are important. The control groups stressed also here that the responses would depend on the situation. This may indicate that the managers are somewhat more oriented toward action than their subordinates unit, a question that was the subject of discussion during the preliminary presentation. These findings may be accounted for by extensive delegating of responsibility so that the individual officer or partners in the same patrol car place importance on obtaining useful information about situations and individuals and through good planning ensure that their tasks are carried out in accordance with routines and regulations. In other words, a thorough analysis of the situation is conducted before making a decision concerning which measures are to be taken and put into effect.

Practical or Philosophical

The results show that the members of the Counter Terrorist Unit have a clear *practical and pragmatic orientation*. The average value on this dimension is 2.14, and more than 90% rate a practical and pragmatic orientation higher than a philosophical and theoretical orientation. During the preliminary presentation of this study, respondents commented that there are a great deal of equipment and devices to be operated and mastered. The police officers reported that they are working continuously with the purpose of finding simple and practical solutions. Nevertheless, they admitted that theoretical knowledge played an important factor in this work, such as the handling of explosives, giving first aid, testing new equipment, and developing new plans.

The practical or pragmatic attitude displays a pattern that is entirely in accordance with findings in international research on police officers. This literature calls attention to, among others, a here-and-now attitude that is descriptive of the situational character of policing. In addition, Fielding (1984) emphasizes personal experiences as a source to understanding situations and solving problems. Some argue that there is an evident anti-intellectualism within the police culture. To the extent it is possible to compare research findings found in British or American social conditions of the 1960s and 1970s with Norwegian society today, this may be an explanatory factor. We assume, however, that the nature of the Counter Terrorist Unit's tasks and technologies as well as the emphasis on developing skills are factors that to a greater extent explain the importance attached to a practical and pragmatic orientation. Blasts, shoot-outs, and driving are examples of activities that contribute to reinforce this orientation.

Security or Challenge

The control group perceived of the dimension *security and safety versus challenges and suspense* as two-sided. On one hand, it is a general feature of the police officers in the unit that they are drawn to suspense and seek challenges to test their ability to master difficult situations. During the interviews it transpired that police officers that chose to apply for the Counter Terrorist Unit were motivated among others by factors related to professional and personal challenges. These findings are thoroughly described in other literature on this field.

On the other hand, we see that importance is given to planning, structure, situation analyses, and training. The significance of security is underlined by the priority given to health, environment, and safety regulations as well as the stress on personal safety in connection with different assignments. These sentiments came forward, among others, at a meeting referred to earlier in this chapter. All the aforementioned factors point in the direction of security and safety. The same factors can also be said to be important for victims of serious crimes. Regarding victims of crime, these factors must be prioritized so that a good solution can be found. Finally, we can see this in relation to humbleness and professionalism where these factors are central.

Democracy or Productivity

Legal protection and democracy versus efficiency and productivity is an important and interesting dimension for the entire public sector. The concept of public ethos might be linked to the question about the role of the police as an institution in society with the right to use coercive force. This dimension is of particular great interest to the police, which act as society's machinery of power. Consequently, the police's priorities in connection with the execution of power have great impact on our democracy. This dimension is also important because the police are action and task oriented, which becomes particularly evident in demanding operative work of the nature of the Counter Terrorist Unit.

The main tendency is that the value legal protection and democracy is valued highly. The average value is 1.71, and more than 80% of respondents chose the two most unambiguous scores. No other question asked in this survey received a clearer answer, which proves that democracy and legal protection are regarded as extraordinarily important by the members of the Counter Terrorist Unit. This is in accordance with the professional attitude displayed by members of the unit throughout all of their missions and with the unit's vision. In the interviews, respondents made it very clear that they looked at illegal and unnecessary use of force as a very negative factor that should not occur in their division. The interviews left an unambiguous and clear impression in this respect.

These sentiments are in line with observations made in meetings and during training. To underline this further, the division's instructions disapprove of illegal and unnecessary use of force. Finally, it may be worth mentioning that the trust in the Counter Terrorist Unit and legitimacy require both a clear attitude and consistent behavior in relation to questions that this dimension affects. The attention the Counter Terrorist Unit naturally attracts implies that any errors committed by the unit in connection with this dimension will have a tendency to produce negative consequences.

Operative work and operative disposition may indicate that the wish to achieve results has priority over values such as legal protection and democracy in practical police work. International research shows that operative cultures rate results higher than legal protection. Certain reservations must be made, however, when the Norwegian or Nordic police forces are concerned. The value democracy and legal protection are viewed as important more often than not. In the annual survey undertaken by the Norwegian Market and Media Institute, the police are consistently the highest-scoring government service. Consequently, the survey gives a general impression of Norwegians as trusting the police.

Police activities are firmly regulated though a large number of laws, instructions, plans, and routines. The Police Instructions and the Criminal Procedure Act are central tools being used to ensure legal protection and democracy. These factors contribute to reinforce the value legal protection and democracy.

Service or Enforcement

The dimension *service and public services versus crime prevention* is central to the police, and the responses vary considerably. A full 13.5% of the respondents prefer service, whereas about 40% favor crime prevention. The average value is 4.73, with about 35% of the respondents choosing the value 4. The main tendency appears to be that the respondents consider prevention to be more important than providing service.

Here, too, it is important to make a distinction between ordinary policing and armed response when examining the figures. The great specter in the responses may indicate that the Counter Terrorist Unit as a whole finds both considerations important. The main tendency can be explained by the unit's character and tasks. However, this goes contrary to the vision of the unit. Police seems to give priority to crime prevention over service, although the latter is frequently discussed.

In everyday policing, police officers demonstrate a healthy attitude toward providing service and a willingness to accept that they are there to serve the public or protect citizens against criminal acts. Knutsson and Granér use the metaphor "I am a guardian too" to illustrate how police officers perceive of what their core tasks are.

Here we also touch on the distinction between preventive and problem-oriented or proactive policing as opposed to the more action-led and reactive perspective of policing. Although it may look like service is a value, which has received more acclaim in recent years, crime prevention is still very central to all police work. According to this survey, the members of the Counter Terrorist Unit appear to be concerned about both their service function and crime prevention and that the matter of priority may be situational but also that they in general value crime prevention higher than providing service.

Boss or Creativity

As for the respondents' attitude toward the dimension *strong and firm management versus freedom, trust, and individual initiative*, there are also great differences. The main tendency is that just below 80% of the police officers prefer strong management. This is in accordance with the findings in the interviews and contributes to strengthen the support for this type of management.

Openness or Loyalty

The values survey closes with the dimension openness and transparency versus professional loyalty and corps/team spirit Once again, the tendency is clear with more than 80% of the respondents preferring openness and transparency. This is a tendency that is contrary to words commonly used to characterize police cultures, such as corps/team spirit, closure, secrecy, and us versus them attitudes (see, e.g., Reuss-Ianni, 1993).

Culture Characteristics

The previous presentations and discussion show that professional loyalty is highly valued. This is also confirmed by the information obtained in the interviews. The same goes for the way the work is organized, which we also have given an outline of in this chapter. Transparency has its limitations in relation to resources, competence, and work methodologies. This is obvious when we know the unit's tasks and responsibilities. The clear line between the unit and other police units is also evident. The intimate work environment, the extraordinarily strong identity, and the relatively great stability among the unit's members may also be indicative of a tendency to prefer professional loyalty and corps/team spirit.

These factors are in line with elements that describe features of police culture internationally. Structural factors can be identified that point in the direction of closure and corps spirit. On the other hand, one may assume that self-confidence, a firm identity, and consciousness about one's own role may counteract this tendency. An important factor in this connection is the manager's priorities and behavior as a role model. This factor shows clearly that both openness and transparency are desired and practiced to the extent this is possible. This applies also in relation to other police units, the police directorate, and the ministry of justice and the police. And so does probably the fact that the Counter Terrorist Unit is a special unit, which easily can find itself subjected to criticism, which may have consequences for both individual members and the unit as a whole. Here we recognize Schein's dimension of external adjustment, which was referred to earlier in this chapter.

Finally, we would like to point out some of the clearest answers assessed on the basis of the average responses in this survey. The survey shows that the police officers in the Counter Terrorist Unit gave the clearest answers in relation to the value legal protection and democracy (1.71). Moreover, they stress that the time is perceived of as fixed (1.83). This is one of the most unambiguous answers in the survey. What is more, it may be mentioned that the police officers attach great value to the informal culture and the value of equality and codetermination. Likewise, they value a practical and pragmatic attitude to their work. Finally, openness and good relations among colleagues are also appreciated.

Both interviews and questionnaires were employed to study the organization culture in the Counter Terrorist Unit. By the help of questionnaires we were trying to make a survey of the dominating values in the Counter Terrorist Unit. The members of the unit were asked to rate what they think are the most prevalent values in the Counter Terrorist Unit along a total of 19 dimensions. The dimensions were designed as opposing pairs of concepts, as shown in Table 13.1, along with the average figure for each dimension. The scale goes from 1 to 7. The first dimension, time is fixed versus floating, gives an average score of 1.83, which means that the respondents are more likely to perceive of time as fixed than floating.

Causal Relationships

Through analyses of statistics we found that the respondents had given very similar answers on a variety of dimensions. This means that these dimensions form one sole factor, which we can call involvement. This new factor encompasses the following dimensions: 7 (competition versus cooperation), 10 (work versus balance), 11 (task orientation versus relation orientation), and 19 (closed versus open or inversed dimension).

Table 13.1 Average Cultural Values in the Norwegian Counter Terrorist Unit on a Scale Ranging From 1 to 7

Number	Dimension	Answer
1	Time is fixed—Time is floating	1.83
2	Change—Tradition and continuity	3.33
3	Individualism—Group orientation	5.44
4	Freedom—Control	3.19
5	Privacy—Public/openness	5.31
6	Informal—Formal	2.33
7	Individual competition—Cooperation	4.81
8	Equality and codetermination—Hierarchy and authority	2.83
9	Short-term focus—Long-term focus	4.38
10	Work most important—Balance work/spare time	4.35
11	Task orientation—Relation orientation	3.31
12	Direct/explicit communication style—Indirect/implicit communication style	2.54
13	Action orientation—Planning orientation	3.85
14	Practical and pragmatic orientation—Philosophical and theoretical orientation	2.14
15	Security and safety—Challenges and suspense	2.40
16	Legal protection and democracy—Efficiency and productivity	1.71
17	Service, visibility, safety, and public services Combating crime and enforcement of law and order	4.73
18	Strong and clear management—Freedom, trust, personal initiative, and creativity	3.73
19	Openness, transparency—Professional loyalty, corps/team spirit	2.52

The variation in the factor referred to as involvement is a consequence of the variation found in the dimensions involved. We identified three significant correlations as shown in Figure 13.2.

Hypotheses 1, 2, and 3 were all supported:

H1: The longer time perspective a police officer has, the higher degree of personal involvement.
H2: The lower degree of hierarchy a police officer experiences, the higher degree of personal involvement.
H3: The lower degree of authority a police officer experiences, the higher degree of personal involvement.

This research model explains 28.5% of the variation occurring in the dependent variable. Statistical analysis of variance (ANOVA) shows that the model is significant. All the coefficients of the independent variables have been measured to have significance, which is stronger than .05.

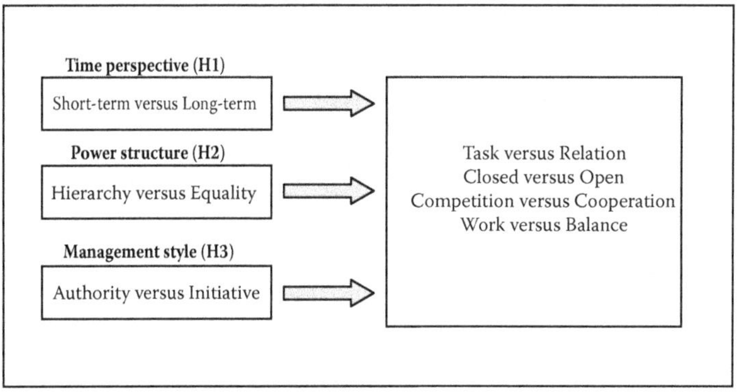

Figure 13.2 Causal model to predict variations.

Conclusion

It is worth repeating that data from this survey reflect the values typical to the Norwegian Counter Terrorist Unit, which was also the objective of the analysis. The analysis may not, however, give an accurate answer to the question of the extent to which the desired values and the values lived by correlate. Nevertheless, we have reason to assume that there is a relatively high degree of correlation.

Consequently, it is possible to describe the following values characteristic of the organization culture in the Counter Terrorist Unit:

- *Competence and development orientation.* The unit emphasizes this value through a great deal of systemization, planning, and routines as well as extensive training, socialization, certifications, and competence-building activities.
- *Safety under the law orientation.* Unnecessary use of force is not tolerated in the Counter Terrorist Unit. This is a value linked to routines, training, and the providing of service.
- *Structure orientation.* The unit is characterized by relatively many efficient and well-developed routines, which express themselves through for example the unit's activity plans, plans for building competence, training programs, and certifications. Moreover, this emphasis also expresses itself through the importance attached to operative routines, rather frequent meetings, and routines for reporting.
- *Performance orientation.* The members of the Counter Terrorist Unit seek vast professional as well as personal challenges. These challenges can be seen in light of a distinct quest for suspense.
- *Task orientation.* Police tasks occupy a central place in the unit's activities, and police officers are constantly looking for new and better ways of solving tasks.

- *Action orientation.* The ability to act is emphasized through training as well as through solving practical tasks. The police officers want to get things done, and there is an inner and collective drive to act and arrive at solutions of the challenges they face.
- *Cooperation orientation.* Throughout the selection process, education, training, practical work, and the ability to cooperate are being stressed. Cooperation implies putting together complementary competence and exploited when tasks are being dealt with. Moreover, cooperation enhances the ability to solve tasks. Finally, cooperation also provides safety for the individual team member.
- *Humbleness orientation.* Humbleness seems to be geared toward the tasks, competence, colleagues, and good connections. Here we find a sense of humbleness when confronted with the risks characterizing many of the unit's assignments. Moreover, it is directed toward themselves in the role as representatives of the Counter Terrorist Unit.

References

Bailey, W. G., Strecher, V. G., Hoover, L. T., & Dowling, J. L. (1995). Occupational culture. *The Encyclopedia of Police Science*, 2d ed. New York: Garland Publishing.

Christensen, W., & Crank, J. P. (2001). Police work and culture in a non-urban setting: An ethnographic analysis. *Police Quarterly*, *4*(1), 69–98.

Fielding, N. (1984). Police socialization and police competence. *British Journal of Sociology*, *4*.

Hofstede, G., Neuijen, B., Ohavy, D. D., & Sanders, G. (1990). Measuring organizational cultures: A qualitative and quantitative study across twenty cases. *Administrative Science Quarterly*, *35*, 286–316.

Kiely, J. A., & Peek, G. S. (2002). The culture of the British Police: Views of police officers. *Service Industries Journal*, *22*(1), 167–183.

Reuss-Ianni, E. (1993). *Two cultures of policing: Street cops and management cops.* New Brunswick, NJ: Transaction Publishers.

Schein, E. H. (1990). Organizational culture. *American Psychologist*, *45*(2), 109–119.

Structural Influences on Police Officer Attitudes Toward Community Policing

14

A Case Study of the Racine, Wisconsin Police Department*

HELEN ROSENBERG
University of Wisconsin–Parkside

ROBERT T. SIGLER
University of Alabama–Tuscaloosa

SCOTT LEWIS
City Attorney's Office (Retired), Racine, WI

Contents

* This project was supported by Grant 96-FJ-CX-0093 awarded by the National Institute of Justice Programs, U.S. Department of Justice. Points of view in this document are those of the authors and do not necessarily represent the official position or policies of the U.S. Department of Justice. The authors wish to thank Dr. Wesley Skogan, Northwestern University, Dr. Lee Ross, University of Central Florida, Orlando, and the reviewers of this article for their valuable suggestions for revision. We are grateful to Chief Richard Polzin, retired and assistant chief John Ernst, retired, for their help.

Introduction

Community policing strives to change the very nature of policing on a number of levels. Officers are encouraged to redefine their roles from servers of the public to community stakeholders, department structures are flattened so that knowledge may be diffused across rank allowing greater discretionary power and increased participatory management among all officers, and police administrators work to expand the role of officers from crime centered to problem-solving centered, working with communities to solve problems rather than working for them (Luen & Al-Hawamdeh, 2001; Skogan, 2003). Implementing such changes in departments has proved difficult. Insufficient rewards to officers for implementing change and supervisors who say they are supportive of change but continue to function as they had before impede efforts for departmental reorganization and power redistribution (Champy, 1995; Hammer & Champy, 1993). Specifically, senior command has been reluctant to transfer knowledge and decision-making power, so police officers have greater participatory management in the department and discretionary power in the community. This separates stated policy from the actual buy-in by officers. Indeed, our research with the Racine Police Department (RPD) indicates that while line officers may "talk the walk" of community policing, they are far from changing their perceptions of their roles as crime fighters and embracing the community policing philosophy. Alternatively, senior command is reluctant to give up decision-making power and provide patrol officers and investigators greater autonomy leading to participatory management. The result is the implementation of a community policing program without the value consensus and common goals for knowledge sharing, transfer of power, and ultimate organizational change required for its success.

This chapter follows the transition to community policing in the Racine Police Department. The city of Racine, Wisconsin, population, 84,298,[1] is located on Lake Michigan, 25 miles south of Milwaukee and 65 miles north of Chicago (U.S. Bureau of the Census, 1992). Racine is an industrial community, home to 300 firms, the most notable of which is S.C. Johnson Wax and Company, producer and international distributor of chemicals for home and industry.

Rather than any specific intervention that marks the onset of community policing in Racine, this study documents officer perceptions to gradual changes implemented over a 6-year period. Some of the changes involved explicit modifications to the structure of the police department, while other changes were more subtle. Organizational changes in the department included the creation of police substations that decentralized the RPD, creation of the community policing unit (CPU), and partnering with other service agencies to reduce crime. In addition, Police Chief Richard Polzin desired to increase communication among officers, especially across rank and to provide the CPU and other line officers increased decision-making power and autonomy. We examine the personal qualities of gender, race, and age as well as occupational status within the organization (rank, length of service) in an attempt to understand officers' opinions of community policing constructs on the basis of the previously mentioned indicators.

Predictors of Support for Community Policing

Community policing since the 1980s has become the dominant strategy of policing for the 1990s. In the United States it has been widely practiced for about a decade (Anonymous, 2002). According to Cordner (2005, p. 401), "Community policing has evolved from a few small foot patrol studies to the pre-eminent reform agenda of modern policing." However, *community policing* continues to be many things to many people. A common catch cry by proponents is, "Community policing is a philosophy, not a program" (Cordner, 2005, p. 402). But there is much confusion over defining what community policing actually means. Wycoff & Skogan (1994), in a national survey in the United States of 1,606 law enforcement agencies, found that nearly 50% of the responding police chiefs and sheriffs did not have a clear understanding of what community policing meant.

If such definitional difficulties are put to one side, it is clear that the core concept behind community policing is that it represents a crime fighting strategy that stresses partnership and problem solving. However, in spite of its current popularity the concept of community policing has its detractors.

Maguire and Katz (2002, p. 504) note, "Critics have argued that community policing represents a slogan without action, style without substance, and rhetoric without reality (Bayley, 1988; Klockars, 1988; Manning, 1989; Weatheritt, 1988). For some, community policing is an empty reform effort characterized by nothing but 'BS and buzzwords' (Hunter & Barker, 1993, p. 157)." Maguire and Katz (2002) further add, "...Some influential reformers have expressed concern that community policing has come to mean anything that is new and innovative in American policing (Goldstein, 1994; Skolnick & Bayley, 1988, p. 510)."

The diversity of the label community policing is a two-edged sword. Community policing is a very flexible umbrella term for a diverse range of activities and programs. "Today, almost every specialised program developed by a police department is labelled community policing" (Walsh & Vito, 2004, p. 57).

It is within this context that this study seeks to explore in more specific detail the types of attitudes that police officers hold that could be used as predictors of support for this very loose label of community policing. A brief review of the literature on such support predictors for community policing indicates that officer commitment to the department and positive attitudes toward superiors have been positively related to rank (Ferdinand, 1980), while cynicism and rank have been negatively correlated (Hou, Miracle, & Poole, 1983; Neiderhoffer, 1969). Hoath, Schneider, and Starr (1998) found that among the variables of age, length of employment, number of years in the current position, and rank, only the number of years in the current position (assignment tenure) significantly impacted on job satisfaction. In this case, lower job satisfaction was associated with higher assignment tenure. Brunetto and Farr-Wharton (2003) found that officer negativity increased with rank up to that of sergeant among those who define organizational process as "poor."

Dantzker (1992) found that patrol officers with a college degree and 5 years or more of experience were less satisfied with their jobs than officers without a college degree and less than 5 years of experience. However, education as a predictor of police attitudes has consistently shown weak effects (Sherman, 1979). It has been posited that socialization into the organization of policing counteracts any effects that education may have on behavior (Christie, Petrie, & Timmins, 1996). This socialization process begins early in police training, which reinforces obedience to authority. The community policing philosophy, which is usually taught after officers are on the force, requires officers to unlearn previously well-established values (Conti & Nolan, 2005). Thus, the literature on demographic correlates of officer attitudes suggests a complex relationship between rank and support for community policing based on attitudes toward supervisors and organizational process. To ascertain further knowledge about this complex interplay of rank and organizational processes the following case study is reported on in relation to community policing attitudes by officers in the Racine Police Department.

Case Study: Racine Police Department

The community policing movement in Racine developed in response to gang and crime problems that increased in the late 1980s and early 1990s. Many of these crimes were in areas that directly impacted commerce (e.g., employees of S.C. Johnson Wax) and created fear among local residents and visitors to the city. In 1991, Chief Polzin secured grants to renovate two buildings in high crime areas into community policing substations. Over time, the number of community policing substations increased to six with one located in a neighborhood shopping mall at the request of retailers who were experiencing heavy levels of shoplifting. All substations were staffed by community policing officers who walked through the neighborhoods during their shifts. Coterminous with the building of community substations was the beginning of a bicycle patrol established to cover park and lake front areas not accessible by car and the Drug Abuse Resistance Education program (DARE), which brought officers into the schools to educate students about the dangers of drugs.

Community policing officers became part of a special unit, the community policing unit. The unit was strongly supported by the senior command in the department who saw officers of this unit as key in mending relationships with community businesses and citizens who had become fearful of gangs in their neighborhoods.

A series of police offensives, called neighborhood sweeps, was begun in 1993. Community policing officers partnering with gang and drug units saturated a neighborhood where home and apartment owners were in violation of building code and health laws (Reiss, 1992). These sweeps functioned to protect Housing and Health Department agents in charge of levying citations for code violations from being harassed and possibly assaulted during routine inspections in high-crime neighborhoods.

The Survey Instrument

We developed a 40-item survey instrument that examined officer attitudes regarding six attitudinal constructs that reflect aspects of community policing (see the Appendix). Officers were asked to rate their agreement with each statement in the survey on a scale of 1 to 5 with 1 indicating strong disagreement and 5 indicating strong agreement and where 21 statements were worded positively and 19 negatively. Scoring was reversed on the negative items producing positive measures of attitudes toward community policing for all items. Scales were constructed on the basis of item content and consistency using Cronbach's alpha.[2] The reported mean for each construct is the mean of all respondents' statements for that construct. The six constructs represent the following:

1. Acceptance of the underlying *concepts of community policing*
2. Support for specific *community policing programs*
3. Approval of police *substations* in high-crime areas of the city to decentralize policing
4. Support for the *community policing unit*
5. Approval of modifications in the *organizational structure* of the department to give line officers more decision-making power
6. Agreement that communication between *supervisors and subordinates* is good

In addition, we asked officers their age, years of service on the RPD, rank, years of education, marital status, and gender. We chose not to ask officers their race, since the department is overwhelmingly White and such a question might be perceived as one way we could identify officers of color on the force.

Study Design and Sample

Attitudes toward community policing were assessed at two time points over a 19-month period—once in February 1997 and again in September 1998 for the population of officers in the RPD.[3] The survey and method of distribution was the same across both waves of the study. Surveys were administered at roll call, and officers were instructed to place completed surveys in one of two boxes or return surveys through the mail using a postage-paid envelope addressed to the University of Wisconsin–Parkside. Each survey was assigned a unique identification number. A blank index card accompanied each survey. The card contained a space for the respondent's mother's maiden name and the respondent's last digit on his social security number.[4] This information was used to match index cards across both waves and to assign unique ID numbers to surveys for each officer in the study.

There were 209 officers in the department for both waves of data collection.[5] A total of 167 officers completed the survey at Wave 1, and 98 completed the survey at Wave 2. During the time that intervened between surveys, an interview in the Racine *Journal Times* with the third author revealed this person to be the assistant city attorney and former legal counsel for the RPD. In addition, the article discussed some of the controversy surrounding items in the survey. Specifically, officers took issue with one statement that described community policing as a cushy job, and officers felt that items, in general, were worded in a negative manner. In addition, officers were suspicious as to why they had to provide their mothers' maiden names and last digit of a social security number if the survey was truly anonymous. These factors influenced the response rate for the second wave of the survey. After the completion of Wave 2, the authors matched surveys across waves on the basis of identification obtained from the index cards. The results from this report are based on data from the 69 officers who completed both waves of the survey.

Measures

Sample

The average age of officers participating in both waves of the study is 39 years, with 40% of respondents between the ages of 34 and 43 years old. Almost two-thirds (64%) have served on the force for more than 10 years. A total of 46% of respondents are patrol officers, 21.7% are either traffic patrol or investigators, 18% are sergeants, and 13.8% are senior command, including lieutenants, inspectors, captains, and the assistant chief and chief of police. Half have completed a college degree or higher, 80% are married, and 95% are male.

Intercorrelations Among Dependent Constructs

The correlation between responses for Waves 1 and 2 for the six dependent constructs indicates a strong to moderate, positive relationship among five of the constructs: (1) favorable attitudes toward community policing concepts; (2) support of community policing programs; (3) support for locating substations outside the central office; (4) support for the community policing unit; and (5) reporting that relationships between supervisors and subordinates are good are all positively related. In addition, in most cases, the size of the correlations increases at Wave 2, indicating greater attitudinal consistency at Wave 2 than at Wave 1. However, there is a negative relationship between those who favor a flattened organizational structure and the other five community policing constructs. This means that those who support increasing decision-making power for line officers tend to have a negative view of the other community policing constructs, and, alternately, those who support community policing do not support increasing decision making for line officers. While this trend is not significant at Wave 1, it is moderately strong at Wave 2. Moreover, those who favor a flattened organizational structure also tend to report poorer relationships between supervisors and subordinates in the department (Table 14.1).

Results

We performed a repeated measures analysis of variance for the six measured constructs for the 69 officers who completed both waves of this study. While we expected significant positive changes in constructs over time, we found that officer attitudes remained relatively stable throughout the study period (Table 14.2).

Overall, officers were somewhat supportive of community policing concepts and the community policing program but were neutral regarding relationships between supervisors and subordinates, placing substations in the community, and desiring a more flattened organizational structure in the department. Officers were slightly disapproving of the community policing unit. Support for the community policing program increased significantly over the study period, but despite its statistical significance support increased slightly and means still remained below the threshold of

Table 14.1 Correlations Among Dependent Measures—WAVE 1 (WAVE 2)

	Favor Community Policing Concepts	Favor Community Policing Program	Approve of Community Policing Substations	Approve of Community Policing Unit	Favor a Flattened Organizational Structure	Good Relationship Between Supervisors & Subordinates
Favor community policing concepts	1.0	.46**(.58)**	.57**(.66)**	.42**(.62)**	–.04(–.32)**	.35**(.46)**
Favor community policing program		1.0	.71**(.70)**	.73**(.60)**	–.03(–.36)**	.36**(.54)**
Approve of community policing substations			1.0	.74* (.62)**	–.16(–.37)**	.47**(.56)**
Approve of community policing unit				1.0	–.21(–.41)**	.57**(.59)**
Favor a flattened organizational structure					1.0	–.54**(–.52)**
Good relationship between supervisors and subordinates						1.0

** $p = < .01$.

Table 14.2 Comparison of Means on Dependent Measures Between Waves

	Wave 1	Wave 2		
Dependent Construct	Mean	Mean	*F*-Value	*P*-Value
Favor community policing concepts	3.562	3.515	0.606	0.439
Favor community policing program	3.314	3.446	5.193	0.026
Approve of community policing substations	3.179	3.275	1.892	0.174
Approve of community policing unit	2.742	2.833	1.339	0.251
Favor a flattened organizational structure	3.216	3.096	2.306	0.134
Good relationship between supervisors and subordinates	3.105	3.119	0.035	0.852

agreement. Examination of the individual items that comprised this latter subscale reveals that statements for this construct focused on community partnerships, including neighborhood watch,[6] National Night Out and the sweeps program, efforts that were targeted by Chief Polzin. Thus, the efforts of the RPD to rebuild neighborhoods through community partnerships received increased support among officers over the study period.

The independent measures reflecting personal demographics and organizational status were entered into a repeated measures multivariate analysis of variance to determine which among these influenced attitudes toward community policing. Age, a virtual proxy for years on the force ($r = .91$), was deleted from the analysis to avoid problems associated with multicollinearity (Weisel & Eck, 1994). Marital status and gender were coded as dichotomous variables with the effects of being married and male entered into the analysis.

At Wave 1, both years of service ($p = .04$) and rank ($p < .01$) were significant predictors of attitudes toward community policing, but by Wave 2 rank was the only significant predictor of officer attitudes. Since there were no significant differences between waves on five of the six dependent constructs, we combined data for both waves and report mean attitudes of officers on the basis of rank alone.[7] Table 14.3 displays the mean ratings for each officer rank across the six community policing subscales and indicates which ranks are significantly different from each other using the Bonferroni post hoc test (SPSS, 2004).

Patrol officers and investigators are least supportive of community policing other than supporting a flattened organizational structure, which would give them greater access to information and decision-making power. Sergeants and senior command are most supportive of community policing, except for their unwillingness to diffuse decision-making power across all ranks. Specifically, patrol officers and investigators have significantly lower mean scores than senior command and in some cases sergeants on their approval for community policing concepts, programs, and placement

Table 14.3 Mean Attitude by Rank for Attitudinal Subscales (Waves 1 and 2 Combined)

Subscale	Rank	Mean	*N*	Bonferroni Comparisons[a]
Policing concepts	Patrol	3.26	64	1 vs. 3,4
	Traffic/Investigator	3.32	30	2 vs. 4
	Sergeant	3.62	25	
	Senior Command	4.02	19	
	Total	3.44	138	
Policing program	Patrol	3.31	64	1 vs. 4
	Traffic/Investigator	2.03	30	2 vs. 4
	Sergeant	3.42	25	
	Senior Command	3.84	19	
	Total	3.34	138	
Policing substations	Patrol	3.09	64	1 vs. 4
	Traffic/Investigator	2.79	30	2 vs. 3,4
	Sergeant	3.33	25	
	Senior Command	3.75	19	
	Total	3.16	138	
Community policing unit	Patrol	2.65	64	1 vs. 4
	Traffic/Investigator	2.35	30	2 vs. 3,4
	Sergeant	2.87	25	
	Senior Command	3.37	19	
	Total	2.72	138	
Organizational structure	Patrol	3.66	64	1 vs. 3,4
	Traffic/Investigator	3.50	30	2 vs. 3,4
	Sergeant	2.65	25	
	Senior Command	2.79	19	
	Total	3.32	138	
Relationship between supervisors and subordinates	Patrol	2.68	64	1 vs. 3,4
	Traffic/Investigator	2.68	30	2 vs. 3,4
	Sergeants	3.49	25	
	Senior Command	3.67	19	
	Total	2.96	138	

[a] All Bonferroni comparisons by rank are significant at < .05 using adjustment for multiple comparisons.

of substations in the community. Apart from senior command, approval for the community policing unit is weak. Investigators have the dimmest view of community policing in the department.

Sergeants and senior command are least supportive of diffusing decision-making power, while patrol and investigators support this. Both patrol and investigators disagree with statements indicating there is a good relationship between supervisors and subordinates, while sergeants and senior command seem to feel that they have a good relationship with officers. In sum, we find conflicting values in the department based on rank.

Discussion

A constraint on interpreting the findings of this study that needs to be borne in mind is that this whole research area of community policing as evidenced in the literature review is plagued with definitional difficulties and confusion. As has been pointed out there is a lot of rhetoric about community policing without much in the way of reality (Maguire & Katz, 2002). The term can mean just about anything depending on who is doing the defining.

Therefore, the attitudinal findings reported on in this Racine case study should be understood at best as tentative rather than substantive, since it is only the police officers themselves who participated in the survey who can fully know in a meaning sense what they are responding to in relation to their own unique understandings of the questions asked and the underlying concept they may hold about what community policing means to them individually.

This is not a unique constraint on this study alone as all attitudinal research faces the same dilemma. What is the issue for this study is that the notion of community policing is an ever muddier concept than most to research. Such a qualification should not be taken to mean such research is invalid or should not be done—only that any research interpretation should be handled with care, as the best proposition we know something about so far.

In relation to this study, we know something about the following. First, responsibilities and privilege within police departments are stratified by rank. Community policing, as a philosophy, challenges this stratification structure. As Zeffane (1996) suggests, it is the responsibility of senior management to make changes in the best interest of the organization. Within the community policing philosophy, this change implies balancing access to information across rank, which ultimately diffuses power and increases participatory management among all officers (Colaprete, 2004; Kelley, 2003). In the Racine Police Department, senior command is resistant to give up this control.

In addition, the community policing unit is resented by most other officers, partly because senior command has conferred greater decision-making power to this unit, creating an imbalance within the department of access to information, privilege, and autonomy (Hughes & Jackson, 2004). Finally, there is a disconnect between senior command and subordinates regarding their relationship, with patrol and investigators reporting that their relationship with senior command is less favorable than senior command perceives it to be. It appears that senior command is unaware of possible resentments that line officers have toward them.

Second, divisions on the basis of autonomy and decision-making power have created informational and ideological silos within the department, that is, distinct units that do not share information and thus are motivated to hide rather than work through organizational problems. This is evidenced by the value differences between ranks that separate senior command from patrol officers and investigators on the six constructs of community policing measured in this study. While community policing advocates for a reduction in the hierarchical organization of departments, the RPD has yet to move on this (Klinger, 2004). The importance of knowledge sharing and communication across rank is strongly indicated. Communication seems to flow from command to rank and file, with little room for response from junior officers (Brunetto & Farr-Wharton, 2003). This lack of knowledge sharing and communication can create uncertainty among officers as to requirements for job performance within the context of a community policing program that does not implement all components prescribed by the program. Sergeants' mean scores are similar to those of senior command, but their role as middle management in the department is crucial to improving communication across rank and moving the organization toward change (Stroshine, 2002).

Such a lack of knowledge sharing as found in this study is not uncommon in the police culture, which has been characterized as being a collection of several subcultures. In fact, according to Dean and Gottschalk (2007, p. 17) the term *police culture*:

> …Is a more or less catch-all phrase which subsumes a number of sub-cultural groupings within its ambit most notably the 'managerial' and 'operational' police sub-cultures which are well documented in the literature (Reuss-Ianni, 1993; Ekman, 1999, Foster, 2003; Paoline, 2003). Moreover, the 'operational' culture of policing can be further sub-divided along the lines other researchers have found, for example, the "investigative culture" of detectives (Wright, 2002, Maguire, 2003, Innes, 2003) as well as the "street culture" of general duties police.

Moreover, the larger framework in which to further understand these findings is that of knowledge management (KM) as a distinct field of study (Alavi & Leidner, 2001). The philosophy of KM is about managing the conceptual outputs of people's tacit knowledge by adopting people-centered approaches (Dean & Gottschalk, 2007). In a policing context such people-centred approaches fit comfortably into a community policing philosophy of shared partnership.

Hence, the tacit knowledge of the community built up by community policing officers in this Racine Study through their involvement in people-centered activities and programs has much to offer an organization that is committed to making the best use of its people as knowledge resources.

Finally, the previously noted findings in this case study of the Racine Police Department have been echoed by other researchers who have found similar results, especially in relation to the lack of real integration of a community policing philosophy and hence the unchanging nature of police departments generally.

For example, Cordner (2005, p. 408) in an up-to-date review of the effectiveness of community policing still concurs with Maguire and Katz's (2002) previous findings by noting, "Many commentators have taken the view that community policing is little more than a new police marketing strategy that has left the core elements of the police role untouched."

The problem these perspectives present for community policing as a philosophy is that in many police departments it is, therefore, relegated to the level of a subunit, not a whole-of-organisation approach. "Although many police departments claim that they are engaged in some form of community policing, the majority of them are still bureaucratically structured and delivering their services based on the strategies of the rational-legal bureaucratic model" (Walsh & Vito, 2004, p. 57).

While some research in Canada indicates community policing still has potential to build proactive policing strategies (Clarke, 2006; Colvin & Goh, 2006) it still begs the question posed by Dean and Gottschalk (2007):

> Is "community policing" no more than an amorphous concept that is largely meaningless and which can be used by police departments as a "trendy phrase" to attach to projects to get more police resources while giving the appearance of legitimacy without making any fundamental or substantive changes to the way "policing" has always been done?

Conclusion

This research provides a very different view of community policing than is typically seen by the public. Conventional knowledge of community policing is one of police engagement within the community. However, officers' views of how community policing should be implemented provides a different perspective. Indeed, community policing completely transforms the legitimacy of officer power in the department and redefines long established relationships among officers (Wilson, 2000). Despite the fact that the RPD attempts to consolidate community policing into a unified policy, departmental subcultures across rank signify divisions within the organization. While officer behaviors may have changed as have public perceptions of policing roles, the traditions and role distinctions in the department that have supported hierarchy and maintained power differentials on the basis of rank are still alive and functioning well for senior command but not for line officers.

What impact might this have on police community relations? First, the role of officer as discretionary policy maker in the community is not possible without the tool of knowledge and the value of shared trust across rank (Gottschalk, 2007). Second, without shared support for organizational change, it is likely that patrol officers and investigators will subvert community policing because they are denied the entitlements of a totally implemented program which includes discretionary power in decision making. Given these barriers, we must ask how we can study variations in perspectives across rank with the goal of balancing access to information that ultimately diffuses power throughout the organization. Can participatory management among the patrol and investigators be viewed as favorable by management and can dissention among ranks be tolerated and incorporated into a dialogue for change?

References

Alavi, M., & Leidner, D. E. (2001). Knowledge management and knowledge management systems: Conceptual foundations and research issues. *MIS Quarterly, 25*(1),107–136.

Anonymous. (2002). Community policing: Essential to homeland security. *Sheriff, 54*(5), 36–37.

Bayley, D. H. (1988). Community policing: A report from the devil's advocate. In J. R. Greene & S. D. Mastrofski (Eds.), *Community policing: Rhetoric or Reality* (pp. 225–238) New York: Praeger.

Brunetto, Y., & Farr-Wharton, R. (2003). The commitment and satisfaction of lower-ranked police officers: Lessons for management. *Policing: An International Journal of Police Strategies and Management, 26*, 43–63.

Champy J. (1995). *Reengineering management: The mandate for new leadership*. New York: Harper Business.

Christie, G., Petrie, S., & Timmins, P. (1996). The effect of police education, training and socialisation on conservative attitudes. *Australian and New Zealand Journal of Criminology, 29*, 299–314.

Clarke, C. (2006). Proactive policing: Standing on the shoulders of community–based policing. *Police Practice and Research: An International Journal, 7*(1), 3–18.

Colaprete, F. (2004). Knowledge management. *Law and Order, 52*, 82–89.

Colvin, C. A., & Goh, A. (2005). Validation of the technology acceptance model for police. *Journal of Criminal Justice 33*, 89–95.

Conti, N., & Nolan III, J. J. (2005). Policing the platonic cave: Ethics and efficacy in police training. *Policing & Society, 15,* 166–186.

Cordner, G. (2005). Community policing: Elements and Effects. In R. G. Dunham & G. P. Alpert (Eds.), *Critical issues in policing: Contemporary readings* (5th edition, pp. 401–418). Prospect Heights, IL: Waveland Press.

Dantzker, M. L. (1992). An issue for policing-educational level and job satisfaction: A research note. *American Journal of Police, 12,* 101–118.

Dean, G., & Gottschalk, P. (2007). *Knowledge management in policing and law enforcement: Foundations, structures, applications.* London: Oxford University Press.

Ferdinand, T. N. (1980). Police attitudes and police organization: Some interdepartmental and cross-cultural comparisons. *Police Studies, 3,* 46–60.

Goldstein, H. (1994). Foreward. In D. P. Rosenbaum (Ed.), *The Challenge of Community Policing* (pp. vii–x). Thousand Oaks, CA: Sage.

Gottschalk, P. (2007). *Knowledge management systems in law enforcement: Technologies and techniques.* Hershey, PA: Idea Group Publishing.

Hammer, M., & Champy, J. (1993). *Reengineering the corporation.* New York: Harper Business.

Hoath, D. R., Schneider, F. W., & Starr, M. W. (1998). Police job satisfaction as a function of career orientation and position tenure: Implications for selection and community policing. *Journal of Criminal Justice, 26,* 337–347.

Hou, C., Miracle, A., & Poole, A. (1983). Assessing determinants of police cynicism in Taiwan. *Police Studies, 5,* 3–7.

Hughes, V., & Jackson, P. (2004). The influence of technical, social and structural factors in the effective use of information in a policing environment. *Electronic Journal of Knowledge Management, 2*(1), 65–76.

Hunter, R. D., & Barker, T. (1993). BS and buzzwords: The new police operational style. *American Journal of Police, 12,* 157–168.

Kelley, J. (2003, November). Overcoming information sharing obstacles and complexity. *Police Chief,* 24–28.

Klinger, D. A. (2004). Environment and organization: Reviving a perspective on the police. In W. G. Skogan (Ed.), *To better serve and protect: Improving police practices* (pp. 119–136). Annals of the American Academy of Political and Social Sciences. Thousand Oaks, CA: Sage.

Klockars, C. (1998). The rhetoric of community policing. In J. R. Greene & S. D. Mastrofski (Eds.), *Community Policing: Rhetoric or Reality* (pp. 239–258). New York: Praeger.

Lewis, S. (1998). Police Officers' Perspectives on Community Policing: The Racine Wisconsin Experience. Thesis in partial completion of the degree of Master of Science. Department of Criminal Justice. University of Alabama, Tuscaloosa, AL.

Lewis, S., Rosenberg, H., & Sigler, R. T. (1999). Acceptance of community policing among police officers and police administrators. *Policing: An International Journal of Police Strategies & Management, 22,* 567–588.

Luen, T. W., & Al-Hawamdeh, S. (2001). Knowledge management in the public sector: Principles and practices in police work. *Journal of Information Science, 27*(5), 311–318.

Maguire, E., & Katz, C. (2002). Community policing, loose coupling, and sensemaking in American police agencies. *Justice Quarterly, 19(3),* 565–578.

Manning, P. K. (1989). Community policing. In R. G. Dunham & G. P. Alpert (Eds.), *Critical Issues in Policing: Contemporary Readings* (pp. 395–405). Prospect Heights, IL: Waveland.
Neiderhoffer, A. (1969). *Behind the shield.* Garden City, NY: Doubleday.
Reiss, A. J., Jr. (1992). Police organization in the twentieth century. In M. Torny & N. Morris (Eds.), *Modern policing* (pp. 51–98). Chicago: University of Chicago Press.
Sherman, L. W. (1979). College education for police: The reform that failed. *Police Studies, 1*, 32–38.
Skogan, W. G. (2003). *Community policing: Can it work?* Belmont, CA: Wadsworth.
Skolnick, J. and Bayley, D. H. (1986) *The new blue line: Police innovation in six American cities*, New York: The Free Press.
Skolnick, J. H., & Bayley, D. H. (1988). Theme and variation in community policing. In M. Tonry & N. Morris (Eds.), *Crime and justice: A review of research* (pp. 1–38). Chicago: University of Chicago Press.
SPSS. (2004). *Advanced Techniques: ANOVA*. Chicago, IL: SPSS, Inc.
Stroshine, M. S. (2002). *Police supervisors and community policing: Supporting or subverting change?* Lansing: Michigan State University.
U.S. Bureau of the Census. (1992). *Census of population and housing: Summary social, economic, and housing characteristics of Wisconsin: 1990 Edition*. Washington, DC: Government Printing Office.
Walsh, W. F. & Vito, G. E. (2004). The meaning of Compstat: Analysis and response, *Journal of Contemporary Criminal Justice, 20*, 51–69.
Weatheritt, M. (1988). Community policing: Rhetoric or reality? In J. R. Greene & S. Mastrofski (Eds.), *Community policing: Rhetoric or reality?* (pp. 153–175). New York: Praeger.
Weisel, D. L., & Eck, J. E. (1994). Toward a practical approach to organizational change: Community policing initiatives in six cities. In D. P. Rosenbaum (Ed.), *The challenge of community policing: Testing the promises* (pp. 53–74). Thousand Oaks, CA: Sage.
Wilson, C. P. (2000). *Cop knowledge*. Chicago: University of Chicago Press.
Wycoff, M. A., & Skogan, W. (1994). The effect of a community policing management style on officers' attitudes. *Crime & Delinquency, 40*, 371–383.
Zeffane, R. M. (1996). Dynamics of strategic change: Critical issues in fostering positive organizational change. *Leadership & Organization Development Journal, 17*(7), 36–43.

Notes

1. This is the population as of the 1990 U.S. Census, which was published 2 years before the first community policing station was established in Racine.
2. Alphas for the constructs representing attitudes about community policing concepts, community policing programs, community policing substations, the community policing unit, and the relationship between supervisors and subordinates ranged from .68 to .75 at Wave 1 and .62 to .81 at Wave 2. Interitem reliability for attitudes regarding the organizational structure of the department was .43 for Wave 1 and .56 for Wave 2.

3. For a discussion of findings from Wave 1, see Lewis, Rosenberg, and Sigler (1999).
4. While we sought to protect officers' identities, we wished to have some system whereby respondents could be matched for each wave of the survey. Mother's maiden name would be unique for all except siblings in the force, and the last digit of the social security number would discriminate among them.
5. A total of 11 newly hired officers replaced 11 officers who left the department after the Wave 1 survey.
6. Neighborhood Watch is a community crime prevention program that educates residents on how to keep their neighborhoods safe from crime. It trains people to assess dangerous situations and contact police when they perceive danger to themselves or their neighbors. National Night Out is held annually during the summer months. It provides neighbors the opportunity to meet each other so they know who lives in their neighborhood, meet with police officers, and learn about crime prevention. Neighborhood Watch and National Night Out are partnerships between police and citizens, while the sweeps program partners police and service providers who are Racine County employees.
7. When comparing mean differences for analyses when years of service is entered into the analysis with rank, years of service has a slight and inconsistent impact on attitudes. Given the lack of substantive significance of this variable at Wave 1 and insignificant effects at Wave 2, we report the consistent and strongly statistically significant effects of rank.
8. For justification of how favorable and unfavorable statements were constructed, see Lewis (1998).

Appendix

Racine Police Department Sworn Officer Questionnaire

Please fill in the blank or circle the correct response as of the date of filling out this questionnaire.

1. What is your age as of your last birthday? ____________
2. How many years of service do you have on the Racine Police Department? ____________
3. How many years of school have you completed? ____________
4. What is your rank in the Racine Police Department? (Circle one category)

    Patrol officer
    Traffic investigator
    Investigator
    Sergeant
    Lieutenant or captain
    Inspector, assistant chief, or chief

5. What is your sex? Male Female
6. What is your marital status? Never married Married Divorced Separated Widowed

Please circle the response that most accurately reflects your attitude. (SA = strongly agree, A = agree, NS = not sure, D = disagree, SD = strongly disagree)

1. Citizen fear of crime is not affected by the patrol saturation (sweep) program. [Programs –][8]	SA A NS D SD
2. There are too many officers currently assigned to the community policing unit. [Unit –]	SA A NS D SD
3. Officers on the street require little supervision or guidance. [Organization +]	SA A NS D SD
4. There has been increased cooperation between the police department and other municipal agencies that enforce ordinance violations. [Programs +]	SA A NS D SD
5. Random patrols in squad cars help reduce crime. [Concepts –]	SA A NS D SD
6. There are too many police substations in Racine. [Substations –]	SA A NS D SD
7. Neighborhood watch programs are ineffective. [Programs –]	SA A NS D SD
8. The Racine police department is too top heavy with shift or unit commanders. [Organization +]	SA A NS D SD
9. The Racine police bicycle patrol is a public relations gimmick. [Programs –]	SA A NS D SD
10. Most of the rank and file, including investigators, understand what the community policing unit does. [Unit +]	SA A NS D SD
11. Citizens show increased support to officers permanently assigned to their neighborhoods. [Concepts +]	SA A NS D SD
12. Community policing unit officers communicate effectively with regular patrol personnel. [Unit +]	SA A NS D SD
13. National Night Out and similar events help call the public's attention to crime related problems. [Programs +]	SA A NS D SD

14. A foot patrol officer has more contact with local citizens than an officer in a squad car. [Concepts +] SA A NS D SD
15. Substations assist police in becoming aware of local community problems. [Substations +] SA A NS D SD
16. An officer walking a beat gets to understand citizen problems better than an officer in a squad car. [Concepts +] SA A NS D SD
17. Front-line supervisors actively seek input from their subordinates. [Relationship +] SA A NS D SD
18. The community policing unit is a plum, cushy assignment. [Unit –] SA A NS D SD
19. The solving of problems of a noncriminal nature should be part of an officer's responsibility. [Concepts +] SA A NS D SD
20. Substations create a police presence in the community that helps reduce citizens' fear of crime. [Substations +] SA A NS D SD
21. The Racine police department needs more front-line supervisors. [Organization –] SA A NS D SD
22. Sanitarians from the city health department should work out of City Hall, not police substations. [Substations –] SA A NS D SD
23. There is little communication between shift/unit commanders and front-line supervisors. [Relationship –] SA A NS D SD
24. The shift/unit commanders are supportive of the community policing unit. [Unit +] SA A NS D SD
25. Saturation (sweep) patrols in high crime areas have little or no effect on crime in those areas. [Programs –] SA A NS D SD
26. Citizen telephone patrols help combat crime. [Programs +] SA A NS D SD
27. Police officers are more effective patrolling in squad cars than on foot. [Concepts –] SA A NS D SD
28. Scout troops can better serve the community when operating out of police substations. [Substations +] SA A NS D SD

29. There is a need for better interaction between investigators and officers assigned to the community policing unit. [Unit +]	SA A NS D SD
30. Front-line supervisors are fair in their performance evaluations. [Relationship +]	SA A NS D SD
31. All officers should be involved in building community contacts and relations. [Concepts +]	SA A NS D SD
32. Police officers shouldn't bother documenting problems they encounter of a noncriminal nature. [Concepts –]	SA A NS D SD
33. The police department top administration is unaware of the concerns of the officers on the street. [Relationship –]	SA A NS D SD
34. A citizen is more likely to report a crime to an officer on foot patrol than to call police headquarters to report the crime. [Concepts +]	SA A NS D SD
35. Officers should have more input in the day-to-day operations of the police department. [Organization +]	SA A NS D SD
36. Discipline is often meted out for trivial offenses. [Relationship –]	SA A NS D SD
37. Assigning officers to substations creates a drain on manpower on the street. [Substations –]	SA A NS D SD
38. Increasing the number of officers in the community policing unit will not improve citizen cooperation. [Programs –]	SA A NS D SD
39. Probation and parole officers do better by meeting their clients at police substations than at the probation and parole office. [Substations +]	SA A NS D SD
40. A police department in a city the size of Racine should operate only out of one central headquarters. [Organization –]	SA A NS D SD

Thank you for participating in this survey. In the extra space provided below, please give any comments you may have on the subjects covered in the questions above or any comments on the survey itself.

Key to Attitudinal Subscales

[Programs –] Specific community policing programs, unfavorable to community policing

[Programs +] Specific community policing programs, favorable to community policing

[Unit –] Community policing unit, unfavorable to community policing

[Unit +] Community policing unit, favorable to community policing

[Organization –] Organizational structure, unfavorable to community policing

[Organization +] Organizational structure, favorable to community policing

[Concepts –] Community policing concepts, unfavorable to community policing

[Concepts +] Community policing concepts, favorable to community policing

[Substations –] Community policing substations, unfavorable to community policing

[Substations +] Community policing substations, favorable to community policing

[Relationship –] Relationship between supervisors and subordinates, unfavorable to community policing

[Relationship +] Relationship between supervisors and subordinates, favorable to community policing

A Law Unto Themselves An Insight Into the Human Rights Watch Report on the Indian Police

15

K. S. SUBRAMANIAN
Council for Social Development

Contents

Introduction

While it is true that the liberal democratic Constitution of India enshrines the human, social and legal rights of the people, the police in India are still governed by the colonial Police Act, Penal Code (IPC), and Criminal Procedure Code (CrPC) with regard to their day-to-day operations and activities. In its 118-page report on the Indian police (2009), the Human Rights Watch (HRW) made a devastating assessment of the pervasive human rights violations by the Indian police and called for serious efforts to reform their structure and reassess their day-to-day practices.

The purpose of this chapter is to examine the HRW report in its historical context, analyze its contents, and highlight its importance in light of the ongoing situation of human rights violations by the Indian police. In the end, this chapter underlines the importance of HRW's recommendations for policy makers.

Indian Police: Human Rights and Reforms

In the 1850s, the board of directors of the East India Company said that the Indian police were "all but useless" in the prevention and "sadly inefficient" in the detection of crime; they were "unscrupulous" in the exercise of their authority with a "generalized reputation for corruption and oppression" (Kannabiran, 2004). The view was largely shared by the Police Commission of 1902. However, the British rulers of India did nothing to remedy the situation.

After independence in 1947, two major police commissions were set up: (1) the National Police Commission (NPC), which submitted eight reports during 1979–81; and (2) the Second Administrative Reforms Commission (SARC), which submitted a report on public order in 2007. The recommendations of both the commissions are still pending with the government of India.

The Congress party, which returned to power in 1980, ignored the recommendations of the NPC set up by the previous government led by the opposition Janata party. It also rejected the report of the LP Singh Committee (1979) on reform of the Intelligence Bureau (IB) and the Central Bureau of Investigation (CBI). Other enquiries on police reforms were made in the subsequent period by (1) the Julio Ribeiro Committee (1999); (2) the Padmanabhiah Committee (2000); (3) the Malimath Committee (2003); and (4) the Soli Sorabji Committee (2005). These inquiries were followed by the SARC report on Public Order (SARC, 2007).

The recommendations of the Sorabji Committee (2006) on the reform of the Police Act of 1861 are under consideration. The Supreme Court in its judgment in the Prakash Singh case (2006) issued seven directions on police reforms to state and central governments, which are being haltingly implemented. The Manmohan Singh government in May 2009 expressed its intention to carry out police reforms but has not followed up the intention with any action so far. The 2006 Supreme Court directed state and central to:

1. Constitute state security commissions to ensure that the state governments do not exercise unwarranted influence or pressure on the police and lay down broad policy guidelines for evaluating police performance.

2. Ensure that the directors general of police at the federal level are appointed through a merit-based, transparent process with a minimum tenure of 2 years.
3. Ensure that other police officers on operational duties (including district superintendents of police and heads of police stations) have a minimum 2 years' tenure.
4. Set up police establishment boards to decide on transfers, postings, promotions, and other matters relating to lower-level police officers and to make recommendations on postings and transfers.
5. Set up a national security commission at the union level in New Delhi to prepare panels for selection and placement of chiefs of the central police organizations (CPOs), with a minimum of 2-year tenures.
6. Set up independent police complaints authorities at the state and district level to look into complaints of police misconduct, including custodial death, grievous hurt, or rape in custody.
7. Separate the investigative functions from law and order functions.

HRW Report: A Synopsis

HRW examined police practices in the three states (i.e., Himachal Pradesh, Karnataka, and Uttar Pradesh) and in the national capital region of New Delhi. It documented ongoing human rights violations by the police and the impunity that contributes to abuse by drawing on the testimonies of 80 police officers and conducting observations at police stations. It found that the police are overstretched and outmatched battling India's most pressing problems (i.e., armed militancy, organized crime, and religious and caste violence). The police were found to have inadequately trained personnel and substandard equipment. In addition, the public, a vital source of cooperation and information, often avoided contact with the police out of fear. Political figures complicate matters by intervening in police operations to protect influential offenders.

Lack of independent investigations into complaints of police abuse contributed to impunity. Poor working conditions coupled with impunity for abuse led to adoption of shortcuts to get around systemic impediments and reducing caseloads by refusing to register complaints. The police also used illegal detention, torture, and ill treatment to punish criminals about whom they lacked the time and the effort to build cases or elicit false confessions. The report recommended reforms and outlined the steps that the authorities should take to end impunity and overhaul the everyday police policies and practices.

HRW consulted national police reform experts and analyzed the extensive research on police practices and human rights records nationwide.

It examined cases arising since 2005 that illustrated the most common human rights abuses by the police. Several victims and witnesses, including victims of police torture or ill treatment or members of their families, were interviewed. Eight individuals arrested or detained on false charges though not suffering torture were interviewed along with six interviews with family members and lawyers of individuals killed by police in alleged shootouts or deaths in custody. A total of 11 interviews were held with individuals for whom police had failed to register or investigate crimes. Group interviews were held with more than a dozen individuals threatened and harassed along with extortion of money on multiple occasions.

HRW visited nine police stations in big and small cities and villages. Some officers spent full days with HRW to give them a better understanding of their day-to-day practices. Police officers of different ranks and constables and others were interviewed inside police stations and outside the presence of officers above the rank of assistant subinspector. Other low-ranking officers were spoken to in the presence of their superiors. Also interviewed were junior-ranking officers who worked as heads of police stations, investigators, and assistants to senior police, many speaking on conditions of anonymity. Several senior-ranking police officers, including chief-ranking officers of Karnataka and Uttar Pradesh, were interviewed along with former police officers, including former members of the National Human Rights Commission. The range of human interest coverage and documentation carried out by HRW was thus impressive and exhaustive.

Nature of Abuses

HRW characterized the Indian police as a "dangerous anachronism," which had failed to evolve from a ruler-supportive, repressive force they were designed to be under colonial rule into a democratic agency. They committed abuses and used threats as the primary tools of investigation and law enforcement. The institutional culture discouraged officers from acting otherwise, failing to give them the resources, training, an ethical environment, and encouragement to develop professional policing tactics. Many officers were ordered or were expected to commit abuses.

HRW examined two separate but linked issues:

1. Abuses by the police against individuals, usually criminal suspects
2. The conditions that facilitated and encouraged the police to commit those abuses

It found that the misbehavior was deeply rooted in institutional practices. Government failure to enforce accountability and to overhaul the structure encouraged abusive practices to continue. HRW found four clusters of issues that needed attention:

1. Police failure to investigate crimes
2. Arrest on false charges and illegal detention
3. Torture and ill-treatment
4. Extrajudicial killings

Historically marginalized groups are especially vulnerable to the first three abuses. Though arising from the biases of the police, the vulnerability was a product of an abusive police culture related to an ability to pay a bribe, trade social status, or call on political connections.

The Sources of Abuse

Part of the problem was the working conditions of individual officers. The civil police, especially constables, lived and worked in abysmal conditions. They were often exhausted, demoralized, always on call, and working long hours without shifts and necessary equipment, only to return to government-provided tents or filthy barracks for a few hours of sleep. On top of all these, junior ranking officers often faced unrealistic demands from their superiors to solve cases quickly. Even if officially encouraged, their use of professional crime investigation techniques was effectively discouraged by the dearth of time, training, and equipment. Local political figures frequently intervened in investigations and sometimes acted to protect known criminals.

To get around these systemic problems, many officers took shortcuts (e.g., refusal to register complaints, illegal detention, torture and ill treatment of alleged criminals, or eliciting of confessions known to be false). Such abuses contributed to a climate of fear in which many Indians avoided contact with the police. Consequently, the police did not get public cooperation that was so essential to solving and preventing crimes. A vicious cycle was created in which the crimes went unreported and unpunished, and the pressure on the police mounted to deal with rising criminality.

The Manmohan Singh government, which came to power in May 2009, has promised to pursue police reform. It faces the challenge of transforming the police institution from one that enables and encourages abuse to one that promotes human rights and rule of law. A critical step is to hold abusive officers accountable. Incentives to officers must change. Disobedience to illegal orders as well as failure to meet superiors' expectation to solve crimes without the necessary means must not be punished. In the long-run, a sustainable drop in police abuses can come only from overhauling archaic police laws and structures and investing in training, personnel, and equipment to build professional, rights-respecting police forces that are needed.

State of Disrepair

Indian police are tasked to tackle armed militancy, terrorism, and organized crime. However, lack of political will to invest in police improvements has overstretched and ill-equipped the police to deal with these major problems. India has just one civil police officer to every 1,037 Indian residents. This ratio is far below the Asian average of one officer per 558 people and a global average of 333 people per police officer. However, the creation of an increasing number of paramilitary police forces is getting priority. Despite law and order and the police being state subjects in the Constitution, the Central Paramilitary Forces (CPF) are growing in numbers. Though meant for specific purposes such as border security and industrial security, they are increasingly deployed in local conflict management on the request of hard-pressed state governments. Manpower deployment for VIP security and misuse of police orderlies as family servants continue. Colonial police laws do not allow lower-rank police to have operational authority or advanced professional training. Constables make up 85% of the Indian police though for the most part they are not trained to investigate cases. Junior officers have little chances of promotion and are subject to the unrealistic demands of the senior officers who are for the most part directly recruited to management positions at the top with no firsthand knowledge of the difficulties of the constabulary.

Political Interference and Stalled Reforms

Partisan policing, including politically motivated refusal to register complaints, arbitrary detention, and torture and killings, sometimes perpetrated at the behest of national- and state-level politicians, have produced unprecedented levels of public distrust and fear of the police. The Supreme Court judgment in 2006 in the Prakash Singh case directed the central and state governments to enact new police laws to reduce political interference. However, the response has been discouraging with the central government, which funds most police activities in the country including state police budgets, holding that police are a state subject in the Constitution and thus passing the buck to state governments and the latter going about the business at their own pace or altogether resisting the move.

Key government officials seem hesitant to accept the need for far-reaching reforms including the need to make the police accountable for widespread human rights violations. The immediate need to improve the living conditions of the subordinate police, which encourage such violations, is also not widely recognized.

Failure to Register and Investigate Cases

Police officers are often under pressure not to register cases on account of political pressure from ruling parties keen to show that the law and order situation in their states is not bad. Many of the victims of such nonregistration of cases belong to the deprived communities such as the Scheduled Castes and Tribes. Crime victims who are poor are often unable to obtain police assistance. They could not afford to pay the bribes that the police demand for registration of cases or for the cost of investigation that the victims are expected to pay on behalf of the police. They may also find it more difficult to elicit political support than the socially more powerful perpetrators of crime.

Illegal Arrest, Detention, and Police Torture

Arrests are often made in retaliation for complaints of police abuse, in return for bribes or due to political considerations or influence of powerful local political figures. Police also often use coercion and torture to elicit confessions to fabricated charges. The procedure indicated in the Supreme Court in *DK Basu V. West Bengal* (SARC, 2007) included production of a suspect before a magistrate within 24 hours of arrest. Severe ill treatment is sometimes intensified over a period of an individual's detention. Individuals who are poor and socially or politically marginal are especially vulnerable to prolonged detention and repeated ill treatment because they are unable to pay a bribe or have no connections with local political figures that can intervene. Arrested children are often not provided the protections required in India's Juvenile Justice Act. Also frequent are sexual and physical harassment of deprived women in custody. Some police officers admit that using force is their primary investigative tool. False confessions lead police to gather faulty evidence, which often leads to cases being thrown out of court or wrongful convictions.

Impunity for Extrajudicial Killings

While the practice is not the norm in most of India, fake encounter killings do occur frequently. The NHRC reported 201 complaints of such killings in the state of Uttar Pradesh in 2007, more than any other state. Police were usually the only witnesses to these alleged encounters, which were typically carried out by junior officials. There was evidence of unofficial sanctions for such practices. Criminal suspects and members of minority communities were often the victims of fake encounter killings.

HRW reports that, in the course of their field work, a police official told them, "This week I was told to do an 'encounter' [referring to the practice of taking into custody and extrajudicially executing an individual and then claiming that the victim died after initiating a shootout with the police]. I am looking for my target. I will eliminate him." On July 2, 2010, the most recent such experience, in an alleged encounter with the Andhra Pradesh police, two Maoist leaders were eliminated (Mainstream, 2010). A peace activist who met the Union Home Minister recently to demand a judicial probe into the incident was told that no such probe was possible since the Maoists were also indulging in such killings of police officers with impunity (personal conversation with Swami Agnivesh, peace activist).

Obstacles to Police Accountability

HRW reports that efforts at police accountability were hampered by systematic police deniability arising from the absence of records, postmortem examination, record of arrest, and detention. Independent investigations were rare in much of India despite the existence of National and State Human Rights Commissions. Investigations undertaken by the police or at the behest of other agencies were hampered by an unwritten code of silence that makes it unlikely that the police would disclose incriminating evidence. Criminal prosecutions by victims often do not take place because of fear of police retaliation. Further, section 197 of the Criminal Procedure Code provides immunity from prosecution to all public officials without government sanction. Efforts by the NHRC have often resulted in police investigating themselves. In most cases, the NHRC recommends only provision of interim compensation to victims without proper prosecution of officers. The country's 18 state human rights commissions (SHRC) vary in resources and willingness to act with local lawyers describing the staff as inadequate in number, lacking human rights training, and biased against complaints. In exceptional cases, the punishment is often temporary suspension or transfer of the accused. Until officers know that they will be prosecuted, fired, or their careers seriously damaged, the problem will not go away.

After noting the Supreme Court direction to set up Police Complaints Authorities at the district, state, and central levels to adjudicate public complaints and make binding recommendations, the HRW report, however, observed that the promise of comprehensive reforms remained unrealized and the momentum it created was dissipating. As of April 2009, only 12 states have passed laws claiming to implement the Court's directives, but the Court has not initiated contempt proceedings against the noncompliant states. In a dangerous departure from the sense of urgency articulated earlier, the Court established a monitoring committee to review the states' compliance. The committee's two reports were unavailable even to the petitioners who took up the matter with the Court in the first place. This has stymied civil society's ability to voice informed concerns over the continued delays. The lack of transparency has made it unclear whether the committee has established a timetable or made minimum demands on noncompliant states. New state laws in some cases were contrary to Supreme Court directives, but the committee would not assess those laws until it could finish reviewing the responses of the completely noncompliant states, a process for which there was no announced deadline.

The HRW report rightly noted that even if eventually implemented, the Supreme Court directives, with their focus on curbing political interference in police work, may fail significantly to reduce arbitrary arrest and detention, torture, and other mistreatment and deaths in police custody. These abuses cannot be ascribed solely to political interference although the problems are linked because of de facto impunity provided by political patrons.

The danger of a reform agenda that seeks to free the police from political control without making them more accountable to the public is also noted. The Supreme Court directions have left undisturbed the police's general immunity from prosecution for serious misconduct, as provided under section 197 of the Criminal Procedure Code. Further, the reform agenda fails to address the working and living conditions of low-ranking police, often the perpetrators of abuses, carrying out illegal orders or operating under a police culture that condones and facilitates such behavior.

HRW further noted that the Supreme Court, while requiring states to establish Police Complaints Authorities to investigate complaints of police misconduct, had not required them to make preventive measures against human rights abuses. While changing laws to prevent undesirable political influence on police functioning, it is equally necessary to ensure that political control is replaced with accountability of the police to the community.

Thus, in noting some problematic issues relating to current police reforms efforts in India, especially with regard to section 197 of the CrPC, the HRW is to be lauded for being in advance of agencies such as the Commonwealth Human Rights Initiative (CHRI), which are yet to take critical positions with regard to the Supreme Court directions, the recommendations of the Police Act Drafting Committee and other similar reform reports by official agencies.

The report contains several case studies of extrajudicial executions by the police in several states and identifies in its penultimate chapter the obstacles to police accountability in India. After analyzing the number of complaints of abuse made and the inquiries made by official agencies, it concludes that impunity is still the norm. Police complaints authorities have not been set up in half of the 28 Indian states and 7 union territories and those that exist do not have staff to conduct independent inquiries. Internal police department inquiries are hampered by the informal code of silence that prevents disclosure of incriminating evidence. Potential for police intimidation or harassment of individuals complaining of abuse is high because registration of the complaint may require a visit to the very police station where the abuse occurred. A major hindrance to criminal prosecution of police is Section 197 of the Criminal Procedure Code, which requires government approval for prosecution of the police. Several constraints affect the functioning of the national and state human rights commissions that have been set up.

HRW concludes with detailed recommendations for action by (1) the Union Home Ministry, Union Territory Police, state home ministries and state police; (2) the Indian Police Service; (3) the Indian parliament; (4) the national Human Rights Commission; (5) the state Human Rights Commissions; and (6) concerned foreign governments and donors.

Insights on the HRW Report

HRW has thus done a commendable service by producing this extraordinary report. In this context, a few broader issues, relevant to police reforms in India, may be mentioned:

- Despite the rhetoric on rule of law, Constitutional provisions and the existence of institutions for human rights protection and promotion, the fact remains that at bottom the Indian police remain a government department with hardly any meaningful autonomy.
- The focus on crime and investigation detracts attention form the fact that the existing Indian police organization is a reproduction of the Irish colonial paramilitary police model with specific characteristics designed to put down political resistance to British rule.
- The provisions of the Indian Penal Code, the Criminal Procedure Code, and the Police Act. All designed during the colonial period focus on security of the state, maintenance of public order, and collection of political intelligence bearing on state security rather than on human rights protection and service provision.
- The sample size of the HRW report is small considering that India is a large country with 28 states and 7 union territories.
- The issues of decentralizing, democratizing the police in India, and empowering Panchayati Raj Institutions (PRI) to oversee police functions remain to be addressed.
- The sufferings of large sections of ordinary people including women and children in the conflict-affected areas of Jammu and Kashmir, the northeastern states and the Central Tribal Belt under the adverse impact of the imposition of lawless laws affecting human dignity needs to be addressed.
- Intelligence systems oriented to security of state and public order, which neglect human rights concerns, are to be addressed.

- The division of the police organization into three separate wings dealing with investigation, law and order, and local police as recommended in the SARC report on Public Order (SARC, 2007) needs attention.
- The role of all India services such as the IAS and the IPS in law and order management needs review.

The Police Unchecked

Institutionalized impunity and lack of accountability for human rights violations by the police have become major issues in Indian politics today (*TLM*, 2010). From Telengana in Andhra Pradesh and the villages in Punjab, West Bengal, and Tamil Nadu to Jammu and Kashmir, the northeast and Gujarat, impunity has emerged as a major part of the police system in dealing with crime as well as political dissent, peaceful, or violent. As the democratic content of governance declines, sanction of impunity to law and order agencies grows. Such impunity can conveniently exist and grow in a working democracy, as seen in the Indian experience since independence. A vulgarized caste structure, repressive of backward castes, scheduled castes, and tribes, has adapted itself to a Western-style liberal democracy and produced a distorted democracy recently characterized as parliamentary fascism (Kannabiran, 2010). A plethora of special legislations enacted over time support the structure: the Prevention of Terrorism Act (POTA), Unlawful Activities Prevention (Amendment) Act (UAPA), Terrorist and Disruptive Activities Prevention Act, and the Armed Forces (Special Powers) Act in some parts of the country. These legislations do not actually achieve their purpose but are widely misused by the security forces in violating human rights (Delhi Solidarity Group, 2009; Singh, 2007).

In the southern state of Andhra Pradesh, custodial killings or the summary executions of political dissenters have been a part of the administrative culture, and during the years 1996 to 2001 more than 200 such dissenters were reported killed each year in fake encounters: "the practice of taking into custody and extra-judicially executing an individual, then claiming that the victim had died after initiating a shootout with the police" (Balagopal, 2009). In Jammu and Kashmir, under the Armed Forces (Special Powers) Act, security forces have had impunity in suppressing political dissent. Fake encounter killings in Punjab, Tamil Nadu, West Bengal, Gujarat, and the northeast have been frequent.

The state of Gujarat, after the genocide against Muslims in 2002 (CCTG, 2002), has witnessed a number of extrajudicial killings of members of the minority community. From 2002 to 2006, a group of Gujarat police officers are reported to have staged five fake encounters, killing 15 "dreaded terrorists" (Sinha, 2010). State manipulation of the 2002 genocide and the subsequent killings are well documented. In the case of a young woman,

Ishrat Jahan, killed in an encounter with the police, the magisterial inquiry found the event to be a fake encounter killing, but the state advocate general challenged the finding and persuaded the High Court to stay the magisterial finding. The Supreme Court of India rejected the proceedings and has ordered that the matter be heard again by a bench of two judges (Sinha, 2010).

In the tiny northeastern state of Manipur (population 2.5 million), a fact-finding team found that the local police commandos extrajudicially executed over 260 persons during the first 6 months of 2009 on the grounds that they were militant underground elements. The number thus killed in 2008 was 300. The state has also witnessed heavy militarization, with about 60 battalions of state and central military and paramilitary forces (in addition to local civilian police) being deployed there to quell the ongoing militancy (Delhi Solidarity Group, 2009).

A vigilante group known as Salwa Judum (roughly, "peace campaign") in the central tribal state of Chhattisgarh has exercised a weird form of impunity in inflicting large-scale violence on the people in the name of fighting the insurgency by the Maoists, though such impunity has not prevented the latter from spreading their influence over 2,000 police station areas in 223 districts in 20 states in the country as admitted by the Union Home Minister himself. In the left-ruled state of West Bengal, pursuit of economic reform policies has contributed to growth of impunity for police killings of protestors in the areas of Singur, Nandigram, and Lalgarh.

In light of these experiences, observers feel that the survival of rule of law in India would depend on successful public action to eliminate impunity for the police forces and to secure the social, economic, and cultural rights for ordinary people (Subramanian, 2007; *TLM*, 2010).

Conclusion

The British colonial rulers devised the Indian police system as a cheaper substitute for the army. The main purpose of the police was to maintain British rule in India. Crime control was only a secondary objective to be achieved through fear of the police (Gupta, 1988). The police structure was paramilitary based on the Irish colonial model with specific characteristics: strict subordination to the civilian administration; secrecy and political significance of intelligence and its growing ties between state and central government; unaccountability to the public and their elected representatives; coercive strength and disposition with frequent use of high levels of state violence; limited understanding of causes of industrial and agrarian unrest; institutionalization of a paramilitary wing within the police organization; and close identification with propertied interests (Arnold, 1986).

The IPC, CrPC, and the Evidence Act enacted by the British put in place a legal framework that equipped the police for the maintenance of British rule by force. The IPC prioritized offenses against the state and maintenance of public order; consideration of traditional crime started only from section 299 in Chapter XVI. Similarly, the CrPC prioritized maintenance of public order and tranquility before starting analysis of investigation and detection of crime. The Police Act gave priority to the collection and communication of intelligence affecting public order. The prevention and detection of crime is mentioned only from section 23 of this act, which is much shorter than the IPC and the CrPC (Gupta, 1988).

This regressive structure not only was retained at independence in 1947 but also was continually strengthened in the subsequent period. The Central Reserve Police Force (CRPF), a tiny force in 1947, stood at 246,689 in 2006 (GOI, 2006) and is continually growing. There are several other paramilitary forces as well and together number over 1 million in strength and are used frequently to maintain order in different parts of the country. This coercive force has been accompanied by new legislations in the period after independence with a view to maintaining public order. Similar growth in strength has been witnessed in the realm of intelligence collection. The Intelligence Bureau (IB), which grew out of the special branches of the previous period, has steadily grown in strength. Thus, the preoccupation with security of the state and public order characteristic of the British period has continued after independence. Crime control and service to the public have taken a backseat. Huge paramilitary forces at the disposal of the central government in New Delhi defy the Constitution of India, which provides that public order and the police are state subjects.

References

Arnold D., (1986). *Police power and colonial rule: Madras 1859–1949.* New Delhi: Oxford University Press.

Balagopal, K. (2009). *Selected articles, combat law. New Delhi.*

Concerned Citizens' Tribunal on Gujarat. (CCTG). (2002). *Crime against humanity* (in three volumes). Mumbai: Citizens for Peace and Justice.

Delhi Solidarity Group. (2009). *Democracy encountered: Rights violations in Manipur: Fact finding report.* Retrieved from http://delhisolidaritygroup.wordpress.com/

Government of India. (GOI). (2006). *Ministry of Home Affairs, Government of India Annual Report.*

Gupta, A. (1988). Law and order in a democratic society. In S. V. Rao (Ed.), *Perspectives in criminology.* Shimla: Indian Institute of Advanced Study.

Human Rights Watch (2009). Broken System: Dysfunction, Abuse and Impunity in the Indian Police.

Kannabiran, K. G. (2010). State impunity as criminal disposition. *Little Magazine, 7*(4–5).

Kannabiran, K. G. (2004). *The wages of impunity: Power, justice and human rights.* Hyderabad: Orient Longman.

Mainstream. (2010.) Heading towards another emergency? Editorial. July 10, New Delhi.

Second Administrative Reforms Commission. (SARC). (2007, June). Second Administrative Reforms Commission, Fifth Report on Public Order, p. 121.

Singh, U. K. (2007). *The state, democracy and anti-terror laws in India.* New Delhi: Sage Publications.

Sinha, M. (2010, July 2). The manipulation by the Gujarat government is now assuming infantile proportions. *Tehelka Magazine.*

Subramanian, K. S. (2007). *Political violence and the police in India.* New Delhi: Sage Publications.

The Little Magazine. (TLM). (2010). Impunity: Getting away with murder. Parts I and II, *7*(4–5).

Appendix: Chapter Abstracts

Section 1: Global Innovations in Policing

Analyzing the Implementation and Evolution of Community Policing in the United States and Scandinavia by James F. Albrecht

Chapter 1

Community policing in the 1980s and early 1990s endorsed neighborhood foot patrol and problem solving by front-line police personnel. With advancements in technology in the 1990s, computerized analysis of crime statistics, trends, and incident mapping became the norm. To ensure optimal results in crime reduction, the responsibility for the strategic deployment of police and other resources shifted from the patrol officer to the police manager. The surprising result was a dramatic reduction in serious and violent crime. These trends, which commenced in New York City and soon expanded to other municipalities in the United States, later shifted to Europe, most notably to the technologically advanced Scandinavian countries. As a result, the traditional model of community policing has evolved into a less community sensitive mechanism. Unfortunately, some media-sensationalized police incidents (e.g., shootings) and the tragic events of September 11, 2001, and the subsequent terrorist attacks in London, Madrid, Moscow, and other major international cities have further resulted in a shift from the envisioned community partnership model to strategically oriented proactive deployment initiatives.

Think Globally, Solve Locally: Security Threats—From Public Opinion to a Proper Response by Gorazd Meško and Darko Maver

Chapter 2

The chapter presents an overview of some security threats in contemporary societies mainly from the perspective of Western civilization and public opinion relative to security threats in Slovenia. Recently established safety and security councils at the local level represent quite a new approach in setting priorities in the field of solving safety and security threats, crime, and disorder problems. Since 1997, there have been more than 130 such councils established in Slovenian local administrations. It is necessary to emphasize that local solving of safety and security problems requires knowledge on global trends in prevention, control, and repression that incorporate respect for state laws and traditions. Safety and security councils are a new form of police and local community cooperation in setting safety and security priorities. Such councils also provide additional support in community policing and civilianization of social control. It is necessary to say that such councils are expected to solve problems that often go beyond their responsibilities and are characterized as informal bodies for the purpose of formal decision making. Perceptions of safety and security threats by council members are quite limited to everyday criminality, disorder, drugs, and traffic offenses. Such perceptions exclude some threats that should be dealt with professionally such as national security threats, financial breakdowns of industry, stock market crime, and other forms of hidden crime. Presently, such councils are ad hoc consultative bodies to the local mayor. The topics and problems dealt with in meetings of such councils seem to require a new arrangement determined by a stricter legal framework and accountability of members of such councils.

It's 2010, But Is Anyone Counting? by Terry G. Coleman

Chapter 3

While community policing has been touted as the operating philosophy of Canadian police organizations since the mid-1970s, the literature suggests that these organizations continue with practices, such as performance measurement and management, which remain inconsistent with community policing. Thus, this study explored to what extent Canadian police organizations have shifted business practices to be congruent with the contemporary public and private sectors, that is, the extent of community policing adoption. Using environmental factors that have shaped contemporary policing and performance measurement, traditional and contemporary policing models were first compared. Next, the measurement and management of organizational performance were examined in the contemporary private and public sectors. Results indicated that many police organizations are perceived as not being managed strategically. In addition, organizations measured activities instead of the end results of those activities. Coupled with an apparent failure to implement performance accountability mechanisms like those found in successful public- and private-sector organizations, the results suggested these police organizations have yet to adopt community policing fully despite claims to the contrary.

Section 2: Responding to Transnational Crimes and Emerging Law Enforcement Issues

The War on Drugs in Chicago: Thinking Locally, Acting Globally by Gad J. Bensinger, Thomas J. Lemmer, and Arthur J. Lurigio

Chapter 4

This chapter focuses on the cultivation and trafficking of cocaine, heroin, and marijuana from Colombia and Mexico to Chicago. The narrative provides a brief historical perspective on Chicago's drug problem and a range of tactics adopted by the Chicago Police Department and other law enforcement agencies in Chicago to counter or minimize the consequences of drug trafficking. The authors maintain that despite the many efforts undertaken by the U.S. government to counter the cultivation, production, trafficking, and distribution of illegal drugs, the ultimate responsibility for successfully fighting the so-called war on drugs lies with local law enforcement. The authors conclude that the Chicago Police Department's antidrug and antigang efforts have disrupted the local drug trade to a greater extent than the federal efforts.

Recruitment Activities of Terrorist Groups: An Analysis of the PKK/KONGRA-GEL Terrorist Organization by Mutlu Koseli

Chapter 5

Although armed struggle against terrorists is essential, this tactic is not enough to permanently end the terrorism problem. Security forces can offer a short-term solution for immediate threats, but other implementations should be considered for a final solution. In this chapter, the recruitment activities of terrorist groups were examined. Taken from the statements of 244 captured individuals who joined the illegal camps, the PKK/KONGRA-GEL terrorist group was found to use private and proximate methods to recruit new members. In addition, a majority of recruitment activities occurred within the political party and through the propaganda of friends. People who migrated from their hometowns were more likely to join the terrorist group, and, likewise, a previous detention for any reason influenced one's decision to join. Individuals also joined to free themselves from family pressures. Finally, most were very young recruits and unemployed. Policy recommendations were proposed to enhance deterrent measures.

Policing and the Mentally Ill: Local Policing and International Standards by Duncan Chappell

Chapter 6

Policing experts acknowledge that encounters with people who are believed to be either mentally ill or mentally disordered are among the most sensitive of all police interactions. For many police executives, the setting of guidelines in regard to the handling of persons with a mental illness, together with appropriate training for officers, is becoming a matter of high priority. At the same time police leaders often face wider problems associated with the inadequacy of public health services for mentally ill persons. As a result, the mentally ill tend to go through a repetitive cycle of hospital admission, while many come into conflict with the law and are incarcerated. This chapter examines contemporary policing issues affecting the mentally ill both in Australia and in an international context. Particular attention is devoted to the way police exercise their powers of apprehension and detention within the framework of the United Nations (UN) Code of Conduct for Law Enforcement Officials, the UN Basic Principles on the Use of Force Firearms by Law Enforcement Officials, and the UN Principles for the Protection of Persons with a Mental Illness and the Improvement of Mental Health Care.

Policing Mental Illness: The Need for a Specialized Police Training Program in Dealing With Mentally Ill Persons by Avdi S. Avdija

Chapter 7

This chapter offers a research-based discussion on police–mentally ill hindrances. More specifically, this chapter focuses on how the problem of mentally ill became the problem of policing and the role that the stakeholders have played in developing some of the police training program to prepare the police properly deal with mentally ill persons. The first objective of this chapter is to discuss theoretical perspectives explaining the criminal propensities of mentally ill persons. In addition, some of the factors that brought about the issue of mental illness on the public agenda will be covered. The chapter also explores one of the most widely used police training programs, the crisis intervention team (CIT) program, which many police departments have found useful in dealing with mentally ill persons. Lastly, the importance of a collaborative effort of mental health services and the criminal justice system in dealing with mentally ill persons or offenders is discussed.

Protecting Vulnerable Young People in Cyberspace From Sexual Abuse: Raising Awareness and Responding Globally by Julia C. Davidson and Elena Martellozzo

Chapter 8

This chapter explores the danger that young people may be exposed to when using the Internet. The first part sets out the context by considering new developments in the U.K. and international legislation and then explores educational moves to protect children. The chapter focuses on findings from research undertaken on behalf of the London Metropolitan Police Service in evaluating the Safer Surfing program designed to enable young people's safe Internet use. In the final part of this chapter it is argued that more must be done internationally both to protect children online and to curb the growing trade in indecent child images.

Section 3: Knowledge Management, Capturing, Sharing, and Sustaining

Patrol Police Officers' Professional Knowledge: An Empirical Study of Knowledge Types in Law Enforcement by Stefan Holgersson and Petter Gottschalk

Chapter 9

A patrol police officer is in need of a variety of professional knowledge to be able to act in an appropriate way. This chapter describes and classifies different types of knowledge that are a part of patrolling police officers' practice. Even though an intervention usually forces a police officer to apply several different knowledge types, this chapter discusses different forms of professional knowledge separately to enable categorization into the value configuration of a value shop. A value shop has the following five primary activities: initial crime scene assessment, assessment of incoming information, selecting appropriate lines of enquiry, case development, and postcharge case management.

Relevant Laws and Empirical Research on Profiling in Law Enforcement in the United States by Katrina W. Berger and Dee Wood Harper, Jr.

Chapter 10

Profiling is defined as a process whereby police officers make judgments about another, relative to possible criminal activity, based on a number of overt and subtle factors that may or may not include such things as a person's race, manner of dress and grooming, behavioral characteristics, when and where the observation is made, the circumstances under which the observation is made, and relative to information the officer may already possess. While there is a great deal of controversy surrounding its use in law enforcement, it is nevertheless an effective tool. This chapter examines relevant case law and empirical research on profiling. We conclude with some policy recommendations regarding the use of profiling with some international applications in drug trafficking and the interdiction of illegal aliens.

Municipal Police Departments' Attention to Crime Analysis: Essential or Impractical? by Brion Sever, Venessa Garcia, and Antonia Tsiandi

Chapter 11

Technologically advanced strategies such as crime analysis have great potential for impacting a department's efficiency, crime reduction, and professionalism. Yet to what extent are they being used or perceived as necessary by police departments? This chapter examines the use of such strategies in New Jersey police departments in cities with a population of 15,000 and above. Specifically, we surveyed 90 police departments in New Jersey in an effort to determine the type of computer technology they possess as well as the extent and manner to which they use crime analysis. We found that although most departments use crime analysis, few use modern strategies in such endeavors.

Challenges in Contemporary Police Leadership by John Middleton-Hope

Chapter 12

Police departments across North America continue to struggle with budget reductions alongside renewed demands to meet community expectations. A highly competitive market environment has emerged in which departments must outmaneuver each other for scarce human resources. While this pressure mounts, policing is experiencing a serious image problem. Exacerbated by a steady diet of media reports of police wrongdoing, modern police administrators must learn new strategies to manage these competing challenges. This chapter examines the ethical, political, and relationship challenges confronting contemporary police leaders such as the erosion of the public's trust and recruitment efforts. Each interrelated perspective assesses the politically charged environment that police leaders face and presents strategies to reduce the possible negative effects of these challenges on the community, the reputation of the department, and the police chief.

Section 4: International Police Practices and Cultures

Organizational Culture in the Norwegian Counter Terrorist Unit by Rune Glomseth and Petter Gottschalk

Chapter 13

The counter terrorist unit (Delta) constitutes a special unit within the Norwegian Police Service. Its organizational culture, among others, has been subject to examination through a value survey. All police officers employed by the counter terrorist unit as of November 2001 participated in this survey, whose objective was to uncover the dominating values among police officers in this unit. Not surprisingly, we found that time is fixed rather than floating in the professional culture of this unit. We also found that cooperation rather than individual competition is a dominating part of the professional culture.

Structural Influences on Police Officer Attitudes Toward Community Policing: A Case Study of the Racine, Wisconsin Police Department by Helen Rosenberg, Robert T. Sigler, and Scott Lewis

Chapter 14

We examined police officer attitudinal changes toward community policing over a 19-month period. Significant differences in attitudes on the basis of rank indicate a split in the department with patrol officers' and investigators' attitudes toward community policing less favorable toward community policing concepts, programming, decentralization of substations, and the community policing unit than sergeants' and senior command's. Both patrol and investigators are equally dissatisfied with communication with senior command, while senior command does not recognize this as problematic. Both patrol and investigators are supportive of a decentralized organizational structure, while senior command disapproves of this. We ask if discretionary power and increased participatory management among all officers can be favorably viewed by management and can dissention be tolerated and incorporated into a dialogue for change?

A Law Unto Themselves: An Insight Into the Human Rights Watch Report on the Indian Police by K. S. Subramanian

Chapter 15

This chapter is a critical review and assessment of a Human Rights Watch (HRW) report. The chapter discusses the historical context of police reforms since India's independence in 1947. It explains the scope of the report and examines its contents in detail. Obstacles to police accountability are brought out. Among the reforms noted are the overhaul of police structure, the improvement of working conditions, and police accountabilities. The chapter brings out the importance and relevance of the HRW report in the context of growing human rights violations by the police and the role of the civil society in effectively articulating the popular urge for radical changes in police structures and attitudes.

Index

I

N

W

X

Y

Z

INTERNATIONAL POLICE EXECUTIVE SYMPOSIUM
WWW.IPES.INFO

The *International Police Executive Symposium* was founded in 1994. The aims and objectives of the IPES are to provide a forum to foster closer relationships among police researchers and practitioners globally, to facilitate cross-cultural, international, and interdisciplinary exchanges for the enrichment of the law enforcement profession, to encourage discussion, and publish research on challenging and contemporary topics related to the profession.

One of the most important activities of the IPES is the organization of an annual meeting under the auspices of a police agency or an educational institution. Every year since 1994, annual meetings have been hosted by such agencies and institutions all over the world. Past hosts have included the Canton Police of Geneva, Switzerland; the International Institute of the Sociology of Law, Onati, Spain; Kangawa Univeristy, Yokohama, Japan; the Federal Police, Vienna, Austria; the Dutch Police and Europol, The Hague, The Netherlands; the Andhra Pradesh Police, India; the Center for Public Safety, Northwestern University, USA; the Polish Police Academy, Szczynto, Poland; the Police of Turkey (twice); the Kingdom of Bahrain Police; a group of institutions in Canada (consisting of the University of Fraser Valley, Abbotsford Police Department, Royal Canadian Mounted Police, the Vancouver Police Department, the Justice Institute of British Columbia, Canadian Police College, and the International Centre for Criminal Law Reform and Criminal Justice Policy); the Czech Police Academy, Prague; the Dubai Police; the Ohio Association of Chiefs of Police and the Cincinnati Police Department, Ohio, USA; and the Republic of Macedonia and the Police of Malta. The current host in 2011 is the City of Buenos Aires, Argentina.

There have been occasional Special Meetings of IPES. Special meetings were co-hosted by the Bavarian Police Academy of Continuing Education in Ainring, Germany, University of Passau, Germany, and the State University of New York, Plattsburgh, USA in 2000. The second Special Meeting was hosted by the police in the Indian state of Kerala. And the third Special Meeting is being hosted by the Swedish Police in 2011.

The majority of participants of the annual meetings are usually directly involved in the police profession. In addition, scholars and researchers in the field also participate. The meetings comprise both structured and informal sessions to maximize dialogue and exchange views and information. The executive summary of each meeting is distributed to participants as well as a wide range of other interested police professionals and scholars. In addition, a book of selected papers from each annual meeting is published through CRC Press/Taylor & Francis Group, Prentice Hall, Lexington Books, and other reputed publishers. A *Special Issue of Police Practice and Research: An International Journal* is also published with the most thematically relevant papers after the usual blind review process.

IPES Board of Directors

IPEs Institutional supporters

The IPES fulfills its mission with the cooperation of a global network of Institutional Supporters.

Abbotsford Police Department (Bob Rich, Chief Constable), 2838 Justice Way, Abbotsford, British Columbia V2 T3 P5, Canada. Tel: 604-864-4809; Fax: 604-864-4725. Email: bobrich@abbypd.ca, swillms@abbypd.ca

Audiolex (contact Kate J. Storey-Whyte, PhD), 9-10 Old Police Station, Kington, Hereford, Herefordshire, HR5 3DP, UK. Tel: 44 7833 378 379 (mobile). Fax 44 154 423 1965. Email: cj@audiolex.co.uk

Australasian Institute of Policing (Ian Lanyon), PO Box 99, Pascoe Vale South, Victoria, 3044, Australia. Tel: 61-3-986-58208; Fax 61-3-986-68325; Cell: 61-9-144-6614. Email: ian.lanyon@aipol.org

Cyber Defense & Research Initiatives (contact James Lewis), LLC, PO Box 86, Leslie, MI 49251, USA. Tel: 517-242-6730. Email: lewisja@cyberdefenseresearch.com

Defendology Center for Security, Sociology and Criminology Research (Valibor Lalic), Srpska Street 63,78000 Banja Luka, Bosnia and Herzegnovina. Tel and Fax: 387 51 308 914. Email: lalicv@teol.net

Department of Applied Social Studies, City University of Hong Kong (Li, Chi-mei, Jessica, PhD, Lecturer), Tat Chee Avenue, Kowloon Tong, Hong Kong. Tel: 27888839; Fax 27888960. Email: Jessica@cityu.edu.hk

Department of Criminal Justice (Dr. Harvey L. McMurray, Chair), North Carolina Central University, 301 Whiting Criminal Justice Bldg., Durham, NC 27707, USA. Tel: 919-530-5204, 919-530-7909; Fax: 919-530-5195. Email:hmcmurray@nccu.edu

Department of Psychology (Stephen Perrott), Mount Saint Vincent University, 166 Bedford Highway, Halifax, Nova Scotia, Canada. Email: Stephen.perrott@mvsu.ca

Department of Social Sciences (Dr. Bankole Cole, Reader in Criminology), 226 Lipman Building, The University of Northumbria at Newcastle, Newcastle-upon-Tyne, NE1 8ST, UK. Tel: +44 (0)191 227 3457. Email: bankole.cole@northumbria.ac.uk

Eastern Kentucky University (Dr. Victor Kappeler), Stratton Bulding 412A, Stratton Building, 521 Lancaster Avenue, Richmond, KY 40475, USA. Tel: 859-622-1980. Email: Victor.Kappeler@eku.edu

Faculty of Criminal Justice and Security (Dr. Gorazd Mesko), University of Maribor, Kotnikova 8 1000 Ljubljana, Slovenia. Tel: 386 1 300 83 39; Fax: 386 1 2302 687. Email: gorazd.mesko@fpvv.uni-mb.si

Faculty of Law, University of Kragujevac, Serbia (Prof. Branislav Simonovic), Str. Jovana Cvikica 1, Kragujevac, 34000 Serbia. Tel: 381 34 306 580; Fax: 381 34 306 546. Email: Simonov@EUnet.rs

Fayettville State University (Dr. David E. Barlow, Professor and Dean), College of Basic and Applied Sciences, 130 Chick Building, 1200 Murchison Road, Fayettville, North Carolina, 28301 USA. Tel: 910-672-1659; Fax: 910-672-1083. Email: dbarlow@uncfsu.edu

International Council on Security and Development (ICOS) (Andre Souza, Senior Researcher), Visconde de Piraja 577/605, Ipanema, Rio de Janeiro 22410-003, Brazil. Tel: (+55) 21 3186 5444. Email: asouza@icosgroup.net

International Police Association, Illinois (Kevin Gordon), 505 N. 10th Street, Mascoutah, IL 62258, USA. Email: Treasurer@ipa-usa.org

Justice Studies Department, San Jose State University (Mark E. Correia, PhD, Chair and Associate Professor), 1 Washington Square, San Jose, CA 95192-0050, USA. Tel: 408 924 1350. Email: mcorreia@casa.sjsu.edu

Kerala Police (Jacob Punnoose, Director General of Police), Police Headquarters, Trivandrum, Kerala, India. Email: JPunnoose@gmail.com

Molloy College, The Department of Criminal Justice (contact Dr. John A. Eterno, NYPD Captain-Reitred), 1000 Hempstead Avenue, PO Box 5002, Rockville Center, NY 11571-5002, USA. Tel: 516 678 5000, Ext. 6135; Fax: 516 256 2289. Email: jeterno@molloy.edu

National Institute of Criminology and Forensic Science (Mr. Kamalendra Prasad, Inspector General of Police), MHA, Outer Ring Road, Sector 3, Rohini, Delhi 110085, India. Tel: 91 11 275 2 5095; Fax: 91 11 275 1 0586. Email: director.nicfs@nic.in

National Police Academy, Japan (Suzuki Kunio, Assistant Director), Police Policy Research Center, Zip 183-8558: 3-12- 1 Asahi-cho Fuchu-city, Tokyo, Japan. Tel: 81 42 354 3550; Fax: 81 42 330 1308. Email: PPRC@npa.go.jp

Royal Canadian Mounted Police (Gary Bass, Deputy Commissioner, Pacific Region), 657 West 37th Avenue, Vancouver, BC V5Z 1K6, Canada. Tel: 604-264-2003; Fax 604-264-3547. Email: gary. bass@rcmp-grc.gc.ca

School of Psychology and Social Science, Head, Social Justice Research Centre (Prof. S. Caroline Taylor, Foundation Chair in Social Justice), Edith Cowan University, 270 Joondalup Drive, Joondalup, WA 6027, Australia. Email: c.taylor@ecu.edu.au

South Australia Police (Commissioner Mal Hyde), Office of the Commissioner, South Australia Police, 30 Flinders Street, Adelaide, SA 5000, Australia. Email: mal.hyde@police.sa.gov.au

UNISA, Department of Police Practice (Setlhomamaru Dintwe), Florida Campus, Cnr Christian De Wet and Pioneer Avenues, Private Bag X6, Florida, 1710 South Africa. Tel: 011 471 2116; Cell: 083 581 6102; Fax: 011 471 2255. Email: Dintwsi@unisa.ac.za

University of Maine at Augusta, College of Natural and Social Sciences (Professor Richard Mears), 46 University Drive, Augusta, ME 04330-9410, USA. Email: Rmears@maine.edu

University of New Haven (Dean Richard Ward, School of Criminal Justice and Forensic Science), 300 Boston Post Road, West Haven, CT 06516, USA. Tel: 203-932-7260. Email: rward@newhaven.edu

University of the Fraser Valley (Dr. Darryl Plecas), Department of Criminology & Criminal Justice, 33844 King Road, Abbotsford, British Columbia V2 S7 M9, Canada. Tel: 604-853-7441; Fax: 604-853-9990. Email: Darryl.plecas@ufv.ca

For Product Safety Concerns and Information please contact our EU
representative GPSR@taylorandfrancis.com
Taylor & Francis Verlag GmbH, Kaufingerstraße 24, 80331 München, Germany

www.ingramcontent.com/pod-product-compliance
Ingram Content Group UK Ltd.
Pitfield, Milton Keynes, MK11 3LW, UK
UKHW020021200926
475702UK00014B/1999
* 9 7 8 1 1 3 8 1 1 2 4 7 6 *